ADLARD COLES'

HEAVY
WEATHER
SAILING

ADLARD COLES'

HEAVY
WEATHER
SAILING

Sixth edition

PETER BRUCE

International Marine / McGraw-Hill
Camden, Maine • New York • Chicago • San Francisco •
Lisbon • London • Madrid • Mexico City • Milan • New
Delhi • San Juan • Seoul • Singapore • Sydney • Toronto

Contents

Acknowledgements

Through Adlard Coles, *Heavy Weather Sailing* became such a respected source of yachting information worldwide that it would have been a formidable task for any normal person to carry out the task of updating it single-handed. I have sought the most eminent and wise counsel that I could find to help me with the task, and have had the script read by as many yachtsmen of scholarship and long experience as possible. Once again I owe much to others in the compilation of the sixth edition of *Heavy Weather Sailing*.

Again Sandy Watson, a member of the Royal Cruising Club, has patiently given up much of his time to reading the script and advising on format, aided significantly by his wife Winki and daughter Sarah. After years of noble proof-reading, Leonard Wesson has gone into well-earned retirement, but happily his place has been taken by Dr Ross Coles, son of Adlard. It is a splendid thing that a member of the Coles family should be so closely and constructively connected to the book again and I am most grateful to him for his painstaking work and sensible suggestions. Other readers who have been of great help are David Hughes, Michael Pocock, Michael Thoyts, Simon Wilkinson, David Wagstaff, Alex Whitworth, Michael Derrick, David Hughes and David Dale. I have also received gallant support from James Beattie, Richard Clifford, Russ Kerslake, David Wagstaff and Robin Leuchars in respect of the parachute sea anchor and drag device trials.

I should also thank Janet Murphy, Editorial Director of Adlard Coles Nautical, for her unsparing encouragement, inspiration and support.

The first part of the book has benefited magnificently from the wealth of knowledge provided by their contributions. They are:

Olin J Stephens II, who must rate highly amongst the most admired yacht designers in living memory, and whose yachts remain ever famous for their good looks, speed and remarkable sea-keeping qualities.

Andrew Claughton, once from the Wolfson Unit for Marine Technology, Southampton, but now with the United Kingdom America's Cup group as Design Team Coordinator, whose chapter enables comparisons to be made between design characteristics of yachts in a way that was previously only achieved by subjective means.

Matthew Sheahan, a highly experienced yachtsman who currently writes for *Yachting World*, and used to work for a leading British mast manufacturer. His book *Sailing Rigs and Spars* was a perceptive contribution to a subject not so often written about, and his chapter in *Heavy Weather Sailing* is a masterly exposition in the same theme.

Richard Ebling, a meteorologist for 41 years who has, for the past 20 years, been providing weather information to the Royal Ocean Racing Club for all its major events and been a member of their Race Team. His chapter on the meteorology of heavy weather takes weather forecasting a step further than most books on the subject.

Dr Sheldon Bacon, from the Southampton Oceanography Centre, has put a new angle on the subject of waves, which is likely to be understood and appreciated by people who, like him, enjoy small boat sailing. He has also responded to an intermittent maze of questions that he answers patiently and carefully and has steadfastly maintained a scientific approach in the face of numerous media revelations.

Hugo Montgomery Swan, editor of the *RIB International* magazine whose offshore feats have astounded other ocean RIB drivers. His assistance with photographs has been of tremendous help.

Dag Pike, rightly famous for racing across the Atlantic in powerboats and rightly famous for a multitude of powerboat books he has written that are based on a lifetime of powerboat experience and acute observation.

Professor Noel Dilly, a professor of medicine, who writes on the subject of seasickness in the most comprehensive manner, but who also has been a source of valuable information on the subject of series drogues, which he has tested from his own small yacht.

Mark Orr, Joint Editor of the magazine *Multihull* amongst many other diverse pursuits. His chapter is based on practical experience, as well as that of his large number of readers.

Richard Clifford, who has sailed worldwide all his life and often single-handed. For example he has crossed the Atlantic seven times, including three single-handed races east to west and has recently sailed out to Australia mostly single-handed. He must rank as one of the tougher and more nimble sailors on the planet and his practical assistance and advice with drag device trials has been most welcome.

I must also thank those who have enriched the text by a contribution from their own experiences, or who have helped in some other useful way. Amongst these are:

    Barry Deakin
    David Ridout
    Frank Kowalski, Safehaven Marine
    Ian MC Campbell
    Jacques Archambaud
    Sverre Haver
    Mike Urwin

I should also thank all those who sent in material for which space has not been found. Much of this material has, nevertheless, been valuable in shaping conclusions.

1 2 3 4 5 6 7 8 9 0 9 8

Published by International Marine
A Division of The McGraw-Hill Companies

First published in Great Britain by Adlard Coles Nautical in 1967. First published in the USA in 1968. Reprinted 1969, 1970, 1971, 1972; Revised and enlarged Edition 1975; Reprinted 1976; Third Revised Edition 1981 (three printings); Fourth Edition 1992 (paperback edition 1996); Fifth Edition 1999; Sixth Edition 2008.

Printed and bound in China by C&C Offset Printing Company, Ltd.

Library of Congress Cataloging-in-Publication Data is available.

ISBN 978-0-07-159290-1
MHID 0-07-159290-3

Questions regarding the ordering of this book should be addressed to
The McGraw-Hill Companies
Customer Service Department
P.O. Box 547
Blacklick, OH 43004
Retail customers: 1-800-262-4729
Bookstores: 1-800-722-4726

Title page photo by
Graham Snook/Yachting Monthly
Contents page photo by Safehaven Marine

Foreword by Ellen MacArthur

During my round the world record attempt, sailing through the end of the Southern Ocean in January 2005 was horrendous. We had a big depression coming through and the winds were 80 knots on the back side of it which, if you're in that, you're probably not going to survive. You have to stay in front of it, so the pressure to maintain a very high speed in extremely rough conditions was really stressful. If you break something, in six hours you're going to be in a cauldron.

I experienced icebergs, swells, pounding hailstorms and waves that were so long, it was like looking across a valley. For three days and nights the wind was so strong that the boat was in danger of going over – like being on a tube train running out of control! I had to take sleep in 10-minute snatches and the effort just to keep standing upright was draining, let alone having to climb the 100ft mast to make repairs, which I had to do twice. It was like trying to hang on to a telegraph pole in an earthquake. You get beaten up black and blue. The biggest risk isn't falling, although there is a risk of that – it's breaking an arm or a leg as you slam against the mast...

...but there is nobody forcing me to do this, so why do I do it?

Yes, I do find myself in some challenging situations, but that is one of the reasons I am compelled to keep going back for more. The Southern Ocean is one of the most powerful and desolate places on the planet, but with the wind, rain and mountainous seas comes great beauty and a unique experience of nature in its rawest form; although a harsh environment to be in, it is one that I have been very privileged to witness.

The oceans can be an unforgiving and unpredictable place, but therein also lies the excitement. Potentially, sailing solo round the world can be a dangerous challenge, but we do everything we can to make the boat as safe as possible and ensure that all the safety procedures are in place should the worst happen. It is crucial to be aware of the risks and have a fundamental understanding of the environment and the challenge you are about to undertake. Ultimately, the risks we take are calculated: I work with the weather analysts to examine the weather ahead of me; I study every aspect of the boat. Knowing that you have covered all you can and learnt all you can on the land before you leave helps to prepare you mentally, but you also have to be prepared for the possibility that some things will be out of your hands – the weather, a breakage onboard. When you are out there, if something breaks you're the one that has to fix it, so it is vitally important that you know the boat inside out.

Ellen MacArthur

Preface

Adlard Coles OBE died in 1985. He left behind him a multitude of friends and admirers, many of whom knew him only through his books. Apart from his ability to write vividly and clearly, Adlard was an extraordinary man. In spite of being a diabetic, a quiet and very gentle person with something of a poet's eye, he was incredibly tough, courageous and determined. Thus it was very often that Adlard's *Cohoe* appeared at the top of the lists after a really stormy race. When reading Adlard's enchanting prose one also needs to take into account that he was supremely modest, and his scant reference to some major achievement belies the effort that must have been required. It is clear that Adlard minimized everything, which does him credit. As an example, the wind strengths he gave in his own accounts in the earlier editions of *Heavy Weather Sailing* were manifestly objective and warrant no risk of being accused of exaggeration for narrative effect.

There were three editions of *Heavy Weather Sailing* undertaken by Adlard Coles and this new edition of *Heavy Weather Sailing* is my third, and brings the total number of editions to 6 over a span of 40 years. This is a record that the Coles and Bruce families, who have often sailed and worked together since 1950, can be proud of. Indeed Ross Coles, Adlard Coles' son, has been closely associated with the production of this new edition.

In writing about a subject that most people do their best to avoid, it should be remembered that to have successfully sailed through a particularly violent storm gives a sailor confidence at sea as nothing else will. Adlard Coles lightly referred to the collection of storms that he endured as being like trophies of a big game hunter, but they are educational and character forming too. After a big storm it will be easier to judge how much a boat and crew can endure before they break, and what the warning signs are.

The ethos of this book is to supply the specialist information that will prepare a sailor for heavy weather, and give honest examples of what happened to people and their vessels that have encountered a severe storm. Most space has been given to the specialist information – the expert advice; as this provides a platform of knowledge to enable the reader to be able to glean the maximum from the storm experiences that follow, and the principles to employ when bad weather approaches. These storm experiences have been carefully picked to cover a wide range of predicaments. They tend to relate to unusually high wind strengths because these rare extreme conditions best prove the worth of a particular course of action. They also illustrate how modern heavy weather seamanship has been able to evolve with the benefit of improved knowledge, clothing, design and materials. The improved knowledge is the most important factor, of course, and the contributors of these accounts have freely given of their experience to help others who may follow in their wake.

Certain storms have become famous, not only because they were storms of remarkable strength but also because they affected a large number of people and were in a position to receive wide media coverage. Amongst the most famous of these was the Fastnet Race of 1979. This storm has been widely publicised, and the time has come to omit the detailed account from this new edition to allow for new sections. The Santander race of 1948, has been retained to keep the connection with *Heavy Weather Sailing*'s legendary original author, and to demonstrate the similarities and contrasts of previous years.

One third of this edition is completely new, and many of the illustrations are new. Material retained from the previous edition of *Heavy Weather Sailing* has been thoroughly revised where appropriate.

PART ONE

EXPERT ADVICE

1

Yacht design and construction for heavy weather

OLIN STEPHENS

HEAVY WEATHER HAS TAKEN ITS TOLL among vessels of all the shapes and sizes that one can imagine, and the survivors have been just as varied. Is it worthwhile, then, to consider the design characteristics of yachts that should best survive the worst that weather can offer; or is handling the only factor? It seems clear that the boat counts too, and could be decisive, although once at sea, the action of the crew is what counts.

To declare the obvious, to survive means to stay afloat, to keep water out of the hull; and further to remain in, or at worst return to, an upright condition. Strength and range of positive stability are first requirements. In the course of this study we shall try to determine how these essentials can best be refined and combined with other characteristics to provide for the safety and comfort of the offshore crew.

A lifetime around the water has shown me the many types of yacht that have come through the extremes of weather on long cruises. I think it must have been in 1926 when my brother Rod and I spotted Harry Pigeon's *Islander* lying in New Rochelle harbour, not far from our home. We were quick to greet him from a borrowed dinghy and to take him for a tour of the nearby countryside after inspecting the home-built 10.4m (34ft) yawl that he had sailed singlehanded around the world. Neither *Islander*'s light displacement nor simple vee bottom form made for

survival difficulties. One was most impressed by the simplicity of the construction and equipment: no engine or electrics of any kind, no speedometer, or even a patent log. We admired the man who made it all seem so easy. Soon we heard that Alain Gerbault and his *Firebird* were at City Island, so we went there. The contrast was in every way disappointing, but the older, heavier boat had made it through some very bad weather.

I had, and retain, a great deal of respect for the work of Dr Claud Worth, the owner, during the 1920s, of several yachts called *Tern*. He must have been a thorough and meticulous student, as well as a practitioner, of offshore sailing. He advocated moderate beam, plenty of displacement and a long keel. I read and re-read his books: *Yacht Cruising* and *Yacht Navigation and Voyaging*.

This background, reinforced over the years, had led me to believe that size and shape can vary widely though I like to avoid extremes. If structure and handling are sound, then the larger the better but the bigger vessel demands more of the builder and crew as the loads increase geometrically with size. Big sails supported by great stability require strength and skill to control; small sails can be manhandled. Similar observations apply to hull, spars and rigging.

Analytical studies, such as those carried out in the course of the joint United States Yacht Racing Union (USYRU) and the

Society of Naval Architects and Marine Engineers (SNAME) study on Safety from Capsizing, and by the Wolfson Unit of the University of Southampton, have noted two characteristic conditions of capsize that have a bearing on design, ie those that occur due to the force of the wind on the rig, and those resulting from the jet-like force of a breaking sea. In the first condition the light structure of a small boat may not be overloaded, but in the second the hull or deck may be smashed, destroying its ability to float like a bottle.

As the terms are often used, size and displacement mean about the same thing, although the terms 'light' or 'heavy' displacement usually refer to the displacement/length ratio, expressed as tons of displacement divided by the cube of 1 per cent of waterline length in feet. Though extreme, one can accept a range of 500 to 50 in that

Yachts should be designed and built to withstand extreme weather, even as severe as in this photograph of the South Atlantic when wave height was estimated at between 12 and 15m (39 and 49ft), and wind speed between 60 and 80 knots. *Photo: Christian Février/Bluegreen*

Figure 1.1
Suggested range of displacement/length ratios for a given waterline length.

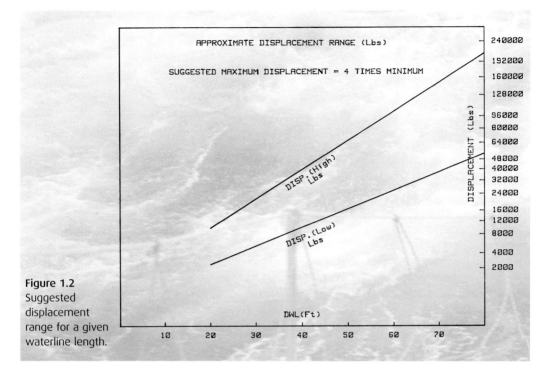

Figure 1.2
Suggested
displacement
range for a given
waterline length.

ratio over a range of 6–24m (20–80ft) in waterline length. In geometrically similar hulls the righting moments increase in proportion to the fourth power of length, while the heeling moment grows only as length cubed. Because of this, small boat designs need more inherent power, ie beam and displacement, while big yachts with similar proportions need very large rigs. Thus smaller boats should avoid the bottom of this range and the larger boats should avoid the top. Figs 1.1 and 1.2 show a possibly over-liberal suggested range. I say 'possibly over-liberal' with the personal feeling that the area just below the middle of the suggested range, say 125 to 250 in the same length range, is best of all.

Displacement is determined primarily by the requirements of strength and stability and, further, for comfort in the sense of motion and of roominess. The yacht's total weight must provide for an adequate structure together with the weight of crew, stores and equipment, and for sufficient ballast to ensure stability for sail carrying power and a good range of positive stability. Truly effi-

cient use of the best materials can give a light hull and rig and, with enough ballast, appropriate design can provide stability, adding up to a lower limit on safe displacement. Though structural materials are not the subjects of this study it should be said that, in the hands of a competent builder, sound light hulls can be built of many different materials including wood, GRP and aluminium alloy. The high-strength, high-modulus materials often used as composites, such as carbon fibre, offer, when used with care and experience, strength and light weight. Steel and concrete are inherently heavier, especially the latter. Boats with light displacement must have light hulls so as to carry a reasonable amount of ballast for the sake of stability. In heavier boats material selection is less critical.

The vertical centre of gravity and hull geometry combine to establish the range of positive stability. A good range, for illustration's sake, over 120° at least, will virtually assure that a capsized boat will right herself in conditions that have caused a capsize. Much lower values may ensure the reverse.

The determination of range depends on a calculation that may be more or less complete in its application to deck structures, cockpits and allowance for some flooding. It also depends on the existing centre of gravity as affected by sails such as those that are roller furled. This suggests the need for some allowance over a stated minimum. It seems unfortunate that racing influences, earlier on the IOR, and still, although to a lesser degree, the IMS, have led to wide beam, and a shoal body: the conditions for a poor range. At least the IMS rule favours hulls with a low centre of gravity, a better situation than the IOR which encouraged an unwholesomely high centre of gravity. Ballasted narrow, deep hulls of the older International Rule type like a decked over 12 metre could go to 180°, representing the full 360° rollover. In beam and hull depth moderation is the best course. Beam offers initial stability and roominess, but too much of it reduces the range of positive stability and results in quick motion. Depth provides easier motion, headroom, structural continuity and space for some bilge water; all desirable, but they are less conducive to high speed. Heavy ballast contributes to range of stability, but also gives quick motion.

A moderate ratio of beam to hull depth seems ideal; say, a beam of not more than three to four times the hull body depth, with the centre of gravity low enough to give a positive stability range of at least 130°. Here one may note that Adlard Coles' three *Cohoe*s fall within the range of proportions that I have recommended. Also, that the damage to *Vertue XXXV*, described in earlier versions of *Heavy Weather Sailing*, was caused by a breaking sea that threw her over and down, smashing the lee side of her cabin trunk (coachroof), a vulnerable structure at best, due to structural discontinuity. The *Vertue*'s small size probably did not permit the incorporation of the material needed for greater strength. A similar occurrence was the damage to *Puffin*, one of my own designs and not quite so small, but hit hard at a weak point. *Sayula*'s survival, after a severe knockdown

in the Whitbread Race of 1973, with great discomfort but minimal damage, contributes to confidence in the larger boat.

The danger of weakness should not be seen as condemnation of the coachroof, which is often needed to provide headroom and can also contribute usefully to range of stability by virtue of its volume if the hull is free of water. It is simply a reminder that all corners or abrupt discontinuities of area in a structure can be sources of weakness, and should be carefully designed and built.

It must be clear to many observers that the trend to keels that are very thin or narrow at the hull juncture weakens an already highly loaded spot by raising even higher the loads in that area, and in turn the stress in keelbolts, the keel and the associated hull structure. Whenever a narrow base is used, the structure must be most carefully considered.

The power to carry sail is quite different from stability range. A naval architect evaluates both at small heel angles by measuring the vertical span between the centre of gravity and the metacentre where, at a small heel angle, a vertical line through the centre of buoyancy cuts the heeled centre plane. The product of this height and the tangent (a trigonometrical function) of the heel angle gives the righting arm at small angles which, multiplied by the displacement, gives the righting moment. The displacement is constant, but with increasing heel the righting moment is strongly dependent on hull shape, varying with the heel angle and the ratio of beam-to-hull body depth. A beamy shoal-bodied boat will have great upright metacentric height without implying a large heeled righting moment that will have been lost with increasing heel when the righting arm shrinks and becomes negative. Good proportions between beam and hull depth will hold that factor almost constant up to angles of 35–40°, while assuring a safe range of positive stability. The first example will feel stiff, but must be kept upright to use the power of the rig, while the deeper boat can benefit from plenty of sail power up to a large heel angle. The beamy, light type depends greatly on crew weight to minimize heel so as to maintain sail power and speed.

Comfort is another characteristic related to beam. Over-generous beam contributes roomy space below, but tends to quicken the vessel's motion and reduce the stability range. While this is not the place to discuss arrangement plans, reference to the importance of air without water in the cabin does relate to safety through the crew's ability to perform. I should like to refer favourably to the Dorade ventilator. Despite its appearance and the many efforts to design something better, it still leads the way in supplying maximum air and minimum water.

Like other vents, the Dorade can admit solid water if fully immersed in a capsize. Preparation for the most extreme conditions should include replacement of the cowl with a deck plate. Similar positive closure for vents of any kind should always be available. In this vein it is well to avoid companionways and other deck openings that are away from the centreline where they are better protected from down-flooding.

Touching briefly on other aspects of safety and comfort we should consider strong, well-located hand rails and we should be sure that sharp corners are eliminated by generous rounding. Galleys should be arranged so that cooks can wedge or strap themselves in place and, if possible, out of the path of spilled hot food. The water supply must be divided between several tanks, each with its individual shut-off valve. This will save the supply in the event of leakage, and also provides control of weight distribution and reduces the large free surface effect of water surging about within the tank. Engine exhaust systems may admit water in bad weather, though careful design can minimize that problem.

Rigs must be designed for the high but uncertain loads of heavy weather. It seems evident that many racing rigs lack the strength to stay in place. Improved analytical methods such as finite element design have not replaced basic calculations based on the righting moment and the consequent rigging loads that apply tension at the chain plates and compression in the mast. Most designers use Euler column methods, often with assumptions on end fixity and safety factors based on their experience. According to such assumptions the safety factors will vary, but they must be generous so as to be ready for the unexpectedly severe conditions of heavy weather sailing.

Rig geometry and sail shape seem to be a matter of personal preference. Under severe conditions, however, the presence of two independently supported masts can be recommended. Strong storm sails and the rigging to set them quickly and easily are essential to a well-found offshore yacht. The storm sails should not be too large. No more than one-third of mainsail area is suggested for the storm trysail and about 5 per cent of forestay length squared for the storm jib. Sail area relative to stability can well be considered in the light of the home port and cruising grounds, and primarily as it relates to comfort more than to safety. Sail can always be shortened, but too large a working rig means frequent reefing or sailing at an uncomfortable angle of heel.

The areas of storm sails given above are very close to those defined in the International Sailing Federation (ISAF) Offshore Special Regulations. Although drawn up for racing yachts there is a great deal of good material in these regulations. I recommend a review of this booklet to anyone preparing to sail offshore.

On the subject of hull geometry I have stressed the ratio of beam-to-hull depth. There are other considerations, less important but still meaningful. Positive and easy steering control is one such. In this day of analytical yacht design there is still no subject more deserving of intensive study than that of balance and steering control. Possibly the lack of understanding explains why there are few subjects that stir greater differences of opinion than the shape of the lateral plane, including keel and rudder. Let me outline some of the problems and some partial answers.

A typical broach by a modern racing yacht, in this case a Mumm 36. If the balance between spinnaker and mainsail is lost, the boat will heel over and forces may be generated that are more than the rudder can correct. The yacht will adopt the angle shown, and due to the buoyancy of the wide stern the rudder may be partly out of the water, making recovery difficult. Although this is a frequent occurrence with modern racing yachts, and unnerving for those who are not accustomed to it, damage to the yacht or injury to the crew is rare.
Photo: PPL

Course stability is often characterized as that condition in which, without the adjustment of the steering mechanism, a boat sailing a given course when diverted by an external force will return to the initial course. This could be a definition of self-steering ability. Many boats can be trimmed to steer themselves under the right conditions, but few will do so on all courses and wind strengths. The forces involved and the direction of their application and the tendency of the hull to turn one way or another at different heel angles and speeds form a very complex system, and one that is difficult to balance. We can accept these difficulties and yet ask for steering that is light and responsive. Even that can be hard for the designer to assure, but I believe that there are a few helpful steps.

A long keel is frequently cited as the best solution. Probably it is, if light weather speed is less important than good manners on the helm, and if the length extends well aft. The disadvantage is the great wetted area that goes with the long keel. Such a keel seems to do two things: turning is necessarily less abrupt and, second, a large part of the lateral plane is abaft the centre of gravity. Think of this the other way around, keel area forward, and visualize a sea turning the boat. It is as though the boat were being towed from a point abaft the pivot point so that the further the new course departs from the original, the further the inertial direction departs from the course, thus causing the boat to turn continually further from the intended direction. Conversely, if the tow point, the CG (centre of gravity), where the force is applied, is forward of the pivot, the CLR (centre of lateral resistance), then the more the course changes the more the direction of the inertial, or tow, force is directed back towards the original course. I should add that this principle of sailing balance is not universally accepted, though to some it seems evident. This principle was first brought to my attention by Dr John Letcher.

Small wetted area carries with it advantages that have resulted in the almost universal adoption of the short keel and separate rudder. Comparatively it means equal performance with less sail area, especially in light weather, or to windward when speeds are low. Using a short keel the required position of the ballast dictates the location of the keel that further dictates the location of the CLR. This disadvantage can be lessened by locating disposable weights as far forward as possible, permitting the ballast keel to come aft, but such gains are limited and the best available strategy to move the CLR aft seems to be to use a large skeg and rudder. These serve the function of feathers on an arrow. Most new boats follow this pattern and, if the ends are balanced, they can behave well, exhibiting no loss of steering control, ability to heave-to or other good seagoing characteristics.

Other characteristics that seem to contribute to good manners are reasonably balanced yet buoyant ends, and moderate to light displacement. Both minimize trim change with increasing heel so that the unavoidable changes in the yacht's tendency to alter course occur gradually and the abrupt application of helm is seldom needed. Easy and positive control is valuable in a big sea.

For the sake of an easy and steady helm the pressure of the water on the hull must be evenly distributed and constant over the range of speed and heel. Long lines, minimally rounded, with relatively constant curvature, make for constant water velocity, and thus constant pressure, over the hull surface. Any short quick curve in the path of the water implies a quick change in pressure on the hull surface and, very likely, a quick change on the helm. Again, a light displacement hull with moderate beam and rather straight lines in the ends best meets these conditions.

The motion of a yacht in rough water is probably better understood than is balance under sail. It depends a great deal on the weight and the way it is distributed. Weight distribution may be considered in any desired plane, usually in longitudinal and transverse senses. It is measured by the moment of inertia and is usually expressed as the gyradius which relates the moment of inertia to displacement. The former is the sum of the products of all weight elements and the squares of their distances from a chosen axis. The radius of gyration, or gyradius, is the square root of the quantity, moment of inertia divided by the total mass. It serves as a measure of the yacht's resistance to acceleration around the chosen axis. Thus a large gyradius, either longitudinal or transverse, tends towards easy motion and is desirable in terms of comfort. In passing it might be observed that the need for a very minimum longitudinal gyradius has become an article of faith among racing sailors. One suspects that they are right more often than not, though studies of resistance in waves show mainly that the weight distribution that results in synchronism with wave encounter is clearly bad; otherwise the effect is small.

Weight itself, or – more correctly – mass, also slows acceleration so that the motion of a heavily built boat tends to be comfortable. Being heavily built, elements of mass such as framing and planking increase the moment of inertia. In this calculation the rig, due to its distance from the centre, makes a major contribution. Anyone who has experienced the loss of a mast in rough water will confirm the quickened motion that followed. Thus, by resisting sudden roll, a heavy rig contributes to both comfort and safety, as studies have shown that, by increasing the transverse gyradius, resistance to capsize in a breaking sea, like that of the 1979 Fastnet Race, is greatly enhanced.

Variations in hull shape are most significant as they relate to displacement and stability, but some other effects of shape are worth noting. I have referred above to balance between the ends. This does not mean anything like true symmetry. My approach was by eye, which spells guesswork, possibly judgement, though today it is easy to check

Figure 1.3 ABOVE The lines plan of *Sunstone*, previously named *Deb*. Her present owners, Tom and Vicki Jackson, live aboard throughout the year and have achieved outstanding success in RORC races.

Figure 1.4 The lines plan of *War Baby*, previously named *Tenacious*, winner of the 1979 Fastnet Race. Her present owner, Warren Brown, has cruised extensively in her.

heeled static trim with a computer, a step towards eliminating excessive trim change.

It is well to avoid flat areas in the hull. These can easily develop in the ends, especially in a light displacement design where the fore-and-aft lines become pretty straight. If sections have a moderate U shape, rather than a V, the flat area that occurs where straight lines cross in a surface will be avoided. Even some slight rounding on a long radius extends the period of impact, reducing the tendency to slam.

Freeboard is another characteristic on which moderation is a good guide. High sides increase stability range but present a large area exposed to the impact of a breaking sea, while a high point of impact increases the overturning moment. Low freeboard leads to the early flooding of the lee deck with its sheet leads and fittings. Related to freeboard is sheer. It can be argued that this has more to do with appearance than seaworthiness, but I think a good sea boat should keep her ends above water without excessive freeboard amidships. Let us agree that the beauty of the Watson and Fyfe boats of the early part of the century was also functional.

Cockpits that can hold a great deal of water can be dangerous, but may be considered in relation to the size and reserve buoyancy of the hull. It is essential that all cockpits will be self-draining through scuppers, which should be large. Deep cockpits offer protection and comfort, but their effect on buoyancy must always be considered. One's priorities may play a part in cockpit dimensions, but the smaller cockpit must be the safest in the end.

The conditions we are considering are less than ideal for centreboarders. They have their supporters and I have been responsible for many centreboard designs. I always tried to advise the owners that capsize was possible (although I hoped very unlikely), but in many cases the stability range was less than I should have liked. In other cases where draft was not too restricted so that the ratio of beam to depth was not too great, and other details such as freeboard and deck structures were appropriate, the stability range seemed fully acceptable. Among S&S-designed centre-boarders, *Sunstone*, previously named *Deb*, seems a good example of a centre-boarder suited to heavy weather sailing (Fig 1.3) due to her rather deep hull.

I hope it has been useful to consider, one by one, a number of specific characteristics. While each has an influence on the ultimate ability of a yacht, it is always the combination that counts. No individual dimension means too much on its own. Good performance can be reached by different paths and, finally, the good combinations are the ones that work (Fig 1.4).

When I think of the boat in which I should be happiest in meeting heavy weather I visualize one that is moderate in every way, but as strong as possible. I should avoid extremes of beam to depth or depth to beam, either very light or very heavy displacement, or a very high rig. I should like the ends to be buoyant, but neither very sharp nor full, and neither long nor chopped right off. Though I have stressed resistance to capsize, in my own seagoing experience I have never been worried on that score, but I have occasionally been concerned about leaks or the strength of the hull or rig. In the final analysis, I recommend moderate proportions and lots of strength.

Comment

At one time yachts were built with colossal strength in reserve, but nowadays, with better knowledge of stress and materials, and the ever-present quest for better performance, yachts are designed with much lighter construction. Olin Stephens' emphasis on the necessity for structural strength is a reminder of current instances when an overly light construction caused disaster.

In 2001 two British lives were lost when an Australian Farr 38 called *Rising Farrster* capsized off the New South Wales coast when her keel broke from the hull. The coroner, John Abernathy, said that 'the primary cause was inadequate hull thickness around the keel washer plates', ie the hull was simply not strong enough to support the twisting force of the keel when the yacht heeled over. It emerged that the hull was built to the minimum standard required by Australian law, but not to the thickness stipulated by the designer, Bruce Farr. Subsequently the chairman of the Cruising Yacht Club of Australia's sailing committee advised participants in the Sydney Hobart Race to 'check the bilge and satisfy themselves that the designed thickness of hull was actually there'. This can usually be achieved quite simply, as will be seen later.

This sad occurrence is not an isolated case, and may be more common than is supposed. Indeed another similar accident occurred in April 2005 when a crewmember died when the keel of his 12.8m (42ft) yacht came off. The building company put out various statements. One of these assumed that the yacht had hit a rock, which was denied by the crews, past and present. The survey report on the damaged yacht stated that 'the bottom section of the yacht as found did not have sufficient strength in the areas designed to take up the forces generated by the keel due to serious manufacturing defects in the laminates and bonding. The wall thickness was between 12mm and 17mm rather than the 25mm or more that was thought appropriate.'

Yacht designers sometimes mention that boat builders do not build a boat exactly to the specification that was designed. Some yacht builders not only adopt their own ideas but simply skimp on the number of laminates used in laying up a hull, thereby saving considerable cost in labour and material. The inexperienced racing owner is likely to be pleased to find his boat is 'down to weight' or even lighter than expected, as to have a light boat is part of a racer's mantra.

There must come a point when lack of structural stiffness leads to loss of boat speed in addition to the danger of losing the keel, or other structural failure. Keeping weight out of the ends of a yacht is also included in the racer's mantra, but the ends of a yacht are the most vulnerable to knocks, such as berthing incidents and, with some modern yachts, the ends are not even built to withstand the minor collisions of normal use, let alone a nudge from a whale. As Olin Stephens simply says, 'a yacht should be built as strong as possible'.

In the case of light displacement yachts, there is little margin of safety in hull design. Thus the designer's laminate specification should be most strictly adhered to. In 2000 a yacht builder in Britain supplied a 10.6m (35ft) 'one-design' racing yacht in which the hull thickness adjacent to the keel was 30–40 per cent less than some other yachts in the class. In this case two different builders had built the class, but the keels and keel bolts were made by the same keel manufacturer who said that all the keels and keel bolts were virtually identical. The second manufacturer produced yachts which were up to 500kg lighter than the first, and it was evident from the exposed height of the keel bolts that there was less hull thickness at the keel intersection, compared to those of the first manufacturer. The matter came to light when external cracking appeared over the length and width of the keel flange, which defied straightforward remedy. It was apparent that the hull, which was bending significantly under load, did not properly support the keel. Such movement was borne out in practical trials, as the saloon table supports happened to be attached to the keel bolts, and thus reflected the keel's lateral movement whenever the yacht tacked.

To assess the depth of the hull at the keel it is necessary only to drill a small diameter hole through to the keel or the keel flange, and measure the depth. Of course the hole needs to be properly filled afterwards, but there is no surer way of knowing the true hull thickness at this vital point. The designer, or the designer's drawings, should give the designed depth of hull adjacent to the keel, and a rough guide is that the hull thickness should be no less than the diameter of the keel bolts.

In the last case mentioned, the floors were reinforced with unidirectional glass fibre, and substantial areas of the keel area were stiffened with up to eight layers of laminate, where access allowed, and no further cracking occurred subsequently. As a matter of interest to racing yacht owners, the scantily built yachts produced by the second yacht builder were never as fast as those built by the first builder, suggesting that, in this case, gain in hull speed through reduction of weight might have been more than offset by the loss of structural stiffness.

Another increasingly common failing is when the keel itself breaks in two, usually near the root. In this case it is almost invariably fabricated steel and composite keels that are to blame. These are sometimes simply not designed and manufactured to cope with the forces involved. An example is when welding has taken place without full penetration of the joint, though any welded structure generally has poor resistance to fatigue.

The EU construction regulations do not apply to racing yachts used exclusively for racing though, in practice, production racing yachts are required to have a RCD certificate. Prospective owners of yachts that do not require an RCD certificate will be wise to make themselves aware of any instances where their vessels do not comply.

I am grateful to Ian MC Campbell, Principal Research Engineer of the Wolfson Marine Unit MTIA, School of Engineering Sciences, University of Southampton, UK for the following information:

In the past, designers used the ABS Guide for Building and Classing Offshore Racing Yachts, and its use was stipulated in Safety Regulations and some Class Rules such as the Volvo Ocean 60s. It was, however, effectively withdrawn by the ABS as were other Classification Society Rules when the Council of European Communities Recreational Craft Directive 94/25/EC, commonly known as the RCD, came into force for vessels up to 24 metres in length. Associated with the RCD is the new harmonized ISO/CEN Standard 12215-5 'Small craft – Hull construction/ scantlings – Part 5: Design pressures, design stresses, scantling determination' but unfortunately this had an extremely long gestation.

The ABS Guide contained clauses concerning keel attachments and included grounding loads so provided a good basis for building robust structures. Indeed there were reports of Volvo 60 yachts grounding at speed and sustaining little serious damage.

The new ISO 12215 standard is due to be published in 9 parts, and whilst the current part 5 contains less about structural details than the former ABS Guide, part 6, which is in draft, and part 9 will be relevant to keel construction and attachment.

There are exclusions to compliance with the RCD, including yachts intended solely for racing, however most European yachts will comply with the RCD and the associated standards.

2

The stability of yachts in large breaking waves

ANDREW CLAUGHTON

Causes of capsize

WHAT CAUSES A YACHT TO CAPSIZE? Sailing dinghies and lightly ballasted day-sailers such as a J24 can be laid flat and capsized solely by the pressure of wind in the sails. In larger yachts the nearest equivalent of this is the broach whilst under spinnaker. In a bad broach the mast can be pressed down as far as the water, but once the heeling influence of the spinnaker is removed, the yacht recovers to an upright position. Experience shows us that, in flat water, gusts alone cannot capsize a yacht. Even when encountering high and steep waves, the story remains the same. The action of wave slope in heeling a dinghy or daysailer may assist the wind in producing a capsize, but a conventional yacht's stability is such that it cannot be capsized by even the combined action of wind and waves, no matter how high or steep.

It is *breaking waves* that cause capsize; if the yacht is caught beam-on to breaking waves of sufficient size, then the exaggerated steepness of the breaking wave front, coupled with the impact of the jet-like torrent of the breaking crest, will knock the yacht down to a point where the mast is well immersed. At this point the yacht's fate is decided by its stability characteristics; it will either return to an upright position or carry on to an inverted position, where the boat may remain for some time until another wave disturbs it sufficiently to flip itself upright. If the wave is high enough or the encounter with it is timed appropriately, then a full 360° roll will be executed.

How big do breaking waves need to be to cause this type of behaviour? Unfortunately, the answer is 'not very big'. During the model tests that were carried out to investigate the problem, when the breaking wave was 30 per cent of the hull length high, from trough to crest, it could capsize some of the yachts, while waves to a height of 60 per cent of the hull length would comfortably overwhelm all of the boats we tested. In real terms this means that for a 10m (33ft) boat, caught in the wrong place, when the *breaking* wave is 3m (10ft) high, this presents a capsize risk; and when the *breaking* wave is 6m (20ft) high, this appears to be a capsize certainty in any shape of boat. The word *breaking* is in italic to stress that it is breaking waves that present the danger, while big waves in themselves are not a problem.

As shown in the photo overleaf, the model tests were done in waves that broke all along their crest at the same time, unlike the waves at sea where short lengths of crest break as the wave systems interact. Once the breaking crest at the point of impact is as wide as the boat is long, then its full effect will be felt.

A fin keel parent model under test showing beam-on 360°capsize.

a Beam-on to a large wave.
b Crest begins to break.
c 90° heel angle (transom visible).
d Upside down (keel and rudder pointing to the sky).
e Nearly upright again.
f Returned to normal!

How can capsize be avoided?

The simple answer to avoid capsizing is to avoid breaking waves. This does not necessarily mean staying tied to a mooring, but rather in avoiding certain sea areas in wind or tide conditions where breaking seas may be thrown up. For example, to help their small-boat fishermen avoid breaking waves, the Norwegian authorities define certain no-go areas as part of their weather forecasts.

Taken a step further, even if caught out in extreme conditions of wind and wave, a technique of avoiding the breakers can be employed, but on a more local scale. During the 1979 Fastnet Race many yachts were able to keep sailing, and actively pick their way through the waves, avoiding the breaking part of the seas, much as a surfer keeps to the unbroken part of the wave by tracking across its face. Once the boat is to one side of the breaking part of the crest the danger is over, and even delaying the moment of impact until the breaking wave has dissipated some of its energy will reduce the capsize risk. The wave is at its most destructive at the point of breaking and immediately afterwards. Active sailing also keeps the boat from being caught beam-on to the seas, which is its most vulnerable position. The risk is that a mistake in steering might cause a broach which results in the boat being left beam-on to the waves. This technique does, however, need a strong and competent crew to execute it for long periods of time. It is nevertheless a well-established and successful technique for dealing with heavy weather.

As was demonstrated by crews' experiences during the 1979 Fastnet, it is not always possible to avoid capsize situations. Due to crew fatigue, or plain bad luck, a yacht, especially if shorthanded, may encounter a capsize or knockdown incident. The research carried out in the wake of the 1979 Fastnet Race has been aimed at evaluating what features of hull design contribute to a safer yacht in survival conditions.

So far I have written in general terms about stability, but we cannot go much further without explaining in more detail the physical mechanisms that keep a sailing yacht the right way up, and how things behave once the mast is below the horizontal.

Fig 2.1 shows a typical righting moment curve; this describes the variation of righting moment as heel angle increases. All of the yacht's weight can be assumed to act vertically down through the centre of gravity, while the buoyancy force opposes this through the centre of buoyancy. The righting moment is the torque generated by the increasing misalignment of the yacht's centre of gravity, which remains fixed on the hull centreline – unless the crew sit out – and the centre of buoyancy which shifts to leeward as the yacht heels. Intuitively one can see that in the normal sailing range of up to an angle of, say, 45°, an adequate righting moment to resist the heeling moment of the sails can be achieved either by a wide beam, so that the centre of buoyancy shifts outboard more, or by a low centre of gravity, so that it is further away from the centre of buoyancy. Whichever way the designer does it, a yacht has to have an adequate righting moment at 30–40° of heel to carry its sail properly. Some boats are stiff, ie the righting moment rises quickly with increasing heel angle, while others are more tender, ie with a slower rise of righting moment. In the latter case, such boats very often require the crew to sit out to produce an adequate righting moment, by shifting the centre of gravity outboard.

At the point of maximum righting moment, the centre of buoyancy is as far to leeward as it is going to get. It then starts to move back to the centre as heel angle increases further. This means that at 90° the righting moment can be quite low, hence the ease with which the broached yacht can be held with its mast close to the water by the flogging spinnaker. A few more degrees past this point and the centre of gravity and centre of buoyancy are in line again, but the wrong way up. This is the angle of vanishing stability (AVS). At this point the boat is balanced in unstable equilibrium like a pencil

Figure 2.1 A typical righting moment curve.

Part of the Atlantic Ocean viewed from a Westerly Konsort of length 8.8m (29ft) in April while on passage from the Azores to Scotland. If this kind of sea breaks just to weather of a small yacht when she is beam-on to the sea she is certain to capsize. *Photo: Douglas Thomson*

Figure 2.2 Body plans of standard series yachts. Length overall 9.75m (32ft).

Fin Keel Parent

Long Keel Parent

High Freeboard Parent

on its end and can fall either way, ie back to upright or to end up floating upside down. At 180° heel – ie upside down – the two centres are in line, and this is another stable position unless the boat is fully self-righting. Before the hydrostatic forces can act to turn the boat the right way up some external force must push the boat back past its angle of vanishing stability.

To calculate the righting moment curve for a yacht, the position of the centre of buoyancy is calculated from the hull drawings, using a computer. The position of the centre of gravity is determined by physically inclining the yacht a few degrees and measuring the heeling moment required.

The ability of a yacht to recover from a breaking wave encounter depends on the hull and coachroof shape. This is not only for its influence on how the breaking wave affects it, but also for its influence on the shape of the stability curve.

The conclusions about capsizing are based on the results of model tests carried out by the Wolfson Unit at Southampton University, UK. The tests were carried out using free-running models in a towing tank 60m (197ft) long x 3.7m (12ft) wide x 1.8m (6ft) deep. The breaking waves were generated by using computer-controlled wave makers, and fans provided a full-scale 40 knot wind over the test area. The behaviour of different hull shapes will be described in the context of the models tested at Southampton University. The results from these tests were complementary to those obtained from the parallel Sailboat Committee of the Society of Naval Architects and Marine Engineers/US Sailing study carried out in the USA.

The three basic hulls tested were: a traditional yacht form, a typical modern 'fin and skeg' yacht, and a derivative of the 'fin and skeg' yacht modified to give it higher freeboard with no coachroof. From these three parent hulls a further six forms were derived, each identical in all respects to its parent with the exception of beam, one narrower and one wider for each type. Models were then constructed from these lines plans to represent 9.75m (32ft) yachts at 1:13 scale. The lines plans of the 9 models are shown in Fig 2.2.

The different characteristics of the hulls allowed individual design features to be evaluated in relation to three aspects of behaviour:
1 Hydrostatic performance, angle of vanishing stability and stiffness.
2 Response to the impact of a breaking wave.
3 Influence on controllability, ie how design features can help an active sailing approach in avoiding a capsize.

Beam

The beam variation tests were done on the wide and narrow versions of the fin keel parent hull. The righting moment curves for the three hulls shown in Fig 2.3 are calculated with the centre of gravity at the same distance above the hull bottom and demonstrate the strong influence of beam on stability and stiffness. The widest yacht is the stiffest and has the highest maximum righting moment, but it also has a very large range of inverted stability. By contrast, the narrow yacht has good self-righting ability but would be hopelessly tender because of the flatter slope of the early part of the curve.

In the capsize tests both the parent and wide hull forms could be inverted by a breaking wave of a height of 40 per cent of the hull's overall length (LOA) while the narrow hull form suffered only a 120° knockdown and recovered. However, a 55 per cent LOA wave caused all the models to execute 360° rolls when caught beam-on to the wave. One of the factors influencing the behaviour of the wider-beam boats was the immersion of the lee deck edge as the boat was pushed sideways by the breaking crest. This dipping of the sidedeck appeared to produce a tripping action that the narrow boat was able to avoid.

= Vertical centre of gravity

Figure 2.3 Righting moment for fin keel yacht beam series; the displacement is 4.5 tons.

1. FIN KEEL PARENT YACHT.   V.C.G. 1.3 ft. ABOVE DATUM
2. FIN KEEL WIDE YACHT.   V.C.G. 1.3 ft. ABOVE DATUM
3. FIN KEEL NARROW YACHT.   V.C.G. 1.3 ft. ABOVE DATUM

Running before the seas, the wide hull proved quite difficult to control and did not show any more willingness to surf ahead of the wave than its narrower sisters.

Freeboard

A comparison was made between the behaviour of the low freeboard with a typical coachroof, and the high freeboard model with a flush deck. Both models exhibited the same propensity to capsize, showing that high freeboard does not increase capsize risk. Once capsized, the yacht with the lower freeboard and coachroof had a greater ability to self-right.

On studying the righting moment curves of the two forms it became apparent that it is the contribution to buoyancy of the coachroof that reduces the area of inverted stability. This is illustrated in Fig 2.4 which shows the righting moment curves for the two hulls. Also of interest is Fig 2.5 where the righting moment curve of the traditional yacht is shown with and without its coachroof, demonstrating how the buoyancy of a coachroof can increase the angle of vanishing stability.

The static stability analysis indicated that a further increase in coachroof size could eliminate the range of inverted stability completely (a concept used with great success in many lifeboats), thus rendering even a very light and beamy craft self-righting.

Figure 2.4 (LEFT) Righting moment curves for the freeboard variation:
1) fin keel parent with coachroof.
2) high freeboard without coachroof.

Figure 2.5 (BELOW) Righting moment for the long keel parent yacht; the displacement is 4.5 and 6.5 tons.

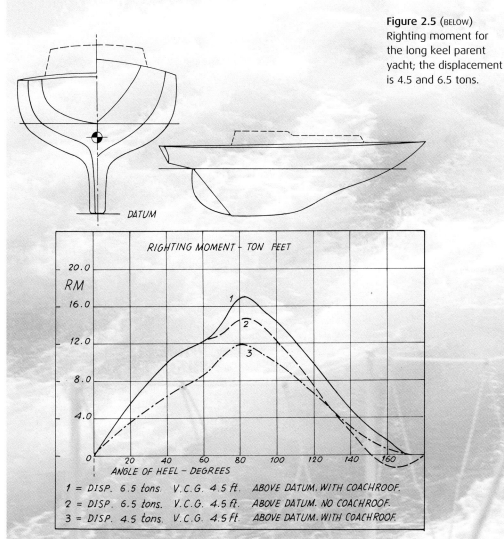

1 = DISP. 6.5 tons. V.C.G. 4.5 ft. ABOVE DATUM. WITH COACHROOF.
2 = DISP. 6.5 tons. V.C.G. 4.5 ft. ABOVE DATUM. NO COACHROOF.
3 = DISP. 4.5 tons. V.C.G. 4.5 ft. ABOVE DATUM. WITH COACHROOF.

Fin or long keel?

One of the most obvious design develop-ments in the last 20 years has been the substantial reduction in the lateral area of the keel. This aspect of design was evaluated not only by comparing the traditional and modern designs, but also by fitting exten-sion pieces fore-and-aft to the fin keel so that the keel area was approximately trebled as shown in Fig 2.6. This produced no dis-cernible improvement in capsize resistance and, more surprisingly, only a marginal improvement in controllability when sailing downwind. A similar result, at least as far as capsize resistance goes, was found when the fin keel and traditional design were compared at the same weight and position of the centre of gravity. Neither design showed a discernible superiority, although of course the traditional design with its narrow beam and larger coachroof had a higher angle of vanishing stability, and therefore recovered more readily from the knockdown.

When it came to downwave controllability, however, the traditional design model was far easier to control and, despite its greater weight, it surfed very readily. The more mod-ern design, by contrast, was hard to keep stern-on to the seas, and once the hull was slightly pushed off course it broached beam-on to the breaking wave and, in this vulnerable position, was prone to capsize. These tests indicated that lateral area, *per se*, does not improve capsize resistance, and downwave control is not influenced only by keel area. It was the more balanced ends of the traditional design that helped its control-lability as much as the larger lateral area of the keel, because, as a wave approached from behind, the stern was lifted less and, conse-quently, the bow was less immersed.

The wider-sterned modern design suffers because the passing wave lifts the stern and buries the bow deeply where it can exert a large turning moment on the hull. This will cause the yacht to broach unless the rudder can be used quickly to counter the turning moment.

The different behaviour of the three mod-els – traditional long keel, fin keel, and increased area fin keel – gave a glimpse of the complex interaction of hull design fea-tures on controllability when running before large waves. The easy surfing and control of the traditional design model was a surprise. The results, however, should not be extended to a generalized conclusion about all tradi-tional and modern boats. While a lighter hull will be carried forward more readily by an advancing wave, to benefit from the effect of the wave, the hull shape must be such that it can be held on course easily. In strong winds, as opposed to survival conditions, the light wide-stern boats can be propelled to high speed by the sails, and any lack of buoyancy forward is compensated for by the dynamic lift generated by the forward part of the hull. This will keep the bow up and will allow the rudder to control the boat with ease.

Figure 2.6
The keel extension.

Extended
keel outline

However, once the driving force of the sails is removed and the boat speed falls – the situation modelled in the tests – it was apparent that balanced ends become an important part of the control equation.

As with many aspects of sailing boat performance, it is the complete combination of design characteristics that is important, and herein lies the designer's skill to blend hull shape, keel area and weight successfully into a harmonious whole.

Displacement, vertical centre of gravity and roll inertia

These three parameters differ from those discussed so far because they can be altered fairly easily on existing yachts, whereas the other parameters are fixed at the design stage and cannot be changed so readily.

Increasing the displacement of the fin keel yacht by 60 per cent while keeping all other

Figure 2.7 Stability curves of models with centre of gravity (left) and that of the parent model (below).

Fin keel parent model (low freeboard)
LOA 32.8' LWL 26.5' Beam 10.8'
Displacement 4.5 tons

1 = VCG 2.6 ft. ABOVE DATUM

2 = VCG 1.6 ft. ABOVE DATUM

3 = VCG 0.6 ft. ABOVE DATUM

factors constant made very little difference to its propensity to capsize; however, the increased displacement did improve the course-keeping qualities of the yacht and its resistance to broaching. This result is not unexpected when viewed in the context of static stability, since an increase in displacement increases the righting moment in approximately direct proportion, as shown in Fig 2.5.

Changes in the vertical location of the centre of gravity (VCG) lead to some intriguing results. The effect of large movements of the VCG on the propensity to capsize was surprisingly small; indeed in some cases the high VCG configuration actually offered more resistance to a knockdown. When considering recovery from a capsize, however, then the high VCG should be discounted as it greatly increases the range of inverted stability. Again, as with increasing displacement, a lower VCG would be beneficial to the control of the craft as it increases stiffness at normal angles of heel. Fig 2.7 demonstrates the influence of the position of the centre of gravity on the shape of the righting moment curve.

Another feature linked to weight and VCG is the roll inertia or radius of gyration. Inertia is increased by moving the component weights of the yacht further from the centre of gravity, and by so doing the yacht is made less easily disturbed by roll-inducing forces, in much the same way as a skater can control the speed of a spin by bringing his arms in and out from his body. In a yacht a high inertia can be induced by using a heavy mast and keeping the ballast as low as possible, preferably on the end of a deep keel. The capsizing tests do indicate that inertia is one of the important influences on capsize resistance. As a rough guide, increasing the inertia of the boat by 50 per cent increases the wave height needed to cause capsize by 10–15 per cent. This is discernible experimentally, but its effect on the overall risk of capsize would not appear to be very great. Beware, however, of increasing inertia by use of heavy spars without a corresponding addition of ballast, otherwise the boat's VCG will rise and the angle of vanishing stability will be reduced.

Racing yachts use crew as moveable ballast, but contrary to a fixed keel, crew weight becomes less effective as the angle of heel increases to higher values. *Photo: Erwan Quéméré/Bluegreen*

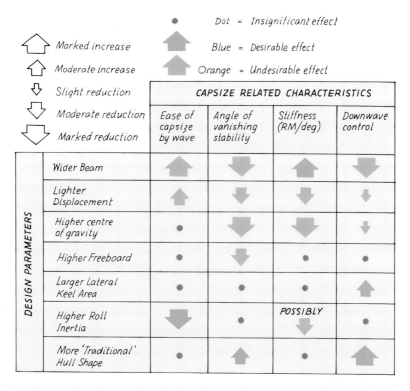

Figure 2.8 Summary of design influences on capsize.

Summary

The model tests and hydrostatic calculations allowed us to discern the influence of several basic design parameters on a yacht's ability to resist capsize, or recover from severe breaking wave knockdowns. Fig 2.8 summarizes the results of the tests and calculations. Fig 2.8 describes how the fundamental design parameters will influence capsize- and stability-related characteristics.

Two of the strongest influences on the vulnerability to capsize are both differences in form. First, a narrow craft appears to have improved resistance to capsize when beam-on to the seas, being able to slip away from the breaking wave. Also, the narrow beam leads to an increase in angle of vanishing stability. Second, the full lateral plane and *more balanced ends* of the long keel design make it less liable to broach and capsize in following seas.

From the tests it was apparent that those yachts having angles of vanishing stability of less than 140° can be left floating upside down for a period after encountering a breaking wave. At the other end of the heel angle range, a high value of initial stability, which makes the yacht 'stiff' in sailing terms, does not provide resistance to the capsizing forces of a breaking wave, and it appears that it is the righting moment values in the range 100–130° of heel that determine the hydrostatic resistance to complete inversion and capsize.

The angle of vanishing stability represents a fundamental measure of the boat's ability to recover quickly from the impact of a breaking wave, and is the design parameter that determines whether knockdown and recovery, or full capsize, results from the impact. The angle of vanishing stability features strongly in the certification requirements for sail training vessels and yachts, and may be estimated from the formula overleaf:

$$SV = \frac{B^2}{R \times T \times V^{1/3}} \quad \text{where}$$

SV = screening value

B   = maximum beam (m)

R   = ballast ratio: $\dfrac{\text{keel weight}}{\text{total weight}}$

T   = hull draft @ B/8 from centreline (m)

V   = displacement volume (m³)

AVS = (angle of vanishing stability)
$$\simeq 110 + 400 / (SV - 10)$$

Examination of the formula shows that beam acts to reduce the range – ie reduces the AVS – while a high ballast ratio, deeper canoe body and higher displacement increase the range.

It must be stressed that the formula is only an approximation based on the actual results of inclining tests and calculations on a number of typical sailing yachts. This means two things. First, it may over- or under-estimate the AVS by up to 10–15° in some cases, and second, it will not work for unusual vessels. Nevertheless, it offers a good guide. If required, the true value of AVS and a complete righting moment curve can be calculated using a well-established procedure of measurements and computer calculations.

The beneficial influences of increased displacement and inertia are also apparent from the tests, but these results highlight the difficulty of designing to minimize capsizability. Many of the design features one might adopt to resist capsize actually mitigate against desirable sailing and living characteristics, which are, after all, the boat's prime function for, hopefully, all of its life. For instance, narrow beam reduces both internal volume and the power to carry sail; high inertia leads to excessive pitching in a seaway, and so on. Finally, even when all the precautions are taken in our models' tests, although discernible trends in resistance to capsize have been determined, no hull form or ballasting combination consistently resisted capsize in a breaking wave with a height of 55 per cent of the yacht's length. Moreover, all the yachts could be rolled to 130° of heel by an appropriately timed encounter

with the 35 per cent LOA high breaking wave. This suggests that alterations in form that improve capsize resistance may be rendered ineffective by a relatively small increase in breaking wave height.

So what is the answer to avoiding capsize? The best and most effective way is to avoid breaking waves by avoiding sea conditions where breaking waves are prone to occur. If caught out in extreme conditions, then by keeping sailing, the boat can be kept away from the breaking crests, or positioned to surf ahead or clear of them. This avoids the dangerous beam-on condition, and delays the encounter with the breaking crest until much of its energy has been dissipated. As discussed earlier, this strategy requires active rudder control and some skill to carry out. Ultimately, the technique may well prove beyond even an experienced racing crew, let alone a shorthanded cruising complement. Once the conditions are so severe that the crew are not able to remain on deck, then the vessel must look after itself. Unfortunately all yachts have a natural tendency to lie beam-on to wind and wave when left to their own devices. This is the most vulnerable position, and it is in this situation that the influence of hull design features on capsize resistance and recovery come into play, realizing, of course, that no conventional yacht design can offer complete immunity from capsize under these conditions. Naturally, increasing the size of the yacht will decrease the chances of encountering a wave capable of capsizing the boat.

After our tests and calculations examining all these different design features, one must admit to a sense of disappointment that no combination of hull form or ballasting arrangement offered a substantial improvement in capsize resistance. Something, say, that if the breaking wave height doubled, a boat could withstand.

It is worth mentioning that the Wolfson Unit continued its experiments, supported by the Royal Ocean Racing Club, to evaluate the influence of a drogue or sea anchor on a yacht's behaviour in breaking waves. This

Yacht capsize and drogue research: the wide fin keel model being held stern-to a breaking wave by a drogue.

research again complemented similar studies in the USA by Donald Jordan. These studies showed that use of a *suitable* drogue, deployed from the stern of the yacht, will cause it to lie steadily downwind and downwave, so that any breaking wave will see only the transom of the yacht and will not be able to exert any capsizing force. Using an appropriately sized drogue, even the lightest, widest fin keel yacht could safely survive the 55 per cent LOA wave with no assistance from the helmsman, whereas lying beam-on it would be easily rolled over by the 35 per cent LOA breaking wave. Indeed, it was only our inability to make higher waves in the tank that prevented us from moving further up the safe wave height range. As will be seen from the sequence of photographs above, the yacht moves steadily downwave with little or no disturbance from the foaming crest.

Thus it may well be that the drogue is the simplest and most reliable way of substantially reducing the risk of capsize.

3

The influence of heavy weather on yacht design

PETER BRUCE

AFTER MANY YEARS OF EVOLUTION IT might be thought that the optimum yacht shape would have been established long ago but, for one reason or another, this appears not to be the case. New yachts appear continually, but none of them are quite like their predecessors.

As yacht design progresses, some desirable design features can be left behind as others evolve. Generally speaking, the boat industry gives people exactly what they want, and clearly people want boat speed, space, grace, comfort, lots of electronics, effortless handling and shallow draft. However, less obvious features, such as seaworthiness – particularly stability – and structural strength, tend to be taken for granted by the buyer.

Unlike cruising yachts, racing yachts are subject to a handicap rule which could be used to pressurize designers towards seaworthiness but, through the influence of owners, the handicap rules are predominantly applied to achieve equality between competitors. It was not always thus. Up to the mid 1970s, certainly in the USA and UK, seaworthiness and strength were paramount considerations for racing yachts. Until then, yachts had a reputation for looking after their crews when it came on to blow; furthermore, it was rare for any yacht to give up a race due to her design or construction, or as a result of gear failure.

Designs of the 1950s & 1960s

Some comparisons illustrate the point. For example, a letter from John McDonell describes a storm that *Cavalier* encountered while returning home after finishing second in the 1963 Sydney–Hobart Race. The 9.4m (31ft) yacht was built of wood by Swanson Brothers in Sydney and, by modern-day standards would be judged as extremely heavy and lacking some desirable accommodation features. Having suffered no damage after being rolled she might also be judged extremely seaworthy. *Cavalier* appears to have stood up to the storm much as one would expect of her traditional design and John McDonell could have had more complaints than he did. His first criticism was that the cockpit did not drain fast enough – a common criticism of that era. The other problem in the storm was that she did not have the speed necessary to keep out of trouble. Yachts which do have such speed and quick response to the helm need to be steered constantly and with some skill, and this situation is satisfactory as long as there are sufficient willing and able helmsmen on board. Racing boats, such as those that do the round-the-world races, will have enough of such helmsmen, but cruising boats seldom do.

One of the interesting aspects of John McDonell's account is how different it is from

A sister ship to *Half Pint*, which is a good example of a strongly built yacht of the 1960s period with balanced ends and accompanying excellent sea-keeping qualities. *Photo: Ben Davies/ PPL*

more recent storm reports where the aim is usually to slow down to achieve a 'comfortable speed'. A possible suggestion, which might have improved *Cavalier's* handling, would have been to use her engine. This would have prevented her from 'stopping dead in the troughs' and would have given water flow over the rudder in the right direction at all times.

The fact is that many traditional yachts are renowned for their sea-keeping qualities, especially those yachts designed by Olin Stephens. Here is an account of one of his designs, *Half Pint*, a Swan 36, in an Atlantic storm, written by her owner Christopher Price, which reinforces the good sea-worthiness of this hull:

Atlantic storm

My partner and I left Gibraltar on 13 December 1968 for Lanzarote in the Canaries, with a favourable weather forecast of light to moderate north-easterlies. On 24 December 1968 we were due north of Casablanca, about 25 miles offshore. The wind had been building steadily through the night and by 0630 was steady at 40 knots from the SW, so I decided to heave-to under a backed storm jib, which made the motion more bearable.

By 1000 the wind had increased to 45–50 knots and we started to run off under storm jib alone, sailing parallel to the coast with a general heading of NE. The seas were very short and even with the storm jib alone the boat was punching into the backs of waves. At about 1530 in the afternoon the boat broached and was knocked flat with the mast in the water. The boat righted herself immediately. We then put out two warps about 20 fathoms each, tied at the ends so as to form a bight, and made off at first the primary and then the secondary winches. The wind was now gusting over the maximum of 60 knots shown by our Brookes & Gatehouse wind speed indicator. By this stage I had no choice but to bring in the headsail and run under bare poles. In these conditions the boat was still making 5 to 6 knots, but the motion was relatively comfortable and the Hydrovane self-steering was able to keep our course with the wind 15 to 20° off our port quarter. The wind remained over 60 knots for most of the night, and at about 0130 the boat was knocked down a second time. We had to pump the bilges at least every half-hour because the boat was being continually swept by green water. Radio reports claimed that this was the lowest depression in the area in the past fourteen years. Throughout the storm the boat behaved very well. We continued cruising for another three years (Brazil, Caribbean, Bahamas, US), but never experienced anything approaching those conditions again.

In this example the Swan 36 ran at a comfortable speed using warps whereas *Cavalier* used none. Not being quite so heavy for her size as *Cavalier*, *Half Pint* might have surfed uncontrollably had she not been restrained. Different methods are appropriate for different boats. More importantly the two accounts suggest that there was not much wrong with the seaworthiness qualities of these two yacht designs of the 1960s, which were genuine cruiser-racers. From the 1960s onwards, racing yacht design evolved according to performance considerations. Yachts became progressively lighter and beamier, freeboard increased; and fin keels and spade rudders became the norm. They also became faster and more exciting to sail.

1979 Fastnet Race

The Admiral's Cup, which included the famous Fastnet offshore race as the last event was, in 1979, considered the premier world cup of yachting. Accordingly a gaggle of international journalists were present at the finishing line in Plymouth to report events. Their accounts of the Fastnet storm, in some cases exaggerated, brought widespread interest throughout the world and remained a major news item for days on end. An anticipated depression had deepened suddenly and the resulting force 10 storm was not well forecast, indeed the first mention of a gale in the shipping forecast was at 1750 on 13 August, by which time the fleet was already experiencing a good force 8. Nineteen lives were lost if the four crew of the catamaran following the course are included, only 28 per cent of the fleet finished, 25 yachts were abandoned, and five sank. The yacht that won overall, and by a wide margin, was the 18.6m (61ft) Olin Stephens design *Tenacious* owned by Ted Turner. She was strongly built in aluminium, had a skeg-hung rudder, balanced ends and had a wide range of stability. Her lines are to be seen in Chapter 1.

Wave height data suggest that the short-lived storm was of rare intensity for the time of year, but not unprecedented, and not excessive by winter standards. Analysis of reports from competitors suggests that there was a band of stronger wind in the region of the Labadie Bank. A notable feature was that the wind swung from south-west to north-west during the peak of the storm, causing a hideously confused sea. It became the standard by which other yachtsmen's storms are judged.

Some heavy yachts with good stability were able to help with rescue work whilst, at the other end of the scale, one yacht with an angle of vanishing stability of 118° remained inverted for some five minutes. There were five yachts that spent more than 30 seconds totally inverted, which gave grounds for concern about their self-righting ability.

A number of useful lessons were learnt from the Fastnet storm of 1979. The Inquiry report highlighted that a yacht is preferable to a liferaft until the former sinks, and remarked on the difference in stability between a Contessa 32 and more modern and faster designs. There was, however, no immediate change in yacht design, specifically regarding stability, and it remained 'performance driven' in spite of the enormous publicity given to the storm. Most of the participants felt that it was the extreme conditions rather than yacht design factors that were to blame.

Happily in 1985, the CHS rule was introduced in the UK: a rule that encourages yachts with a greater range of stability. Now renamed as the IRC rule, it appears still to be growing in popularity worldwide, and has brought a more healthy trend to yacht design in countries where it is used.

1984 Vasco Da Gama Race

After all the tremendous publicity that anything to do with the race had generated, many people felt that the lessons of the 1979 Fastnet must surely have been learned.

Round-the-world race yachts tend to have a good stock of helmsmen. *Photo: Philippe Schiller/PPL*

However on 26 April 1984 an unforecast storm brought havoc to the 29 entries in the Durban to East London Vasco Da Gama Race. Winds of at least 60 knots over a period of 6 hours blowing in the opposite direction to the Aghulas Current created seas which caused three yachts to sink and the Lavranos 2-tonner *Sensation* to be wrecked on the coast. One of the yachts that sank, *Rubicon*, was lost without trace. Three yachts experienced 360° rolls. For example, in the case of *Spiffero*, a Dufour 34, the 360° roll dismasted the boat, and the deck-stowed liferaft, the engine and battery became detached from their mountings. The liferaft was lost and when the wreckage had been cleared away the yacht was rolled through 360° for a second time.

The official report, which there is no reason to doubt, said that the yachts were competently crewed and that safety regulations had been properly applied. The question that remained is whether modern performance yachts are sufficiently optimized for extreme weather.

1987 The Great British and French October storm

In October 1987, a short-lived but unusually fierce storm with winds of over 100 knots caused massive destruction to buildings and woodland in both France and England. This storm was accurately forecast in France but not properly forecast, even denied, in England. Two of four yachts caught out in this storm survived without being inverted, a Contessa 32 and a Hallberg Rassy 42. Another yacht with shallow draft but a conservative hull type survived a 360° capsize, and the fourth and more performance-oriented design, with a comparatively low range of stability, was rolled through 360° and after colliding heavily with the rescue ship was abandoned and was never found. Both of the latter yachts were lying a'hull. No lives were lost. It so happened that the largest yacht with a low range of stability came off worst, but it would be wrong to draw firm conclusions from such a small sample.

1991 Japan–Guam Race

No further offshore races were to run into serious trouble until 1991, but then the matter of stability, coupled now with the strength of racing yacht structure, raised its head again. The Japan–Guam Race tragedy did not receive much publicity in the western world, yet 14 yachtsmen lost their lives. I am grateful to Barry Deakin from the Wolfson Unit who, in 1992, wrote the following description:

Capsize in the Pacific Ocean

The 7th Japan–Guam Yacht Race began at midday on 26 December 1991 off the Miura Peninsula just south of Tokyo. Nine yachts crossed the start line in wintry conditions, heading for the tropical island of Guam over 1300 nautical miles to the south.

On the afternoon of the following day, with winds of 30 knots and waves of up to 6m (20ft), two yachts retired from the race. One, a Van de Stadt 71, was dismasted and the other, a Frers 48, had a torn mainsail. At 1540 a crew member, who was not wearing a harness, was lost overboard from the yacht *Marine Marine*, a Yokoyama 39, while trying to untangle a running backstay. He could not be found.

At midday on 28 December a female crew member of *Marine Marine*, exhausted and incapacitated by severe seasickness, was transferred to a patrol boat that had attended to assist with the search.

Twenty-four hours later with the rough conditions persisting, *Marine Marine*'s engine was started but a rope was around the propeller and the engine stalled. A tow was requested from a second patrol boat which made five unsuccessful attempts to pass a line to the yacht. That evening one of the crew became aware that the rolling motion of the yacht felt unusual and transfer of the crew to the patrol boat was requested. It was decided however that it would be too dangerous in the dark and rough conditions. The crew put on lifejackets and a liferaft was prepared.

At around 0530 on 30 December the keel parted from the hull, which rolled upside down and filled rapidly with water. One crew member escaped through the hatch on his second attempt, finding it difficult to dive through it with the lifejacket on, and was joined a little later by two others. The incident was not seen by the patrol boat which had lost visual and radio contact with the yacht, although the empty liferaft was found at 0700. At 1020 an aircraft, which had joined the search, located the yacht with one surviving crew member. There was a hole in the hull roughly the same size as the root of the keel. A transverse frame was seen to have remained intact inside the hull. Seven members of the crew were drowned: four of their bodies were found inside the yacht.

On 29 December at 2030, while the crew of *Marine Marine* were beginning to worry about the motion of their yacht, *Taka*, a Liberty 47 about 230nm to the south, was capsized by a breaking wave while sailing under storm jib in a quartering wind of 32 knots. The maximum wave height in that area was in excess of 6m (20ft). The yacht remained upside down and after more than half an hour, the four crew inside the yacht made their way out through the hatch. Their EPIRB, which did not appear to be functioning correctly, was lost at this time. They found that one of the three crew on watch had drowned. After a further 15 minutes the yacht rolled upright. The upper washboard was lost and, as the yacht was half submerged, water continued to flow in. The mast was broken and the bilge pump tangled with ropes. The liferaft was inflated but capsized soon after with the loss of some of the gear.

The loss of *Exide Challenger's* keel in the 1997 Vendee Globe Race led to an epic Southern Ocean rescue. To optimize performance, modern keels have become extremely narrow and thin at the root, and require very careful design and construction. Even then they are vulnerable to running aground. *Photo: 92 Wing RAAF Edinburgh*

The six remaining crew boarded the raft and drifted. Despite the mobilization of 11 patrol boats and 52 aircraft, the raft was not found until 25 January when it was spotted by a British cargo vessel. Only one crew member remained alive, the others having died between 10 and 16 January.

The remaining five yachts finished the race between 1 and 3 January. *Marishiten*, a Nelson/Marek 68, broke the race record with an average speed of 10.1 knots.

An analysis of weather records for this and previous races reveals that, with mean winds of more than 30 knots and gusts of up to 50 knots during the first two days, this race was subjected to more severe weather than before. The margins are small however, with mean winds of 30 knots or more experienced during every race except one. Furthermore, such weather is typical at that time of year and so crews should anticipate that they might encounter very rough conditions.

The race is classified as ISAF Offshore Special Regulations Category 1, and all yachts must meet the appropriate ORC special regulations in addition to a series of Nippon Ocean Racing Club Regulations. All yachts must be at least 10m (32.8ft) overall.

The NORC wasted no time in forming a research committee to investigate the casualties, it being officially approved on the same day that *Taka's* liferaft was found. The man overboard was caused by human error, demonstrating the value of safety harnesses and lines, but the keel failure and the inability of *Taka* to return upright after a capsize suggest design deficiencies which were the subject of extensive research in Japan. Two lines of investigation were followed. In the first, the detailed arrangement of *Marine Marine's* keel attachment and local GRP structure was studied from drawings, and calculations were carried out to assess the strength. It is not clear from the report on the investigation whether the keel was attached to a fair canoe body or a laminated stub, but detailed drawings of the local laminate configurations and the attachment of transverse floors show features that the Wolfson Unit considers bad practice.

The laminate thickness met the requirements of the ABS rules and the calculations indicate a safety factor of 2.71 when the laminate shear strength is compared with the static load of the keel with the yacht at 90° of heel. This load is chosen in the absence of any information on actual keel loadings caused by a yacht rolling in a seaway, and it is therefore difficult to draw firm conclusions from the value for fatigue considerations.

Disturbingly, the report suggests that the hull failed in shear around the outline of the keel and at the keel bolt washers, probably as a result of fatigue, implying that other well used yachts may lose their keels. The hull's shell had become detached from the transverse frame. The yacht was built in 1983 and had competed in many offshore races. She had run aground five years before the failure and required some repair to the hull-keel joint but details of the damage were not included in the report. The authors assumed that delamination between the shell and the frame may have occurred at that time and gone unnoticed by the repairers.

To take this study further, destructive tests were conducted on full size samples of yacht hulls with fin keels attached in various configurations. Hulls with and without stubs were used and a range of laminate thickness was tested. The samples represented a yacht of only 7.5m (24.6ft) compared with *Marine Marine*'s 11.9m (39ft), and the sample keel weight was only 20% that of the failed yacht's, so use of the data must be made with caution. The tests revealed that the breaking load in bending increases in proportion to the square of the laminate thickness, so any deficiency in the laminate will reduce the strength significantly. A safety factor of 3.3, similar to the calculated value for *Marine Marine*, was obtained with a local hull laminate thickness of 14mm which is also the same as *Marine Marine*'s, but the keel moment at 90° for *Marine Marine* was over eight times greater than that for the sample yacht.

Although there are insufficient details published in the report for a direct comparison, these figures suggest an inadequacy either in the structural design or in the assumptions used to calculate the keel loadings and hence the safety factors.

In the other avenue of research, the capsize of *Taka* prompted the Japanese to investigate its range of stability as derived from the hull measurements as part of the IMS rating process, and from drawings of the complete hull, keel, coachroof and cockpit arrangement. The IMS stability curve indicates a positive range of 108° (the angle beyond which the yacht would capsize in calm water) and when the cockpit and coachroof were taken into account in the independent calculation a range of 114° was derived. This range is below average for the fleet of 56 IMS yachts used for comparison, but seven yachts had lower values. The IMS rating system uses a 'Stability Index', which comprises the range adjusted by the size of boat and its displacement/maximum beam ratio, and *Taka*'s value was only marginally below average for the fleet.

The effects of flooding of the yacht were investigated, and it was concluded that when upside down the stability gradually reduces as the amount of flooding increases. Thus the yacht remained inverted for a considerable time despite some flooding, but after the main hatch was opened the rate of flooding increased and the yacht righted herself, albeit in a seriously swamped condition.

These calculations and conclusions will be familiar to those who have studied the 1979 Fastnet Race Inquiry Report, which contains precisely the same results as computed by the Wolfson Unit in response to that disaster. At that time the Wolfson Unit was also commissioned to conduct a series of model tests to examine the behaviour of yachts of various forms, both traditional and contemporary, in large breaking waves (see Chapter 2). This work has been published and discussed at length at various times and has been complemented by parallel work conducted in the USA and the Netherlands. None of this work is referenced in the report, however, and the Japanese researchers have undertaken their own experimental study of breaking wave capsize. Their experimental technique was very similar to that used by the Wolfson Unit, and their results and conclusions reinforce the findings of the work done previously.

At a scale of 1:10, they modelled two basic hull forms: a typical IOR form of 9.3m (30.5ft) overall, and a traditional long-keeled cruising yacht of 9m (29ft 6in). The first had a range of stability of 120° and the latter a range of 165°, both of which are typical for such types. The IOR yacht was capsized and remained inverted after the impact of a 3m (10ft) wave. That is a wave height equal to the beam of the yacht. The traditional yacht could not be capsized though, it should be noted, the maximum wave height available was only 3.4m (11ft). With the masts removed the IOR yacht capsized in waves of over 2.2m (7.2ft) and the traditional yacht was rolled through 360° by waves in excess of 3m (10ft). Because of its large range of stability it would not remain inverted.

The yachts modelled were 9m (29.5ft) long and, if it is assumed that the principal characteristics of a yacht remain in proportion as size increases, we may infer that a wave of more than 4m (13.1ft) high would be required to capsize *Taka*. The maximum wave height was well in excess of that at the time.

It did not require an extreme wave therefore to cause the capsize, but rather the combination of being caught beam-on to, or broached by, a wave of above average height which happened to be breaking at the time of the encounter. Perhaps the other competitors were fortunate enough not to have been caught in such a situation since the fleet stability statistics do not imply that they would have fared any better.

At the Wolfson Unit we would consider a range of stability of 114° to be insufficient for a yacht of this size undertaking an offshore passage. Indeed the yacht would not comply with the Department of Transport's Code of Practice for sail training vessels that would require a minimum range of 125°.

Some items covered by the ISAF Special Regulations, which have been introduced to minimize the effects of failures such as these, were also inadequate. For example, washboards must be secured to the boat, but those on *Taka* were swept away. Bilge pumping arrangements on *Taka* were inadequate because one pump was disabled. Two pumps are required by the regulations but the other was presumably submerged in the cabin.

It is important to note that neither *Marine Marine* nor *Taka* were anything other than typical offshore racing yachts, and the force 7 to 8 conditions in which they failed were not particularly extreme. They were to be expected in this race.

It is unfortunate that the lessons learned since the Fastnet disaster do not seem to have changed design trends significantly and, furthermore, they appear to have to be re-proven when a fresh incident occurs.

1993 Sydney–Hobart Race

The points made in Barry Deakin's report are clear, but did not appear to have had much effect on yacht design. Perhaps there would have been an effect had there been loss of life in the windy and rough Sydney–Hobart Race of 1993 but happily there was not. One of the smaller class winners and third overall was the 20-year-old S&S 34 *Marara*, a close relation

of *Half Pint*. After a brief period of tail winds on leaving Sydney, most yachts were on the wind for three and a half days in gale or storm force winds. The 2 knot south-going current met the north-going wind causing steep breaking seas. Hulls delaminated, yachts sank, yachts were dismasted, yachts lost their keels, and the skipper of one yacht spent five and a half hours in the water before being rescued. The New Zealand yacht *Swuzzlebubble VIII*, a Davidson 40, when under storm jib and trysail was rolled through 360° by a breaking wave, dismasted, damaged and swamped. Her doughty crew, by the way, cleared away the mast wreckage, put a No 3 genoa out as a sea anchor whilst bailing, managed to start the engine, and put into harbour unaided. Another yacht, a Farr 40, was doing 7.2 knots boat speed in 46 knots of wind when she fell off a wave. Next moment the starboard side of the main bulkhead, to which the chain plates were attached, appeared through the deck and then disappeared over the side complete with mast and rigging. There were no casualties in spite of all this.

Some instructive comments came from the winners and losers. Winners commented on strong crew teamwork, on the need for strongly built boats and the necessity of having three slabs in the main rather than 'the two sailmakers try to persuade you to have'. Clearly storm trysails proved their worth as well. Comments made by those not so lucky were that the average modern racing yacht is more suited to inshore 'round the buoys' racing. The latest handicap rule (IMS) was encouraging light, shallow rocker craft which were very difficult to steer and would slam badly in a sea. Keels were not strongly enough attached, rigs were too light, and cockpits gave little protection in severe conditions. It was said by some that they were impossible to slow down too.

1994 The Queen's Birthday storm

The Queen's Birthday storm was described as both a tropical storm and a 'bomb'. Seventeen yachts were caught up in the direct path of the storm that deepened suddenly, much as the 1979 Fastnet depression had done. In this case the storm lasted longer and the yachts were generally larger, were cruising orientated and had family crews. Twenty-one crew were taken off seven of the yachts.

There were fatalities in only one 40ft (12.2m) yacht where a family of three adults

were lost. After putting out drogues, the crew were down below relying on their auto helm to steer. Only the liferaft was ever found, from which it could be seen that that it must have had at least one of the crew on board at some time, as seasickness pills and water had been used. Beforehand, the yacht had talked to a shore radio station, reporting a series of severe knockdowns, crew injury and concern about the windows. The owner had put out a Mayday call, which he had subsequently cancelled. Their EPIRB beacon was detected nearly three hours after the last communication. The presumption was that the people in the liferaft had been carried out by a wave. Because no bodies were found, it is possible that the crew were not wearing lifejackets, which could suggest a hasty entry into the liferaft.

The boat came from a designer of racing yachts and, though well constructed, she was more lightly built than the norm. At the other end of the displacement scale, two steel-built smaller yachts came through the storm with negligible damage. As far as yacht design was concerned, the most significant finding of the Queen's Birthday storm was that the lighter yachts experienced the most knockdowns.

A full account of this storm is given on pages 244–56.

1998 Sydney–Hobart Race

Conditions were more severe in the 1998 Sydney–Hobart Race and, sadly, there was loss of life. After the race had started a low formed suddenly in the Bass Strait, bringing winds of hurricane strength for a period of 10 hours from a westerly direction. At the Esso Kingfish B Platform in the Bass Strait, average wind was 55 knots, gusting 64 knots, an unusually high strength for summer time and rather more than had been predicted. The south-going coastal current had been running strongly, but by the Bass Strait it had largely dissipated and its influence was probably small. The Esso Platform recorded a wave height of 11.8m (39ft).

Six people died, 55 people were rescued out of a total of 1135, six yachts were rolled, and seven yachts were abandoned, some of which sank due to structural failure. One of these was the 1942-built 15.8m (52ft) wooden cutter *Winston Churchill*. When she was thrown into a trough it seems that her hull was opened up as part of her port bulwark was torn off by force of water. Help was not at hand and three of the crew were lost from the liferafts.

Two more died aboard the Farr 40 *Business Post Naiad* (built in 1984) which capsized twice. On the first occasion the yacht was doing 4 knots under bare pole when a massive breaking wave rolled her over, breaking the mast and causing major structural damage. Harnesses held the crewmen on deck, and after the mast had been secured the yacht set off under power for shelter at Gabo Island. Some hours later another large breaking wave turned the boat over and she remained upside down for a period of five or six minutes. While the boat was inverted the owner-skipper suffered a fatal heart attack, and a crewman on deck was drowned through being unable to detach his safety harness in the same circumstances, probably, as when *Taka* capsized in the Japan–Guam Race of 1991.

It transpired that *Business Post Naiad* had lower stability than other yachts in the race, which accounts for the long period that she was inverted. She did not meet the minimum requirement of 110°.

Finally the helmsman was lost overboard from the Reichel/Pugh 43 *Sword of Orion* (built in 1993) when she was rolled through 360° as she headed back to Sydney after retiring from the race. As the yacht rolled, force of water broke the stanchion to which the boom had been lashed. The freed boom smashed the wheel and swept the helmsman

over the side, parting his safety line. The mast was wrapped around the hull; the engine was unserviceable; the steering wheel unusable; many starboard ring frames had broken and the deck to hull joint had split between the cockpit and the stern. The crew cut away the mast and deployed the anchor over the bow on a warp, which kept the bow into the wind. After some hours the remaining crew were taken off by helicopter.

Other yachts rolled and dismasted were the Young 12m VC Offshore *Stand Aside* (built in 1990), the Bashford Howison 41 *B52* (built in 1995), which remained inverted for three or four minutes, and the Tartan 40, *Midnight Special* (built in 1995), which was rolled twice and just stayed afloat long enough for the crew to be rescued by helicopter. The Swan 44 *Loki* was rolled and had her cabin windows broken by an enormous wave, and the sturdy Cole 43, *Solo Globe Challenger* (ex *Rangatira* and built in 1984), a renowned seaboat, was rolled to 135° which caused loss of her mast, and a skylight hatch to break, allowing flood water to render inoperable all the essential electrics. Most of the crew were injured and were taken off, one with a broken leg, leaving just three to bring the boat in.

The 19.8m (65ft) *Team Jaguar*, after losing her mast, was struck by a breaking wave that submerged the boat to the companionway and brought her to a near vertical angle. All her deck beams were sprung and, as might be expected, there was a real mess down below.

There is always something to be learnt from those who did completed the race successfully and accounts follow from the skippers of the winners of the three major classes. Firstly that of Ed Psaltis, skipper of the overall IMS winner *AFR Midnight Rambler*. She was tenth to finish, beating numerous larger yachts. He comments:

The 10.5m (35ft) *AFR Midnight Rambler* is of exotic GRP construction. There was no sign of hull/rig, keel joint damage although we put her through a horrible pounding. As long as no extremes are taken, modern construction does work. The fin keel is of lead, with no bulb, and she has no internal ballast. The angle of positive stability is 123°, and while still a modern, light competitive IMS design, her stability is higher than some of the very recent IMS designs. In addition to worldwide experience, the crew of seven had 50 Sydney–Hobarts between them.

During the eight hours when the breeze was 70 to 80 knots with very big waves, we just had the storm jib up. We were overpowered at times but mostly the helm felt good with just enough weather helm. Attempts were made to set a trysail but it created too much weather helm.

We had two important defensive weapons: speed and acceleration. Our usual speed was 7 knots and after a bad knockdown or confrontation with a big wave the speed would quickly accelerate up to this speed again due to the modern lightweight (while not extreme) design. Having speed and manoeuvrability was essential to steer through the big and confused seas. We were able to position ourselves best for each wave as it came, or steer around it. Otherwise the boat would have been a sitting duck.

Importantly during the storm we changed to a 'survival' watch system and had only two on deck at one time. One sat on the rail facing the storm, sheltering the helmsman from the bullet-like spray and called 'wave' when a big one came. The helmsman altered course to bring the bow into the wave, then pulled away sharply on the top of the wave and back onto the normal course. No helmsman should stay on watch for more than an hour in extreme conditions for, if concentration lapses, the outcome will be devastating.

AFR Midnight Rambler, designed and built by Robert Hick in 1995, has enough stability to keep going with the crew down below. I am told that some of the latest IMS yachts could not make ground to the south during the storm without all the crew on the rail.

I would never recommend a yacht to turn and run with the weather. Much better keep going into the wind and seas at about 60° apparent. Most boats that had severe trouble had retired and were running with the storm. In addition I would suggest that crew hook their safety lines to strong points situated at the main companionway before they come on deck and that they carry a personal strobe light or at least a waterproof torch in their wet weather gear.

A second account comes from Alex Whitworth, owner and skipper of the *Berrimilla*, a Brolga 33, designed by Professor Peter Joubert in 1969. She finished first overall in the Performance Handicap System division out of over 45 yachts, and had the big disadvantage of having to weather the storm in the night. The Brolga 33 is somewhat similar to an S&S 34, with deep vee-shaped underwater sections, pronounced tumblehome and long overhangs.

She is described by her owner as very strong and very stable with a range of stability of 136°. She came through the storm undamaged, though, he says, the hull took a real beating.

During the storm the same watchkeeping regime was adopted as *AFR Midnight Rambler* (ie two on deck, and changing every hour). The crew had 15 Sydney–Hobarts between them. Steering was made difficult by darkness and was mostly done by feel.

We sailed through the storm with just the trysail because I felt that we would have been seriously overpowered with the storm jib as well and she was handling all but the biggest breakers with no dramas. The trysail was sheeted to the spinnaker turning blocks on each quarter. We were sailing at around 60–70° apparent, averaging about 4 knots. It was generally possible to set the boat up for each wave, or avoid it, but the occasional breaker was either going too fast or coming from further abeam. On about ten occasions the boat was caught by one of these bigger breakers. She would be carried down the wave front at about

The 10.7m (35ft) *AFR Midnight Rambler* built in 1995 making steady progress at the height of the storm. She went on to win the IMS Class overall. *Photo: Richard Bennett/PPL*

an 80° angle of heel (ie on her beam-ends) on a wild surf, with the wave breaking right across the boat and filling the cockpit. A technique that evolved during this situation was to put the helm over to push the bow down the wave as the boat was being carried bodily sideways. In this way the sideways motion was converted into some forward motion and lessened the tripping effect of the keel. I am convinced that this technique helped us to avoid the worst effects of the breakers that did get us.

The boat is so stable that, once in the trough, she immediately stood upright, gathered speed and went on sailing, though on one occasion the boat was turned through 180°. With just the trysail up we could not tack so had to gybe which we felt was particularly hazardous. A wave breaking over the boat would fill the cockpit entirely and the storm boards were very necessary to keep water out of the cabin. The four cockpit drains are just about on the water-line when the cockpit is full and it takes an age to empty. Having a small swimming pool at the back of the boat tends to slow us down too.

Modestly, Alex Whitworth says that he suspects that *Berrimilla* was behind the worst of the storm and was quite lucky not to get rolled. The morning after the storm they saw a helicopter that was looking for *B52* which had been rolled in their area. Incidentally Professor Peter Joubert, who designed *Berrimilla*, was in the race in a larger but similar very stable design. His 13m (43ft)

Kingurra, with 6 tons in her keel, became almost totally inverted by an enormous breaking wave but she righted herself 'in about five seconds'.

The winner, by some 12 hours, of the CHS division, comprising 12 yachts, was *Aera*, a Swan 46, a well known solidly built class of yachts renowned for the quality of their construction. The skipper said:

A satellite photograph of the
storm taken at 1615 on 27
December 1998.

At midday on 27 December the storm hit with the wind building rapidly up to 60 knots from
the west. Long experience of sailing a Swan 46 in heavy airs shows that the boat goes as fast
under headsail only as she does with a mainsail set on almost all points of sailing. Thus, with
an assured storm forecast, by this time *Aera* was under only her storm jib.

As the waves built up to a maximum of 10m (33ft) it became clear that it would not be
safe to maintain the rhumb line so we bore off some 30–50°, bringing the true wind angle
to 110–130°. The wind continued to build and was too much even for the storm jib, so we
peeled to the storm staysail, maintaining our course and 10–11 knots.

The wind strengthened to 70 knots for a period of two hours with gusts to 75 or 80 knots.
Fifteen per cent of the surface was breaking and the wind was blowing the top off every
wave. As a result there were long streaks of wind-blown water joining one crest to the next.
The sea looked as if it was covered in a layer of smoke. Wavelength was about 100m (330ft)
and the waves were not long-crested as one might expect, but diamond-shaped. During this
period we suffered three or four small knockdowns, none more than 45°, and the cockpit
filled seven or eight times. We kept a full watch of six on deck throughout, the most vulnerable person being the helmsman who was washed up against the stern pulpit a couple of
times when a wave filled the cockpit.

In the next couple of hours the wind abated to 50 knots and we were able to set the storm
trysail in addition to the storm staysail, and alter our course by 20–30° towards the rhumb
line. However at about 1700 cloud cover became complete, we had sheeting rain and the
wind built up to 65 knots. We were forced to drop the trysail and bear away to the old course.
By now wavelength had increased to 150–200m (500–650ft).

Though we had been heading south-east at about the same speed as the low-pressure system we considered this safer than trying to turn back. However, the system was soon to
move quickly towards the south allowing us to resume the rhumb line course and set more
sail. By morning the storm was over. Our biggest problem had been our auto-inflating lifejackets that inflated when solid water came on board.

The stiffness of the Swan prevented us from ever being knocked beyond 45° and it seems that the boats that got into difficulty were generally of lighter construction than *Aera*. Even so, we were unable to maintain the rhumb line course safely at the peak times of the storm. Many yachts were knocked down by seas on their beam. For example, *Loki*, a Swan 44 of similar design to *Aera,* tried to sail the rhumb line course but was knocked down beyond 90°, suffering a broken coachroof window that caused her to retire.

However, I believe there were other factors that allowed us to finish the race. Firstly, many yachts' storm jibs were too large for the conditions. Secondly, a very large number of yachts suffered gear failure. *Aera* was extremely carefully prepared by her regular crew and suffered no gear failure at all. It is worth mentioning that a small failure often leads to other problems, so the greatest attention to detail before the start of the race is vital. Finally, *Aera's* crew was very experienced with over a hundred races of similar length between us and many of these races had been on the same boat. Familiarity with each other and the boat was another important factor.

Some interesting comparisons can be made from these three accounts. We have three distinct types of yacht: a fairly moderate modern IMS type, a 30-year-old design, and a modern but conservatively designed Swan.

The IMS yacht, *AFR Midnight Rambler*, managed to avoid getting into trouble by displaying great skill. She also had the advantage of daylight; nevertheless, at the same time several roughly similar but larger designs were rolled and suffered severe structural damage. The 30-year-old design, *Berrimilla*, resolutely and intelligently crewed, found quite big trouble in the dark but somehow every time flipped upright and undamaged. The large, stiff, strong, well-pre-pared Swan, *Aera*, again experienced the worst part of the storm in daylight, with her experienced crew never becoming seriously worried at all. It is noteworthy that she carried a storm staysail as well as a storm jib. If the wind speed increases from storm to hurricane levels, sloops will need a spitfire jib, ie a storm jib of yet smaller size, if any sail is to be carried.

In the preceding chapter we learnt that if a big enough wave breaks at a critical moment catching a yacht beam-on, she will capsize whatever her stability, but it is what happens afterwards that may be critical. Will she come back up again in about five seconds (as Peter Joubert's *Kingurra* did) or will she remain

The stricken VC Offshore *Stand Aside* with part of her coachroof ripped off. *Photo: PPL*

inverted from four to five minutes? Had *Business Post Naiad* recovered from her inversion as quickly as *Kingurra*, at least one life would not have been lost.

Comparing *Berrimilla* with *Midnight Rambler* one finds in *Berrimilla* a boat with more factors of safety built into her, but one capable of only half the speed. Incidentally it was extremely interesting to discover from Alex Whitworth that it may be possible to reduce the chances of being rolled by use of the helm to bring the bow down the wave.

Comparing *Aera* with *Midnight Rambler* we find a boat again with big factors of safety, not quite so elating to sail and, perhaps, twice the cost. *Midnight Rambler* probably represents a very good example of an IMS design. Nevertheless it remains questionable whether racing yachts in more extreme form are 'capable of withstanding heavy storms and are prepared to meet serious emergencies without the expectation of outside assistance', the supposed criteria for a Category 1 offshore race. The answer may never exactly be known, as human factors in storms tend to weigh so heavily.

The Cruising Yacht Club of Australia's report on the storm stated that yachts that continued to 'sail actively', using speed and power to negotiate the waves, generally fared better. Asked to describe the trim under which yachts fared best, a comfortable majority reported 'when eased off the wind up to 15°'.

Among the many compulsory changes in the safety rules that came out after the 1998 Sydney–Hobart Race were:

1 A minimum of 115° positive stability for all classes.
2 50 per cent of the crew should be 'experienced'.
3 A minimum age of 18 years.
4 30 per cent of the crew to have attended training seminars.
5 Safety harnesses to be replaced every-seven years.
6 406MHz EPIRBs should be the primary EPIRB. There should be one EPIRB per liferaft carried.

7 One waterproof handheld VHF should be carried in addition to the ship's VHF.
8 Sheets of storm jibs and trysails should be permanently attached to the sail.
9 Four white parachute flares should be carried in addition to current flare requirements.
10 At least one of the ship's batteries should be of the closed cell or gel type for the purpose of starting the engine after an inversion.
11 Kapok filled lifejackets will no longer be acceptable.
12 Personal strobes or high intensity lights and dye markers should be carried by all members of a crew.
13 Yacht names should be limited to two words for the purpose of radio communications.

The trend from the stormier Sydney–Hobart Races suggests that something has changed over 40 years:

> 1956 – 30 started, 28 finished (93%)
> 1963 – 44 started, 34 finished (77%)
> 1970 – 61 started, 47 finished (77%)
> 1977 – 131 started, 72 finished (55%)
> 1984 – 150 started, 46 finished (31%)
> 1993 – 105 started, 37 finished (35%)
> 1998 – 115 started, 44 finished (38%)

Since 1998 there have been no particularly stormy Sydney Hobart Races, though as major coverage is given to all incidents that occur due to the weather, the impression is sometimes given of more severe weather than has actually occurred.

Unless Australians are becoming soft, or storms are steadily becoming worse, neither of which seems likely, one might well feel that the trend is further evidence that commonly used racing handicap rules may be encouraging performance-orientated yachts to become less fit for ocean passages. The failure of some yachts to finish was solely due to mast/rig deficiency or structural problems, but in other cases failure to finish can be linked to low stability.

The IMS rating rule and its offshoots may have passed its zenith, while the IRC rule, that started as the CHS rule in 1985, appears to be still growing with over 7300 measurement certificates be issued in 2007. On the one hand the IMS rule does not encourage stiff yachts, whereas on the other hand the IRC certainly does.

Stability of racing yachts

I am again grateful to Barry Deakin of the Wolfson Unit for his thoughts:

Traditionally, small cruising yachts had a range of stability of at least 150° and would therefore always return to upright if capsized. Such a stability range requirement is generally considered by modern designers to be unnecessarily conservative, and is certainly not readily achievable with a modern hull form. In general, traditional forms with narrow beam and a deep hull were more resistant to capsize, but breaking wave height in relation to boat size is the overriding factor. Larger yachts are therefore safer in a given sea state, since they are less likely to encounter a breaking wave of sufficient size to result in capsize. This fact has led to proposals for stability requirements that vary with size (see Fig 3.1).

There is no doubt that there are many yachts which are vulnerable to being inverted by breaking waves, and some of them are also unlikely to return to the upright, despite being in storm conditions where further large waves will be encountered.

Casualty data appear to validate the standards developed, and suggest that the lessons of the 1979 Fastnet Race may not have been taken to heart by the industry or the authorities, despite further high profile casualties around the world. Unfortunately, as we all know, those characteristics that have an adverse effect on safety in survival situations make the yacht fast, spacious and comfortable in favourable conditions. They are valuable assets in the modern yachting market, and authorities will be reluctant to try to enforce unpopular restrictions.

Buyers of sailing yachts should be provided with information to indicate realistically the type of operation for which they are suitable. It would be irresponsible to market yachts as ocean cruising yachts if they are vulnerable in terms of stability, or indeed any other aspect of safety. Every individual is entitled to take measured

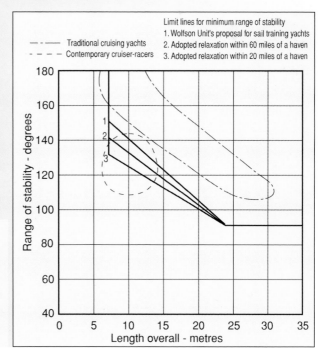

Figure 3.1 The two sets of pecked lines show that modern racing yachts lie in an area of a substantially lower range of stability than traditional cruising yachts.

risks, but one should not be misled by marketing strategies into underestimating those risks.

Most yacht design offices now have facilities for computing the stability characteristics of new designs and many incorporate a calculation of the range of stability into the design process. Not all of these computer programs are able to include the effects of coachroof and cockpit however, and these are of course fundamental to the stability at very large angles. There are many individuals and small companies involved in yacht design who do not have such facilities, and it is unlikely that they will commission a consultant to produce stability data, since there is no legal requirement nor public demand for such information.

Yacht designers tend to rely on their calculations for displacement and centre of gravity location. Inclining experiments, which are used to measure these values accurately, are virtually unheard of for cruising yachts, unless of course the yacht is also to be raced and undergoes an inclining experiment as part of its rating measurement. Since there have been no stability regulations for yachts, some designers have adopted their own targets and generally they appear to regard a range of stability of about 120° to be the basic requirement. This value may have been selected as a result of considerable publicity given to the USYRU recommendations in the mid-1980s, rather than being arrived at independently by the individuals.

There has been a reluctance on the part of rating authorities to demand detailed stability calculations from the designers of racing yachts. Until perhaps 30 years ago the technology was not readily available but more recently, with numerous computer programs available, specific stability requirements could have been incorporated into their rules. Fears of additional cost to the designers and problems associated with approval of results have perhaps deterred them. This attitude has led to an increased tendency to rely on approximate methods of assessment, based on a small number of principal dimensions.

An alarming illustration of the dangers of approximate assessments is given by a comparison of the stability curves for two examples of the same class of 8.7m (28.5ft) production cruising yacht (see Fig 3.2). The yacht with a range of 127° has a conventional rig as designed. The other with a range of only 96° has a mast furling mainsail and roller furling headsail fitted. The additional weight aloft on this yacht has reduced its range by 31°. The only way to identify such effects accurately is with an inclining experiment and a conventional stability calculation.

Thus, there are two aspects to stability assessment: the range needs to be determined properly: and there needs to be a sufficiently conservative minimum requirement. If an approximate method must be used an increased factor of safety should be introduced, for example by increasing the minimum requirement.

Stability curves for two yachts of the same class with different rigs

—— Conventional rig
- - - - Roller furling rig

GZ - righting moment

Angle of heel - degrees

Figure 3.2 A dramatic illustration of how a small yacht's range of positive stability can drop with modifications to the rig.

Whitbread Rule

Yacht racing will never be 100 per cent safe, but if the authorities wish to minimize the likelihood of fatalities through yachts having insufficient stability, the knowledge and techniques are there to be used, and they are now available at an acceptable cost. It appears that the result of existing racing rules has been to keep existing fleets competitive rather than to encourage increased safety in new designs. Improvements were introduced into the Whitbread Rule, and subsequently incorporated into the Volvo Rule, and if this example were followed by other race authorities, with a sufficiently stringent requirement, the general standard of safety would be raised. Researchers are making progress but the authorities seem to be hesitant about incorporating their findings.

Clearly *Taka*'s stability range of 114° was not enough for an ocean storm if a yacht is to right herself quickly in the event of a total capsize. Compromise is allowable as vessels get bigger and Barry Deakin's figures in Fig 3.1 are worthy of note. He adds that the approximate methods of establishing the range of stability are acceptable for more stable craft but more elaborate and accurate methods are necessary for craft in the lower range. This will include most racing boats.

Not only will a yacht's stability be significantly reduced by furling sails (Fig 3.2), but equally for radar, radar reflectors, spinnaker poles which fold up the mast, and mast steps. Even just loading up a yacht with equipment stowed above the waterline, will have the same effect to a lesser degree; for example: outboard motors, liferafts, and drums stowed on deck. The problem is not confined to smaller yachts. There are a number of superyachts that only set their sails in gentle conditions due to heavy top hamper combined with shallow draft.

It was interesting that *Taka* self-righted after 45 minutes. A yacht should eventually self-right if she floods, and the effect of free surface water is to accelerate the process. Once righted there will usually be enough internal fore-and-aft structure to break up the free surface and discourage the yacht from inverting immediately, but there will be several tons of water to get rid of. Pumping out, by the way, is almost always preferable to taking to the liferaft.

The less lucky participants in the Vendée Globe Challenge singlehanded race of 1996–97 showed that there was a rash of keel and stability weaknesses around the racing circuits. Far from bringing good ideas in for the cruising sailor, this race seemed to be breeding unsafe yachts. At least the Vendée Globe type of yachts are now designed, like multihulls, with capsize in mind, eg with escape hatches fitted in the stern, etc, but it would be preferable that they have sufficient stability to right themselves quickly. One well-known case was Thierry Dubois's Open 60 *Amnesty International* which, in the 1996–97 Vendée Globe Race, remained firmly capsized in spite of large waves and the flooding of one of her stabilizing water tanks. The designer said that the boat had flooded as much as she was going to, and for the boat to right herself it would have been necessary to vent off air through a seacock to bring more water inside. In this event it might be prudent for competitors to establish at some point before the race the water level inside the boat which will cause her to sink! That Isabelle Autissier capsized in the South Pacific in February 1999, whilst taking part in the Around Alone race, and abandoned her yacht after being unable to right her, suggested no progress was being made then in the realm of single-handed competition yacht design.

The stability characteristics and, in particular, the angle of vanishing stability is information that can and should be obtained

Thierry Dubois clinging onto his capsized yacht which, by virtue of her extreme beam, is stable when inverted. Only by venting air from inside will she right herself. *Photo: AFP/PPL*

before a yacht is purchased for ocean voyaging. This information should include the effect of modifications such as furling sails, radar and other mast hamper, and also increasing displacement by the addition of fuel drums and motor cycles on the upper deck and large quantities of stores and equipment down below. With this information one will have a good guide as to how stable a boat really is. In certain cases racing boats have acquired adequate or even abundant stability through using a bulb on the end of a high aspect keel, but such yachts have an unsuitably large draft should they ever be considered for cruising.

Other yachts have not righted themselves, as might be expected, when the keel has broken off. High aspect ratio keels, by virtue of their extra depth and smaller cross-sectional area, need considerable extra support. It is not so easy to tell at a glance how likely it is that such a keel will detach itself from the hull, though a surveyor is likely to give good advice. There is little to be lost in perfor-

mance, or any other characteristic, by increasing the factor of safety in this region. Many designers will build in strength at the design stage to allow for groundings. Of course keels of old-fashioned yachts are most unlikely to break off, but there is no need to go back to this style of design to achieve adequate strength.

Questionable design features

Other modern features which buyers should be wary of are: large Perspex (acrylic) windows, weak coachroof structures, open centreboard casings, weak cockpit locker lids, weak steering arrangements, 'high tech' but unproven composite hull construction, off-centre hatchways, weak and unsecurable washboards, objects that rely on gravity to stay put, such as engines, batteries, anchors, fuel and fresh water tanks, and exhaust pipes which are not sufficiently well designed to stop water flooding back to the engine. Many racing yachts, these days, have large shallow open cockpits with little protection from the elements, insufficient lockers, and Spartan accommodation. The IRC rule encourages a strong rig so the fragile multi-spreader 'fishing rod' type masts with running backstays are no longer popular where this rule applies. Under all handicap rules ever narrower bow entries and broader sterns that create a decidedly unbalanced hull remain in fashion.

Racing yacht keels have become of extreme high aspect ratio with a bulb on the end and, though tending to increase the range of stability, these keels need great care in their construction and attachment. Failures of fabricated steel and composite keels have markedly increased, and the hull structure at the keel intersection has in a number of cases been found to be insufficient. Twin rudders are used more often in modern yachts, the rudders being offset from the centreline and angled outwards. Rudder damage can occur with this configuration owing to the keel no longer giving protection, and if one rudder is damaged the alternative one is usually only effective on one tack. A slightly questionable compromise has been adopted in one round the world class with the use of 'kick up' rudders, that yield to an excessive force. The very high aspect ratio rudders of racing boats require two enormous bearings beneath their cockpit floors to function, and the bending moments are huge in return for small gains in

Wild Thing in the 1995 Melbourne–Hobart Race demonstrates the full potential of modern racing yachts given an alert and competent crew. *Photo: Richard Bennett/PPL*

efficiency. Structurally, a rudder supported by a skeg should be stronger than a blade, thus there is a good argument for using a skeg in the case of boats intended primarily for cruising. Not only should the rudder be better supported and protected but also it is much less likely that the rudder will stall. It is not sufficient just to have a skeg; the skeg must be built to withstand the most extreme loads that the rudder can give. The owner of one of many yachts that encountered a bad Atlantic storm gave an illustration. Most of the yachts put into the Azores after the storm and quite a number of them were hauled up on the slipway with broken rudders; skeg-hung rudders being about equal in number to the blade type. The wry comment was that in some boats the whole skeg had been torn off, leaving a hole in the hull, a disadvantageous situation compared to the blades.

Straight or plumb bows are another characteristic of modern yachts encouraged by a rating rule. The elegant overhanging bow allows an anchor to be deployed with much less chance of damage to the bow. In many cases an unsightly strut has been used to carry the anchor and its chain clear of a plumb bow, negating most of the plumb bow's original advantages.

The charter business has become strong enough to dictate its own style of yacht and in some cases these purpose-built yachts display attractive accommodation features and shoal draft that compromise ultimate stability. They are characterized by wide beam, low aspect ratio rigs, and a shallow low aspect ratio keel. Sometimes performance lost by cutting down sail area has been compensated for by the use of over-light construction, which also has a cost benefit. Notwithstanding the dangers of over-light construction, in some cases these yachts have such a poor range of stability they are hardly fit for the open sea on these grounds alone.

Conclusion

One must appreciate that designers and builders are bound to try to give cruising yachts the sparkling performance characteristics of a racing boat if this is what people want. Thus every would-be buyer of an ocean cruising yacht clearly needs to be careful that he has a boat truly designed and built for the job – allowing for the extras he has in mind. Would-be buyers of performance yachts have to be more careful still. The quest for performance and excitement has, in some cases, been at the expense of passable stability, seakeeping qualities and strength. Moreover, in a fresh wind, this quest is possibly beyond the ability of an enthusiastic 'amateur' crew to control.

The implications for the prudent ocean cruising yachtsman might simply be to purchase a strong, stable proven design of vessel, unrelated to the current racing breeds and influenced by the sensible design characteristics given in Chapter 1 by Olin Stephens, the master designer of seaworthy yachts. Such thinking should produce a sensible craft. There is another argument worthy of consideration. If offshore or ocean racing crews are in need of help from the rescue services every time it blows more than force 8, there will come a time when governments will decide that yachtsmen are not able to manage their own affairs properly. They could take control of leisure craft safety regulations by creating all kinds of expensive and unsympathetic new legislation, to the detriment of all.

It is to be hoped that improvement of yacht design will continue, but not at the expense of good stability, keel integrity, hull strength and similar less obvious but important design features. Onus should always be on racing rule-makers to give precedence to seaworthy characteristics instead of equality of handicap.

4

Spars and rigging for heavy weather

MATTHEW SHEAHAN

COASTAL-HOPPING IN HEAVY WEATHER conditions is one thing, long-distance blue-water cruising quite another. When the going gets tough many miles from land, self-sufficiency and confidence in the boat and her equipment are essential requirements.

As the primary driving force aboard the boat, the rig is fundamental to the crew's well-being in more ways than one. Lose the rig and there is a risk of having to cope with more than just the initial loss of motive power. Communications can be made inoperable and a longer passage time will put the food, water and fuel supplies in question. Depending on the type of craft, the motion of the boat may change completely as well, especially in bigger seas, and can make life very uncomfortable.

Prevention is always better than cure, and although it is never possible to guarantee the security of a yacht's rig, there are several ways of minimizing the risk. It is this approach that will be looked at first in this chapter, and then what to do if the worst does happen. But first a brief explanation of some of the most common types of rigs and what sets them apart from each other.

Rig configurations

Although there are many historical reasons for the development of the wide variety of rigs in evidence today, the main reason for the differences is the practicality of handling a given sail area. Modern-day furling devices and reefing systems have done much to nudge up the size of sail plans that can be handled easily by, say, a crew of two. As boats get bigger, the configuration of the rig starts to play an important part in the manageability of the sail plan.

For boats of up to around 12m (40ft) LOA, Bermudan sloop rigs are by far the most popular as they are simple and easy to manage. However, above 12m (40ft) the cutter rig can provide advantages. With this configuration, a staysail is set from an inner forestay either instead of, or in conjunction with, the primary headsail. Breaking down the fore-triangle area into two sails does make life easier for trimming, tacking and changing headsails. The configuration is particularly popular for coping with heavy weather when just the staysail and a deep-reefed mainsail can be used.

Since the advent of modern sail-handling systems, ketch and yawl rigs have become less popular. Yet they still have their place in reducing the total sail area into manageable sizes, especially on boats of 16m (52ft) LOA

In the 1981–2 Whitbread Round the World Race, *Ceramco New Zealand*, skippered by the late Sir Peter Blake, lost her mast 150 miles north of Ascension Island when the port lower intermediate rod shroud broke where it had been bent around the lower spreader. The 15m (50ft) top section was recovered and lashed to the 3m (11ft) stump using a breadboard as a baseplate. The destination of Cape Town was 2455 miles away, but it was necessary to sail over 1000 miles more to stay in favourable winds. During the passage, *Ceramco*'s crew achieved one day's run of 238 miles. *Photo: PPL*

and above. Furthermore, having two masts means that there is at least the possibility of a spare mast, albeit smaller, in the event of losing the main mast. However, this will not always be the case, especially if a triatic stay – running from the top of the main mast to the top of the mizzen – is fitted. Having a mizzen mast can also provide a well-balanced heavy weather rig configuration too, where a staysail can be set on the main mast and a mizzen sail set aft.

Schooner rigs, where the forward-most mast is the shorter, offer similar advantages to ketches and yawls, where the total sail area is divided up into smaller individual areas. Again, this allows more options when it comes to balancing up the sail plan for heavy weather sailing on a given point of sail. And once more, in the event of losing one mast, there is at least a chance that there will be another still standing.

Although less popular, the unstayed mast configurations should be mentioned too. These are cat rigs with single large mainsails, swing rigs with a rotating mast and boom fixed unit, and junk rigs.

While providing several solutions to some of the potential problems and shortcomings of conventionally rigged spars, such configurations do have disadvantages of their own, particularly for the long-distance sailor. Having no rigging does mean that the spar is more likely to flex and, depending on the spar's material, is therefore more susceptible to fatigue in certain areas. Most builders of these types of spars are well aware of the problems, and it is true to say that this is less of an issue with carbon masts than those built in alloy. Nevertheless, while compression is the biggest problem for stayed spars, fatigue through flexing is the unstayed rig's biggest enemy. Lack of rigging also makes it more difficult to go aloft, especially while under way. A blessed excuse perhaps, but take time to consider how you would cope in such an event, before it happens for real.

Perhaps the most important factor to bear in mind, though, is that of setting storm sails. Few unstayed masts have attachments for inner forestays onto which storm jibs can be hanked, and some mast/mainsail arrangements have problems in fitting a trysail track. Such considerations must be borne in mind before heading off over the horizon.

A seaworthy spar?

The biggest dilemma for many designers and prospective owners is whether to opt for a deck-stepped or keel-stepped mast. There is a continuing debate as to which is the most suitable for long-distance cruising, and there are advantages and disadvantages on either side. From a structural and spar design point of view, a keel-stepped mast should always be lighter, yet no less secure, than the same rig stepped on deck. Keel-stepped masts derive a large part of their security from the fact that they are 'built in' – as engineers would say – being supported at the mast heel and at the deck.

To use the same engineering terminology, deck-stepped masts on the other hand are 'pin-jointed' structures. In other words, without the rigging, a deck-stepped mast would fall over straight away. A keel-stepped mast would not – at least, not so easily!

When it comes to designing the mast section, a deck-stepped mast should always be constructed from a stiffer mast section – one having higher moments of inertia – compared to the keel-stepped alternative. Heavier masts can have a considerable effect on the stability and motion of the boat, as well as her performance, and although this may not be a key issue in some cases, it is nonetheless an important consideration.

Keel-stepped masts do have their disadvantages though. While it can be avoided

Lowest halyard exit

Tube for mast cables

Sealant

Foam plug shaped to fit mast section

Cables for Tri-colour navlight, V.H.F., wind instruments, etc.

Figure 4.1 An example of a means by which a keel-stepped mast can be made to drain on deck rather than in the accommodation area.

(Fig 4.1), the most common is water leakage down the inside of the mast into the boat. A boat with a deck-stepped mast does not suffer this problem. In the worst case scenario of being dismasted, the bury section (the section below decks) of keel-stepped masts can sometimes cause damage below decks too, especially if the heel comes away from the mast step. This can happen if the boat is rolled or knocked down.

Although this type of damage is rare, a recent case in the Southern Ocean contributed to the loss of the boat as a watertight bulkhead was damaged. So preventative measures are important. They are simple too. Fastening the mast heel down to the mast step either by through-bolting, or by attaching a rigging screw strop to a hull attachment, is usually sufficient.

But what about the rest of the rig: what should be looked for or specified in a set of

With only the top section of the mast lost, after some sorting out, it may be possible to still use a reefed mainsail. Spinnakers flying free up the mast can usually be recovered by sailing or motoring dead downwind. *Photo: David Harding*

spars that will be fit for bad weather? Spreader roots, gooseneck attachments, shroud tangs and masthead units are the main areas to focus on. Although they all perform separate tasks, they do tend to fall into three categories: cast aluminium units, fabricated aluminium fittings and fabricated stainless steel fittings.

Cast alloy fittings are popular among production spar manufacturers as they are cheaper to produce in numbers and simple to fit to the spars, requiring only a few rivets or machine screws to fasten them (Fig 4.5). Although fine for normal coastal and occasional offshore sailing, castings like these can present more of a problem for longer-distance sailors for a number of reasons.

Aluminium castings are brittle when compared with alloy or steel fabrications, and consequently do not fare well if they receive sharp blows. In the case of a gooseneck, a crash gybe, transferring high shock loads along the boom, could be enough to damage a casting irreparably, whereas it might simply bend or distort a fabricated unit. Cast fittings do not like being distorted either. A spreader set at an incorrect angle can, when loaded, distort a casting to the extent that it fails completely. Again, a fabrication may be more tolerant of such misalignments.

But it has to be said that there are different views on this subject. One justification

in favour of simple screw or rivet-on castings is that they are usually a stock item for the spar builder. As a result, they can easily be sent almost anywhere in the world and can often be fitted without specialist tools. The balance that needs to be struck when considering which system to go for is between the likelihood of failure, against the difficulty of repair.

In this respect there is one type of fitting that is not suitable for those travelling far afield. Spreader root castings welded to the mast wall itself should be avoided where possible, as not only are they more susceptible to failure, for the above reasons, and often reduce the strength of the mast wall locally, but should they be damaged, it is often difficult to repair the mast as the fitting cannot be removed easily. Indeed any arrangement where the spreader transmits its thrust to the mast wall rather than a through bar is to be avoided.

On the other hand, welding masthead units and sheave cages into a tube is not only acceptable for a robust spar, but also desirable, so long as the work is carried out properly. To achieve full strength, most types of aluminium alloy need to be heat treated from a 'soft state' to a 'hard state'. Subsequent welding heats up local areas of the mast section, usually at critical points, and lowers the mechanical properties of the alloy back towards the soft state.

Figure 4.2 Poor articulation will result in fatigue for this forestay, especially when going downwind when the stay is slack.

Figure 4.3 Stemball systems may be neat and simple but often lack articulation under load.

Figure 4.4 Traditional pin and eye attachments. *Photos: Peter Bruce*

The optimum procedure is to perform all welding tasks such as tapering, attaching masthead units, forestay attachments and sheave cages while the tube is in its soft state. Once complete, the tube is then heat treated to achieve its full strength. As far as finish is concerned, anodizing is technically the best means of protecting a mast against corrosion and is normally the most cost effective too for boats of up to around 13m (43ft) LOA.

Painted spars are the next best thing for larger boats, as there are few anodizing tanks that can cope with the size and length of large yacht masts. Furthermore, many people consider a paint finish to be prettier.

Paint finishes have improved significantly, and can offer good protection for an alloy spar so long as the surface is not damaged, but maintaining a perfect, scratch-free mast is a near impossibility. Although scratches and flaking paint are unlikely to cause structural problems themselves, one must keep an eye on any unusual signs that may indicate more serious corrosion beneath.

Staying the rig

There are few statistics to prove it, but most spar manufacturers would agree that aside from poor maintenance and set-up, fatigue and rigging failure are among the most common reasons for dismastings aboard cruising boats. Fatigue cycles, where the fitting is effectively work hardened through repeated flexing, usually start as a result of poor articulation. This is particularly true of the shroud attachments to the mast where the less articulation that is present, the greater the risk of fatigue and subsequent failure. As is so often the case, all it takes is one inexpensive fitting to break to cause far more serious and costly damage to the mast.

So how is it possible to be sure that attachments are suitable? As a rule of thumb, pin and eye attachments are structurally the best as there is a greater chance of the eye rocking on the pin to accommodate different alignments (Fig 4.4). Fittings designed as ball and

Figure 4.5 (ABOVE LEFT) Cast spreader brackets are straightforward to replace if damaged.

Figure 4.6 (ABOVE RIGHT) Good articulation for the forestay and the spinnaker halyard blocks will help to minimize chafe and fatigue – note the plastic ties to lock the shackles.

LEFT Serious chafe leads to extra hoisting work before the failure of the block.

Photos: Peter Bruce

sockets – often referred to as stemball systems – have greater friction between their surfaces and are less likely to articulate (Fig 4.3). The result is fatigue cycles somewhere else in the fitting, usually some way down the stem of a swaged fitting or at the point where the wire exits the end fitting.

T-terminals and similar devices may well be suitable for many applications, but it has to be borne in mind that they will articulate less and need to be replaced on a more regular basis. The big problem is that, apart from the considerable expense of X-raying the terminals, there are no visual indications of how far the fatigue problem has progressed.

Another factor to consider is that few masts remain rigid in one place. Indeed, if they did, high shock loads would be transferred throughout the boat. Instead, masts do move in the boat and the rigging should be able to accommodate the full range of movement. But what is an acceptable amount and how should a mast best be stayed?

The wide range of basic configurations,

plus the added combinations of the variety of multiple spreader arrangements, makes this area a difficult one to define precisely. If it was not for considerations of sheeting the headsail, the wider the chain plate base the better. But as a small sheeting angle is essential for good windward performance, a narrow chain plate base has to be offset by an increase in the number of spreaders up the mast. Larger craft often require discontinuous rigging once three or more sets of spreaders are used.

Generally, most boats are adequately stayed in the athwartships plane. It is achieving sufficient fore-and-aft support that causes most problems. Beating into a heavy seaway with a deep-reefed mainsail can be one of the most punishing situations for a mast. High shock loads transferred through the rigging, as the boat pitches and slams through each wave, can cause the mast to pump fore-and-aft. A deep-reefed mainsail can make the situation worse as the sail tries to pull the middle of the mast aft. Unless checked, this can cause a full inversion of the mast, ie when the middle of the spar bows aft. Under these conditions, masts can and do fail due to the high compression loads, especially when the boat drops off a wave. To prevent this it is important to stop the mast from moving too much in the fore-and-aft plane. Checkstays and running backstays prevent the mast from moving too far forward. Forward lowers or a babystay can help to prevent the mast moving aft, but the small angles where the stays meet the mast mean that an inner forestay should also be included for a belt and braces approach.

The inner forestay, as with the running backstays and checkstays, need not be permanent features and can be stowed by the mast in normal conditions. But for anyone considering trips where they may encounter heavy conditions, such stays are a must, especially on masthead rigged boats.

With the wide popularity of furling headsail systems, it is advisable to make provision for an emergency forestay. Although generally reliable, furling units can fail, and to be left with no headsails at all is inadvisable. Furthermore, even if the furling system works perfectly, when reefed heavily the shape of the remaining scrap of sail is too full and positioned too high up the forestay to act as a sensible storm jib. Setting a flat storm sail, low down, will drive the boat better and reduce heel – providing a much more comfortable ride. In most cases, an emergency forestay can easily be fitted to existing masts as well as new ones. A tang fitting positioned on the forward face of the mast, just below the main forestay fitting, and a tack fitting on deck are usually all that is required.

One popular concern of long-distance sailors is whether rod rigging should be chosen rather than the more conventional 1 x 19 wire. Although rod-rigged systems are generally more expensive than their equivalent in wire, the decision will usually depend upon ease of maintenance.

Conventional stainless steel wire is commonly available around the world and is easy to work with. Swaging tools are found in most popular ports and sailing areas, but for those

travelling much farther afield, bolted cone and socket type (or swageless) fittings, such as the Norseman or Sta Lok-type terminals, require just a hacksaw and spanners to fit them. A further advantage is that these terminations can easily be re-made if any local damage to the wire is found or suspected.

Rod rigging, on the other hand, requires specialist tools to make the terminations and can be more prone to fatigue with few outward signs. Rod rigging does have advantages though. For a given diameter, rod stretches less than wire. This means that a mast can be secured more efficiently in the boat with less deflection of the mast itself, and that weight aloft can also be reduced, improving the performance and motion of the boat. It should also be said that on large cruisers, the scaling effect means that weight aloft becomes a serious issue for which rod rigging is frequently the only sensible option.

Shortening sail

While highly practical, affordable and, best of all, simple, roller reefing systems for main or genoa do have a few drawbacks that should be considered. Headsail furling gears are generally easier to get at than those used for in-mast mainsail furling and present less of a problem in the event of a failure. Furling mainsail systems can snag with the sail jammed in the section and refuse to come in or out which, in the teeth of a gale, could be very awkward. Even if the system is to be trusted completely, provision should be made for some other means of storm mainsail that doesn't rely on the furling device, such as a trysail track.

Unlike slab reefing systems or boom furling systems, where the weight is lowered each time a reef is taken in, vertical furling systems mean that the sail weight remains at the same height above the waterline. Keeping weight high up means that there is no stability improvement as the sail plan is reduced. This can lead to a slow heavy motion due to the inertia of a heavier spar with a furled sail inside it. Furthermore, with furling headsails, the increased windage of a rolled-up headsail over a bare forestay is much greater. Another significant drawback is that if the sail cannot be fully furled, the only way to get it down is to open it out fully before lowering it. This may not be feasible in severe conditions.

In-boom furling systems offer some advantages over their in-mast equivalents, especially when it comes to reducing weight aloft, but the problems of an even furl and the distance of the luff back from the aft face of the mast can cause problems.

Slab reefing is a practical and reliable method of reefing. The comforting thought is that in the worst case, there is a better chance that the sail can be lowered, although this is still by no means guaranteed, especially if a headboard car or batten sliders are fitted. Fully battened and semi/fully battened mainsail systems make the reefing process simpler to manage, especially if lazyjacks are fitted, by reducing the flogging of the mainsail as it is lowered. The sail

also stows more easily on top of the boom.

Single line reefing systems, where the tack and the clew of the reefed mainsail are controlled by a single line, are also very popular and allow a mainsail to be reefed quickly and without having to leave the cockpit. However, one of the potential drawbacks with any control line led back to the cockpit is friction. In order to make the system work as smoothly as possible it is very important to ensure that the reef lines or halyards are kept as free from abrupt turns around lead blocks wherever possible.

Checking and maintaining the rig

How often the rig should be checked will depend entirely on the type of sailing undertaken. While every sailor should keep an eye on the rig all the time, there are practical limits. At the very minimum, weekend,

In the 1992–3 British Steel Global Challenge a number of bottlescrews cracked, and aboard *British Steel II* the mast was lost after the forestay bottlescrew failed on the leg between Rio and Auckland. A jury-rig was made using the boom and spinnaker pole, staysail sheets and reefing lines but, having been refuelled by a P&O tanker, she was able to complete much of the leg under power. *Photo: PPL*

home-based sailors should check their masts at the beginning and end of every season, with the mast being taken out of the boat for a thorough check at least every three years. At the other end of the scale, checking the mast and rigging while on passage should be a daily event. Whatever type of sailing is undertaken, the potential causes of damage or failure are more likely to be as a result of chafe, fatigue or corrosion than from the effects of overloading. In most cases, tell-tale signs of problems can be identified visually, while the mast is in situ, which is just as well as X-raying the mast and fittings would in most cases be impractical, extremely expensive, and sometimes inconclusive.

Aluminium alloy used for most spars has a high natural resistance to corrosion, resulting from the formation of the tough impervious oxide film on the surface of the aluminium when exposed to air. This oxide film, which is grey in colour, is self-repairing. So if removed by chafing or scratching, it will protect the aluminium from further corrosion, provided no dissimilar metals are in contact with the aluminium to cause electrolytic corrosion. However, any substantial corrosion at the base of the mast and at deck level should be treated seriously as these are high load areas for the mast. In these areas, dents in the mast wall can be a problem too and could cause the mast to buckle. This type of damage is not easy to repair without any specialist tools and help.

Cracks are a particularly common starting point for mast or rigging failures and can be remedied so long as they are caught before they have had a chance to propagate too far. The areas to look at are wherever there is an exit or hole in the mast wall – especially if it is rectangular – for example, around halyard exits and where mast fittings penetrate the mast wall. Drilling a small hole at the end of the crack can, in most cases, stop the crack from travelling further, but it will only be a temporary measure and will need more elaborate attention as soon as possible.

Ensuring that all fastenings are secure is perhaps an obvious check, but one that is often overlooked, as is the free running of sheaves which, if jammed, can cause premature chafe and failure of halyards and control lines. If the mast is keel-stepped, another area that is frequently ignored is the deck-level chock arrangement. The chocks should be so secured in place that the mast is prevented from moving at all.

While there are ways in which rigging terminations can be checked using electrical methods, a few simple checks can often reveal potential problems. Looking for broken strands or corrosion within the wire is the most obvious. Elongated eyes or bent pins are an indication of overloading and should be replaced. Alignment of rigging is another important check, as a stay or shroud that is distorted may fail from fatigue. As has already been mentioned, poor articulation is also very important and a common cause of fatigue-related rigging failures. All standing rigging attachments should have some degree of articulation in as many planes as possible. Another simple but essential check is to make sure that the standing rigging is secured to the spreader ends.

Heavy weather procedures under way

Preparation in all areas of the boat is the key to riding out heavy weather conditions, and nowhere is it more important than with the rig. As with many other dramas at sea, all too often a catastrophic event is the culmination of several otherwise controllable or avoidable incidents. Be prepared. Ensure that the trysail will fit in its track by hoisting it, preferably without having to climb above deck level. Have enough sail ties ready to strap down the mainsail if it has to be lowered altogether, and ensure that there is a secure means of lashing the boom to the deck to prevent it being hurled about the cockpit. Life will be difficult enough with the boom in the cockpit instead of overhead, without the further complication of the spar sliding from one side of the boat to the other as the boat rolls in big seas.

Just as important is to ensure that all the heavy weather sails have been tried out, not just when tied up to the pontoon or swinging at a mooring, but under way and preferably when it is blowing. Anticipation is important too as it is far easier and safer to throw out a reef in calm waters, than it is to put one in when the weather has deteriorated. Anticipating the weather is particularly important if furling sails are used. A furled headsail can present considerable windage in gale conditions, to say nothing of the weight aloft. If the forecast is for heavy conditions, it may be prudent to take the sail down altogether and this means unfurling it completely – the last thing to be doing in 40 knots of wind! This also goes for furling mainsails. Although there is no additional windage when the main is furled, in extreme weather it may be sensible to lower the mainsail to reduce the centre of gravity.

When the worst happens

Mast failures are frequently a result of rigging failures, and in many cases quick thinking can save the day – just. A shroud failure, be it a wire or terminal problem, often results in losing the mast. But if the helmsman is quick enough, and it is safe to do so, a smart tack with the jib left cleated will cause the boat to heave-to and allow the mast to be jury-rigged. In some situations it may not be possible to spend much time in this position, but at least it provides time to think about how the mast can best be supported. If a halyard is used to replace a shroud, bear in mind that the angle at the masthead will be very small as the halyard won't run over the spreaders. Using a jockey pole or spinnaker pole just above deck level as an outrigger may help to increase the angle at the masthead and improve support of the spar.

A forestay or backstay failure is less likely to result in an instant dismasting, but it is still a serious problem and should be dealt with quickly. In this case the most important thing to do is to turn either downwind or upwind to take the load onto the intact stay, depending on which one is broken, and then rig temporary support using a spare spinnaker or genoa halyard. If the backstay fails upwind, don't panic. Leave the mainsheet cleated as the leech of the mainsail will help to support the mast. In many cases, be it shroud or stay that fails, it is important not to be too quick to lower the sails, especially if there is a big sea running, as the sails can often help to stabilize the motion of the boat and prevent the mast from panting. However, if the rigging failure happens in flat water and is simply a result of overstressing, dropping the sails may be the best option.

If the worst does happen and the mast falls over the side of the boat, there are two golden rules – get the spar away from the hull and don't start the engine until you are absolutely sure that the rigging cannot foul the propeller. Hull damage is a major consideration in the case of a dismasting, as is the issue of remaining safe on deck and not getting dragged overboard by tangled rigging. Extreme care is required, but also swift action. Cut the rig free to protect the boat, but do remember that the more that can be salvaged the better the chances are of setting up a jury-rig. Sometimes it is not possible to save any of the rig, so it is a good idea to think about how a jury rig might be arranged with just the boom and the spinnaker poles.

Spares and tools

The ideal tool kit is one that provides tools to deal with every component aboard. In reality, this is impractical and a compromise has to be reached. Basic tools should include drills, knives, hacksaws, screwdrivers, spanners, grips and wrenches, which are usually considered essential for all kinds of shipboard

A rain squall struck contenders for the British Admiral's Cup Team seconds after the start of a selection trial race, dismasting Yeoman 25. Her mast failed in compression as a result of the mainsail luff rope pulling out of the track, which allowed the mast to bend forward out of control until it broke. *Photo: Peter Bruce*

tasks. A battery-powered angle grinder can make swift work of removing rod rigging. Tools that are needed specifically for the rig might include the following:

- Rigging cutters (eg Felco) if 1 × 19 wire rigging is used. (Note that only an HT grade hacksaw blade, an angle grinder or a hydraulic cutter will cut rod rigging.)
- Club hammer
- Pipe wrench
- Extra large adjustable wrench and a length of hollow pipe to fit over it
- Sharp cold chisel
- Marlin spike
- Long tape measure
- Rivet gun

Spares
- Clevis pins
- Split pins
- Shackles

- Nuts and bolts
- Screws: machine and self-tapping
- Blocks
- Toggles
- Rigging terminals: swage and swageless
- A length of wire, longer than the longest stay aboard and no less than the biggest diameter, plus swageless fittings to match
- Bulldog clamps
- Mast and boom sleeving kit
- Rivets
- Zinc chromate paste (or other insulating material)
- Seizing wire
- Tape
- Rope and cordage
- Hacksaw blades

5

Storm sails

RICHARD CLIFFORD

SAILING OFFSHORE REQUIRES SMALL, strong sails to cope with extreme wind conditions. On some cruising boats no sail can sensibly be set once the wind has reached storm force, whilst other yachts have so much power that they can keep sailing in surprisingly heavy weather. In winds of gale force or stronger, the two sails that will be of most use to a sloop are a storm jib and a trysail, and yachts racing under ORC racing rules are required to carry both a storm jib (which must be able to be set independently of a luff groove device) and, in races of extended duration, a trysail.

If it is still possible to carry sail at all in gale or storm conditions, the combination of storm jib and trysail enables progress to be made to windward, and if the wind is abaft the beam then the storm jib alone is often satisfactory. As the wind continues to increase, and, depending on the sea state, it may be necessary to use other tactics such as deploying a sea anchor or, if there is enough sea room, lowering all sail and/or running under a bare pole, with or without some drag device. This chapter applies mostly to smaller displacement yachts travelling more slowly than the waves.

Storm jibs

Before furling foresails became the norm, cruising yachts carried a separate storm jib, which was hanked onto the forestay, though this arrangement is now less common. It is a mistake not to have a storm jib, as by the time the furled sail has reached the size of a storm jib it has usually become baggy and will not form an efficient windward shape. It is also likely to be quite high up the forestay thus increasing the heeling moment, and in extreme conditions it is liable to become stretched or damaged. However, if running downwind the shape of the sail does not matter so much and a well-furled foresail is a reasonable option. Indeed a scrap of the furling sail may provide the necessary control while running under conditions when either the storm jib is too large or it would give too much speed for safety. Racing yachts are required to carry a storm jib of no more than defined dimensions[1]. In practice a sail made to the specified size may be too large for gale or storm conditions, and it may be wise to carry an even smaller storm jib called a spitfire jib, as one size of storm jib will not suit a large range of wind speeds, say between 35 and 60 knots.

---

[1] The ORC rules state that the maximum area of the storm jib should be 5 per cent of the height of the fore triangle squared (I2) and it must not exceed 65 per cent of the height of the fore triangle.

LEFT The Storm-Bag storm jib coming out of its bag. RIGHT The Storm-Bag storm jib sets well, though precautions may be necessary to avoid chafe. *Photos: Peter Bruce*

The weight of cloth used for a storm jib should be similar to that used for an offshore cruising mainsail and modern fabric is so strong that there is less need to reinforce than was the case in the past. Nevertheless, abundant strength at the clew is necessary to prevent damage when flogging. Edges should be taped and not just turned over and stitched. Some sailmakers add non-adjustable leech and foot lines within the tapes to add strength. The sail should be cut so that the foot is well off the deck and, if necessary, a strop of wire, Dyneema, or similar low stretch material, can be added both to keep the sail above green water on deck and to adjust the height to bring the clew to a better position for the sheet car. Consideration should also be given to using a high visibility coloured fabric or, failing that, to the addition of a highly visible patch (eg in day-glo orange, pink or yellow) to both sides of the sail. Cloth manufacturers now make orange sails in a wider range of material weights, but it should

not be forgotten that the correct weight and material of cloth is more important than colour. The Offshore Racing Council special regulations prohibit the use of aromatic polyamides or carbon for either storm jibs or heavy weather jibs, though Spectra and Dyneema are acceptable.

An option could be to replace the furling foresail with a storm jib on the grooved forestay (headfoil) but in most circumstances when a storm jib would be set, unfurling, lowering and replacing the furling sail would be difficult and hazardous. Attachment of a storm jib over the furled sail is a possible solution, and devices such as the Gale Sail and Storm-Bag are available on the market. Another arrangement is to set a conventional storm sail with three or four layers of parrel beads to secure the sail around the furled headsail.

Most cruising yachts would use a stretchy 'braid on braid' spinnaker halyard to hoist the storm jib, and the vertical movement of the halyard acting on the furled headsail, and hard points such as parrel beads, will sooner or later cause chafe. Though chafe is obviously most undesirable in the furling headsail, the damage can be patched by making a localized repair that initially may only affect the sun strip.

When the Storm-Bag was tested it was found quite easy to put into position and to hoist, and the double sail system sets well, so will be efficient in extreme conditions. At some point chafe damage would be likely to occur at the points where the halyard is attached and where the top tack knot are up against the furled headsail. By using tape straps sewn to form a loop for the cringles and taken above and below the furled sail, the hard points will be clear of the furled genoa, and the chafe will be substantially reduced though probably not eliminated. The sheets are supplied with a snap shackle to attach them to the clews, but a traditional bowline will probably be better if the flogging clew was to strike a person. The clew rings are a bit on the light side, and the Storm-Bag can be quite difficult to rebag at sea.

Hoisting a storm jib loose-luffed can be unsatisfactory owing to the difficulty of obtaining a straight enough luff, and to the difficulty of hoisting the jib in windy conditions with the likelihood of a halyard wrap at the top of the mast or around the spreaders. The balance of the storm sails should also be taken into account when deciding the position for the storm jib, and generally it is better to have the inner forestay as far forward as the situation allows rather than aft. There are instances of cutter-rigged yachts where the inner forestay has been so far back that the boat will not tack.

So the better option is probably to have a separate storm jib that is hoisted independently of the furling headsail and, for sloops with furling headsails, to provide a separate inner forestay onto which the storm jib can be hanked. Conventional cutter rigged yachts have the option of setting the storm jib on the inner forestay. Alternatively, if a small furling staysail is used, in some cases it will furl down adequately to be used as a storm jib, especially if it is made from material with a low stretch character.

The siting of a separate inner forestay for the storm jib is critical. When required it should be easy to fit, and when not in use it should be out of the way. It must also be sufficiently clear of the furling forestay so that it is possible to operate the furling sail with the inner forestay in position, and positioned so the hanks of the storm jib cannot chafe the furled sail. It must be possible to tension the inner forestay so that the storm jib will set efficiently. Additionally, the top of the stay must be attached at a point that is below and clear of the furling gear to prevent halyard wrap, and at the foot of the stay a single strong point is needed which is comfortably clear of the furling drum. There are various levers and systems on the market that can be used to tension the inner stay, which include a wheel-operated rigging screw and a Highfield lever. When no single strong point is available, the rigging screw can be attached to a four-legged bridle with each leg going to a strong point on the foredeck, but this method does present extra difficulty when working on the foredeck.

Once the inner stay is set up, it may seem necessary to roll the furling headsail before tacking or gybing but, with practice, this is usually only a problem when short tacking. The inner stay can also be used for twin headsail running as well as a back up should the main forestay fail and it is common practice to passage-make with the inner forestay set up for additional security. When not in use the inner stay needs to be kept clear of the mast, spreaders and running rigging; for example it can be secured on a pad eye on the coachroof designed so that both ends of the tensioning device are held firmly. Yachts with in-line spreaders can stow the inner forestay on the toerail between the cap shroud and the forward lower shroud provided the point is clear of the genoa.

A separate halyard is needed for the storm jib, and this halyard needs to lead clear of the furling gear at the top of the mast. It should

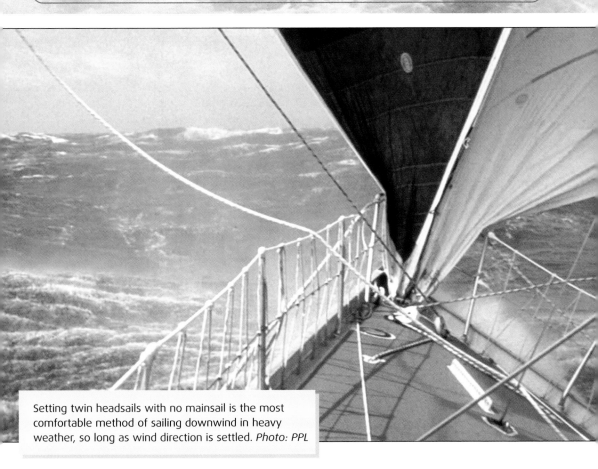

Setting twin headsails with no mainsail is the most comfortable method of sailing downwind in heavy weather, so long as wind direction is settled. *Photo: PPL*

either leave the mast just below the attachment point for the inner forestay, or run from a sheave at the truck down to a fairlead that is below the attachment point for the top of the inner forestay. The spinnaker pole topping lift, if made of low stretch material rope, can sometimes double as the storm jib halyard but it is always better to have a dedicated storm jib halyard.

The correct sheeting position for the storm jib should be established in calm conditions and a tack strop is often necessary to achieve an acceptable sheeting angle. If a tack strop is fitted it may be useful to have a hank, snap shackle or even just a lashing in the tack cringle to attach to the forestay in order to stop the sail pulling away from the stay and stressing the lowest hank. In any event it will be advantageous to raise the tack clear of breaking seas and improve visibility forward.

In some cases the storm jib may have its own sheets and its own cars but if the sheets are permanently attached to the storm jib two people may need to go forward to set it – one to hank on and the other to run the sheets. Unless the storm jib sheets have been meticulously coiled and lashed they can come out of the bag snarled up, and it may be easier to have two sheets permanently set up with the cars positioned, so that the sheets can be secured after the sail is hanked on. If using non-furling headsails, the sheets from the previous sail can often be used and, in some yachts, the storm jib tack strop is arranged so that the sheeting position of the smaller genoas is the same as for the storm jib and there is no need to move the cars.

The storm jib needs to be stored in its bag together with all its shackles, strops and blocks in a reasonably accessible stowage, and brought out from time to time for examination and for practice in setting.

When it becomes apparent that the storm jib will be required, the first action is to prepare the inner forestay and ensure it is appropriately tensioned and clear of any running rigging that may be flapping around the mast. The storm jib halyard will require a winch, which may mean clearing the winch that is normally occupied by the halyard for the furling headsail. The storm jib then needs to be taken forward in its bag and attached to the inner forestay – a hank or karabiner fitted to the bag is useful to secure the bag while the storm jib is being taken out. Pre-rigged sheets can save a lot of work in difficult conditions.

After the sheets have been attached, the foresail should be furled and then the storm jib hoisted and sheeted in as quickly as possible, preferably with a bit of windward sheet tension to control the flog, preserve the clew and to ensure that the bowline does not shake itself undone. Just how much sheet tension used is boat specific and is learned by trial and error. It may be necessary to ease the sheets of the furling sail or to secure them well forward to prevent them catching on the storm jib as it is hoisted, or chafing when the storm jib is eased. Likely causes of chafe are from the hanks of the storm jib, or inner stay, rubbing on the furled headsail, and from the sheets of the furled headsail rubbing on the storm jib, which may need to be temporarily re-routed. The sheets of the furled headsail or even a small area of foresail can be useful to contain the storm jib as it is lowered.

Of all these points, the need for a storm jib, which can be set separately from the furling headsail, is the critical factor if windward progress in heavy weather is to be possible.

Trysails

The trysail is a triangular sail, which is attached to the mast but is set loose-footed and can be sheeted independently of the main boom. The traditional use of a trysail is to replace the mainsail in heavy weather in order to balance the storm jib and to improve the ability of the yacht to sail to windward. It has secondary uses such as to replace the mainsail if it has been damaged or blown out or if the boom or gooseneck has broken. An example of this use of a trysail was when Hugh Clay in *Aratapu*, having broken his gooseneck, sailed under trysail for most of the passage from Tasmania to Chile. The Offshore Racing Council requires yachts racing in Categories 0–2 (Trans-Ocean in offshore or large unprotected areas where a high degree of self-sufficiency is required) to carry one storm trysail and it specifies the maximum size and some aspects of sail construction[2].

A trysail needs to be strong and should be made from a fabric that is the same weight but softer than a mainsail, perhaps using a high visibility colour. The major consideration in construction is strength at the three corners and in particular at the clew that, due to the narrow angle at the aft end of the sail, is a high-stress area and made weaker by the insertion of a cringle eye to take the sheets. All three corners thus need reinforcement patching, backed up with webbing straps, and the eyes need to be fitted using a hydraulic press. The sail can be leech-cut, with the seams parallel to the leech to maintain continuity of strength along the most highly loaded edge of the sail, or cross-cut with the seams perpendicular to the leech, giving less stretch. If slides are used on the luff, the top and bottom

---

[2] The rules state the trysail is to be capable of being sheeted independently of the boom and of an area not greater than 17.5 per cent mainsail luff length x mainsail foot length. There should be neither headboard nor battens. The yacht's sail number and letter(s) shall be placed on both sides of the trysail in as large a size as is practicable. Aromatic polyamides, carbon fibres and other high modulus fibres shall not be used in the trysail.

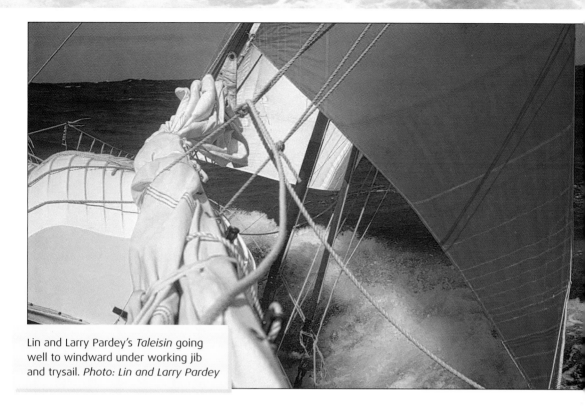

Lin and Larry Pardey's *Taleisin* going well to windward under working jib and trysail. *Photo: Lin and Larry Pardey*

slides should be aluminium or stainless steel while the others can be plastic, but all should be attached to the sail with webbing rather than the weaker plastic shackles often used on mainsails. If lacing or parrel beads are used, care should be taken to avoid snagging points on the mast.

One of the many comments that came out of the Sydney–Hobart Race storm in 1998 was the fact that skippers thought their trysails were too big. Tim Trafford thought the same as he was closing the coast of Chile on passage from Easter Island in 1998. While sailing the 16.7m (55ft) yacht *Ardevora* he was caught in a northerly storm with a strong northerly current running whilst on the edge of soundings, and refrained from setting his trysail as he thought it was too big for those conditions, using instead a sea anchor which, incidentally, proved to be too small.

The issue of size must therefore be considered carefully and one might even consider carrying two trysails; one made close to the ORC maximum recommended size to substitute for the main in case of damage, and the other made much smaller for use as a storm trysail in more severe conditions. An alternative might appear to be to add reef points on the larger trysail, but to attempt to reef such a sail in severe conditions would be adding another operational hazard so this is not practical.

Sheets can be permanently bent to the sail using a single line, halved at the clew. Although one sheet can be sufficient as tacking is unlikely under trysail, better control will be possible with two. The lead should be judged from the cut of the sail, and a block fitted to the appropriate point on deck. Sheeting to the end of the boom is another possibility when the boom is not damaged, but the downward angle of the leech from the mast to the clew is likely to be very flat and therefore an inefficient carrier of the combined weight of boom, mainsail and perhaps 50 litres of water, so the boom would need support from a topping lift or possibly a solid vang. An inadvertent gybe involving the boom in storm conditions can be disastrous, for example the binnacle can be picked up and damaged or the

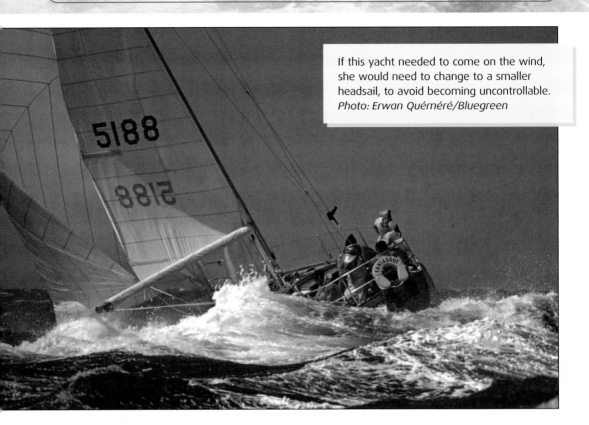

If this yacht needed to come on the wind, she would need to change to a smaller headsail, to avoid becoming uncontrollable.
Photo: Erwan Quémére/Bluegreen

boom mainsheet fitting can fail. But with just the two sheets in use without the boom, inadvertent gybes are no problem – the sail just flops over. When sailing downwind the clew of the trysail sheeted to the boom and held by a fore guy can be more efficient and more convenient than using double sheets and no boom, but it is even better to set twin headsails. When sheeting without using the boom, a block on the quarter or the spinnaker sheet block will be suitable. Yachts with a limited number of winches may need to lead the sheet across to a windward winch. As with setting the storm jib, a little practice in light weather will determine the best arrangement and prove invaluable when the sail has to be set in anger.

Small yachts may have only one mainsail halyard and a topping lift, in which case transferring the halyard needs to be done with care due to the risk of losing the shackle, allowing the halyard to fly loose or allowing the halyard to wrap around a mast fitting. A safety line from a cleat to the thimble on the

halyard is a wise precaution, as is seizing the shackle (which should have a captive pin) to the halyard. A spare main halyard will make the transfer a bit easier, and if the topping lift is made of a sufficiently low stretch material, it can double as the spare halyard, although this does assume that either a solid kicker is fitted or that the boom will be lashed to the coachroof or deck when the trysail is set. Ideally a set of boom gallows should be fitted, which allow the boom to be firmly secured when the main is lowered, and should accommodate solid kicking straps and spray hoods, making the task of changing sails aft of the mast safer and easier.

Another consideration is that the halyard from the masthead down to the head of the trysail is liable to flog tiresomely against the mast when the trysail is hoisted. Changing the halyard tension simply alters the frequency, and in storm conditions it is obviously impossible to get up there and secure it. A remedy, that may be unacceptable to some due to the increase in complication,

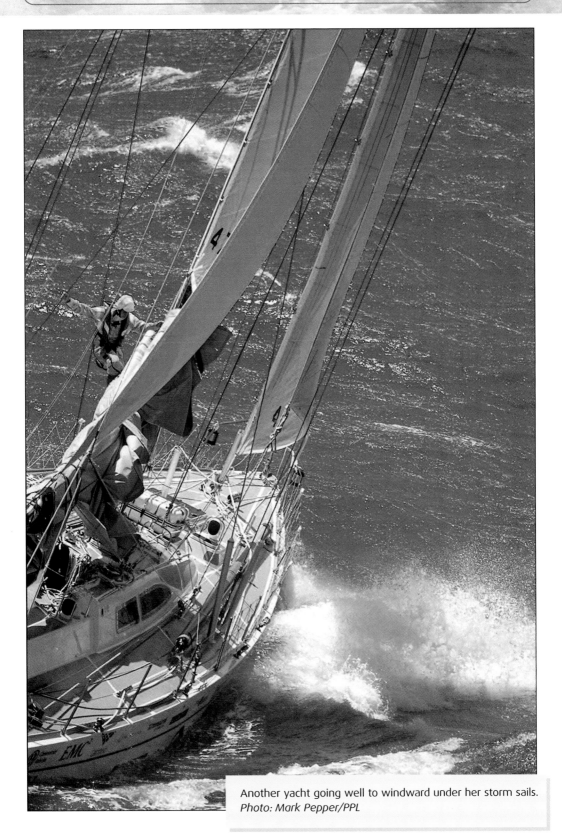

Another yacht going well to windward under her storm sails.
Photo: Mark Pepper/PPL

is to add a long reinforced tape fitted to the head of the trysail with slides at appropriate intervals, long enough to reach to about half a metre from the halyard sheave. The tape must be carefully fed untwisted into the mast luff slot and flaked and tied before stowing.

The tack of the trysail needs to be fitted with a tack line that should be attached to a strong point below the boom and be long enough for the trysail to set above the handed and bundled mainsail. Finding a suitable securing point may require some thought on yachts with aft-led halyards because if the tack is secured directly to the gooseneck it may foul and chafe the stowed mainsail; moreover it is possible that the gooseneck may have broken.

There are several different systems for hoisting a trysail. When Bermudan rigged yachts had wooden masts, many had two tracks, one for the mainsail and the other for the trysail. A system of lacing the luff of the trysail to the mast is impracticable on most masts due to the lacing snagging on a mast fitting. Some yachts had a very short secondary track with a junction and gate system so that once above the top slides of the handed mainsail the secondary track joins the main track. Gaff rigged yachts had a trysail bent onto its own gaff. Today, with the predominance of aluminium masts, a second track can again be fitted alongside the main track and, although it is not often seen, it is the best system for hoisting a trysail. Ideally the track should lead down to near deck level so that the bagged trysail can be put at the foot of the mast with its tack made fast and all the slides in the track, ready to hoist at short notice.

Both Willy Ker and Michael Thoyts, two experienced singlehanded ocean sailors, habitually sail with their trysail at the base of the mast all ready for the moment it is required, but this has potential disadvantages of the risk of chafe from non-slip deck paint and the possibility of loss or damage through the sail living in such an exposed stowage. Those with in-mast reefing may unwisely consider that they do not require a separate sail as they can reef the main until it is very small, provided that it is made sufficiently strong in the clew area. This will be true until something jams or breaks. Masts fitted with a retrofit in-mast reefing system sometimes have a track or luff groove for another sail within the housing, and this may serve for use with the trysail.

The trysail should be the easiest sail on the boat to set but, perversely, it is often the most difficult. If no second track is fitted it is necessary to drop a tightly reefed and bundled main out of the only track, secure it and then fit the trysail slides into the track – a difficult task in conditions in which a trysail might normally be set and consequently one which needs to be tackled early as it may be the only means (in conjunction with a storm jib) to make to windward, perhaps off a lee shore.

Those owners who have a gate on the track above the bundled mainsail may find operation difficult due to the height of the gate off the deck and in most cases the gate is located part way up the stowed stack of slides, resulting in some or all of the mainsail slides having to be removed before the trysail slides can be inserted. This operation is impractical with a fully battened mainsail. With a boltrope system, once the mainsail has been lowered it is easier to insert the boltrope of the trysail and hoist the sail, but lowering a mainsail without sliders can be hard to control, even with several strong crew. All in all, the best system is to use a long, second, independent trysail track fitted for sliders.

In most modern yachts the most convenient method of securing the boom when not in use is to set it up tight on the topping lift or rod kicker and sheet it in hard, although this will cause most windage. In the days of long heavy booms the answer was to either secure the boom firmly in the gallows, or lower the end of the boom to the quarter and secure it well; but lowering to the quarter may be difficult on yachts with rod-kickers, fixed windscreens, or spray hoods. The end of the boom lying on the deck is also an obstacle for green water breaking across the deck, and if the boat is tacked and the boom is up to windward it is yet more unsatisfactory. In the Sydney–Hobart Race of 1998, a helmsman was tragically swept overboard and lost when the stanchion, to which the boom was lashed, carried away. Unless a boom crutch is used, the preferred method is to have the boom hoisted and held firm with two preventers, or the mainsheet and one preventer, as using the mainsheet alone allows too much movement. It is important to remember to set the boom lower than the foot of the trysail and to set the leeward trysail sheet on the correct side of the topping lift.

It has been known for a knockdown wave to blast a hole through the flaked mainsail, so it is vitally important to have the main as tightly furled as possible, perhaps using spare line to wrap the sail so as to present a minimized target. Whatever solution is adopted, care must always be taken to prevent any chafe, which could hole or damage either mainsail or trysail.

Some yachts will heave-to best under trysail rather than mainsail and storm jib, though not forereaching at such speed as to be uncomfortable, while other yachts will heave-to best under storm jib alone. In my own yacht a trysail alone works best.

One successful use of a trysail was by David Cowper when rounding Cape Horn on his second single-handed round-the-world passage in *Ocean Bound* when he went to windward in a series of storms up to force 11, which had been blowing for a week. He put up his orange trysail and found the motion of the boat was easier and any shipped water was quickly shed. However, in over 200,000 miles largely in the higher latitudes, he only used his trysail twice. In many ocean miles Willy Ker has also only used his trysail twice. I have used mine many times, but mostly in milder conditions when comfort was more important than speed. In the 1979 Fastnet Race storm 12 yachts in the fleet of 303 used a trysail, and in the Sydney–Hobart Race in 1998, out of 115 entries, 47 yachts used their trysail, though most thought them too large for the force 12 conditions. *Berrimilla* was an exception, her trysail was not too big, and although she was knocked down a few times, all the solid water tended to go below the sail with just froth going into the sail, and the boat behaved exceptionally well. Some believe that when sailing off the wind it is better to sheet in the trysail hard to avoid giving dirty air to the jib, but better still is to use the trysail only as a windward sail, taking it down off the wind and using just a headsail.

There are offshore cruising yachtsmen who prefer to carry a spare mainsail and a small storm trysail. Some sailmakers, for example in New Zealand, place mainsail reefing points in such a way that the boom lifts higher with every reef (for example 45cm (18in) per reef for a 11m (36ft) yacht), to make it less likely that the boom will dip into the sea. The main boom fore guy or preventer led from the top of the kicking strap often leads to boom breakage in the open ocean, so it should be led forward from the end of the boom if there is any chance that the end of the boom will drag in the sea when heeled; a length of rope from the end of the boom can be permanently led under the boom to ensure that the preventer is immediately available when required.

In conclusion, offshore yachts should carry at least one storm jib and trysail of appropriate size and strength with appropriate rigging arrangements, and their use should be exercised from time to time in normal conditions.

6

Preparations for heavy weather

PETER BRUCE

AFTER SHIPS OF HIS US PACIFIC FLEET were seriously damaged or sunk in Typhoon Cobra on 18 December 1944 with the loss of 790 officers and men, Fleet Admiral Nimitz wrote a letter to the fleet which ended with the following comment: 'The time for taking all measures for a ship's safety is while able to do so. Nothing is more dangerous than for a seaman to be grudging in taking precautions lest they turn out to have been unnecessary. Safety at sea, for a thousand years, has depended upon exactly the opposite philosophy.'

Whilst some heavy weather is almost the inevitable lot of the ocean voyager, the majority of coastal sailors will be in a position to avoid it most of the time, very sensibly, by the exercise of discretion and by good planning. But meteorology is not an exact science, so there is always a chance of being caught out in a blow at sea, however carefully one has studied the weather and listened to the weather forecasts. One can find oneself caught out in a storm anytime and anywhere. If this does happen, the aim should be to come through the experience safely, without damage, independently of outside assistance, and in as much comfort and good humour as the circumstances permit.

To achieve this aim, the wise skipper will make contingency plans and will practise for heavy weather either in harbour or in calm weather, knowing that he should expect no more than simple tasks to be undertaken by his crew when it comes on to blow. Storms can creep up insidiously on the crew of a vessel at sea; in a sailing boat, this often happens after a period of exhilaration as wind and wave exceed normal expectations. The time comes later when crews show a gradually decreasing tendency to make any additional effort, save, one hopes, that of attending to necessary reductions of sail. Their main interest will lie in adjusting to discomfort or reconciling themselves to seasickness.

Clearly, a crew's energy and resources are best reserved for matters that cannot be anticipated. A skipper with no inner doubts about the fitness of his vessel and equipment will find it easier to inspire his crew to make the special effort needed in a storm. This chapter is written without a particular level of severity of weather in mind, but rather in acknowledgement of the fact that an unexpected encounter with heavy weather may occur at any time.

Harbour preparations

One cannot buy safety nor guarantee survival, but one can buy equipment that in practised hands can improve safety. Predominately it is a crew's skill that will mostly affect the issue in an emergency.

A well-prepared and strongly built vessel should be able to withstand any breaking sea, but caught beam-on to waves such as these, there will be a high chance of capsize. A yacht with good stability will tend to right herself in seconds and a yacht with poor stability may not right herself for many minutes. *Photo: Safehaven Marine*

Safety equipment comes in many forms and will vary according to the extent of the voyage. As mentioned by Olin Stephens in Chapter 1, a useful list of seamanlike measures to cope with eventualities in bad weather is provided by the ISAF Offshore Special Regulations. These regulations are compulsory for yachts in most offshore races worldwide, but cruising boat owners would also do well to study them, as they have been distilled from many years of experience. If he, or she, is to face bad weather with confidence, a skipper needs to do more than buy and mount the safety equipment that his conscience dictates, or that complies with regulations. He and his crew must know how to use it through testing it in a non-threatening situation.

In addition to safety equipment, even the owner of a new vessel may need to make an occasional effort to keep on top of defects in a vessel's general equipment; in the case of an older boat, a constant effort may be necessary. In calm weather, the adaptable human quickly reconciles himself to such things as small leaks, quirky navigation lights, a seized hull valve, a defective pump, a blocked drain and so on. Such shortcomings can assume enormous proportions in rough weather, creating an emergency out of something previously regarded as a trivial problem. Recording such faults in a 'defect book' is a helpful means of maintaining a boat in seaworthy condition.

Storm sails tend not to be used very often, and after use are usually returned to their bags with little thought for the future. It is wise, therefore, to wash the salt out and check them for weak or broken stitching and sticky hanks at the end of every season.

In addition to commonplace failures, another potentially weak area lies with standby equipment. For example, when the jib furling gear breaks, is there an alternative system and will it be operable? When the GPS fails in fog, will the batteries for the standby be charged, and will it work? Likewise, the reserve bilge pump, the emergency navigation lights, and so on.

It has to be said that not all new boats are fit for heavy weather on delivery, particularly production boats. Apart from the need for inherent structural strength, serious offshore owners will often have to carry out numerous modifications. For example, a separate trysail mast track can be added which runs down to near-deck level, allowing the sail to remain bagged at the foot of the mast ready for instant use. Lee cloths may have to be changed for ones of adequate size and strength; bolts may have to replace screws; penny washers changed for proper backing pieces for deck fittings; anchor well lids may need fastenings; mainsails may need more reefing points; arrangements may be necessary to set a storm jib; adaptations may be necessary to deploy a parachute sea anchor, and so on. A surveyor's advice can be helpful in this situation.

When planning a vessel's chart portfolio, either before a voyage or during the lay-up period, it should be ensured that there is adequate information in the event of being blown well off course, or having to find an unfamiliar port of refuge under the stress of bad weather. It is easy to imagine the anguish of being forced into an area of shoal waters without a chart.

Planning for dire situations

A good heavy weather principle is to hope for the best and prepare for the worst. For example, Chay Blyth used to prepare himself on a flat calm day by staging the onset of a fictitious gale and working through his sail wardrobe from full sail to storm sails.

Another method is to plan and practise for dire circumstances. Such action can have a negative effect on less experienced crew, so give them notice, ie 'Tomorrow morning at 10 am we will do safety drills!' Among the worst of all the dire situations that should be considered are: one or more members of the crew falling overboard; the necessity to make to windward under sail in heavy weather to clear a lee shore; fire; capsize; or the need to abandon ship.

Man overboard

Looking at these events in turn, the man overboard situation comes to mind first. The UK's Royal National Lifeboat Institution deals with more fatalities from people lost overboard than any other cause. There are four phases involved when someone is lost overboard: location; attachment; recovery on board and treatment.

At the risk of stating the obvious, location is much assisted by immediately nominating someone to keep the casualty in sight. One cannot assume that this will always be possible in big seas, so it is of equal priority to practise recording the vessel's position, both with appropriate buoyant safety gear, and by using such navigational aids as may be available. In a real situation, in addition to the measures taken on board, outside help should be summoned without delay.

Two different methods for the retrieval of man overboard are in favour – the 'quick-stop' and the 'reach-tack-reach' method. I instinctively adopted the 'quick-stop' method with a satisfactory result in my 7m (23ft) yacht *Scarlet Runner* in 1973, when surfing downwind under spinnaker in an English Channel race. Immediately after the man was lost over the bow, the yacht, which had no engine, was turned into wind as the spinnaker was dropped. The sail backed across the fore triangle and was successfully gathered in as the boat beat back under mainsail to the man in the water. He was hauled in

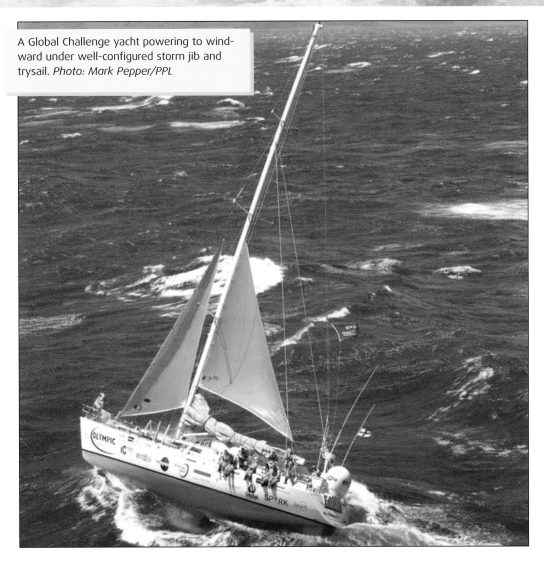

A Global Challenge yacht powering to windward under well-configured storm jib and trysail. *Photo: Mark Pepper/PPL*

from the lee side at a point just aft of the shrouds.

The other method, taught by the Royal Yachting Association for many years, involves turning onto a reach, followed by a tack and a reach back to the victim. It is preferable to spend time trying either one of them, rather than spending the time discussing which one to employ.

At first, it may be found that an effort may be necessary to persuade a crew to exercise a man overboard drill, but thereafter it will almost certainly be perceived as an important evolution, worthy of practice and discussion. The quick and seamanlike retrieval of some suitable object from the sea, without the use of the engine – as propellers so often catch a rope in a crisis – also provides a source of deserved satisfaction within a crew. Equally important is to prove by practical trial that the equipment intended for quick deployment, such as a horseshoe lifebuoy with a flashing light attached to it by a lanyard, can be used effectively in stressful circumstances. Experience, supported by trials in the USA, shows that a tangle is likely at the first attempt.

Every boat should have at least one means of lifting a casualty back on board. A stern bathing ladder is not the answer in a seaway.

In particular, couples who sail on their own together should consider how to cope with the situation where the stronger and heavier partner has fallen over the side. The Seattle Sailing Foundation was inspired to study this aspect of the man overboard problem by some understandable but heartbreaking local tragedies. In one case a man, an experienced sailor, went overboard on a blustery day from the foredeck of his yacht. His wife, his sole crew, who was not experienced, had no idea what to do. Frozen with horror she steered straight which was what her husband had always told her to do when she was at the helm until she hit the beach some time later. Her husband was never found. In another case, a skipper was lost and drowned even after being brought alongside, due to difficulties in hoisting him on board.

There is some very good equipment available to aid the recovery of a man overboard. At the same time one should be aware that there may be a tendency these days to place too much reliance on technology, so it is best only to buy items that have withstood the stringency of thorough testing. Mike Golding carried 'personal EPIRBs' in the 1997 BT Round the World Race. Rather than have the crew wear them, one or two were placed within easy reach of the helmsman who was instructed to throw them over the side if someone was lost.

A small waterproof torch carried in a foul weather jacket pocket as a back-up device is not only useful for finding things down below at night without disturbing the off-watch crew, but the torch might also provide a position indicator should one ever involuntarily part company with one's vessel. Of course a personal strobe light is ideal for this purpose.

Obviously prevention is better than cure, and in addition to non-slip surfaces and foot-gear, the value of a well-designed safety harness, built to the standard Offshore Racing Council specification and adjusted so that one will not slip out, cannot be overestimated. Foredeck crews are most exposed, but they tend to be nimble and aware of the haz-

ard, whereas those not used to being on the foredeck can be equally exposed so more at risk. Less obvious moments of exposure, but ones that have claimed lives, are those when crews unclip their safety harnesses to go below or have not yet clipped on when coming on deck. It is good practice to pass the clip up for the on-watch crew to clip on before progressing to the cockpit and vice versa. With practice, education, well-positioned strong points and jackstays, it should be possible to avoid ever being unclipped when on deck. The harness should be clipped on in a way that prevents a person falling over the side rather than merely preventing him from being separated from his craft having done so.

Another point worth bearing in mind is that the stitching of safety harnesses deteriorates in sunlight. The racing authority in Australia now requires that safety lines are replaced every seven years.

In spite of more general use of safety harnesses, there still remains a chance of losing someone overboard. Two more common examples are when gentlemen are relieving themselves over the side, and when crew members are struck on the head by the boom in an unexpected gybe. Chances of survival, once in the water, are obviously much increased when a lifejacket is being worn. In the latter case, when the victim is unconscious, the facility of automatic inflation is desirable, but automatic inflation leads to extra expense and effort as it often activates when not required. Mike Golding disarmed the auto inflation capability during the BT Global Challenge Race of 1997.

There is something to be said for foul weather jackets with built-in safety harness and lifejacket, as the decision to put them on is then directly linked with windy or bad weather, and little effort is required. However, it is difficult to design built-in life-jackets with features to make them effective in rough water. For example, the experience of man overboard from the yacht *Hayley's Dream* in the 1989 Fastnet showed that it is necessary to incorporate a crutch strap, to prevent the lifejacket riding up over the casualty's head. Another man overboard case, which occurred in the 1989–90 Whitbread Round the World Race, draws attention to the value of a spray guard to prevent the casualty drowning from inhaled spray, as in stormy weather the layer above the sea surface is more water than air. All such features can be achieved when the lifejacket is combined with a safety harness, rather than an oilskin jacket, an arrangement that would appear to optimize both safety and convenience.

In concluding this subject, it should be remembered that drowning, rather than hypothermia, is the predominant cause of loss of life in man overboard incidents.

A lee shore

The next eventuality to be considered is to be close to a lee shore, which was once such a terrifying prospect to the crews of square-rigged vessels. Such is the weatherliness of modern craft that a lee shore is not now such a common cause for concern. Nevertheless, circumstances can come about when a yacht will only be saved from shipwreck by having the ability to make to windward under storm sails. Those who have a roller headsail system should be aware that, as the headsail is rolled in, it becomes baggy and increasingly inefficient as a windward sail. Some standard production yachts are neither supplied with storm sails, nor with provision to use them. To reduce the cost of the sail inventory, others are supplied with sails described as storm jibs that are too big for use in really severe weather.

Even when in possession of a sensibly sized storm jib, it should be remembered that, to be effective to windward, sheet leads and the point at which the jib is attached to the foredeck need careful assessment. Ideally, the tack of the storm jib should be taken to a point somewhat aft, but not too far aft, of the stem fitting to obtain optimum balance and interaction between it and the mainsail/trysail. But to achieve this, a properly designed independent forestay, supported by running

Caught on a lee shore: *Gypsy Moth V* beached on the rocks during the BOC Challenge Race 1982. *Photo: Ace Marine/PPL*

backstays, will be necessary. A tack pendant is often advisable to raise the storm jib to give greater clearance to waves breaking over the foredeck and can also serve to allow the clew of the storm jib to suit a particular sheeting point. In addition, sheet leads for a storm jib will need to be positioned further outboard than for the larger headsails to give a greater angle from the centreline with the aim of achieving an efficient rather than a high pointing windward sail. Finally, for yachts that use a headfoil system rather than hanks, consideration needs to be given to coping with an unusable foil. Headfoils are tough, but can be crushed by a spinnaker pole. Moreover, plastic versions have been known to fragment through cold temperatures or prolonged exposure to natural ultra-violet light.

Mainsails are often supplied without a sufficiently deep reef capability, ie the ability to reef to 25 per cent of the full area. This is, presumably, on the risky assumption that the engine will be used if it becomes too windy to sail, or that most owners are not out in severe weather. Even if a good deep reef provision in the mainsail has been made, it is still important to ensure that the reefing line is located to create a really flat sail. A well-reefed but over-full mainsail can create more heeling moment than an unreefed but well-flattened sail.

Assuming conditions warrant its use, a trysail is a most efficient sail, but it is usually difficult to set, due to the necessary height above the deck of the luff fastening arrangement – normally a slider gate – coupled with the proximity of the mainsail. Ideally, a separate mast track should be provided for the trysail. This allows the trysail to be bent on before the mainsail is lowered. Whatever system is used, a new trysail must be given at least one airing in calm conditions. Clearly, it is better to find that the sliders are the wrong size for the track in harbour, than when drifting onto a rocky lee shore in a force 10 storm. Sheeting positions should be tried with and without a serviceable boom. A good opportunity to put up storm sails might be when forced by lack of wind to make a passage under engine, or when racing has been cancelled due to bad weather.

Further details of suitable arrangements for storm sails will be found in Chapter 5.

Fire

Fortunately fires at sea are rare, but if one does occur in stormy conditions, as well it can, the fire is yet more difficult to deal with. The confined space of a yacht will rapidly fill with smoke and will probably have to be abandoned immediately, with the possibility that there is no access to the radio, the life-raft or the flares. Quick thinking and action is imperative in this short period.

Electrical fires are most likely in rough weather, caused by an ingress of salt water or by the yacht's movement creating a short circuit. Good design and construction will obviate most problems but the owner must ensure that his battery fastenings can stand extreme angles of heel and heavy shock without the possibility of a short circuit being created. If an electrical fire does occur, switching off power will help the situation if the problem is down-supply from the switch. However, many fires occur at the main power leads near the battery and these cannot be isolated by breakers or fuses. It is essential that the batteries cannot shift nor that anything can shift onto them. For example, there is a case where a fuel tank broke loose, shifting the battery, which then caused the main supply to short, hence causing a fire.

ISAF special regulations require all racing yachts to carry two fire extinguishers 'readily accessible in suitable and different parts of the yacht'. For trans-oceanic vessels three dry powder extinguishers of 2kg, including one extinguisher or system suitable for dealing with a fire in a machinery space, are required, plus a fire blanket adjacent to the cooker. In my own experience of a fire at sea, having four buckets in a deck locker proved valuable, as it was seawater thrown from the buckets that put out the fire, not the fire extinguishers.

Capsize

The importance of a stable, strong and water-tight hull has been referred to in earlier chapters of this book. The need for these features is particularly important in the dire situation of a capsize. To be prepared for a capsize, one should try to imagine one's vessel being placed upside down in the sea, with ventilator plugs in place. Thus orientated, a well-designed and soundly built craft should have minimal leaks, even through the companionway or the cockpit lockers. Clearly, heavy items such as the engine, the galley stove, the deep freeze, all anchors – especially that extra-heavy emergency anchor deep in the bilge – batteries, gas cylinders, tanks and internal ballast should be installed with total inversion in mind. If yachts were subject to an inversion test with full tanks when new, not all would come through unscathed.

It might be thought that floorboards do not come into the category of items that should be secured, on the grounds that access to the bilges can often be useful, and perhaps essential in the event of being holed. A compromise is the best solution. One should leave the floorboard that gives access to the strum box unsecured, while other floorboards are screwed down with a minimum number of fastenings that can rapidly be removed in an emergency, or for cleaning.

Securing heavy items properly is half the battle; the other half entails educating the crew to conform to the time-honoured mariner's practice of 'securing for sea'. Adequate locker space and proper stowage are necessary to give this prescription a chance, but even so it will be found that stowing and securing all loose gear before leaving harbour, and keeping a vessel tidy thereafter, does not come naturally to most mortals. Nevertheless, unexpected events at sea can be so confounding that it does not always need a capsize to prove the wisdom of an orderly ship.

If a yacht is turned through 360° the mast is usually broken due to rig failure. It may be unrealistic to strengthen the rig so much as to make such failure impossible, but as most yachts are designed for 'ordinary' sailing, a degree of beefing up may be wise for ocean-going sailors.

While on the subject of capsize it should be mentioned that a safety harness line should have a clip at both ends so that, in the event of a prolonged inversion or a vessel foundering, crew have a means of releasing themselves within reach.

A sinking vessel

Our final worst situation is that moment when a liferaft will shortly be the only craft left afloat, and the moment has come to pull the inflation cord. An example of such a situation took place in a force 9 gale a mile off Salcombe on 11 August 1985. The 9.1m (30ft) sloop *Fidget*, built of mahogany on oak by Camper & Nicholson in 1939, fell about 6m (20ft) off the back of a wave in a very large cross-sea. She opened up and sank in about 30 seconds. The skipper, Simon Wilkinson, who habitually keeps a knife in his foul weather jacket pocket, only just had time to cut the liferaft and uninflated tender free from their lashings before *Fidget* foundered, and the crew were left swimming. It was fortunate that they were already wearing lifejackets, because there was an interval before the inflation cord, which was still attached to the yacht, came taut, and the liferaft inflated. Simon Wilkinson thinks that he and his crew might well have drowned if they had not been wearing lifejackets.

Should a vessel sink far from help, the best chance of being found lies with an emergency indicator beacon (EPIRB). This is a radio device that operates on 406MHz in conjunction with a satellite system. It has worldwide coverage, gives the identity of the casualty, an accurate position, and is not prone to spurious activation.

The kind of event that *Fidget's* crew experienced is not one likely to have been practised, though courses of instruction in survival exist and are rated as good value. Apart from those who carry a Tinker Tramp combined dinghy and liferaft, the operation of a conventional liferaft is usually taken on trust. However, an opportunity to learn about one's liferaft occurs at the time of its inspection, when it will have to be inflated anyway. To witness an inflation, it is best to make an appointment with the servicing agent, who should be one authorized by the manufacturer, for an 'opening day'. If you are lucky to find an inflated version of your own liferaft on display at a marine or boat show, this presents a good opportunity to check it out. A garden or marina inflation in the company of the crew is entertaining, but will certainly lead to extra cost. For example, the gas bottle is not used for a test inflation but is merely weighed and inspected, and replacement bottles are expensive to recharge and retest. Besides, it is quite easy to damage the fabric of a partially deflated liferaft when in transit back to the servicing agent. Nonetheless, it is possible for an owner to inflate the liferaft without using the gas bottle, and those who can trust their own judgement and know the technique for repacking, do speak highly of carrying out their own inspection.

The merit of having additional items to supplement the liferaft's safety equipment pack will depend very much upon the circumstances; however, the concept of a grab bag, or calamity-bag, filled with suitable sundry items deserves recognition. For example, a waterproofed VHF radio, dry clothing, space blankets, extra flares, food, water, writing materials, passports, money and crew medicines may one day reward the foresight involved. *Fidget's* crew, for example, were not to know they had been spotted, and would have been glad to have had some drinking water during the interval of 40 minutes while they were waiting to be picked up. Also, they were short of flares, one being faulty, and the others having been used immediately.

Sea preparations for imminent bad weather

A skipper should delegate various tasks within his crew to spread the load, and to take care of the situation if he himself were to be incapacitated or lost overboard. This means an organizational structure has to be formed, and though some people may go sailing to escape such duress, there is a clear need for it in times of crisis.

Likewise, it is always desirable to establish and maintain a watch routine so that crew can rest properly when off watch. With an experienced crew the watchkeeping routine will need no adjustment with the onset of bad weather. A less experienced and less well-prepared crew may find some members opting out through seasickness while others are involved in one drama followed by another, leading to whole-crew exhaustion. This can be a recipe for disaster, as people do not tend to make good decisions when they are cold, wet, anxious and tired.

Quite often the situation, bad though it may be, does not require the whole watch on deck. Two people or even one person on deck may be enough to ensure the safety of the boat while conditions are stable. Others on watch may best stay down below where it is warmer and drier.

It is suggested that all craft likely to be in the open sea could benefit from an owner's checklist covering actions to be taken in the face of an impending storm. Such measures will depend very much on the circumstances, such as the experience of the crew, the type of craft and her distance from base. The following list (in no particular order) may be helpful to some, while others may consider the suggestions given here as being standard procedure before going to sea:

1   Issue seasickness pills.
2   Charge batteries.
3   Bring dinghy inboard and stow securely. Deflate an inflatable and stow below deck.

The Dutch yacht *Doortje* sinking in mid Atlantic during the 1988 OSTAR. The owner Roel Engels took the photo from his liferaft shortly before she sank. The boat had hit an unknown object, thought possibly to have been a container. A passing ship rescued him later. The event makes an argument for taking on board both a liferaft and EPIRB. *Photo: Roel Engels/PPL*

4 Remove mainsail and stow in bag below decks. Set up inner forestay for storm jib, if appropriate. Rig trysail. Remove cockpit dodgers. Fold or remove cockpit sprayhood.

5 Check that windows and hatches are tightly closed. Fit or have ready ventilator cover plates. Attach hatchway and window storm screens. If appropriate, put stopper, such as cork or plasticine, in navel pipe.

6 Move storm sails, buckets, warps or other drag devices to a handy position, bearing in mind that it may be difficult and dangerous to open cockpit lockers during a storm.

7 Shut WC seacocks after a good pump through unless experience has shown that sea water will not flood back into the boat. Experience may also show that other cocks need to be closed during bad weather. If shutting such seacocks could cause catastrophic results, an appropriate

notice should be displayed. For example, a sign saying 'Engine cooling water cock closed' taped over the engine starter.

8 Plot position and, if a survival situation is anticipated, report this and intended movements to coastguards or shore authority. Put a dry towel, or absorbent material, within reach of the chart table. Start recording frequent barometer readings, or better still refer to a barograph.

9 Check security of batteries and other heavy weights stowed below, such as anchors, toolboxes and tanks. Use additional lashings or sail ties as necessary.

10 Plan for much colder conditions. Put on appropriate clothing, such as thermal underwear, seaboots, gloves, etc. Drysuits are remarkably good in gale conditions.

11 Pack a 'grab bag'. In addition, seal spare clothing, bedding, matches, lavatory paper, food, water, handheld VHF radio, etc within clear heavy-duty polythene bags.

12 Pump bilges. Check pump handles are attached to the boat with lanyards and check the whereabouts of spares.

13 Put washboards into position, and secure their fastening arrangements so they can't fall out if the boat inverts.

14 Firmly secure latches of cockpit locker lids.

15 Check that cockpit and anchor well drains are free. If narrow it may be helpful to blow through with an inflatable dinghy air pump or sink drain clearer.

16 Check deck items, such as the spinnaker pole, anchor, anchor well lid and liferaft, are properly secured. Winch handles should not be left loose, and a spare should be kept below decks.

17 Check halyards are not twisted and the free ends of the lines on deck are stowed, so that they are not likely to go overboard and foul the propeller. Lead spare halyards etc clear of mast (to reduce noise).

18 Check navigation lights are working; hoist radar reflector.

19 Consider renewing torch batteries and changing cooking gas cylinder.

20 Make up thermos flasks of soup and coffee. Make sandwiches and place in a watertight container.

21 Give the crew a good hot meal.

22 Secure and stow loose items below, especially in the galley area. If containers made of glass have to be brought onboard, such as coffee or jam jars, they must either be packed away with great care or ditched.

23 Put bagged sails at strategic points to break the falls of the crew.

24 Instruct crew members to put on their safety harnesses and lifejackets. Ensure that they are adjusted to fit snugly over storm clothing so that the wearer cannot slip out. Also, that the crew are familiar with the operating features and strap design so that they may be donned rapidly without assistance, if need be, in violent motion and darkness. Safety harnesses and lifejackets should usually be worn during the period of the storm.

25 Change down to storm canvas in good time.

26 If running, rig a heavy-duty main boom preventer to avoid accidental gybes. Ideally this should be rigged round a leading block forward and led back to the cockpit.

27 Rig a rope lattice within the cockpit to give greater security to its occupants. This action may be appropriate for large, shallow cockpits.

28 Brief the crew on what to expect. Remind them of the importance of being hooked onto something really strong when on deck, of maintaining a good lookout, especially to windward, and the whereabouts of flares, grab bag, liferaft, sharp knife, etc.

29 Check rigging cutters. Ensure there is a lanyard on them.

30 Tape up all lockers without positive locking arrangements.

The well-prepared vessel, applying Admiral Nimitz's doctrine, is much more likely to come through a gruelling storm with only minor problems. Yet storms can be a tremendous test of endurance and, despite very careful preparation, much may still depend upon the cool judgement, courage, physical fitness and tenacity of the skipper and crew.

7

The use of drag devices

PETER BRUCE

WHEN IT REALLY COMES ON TO BLOW it is safer to lie with the bow or stern into wind and wave, rather than beam-on. Choice of heavy weather tactics has been increased by the availability on the market of a large number of drag devices, the generic term for objects used over the bow or stern to hold a vessel end-on, and slow her down. The requirement to reduce speed is seldom necessary for strongly manned racing yachts such as those taking part in round the world races; on the other hand, for lightly crewed cruising yachts, slowing down can be a matter of dire urgency in stormy weather due to a crew's need to rest.

Drag devices fall into two categories: sea anchors in the form of *parachutes* that are streamed over the bow on a long line called a rode and are intended to hold the boat head-to-wind with a low rate of drift, and *drogues* that are trailed over the stern, and are designed to slow a boat down to a comfortable speed, keep the boat's stern into the sea, or act as an emergency steering device. At one time the term 'sea anchor' could mean 'a drogue' and vice versa, but now they are coming to be thought of as different devices used in entirely different ways.

Once a parachute sea anchor has been successfully deployed in severe weather, the boat should need little further attention and the crew can relax. It is usually necessary to continue to steer when using a drogue, but in some combinations of hull and drogue the boat can be left to look after herself.

Use of drag devices is gaining in popularity as they repeatedly prove their effectiveness. Simplicity and ease of use are important factors for the successful use of drag devices in unfavourable conditions; but a degree of skill and some specialized seamanship is necessary, as heavy loads are involved, especially for larger parachutes.

Sources of information

Information on drag devices can be obtained in a number of books from the USA. First is the *Drag Device Data Base*, written by Victor Shane and published by Para-Anchors International – not to be confused with Para-Tech International or Para·Anchors (Australia). A second book is entitled *Heavy Weather Tactics Using Sea Anchors and Drogues* by Earl Hinz. Another book is *The Sea Anchor and Drogue Handbook* by Daniel Shewmon. There is also a book by the exceptional sailing couple Lin and Larry Pardey called *Storm Tactics Handbook*. Finally there is a significant report by the Wolfson Unit for Marine Technology, University of Southampton, UK (1988) giving results of tank tests of parachutes and drogues.

Victor Shane, author of the *Drag Device Data Book*, records the use of drag devices from all the different manufacturers. He has tremendous enthusiasm for drag devices and has collected over a hundred accounts of their (mostly) successful use. The style might leave some readers feeling a bit pressurized; nevertheless, the content is of very great interest and covers the use of drag devices of all sorts, many in really heavy weather. A number of skippers finish their report by stating that they would never go to sea again without a parachute sea anchor.

Earl Hinz has written a comprehensive book with much detail on a wide diversity of parachutes and drogues and their use.

The Shewmon book is a fund of independently derived detailed data, much of it constructional. He also highlights the characteristics of parachutes of his own design and compares them with the Para-Tech design.

The Wolfson Unit's report is based on tank tests. It is particularly interesting as in the ocean no one wave is exactly similar to another, so comparisons are not always valid. In the tests an exactly repeatable breaking wave equivalent to 5.85m (19ft 2in) in height was created in a tank in a wind of 40 knots. A number of 'typical hull shape' yacht models, equivalent to 10m (33ft) overall in length, were used in conjunction with two sizes of parachute and two types of drogue. Drogues were trialled both individually and in series.

The results demonstrated that, without assistance from a drogue, the models drifted broadside on to the breaking wave and were invariably capsized, sometimes by the breaking wave of 3.3m (11ft) which preceded the main one. What was surprising was that parachutes did not prevent yachts in the tank from being capsized. The sudden huge force of the breaking wave caused the parachute line to stretch and then, after the wave had passed, the model yacht would be carried forward by the elasticity in the line. Her momentum would take the boat past her original position, allow the line to go slack and cause the parachute to collapse, especially if the parachute had been pulled near the surface. Though this does not seem to happen at sea, the yacht would then turn beam-on to the direction of the waves and,

before the parachute had redeployed itself and the slack in the line had been taken up, she would be capsized by the 3.3m (11ft) wave that followed the main one.

The drogues tested by the Wolfson Unit were more successful. Provided there was tension in the drogue line when the breaking wave struck, and the yacht model was roughly stern-on to the breaking wave, she would invariably *not* capsize. Additionally, use of a drogue made it much easier for the rudder to hold the stern into the sea.

In summary, the Wolfson Unit trial results favoured drogues rather than parachute sea anchors, and series drogues rather than individual drogues. Of course no tank test can exactly reproduce conditions at sea, and the Wolfson Unit findings regarding parachutes is seldom, if ever, borne out in practice, possibly due to the difficulty of matching the parachute line to the line in the tank, but there are records at sea of the parachute line becoming slack, as happened in the tank, followed by a near capsize of the vessel. The possibility gives food for thought. It may be that the rode can be too long as well as too short.

The *Storm Tactics Handbook* by Lin and Larry Pardey, among other valuable advice, gives detailed instructions on using a parachute sea anchor with a bridle or pendant line to angle a yacht some 50° from the waves, an ingenious refinement upon the basic system that improves comfort considerably.

The need for further evaluation

The original need was to reconcile theoretical and practical assumptions from an impartial standpoint and learn the techniques for the deployment of drag devices. Thus sea trials were undertaken between 1996 and 2006 to evaluate, particularly from the practical point of view, purpose-built sea anchor type parachutes, a much cheaper and smaller 'Bu-Ord'

Deployment of a parachute sea anchor. The deployment bag can be seen in the foreground with the parachute beyond, which will fully open out when the load comes on.
Photo: Peter Bruce

parachute, makeshift alternatives, and commonly used drogues. The trials were based on drag devices that were available in the UK and were offered for evaluation.

The trials were initially undertaken in calm weather with a view to working up to heavier weather using well-known types of cruising boat. These were a Najad 391, a Maxi 1100, a Rustler 36, a Hallberg Rassy 36, a Warrior 35 and a Contessa 33.

For understandable reasons, force 6 to 7 was about as much wind as most owners wanted to go out into deliberately. Thus the trials were confined to conditions below which drag devices would normally be used. In spite of this anomaly, it was felt that much was learnt from the trials. It was observed when using the parachute anchor that the behaviours of the yachts were surprisingly consistent through the wind range experienced, giving some reason to believe that their behaviours would be similar in higher wind speeds. Subsequent trials up to 2006 have involved Para·Anchors of Australia, Para-Anchor, and Para-Drogue. Richard Clifford, mostly sailing single-handed, has carried out his own trials worldwide. He has made a number of suggestions in this chapter based upon his own experiences and has played a vigorous role in local testing.

Parachute sea anchors

Early sea anchors used over the bow

John Voss, a retired Canadian sea captain of great experience who sailed around the world in a 11.6m (38ft) Indian war canoe at the turn of the 20th century, was one of the earliest successful proponents of the sea anchor. His canoe had a low rig with a small mizzen well aft, only 1.7m (5ft 6in) beam and only 0.6m (2ft) draft, all features that should suit the use of a small cone-shaped sea anchor. Subsequent attempts to emulate Captain Voss with similar sea anchors probably failed owing to the sea anchor having insufficient cross-sectional area and thus allowing excessive stern way.

In 1963 there is a brief record of Arthur Piver using a parachute as a sea anchor to ride out a great storm near Rarotonga aboard his trimaran. In 1965, on an expedition to Heard Island, the great explorer Bill Tilman hove-to by using a 9.8m (32ft) diameter parachute led from the bow of a 19.2m (63ft) steel schooner. He was surprised how well the parachute held a vessel of such size and weight into the wind until the bronze ring broke, to which the rigging (or shroud) lines

Figure 7.1 Sea anchor as used by the Casanovas for their trimaran *Tortuga Too*.

were attached, and the parachute was lost – a point worthy of note.

Use of parachutes has probably come about from the availability of special ex-military parachutes. The tuna fishing boats came to use them at San Pedro, California, as did the multihull owners John and Joan Casanova, and the Pardeys in the late 1960s. The Casanovas used a parachute both to weather a succession of extreme storms experienced over many years of sailing in their trimaran *Tortuga Too*, and also simply to rest. At about the same time the Pardeys were experimenting in their monohull as well.

Why use a sea anchor?

When at sea in a small boat far from land the concept of a sea anchor, which could be compared with a mooring, is most attractive. Parachutes of appropriate size have little 'give', as if they were in hydraulic lock. There is a lot to be said, too, for presenting the bow into the wind and waves during a storm, as a boat is designed to take water flow from ahead. Besides, placing the bow into the sea by heaving-to or motoring into it are tactics with a good record of success.

For some yachts heaving-to is not straightforward. Many modern light-displacement yachts with fin keels do not heave-to comfortably. They are too lively and have insufficient underwater lateral area, so they yaw about and make tremendous leeway. It cannot be certain that the bows will always face close enough into the waves to prevent capsize by an unusual wave, and the boat may be thrown backwards by a breaking wave causing damage to her rudder. It may be that some of the features that make a yacht unsuitable for heaving-to, such as low wetted surface area, are features that make her suitable for lying to a sea anchor. On the other hand, certain yachts, usually of heavy displacement, low freeboard and long keel, heave-to so well that their owners may feel that no other tactic is ever likely to be necessary.

Motoring into the sea can be another good storm tactic. The bow can be kept pointing into the waves and one can, to a certain extent, pick one's way around them. The disadvantages are that the tactic requires a skilful helmsman, a powerful engine, adequate fuel and ideally a large slow-turning three bladed propellor.

Properly conceived parachute sea anchor systems have none of the above disadvantages, and might appear to some to be the ultimate solution and main line of defence (see Fig 7.2).

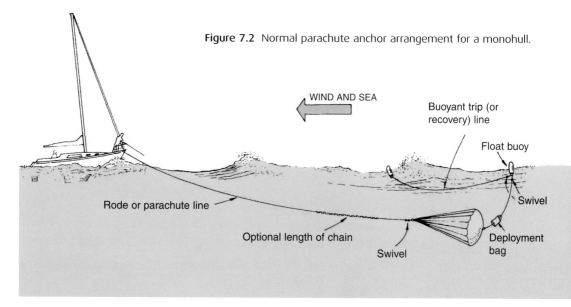

Figure 7.2 Normal parachute anchor arrangement for a monohull.

WIND AND SEA

Buoyant trip (or recovery) line

Float buoy

Rode or parachute line

Swivel

Optional length of chain

Swivel

Deployment bag

The parachute

At one time the only parachutes obtainable were those designed for aerial purposes. A good example is the Bu-Ord parachute – the name originates from *Bureau of Ordnance*, which is a chain of American military surplus stores and can be found via the Internet. They were designed to haul a load out of the back of an airborne aircraft and are thus designed to take shock loads. These can work comparatively well for small craft and can be obtained cheaply. Sizes are said to go up to 5.5m (18ft) diameter, but smaller sizes are more generally obtainable. For years fishermen in the USA have used Bu-Ord parachutes for lying to at night or in bad weather rather than returning to harbour. They have been known to overcome the difficulty of obtaining larger sizes by putting a number of Bu-Ord parachutes in series. One should remember that such ex-military stores are made available presumably because they are no longer suitable for their original purpose. They may be cheap, but are not necessarily fit for use at sea, although some have lasted for years. Purpose-built parachutes, designed for use as a sea anchor, manufactured in the USA, Australia and New Zealand in several sizes, are more likely to be effective and reliable.

On the one hand too large a parachute is not advisable, as the larger the parachute the larger the loads and the greater the handling problems. On the other hand too small a parachute will not hold the boat into the wind. The US Sailing's *Recommendations for Offshore Sailing* specifies a parachute diameter of 35 per cent of the boat's overall length, and of course parachute manufacturers will give advice. The UK trials showed that long-keeled yachts tend to need larger parachutes than fin-keeled yachts because many long-keeled yachts take up a very stable broadside-on attitude.

Para-Tech Engineering Co, Colorado; Fiorentino, c/o LIS International Group, California; Para-Anchors of Australia, Victoria; WA Coppins of Motueka, New Zealand have a range of sizes of parachute, and there are Shewmon parachutes that are smaller for the same length of craft. There are other manufacturers and other less conventional forms of parachute such as the cruciform, and there are makeshift options. For example my brother, in his Hallberg Rassy 29, successfully lay bows-to an Atlantic storm in 1998 using a square-shaped builder's hoisting bag of low cost, said to be strong enough to lift a ton of sand.

It is more convenient if parachutes are supplied in a deployment bag, a fabric

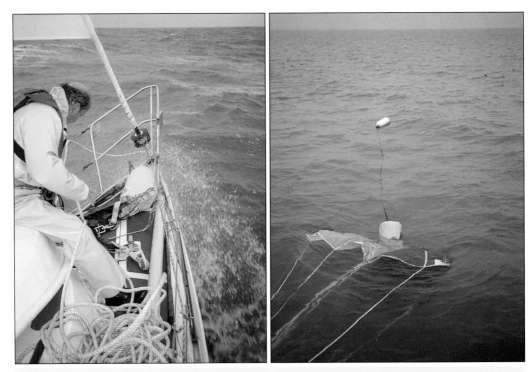

LEFT Preparing a parachute sea anchor for deployment. RIGHT The parachute sea anchor has been pulled from the deployment bag. Note the float buoy in the form of a white fender. The red recovery buoy lies beyond. *Photos: Peter Bruce*

container that enables the parachute to open after it has been launched, rather than on deck when the wind can severely hamper operations.

Foredeck work

Some sailors prepare their sea anchor by attaching the gear to guard rail stanchions with cable ties before going to sea, but most will not want to risk damage and deterioration through berthing incidents, neglect or ultraviolet light. Thus sea anchors will require foredeck work at some stage and, if this work is left too late as a storm builds, it can become difficult and dangerous. For example, when Robin and Maggi Ansell set off in *Orca* (16.8m (55ft)) through the Great Barrier Reef bound for Alaska, they decided to deploy their new sea anchor in the early stages of Cyclone Justin. Even though use of the sea anchor had been rehearsed, the task

was not easy and after two hours of struggle the difficulties with the chafe guard had still not been resolved. Maggi Ansell said later that only with superhuman effort had Robin Ansell detached 3m (10ft) of 12mm ($\frac{1}{2}$in) chain from the stern anchor, crawled forward again and attached it to the end of the parachute line. The yacht's motion was very severe, and when the load came on the chain, his ankle was caught between it and the toe rail and he was lucky to get away with severe bruising. She thought that to go on deck hourly to 'freshen the nip' would have been suicide.

It will be useful to pass the parachute line through the stem fitting at the first indication of a possible storm rather than wait for the moment when it is decided to deploy the parachute. Generally speaking, an anchor at the stem fitting should be removed if possible, both to clear the way for the parachute line chain and to prevent chafe.

If stormy conditions are expected, it is better to put the parachute line in position before leaving harbour. It should be led aft to the deployment bags in the cockpit locker along the outside of the guard rail, secured by breakable line.

Load

In addition to possible handling difficulties, the loads exerted by parachute sea anchors on their attachment points in heavy weather can be tremendous. Cleats, their fastenings, backing pieces and adjacent structure need to be up to the job. The Wolfson trials suggested that these should be enough to carry 80 per cent of the weight of the boat. An illustration of the sort of loads created is given by an account of a 12.2m (40ft) yacht, lying to an 5.5m (18ft) parachute in a North Sea gale of some 45 knots, with the parachute line attached to the windlass. When the first heavy load came on the line the windlass was torn out of the deck, taking with it the bow roller and most of the stem fitting. When cleats are judged to be not strong enough on their own, additional lines can be used to spread the load over the boat. For example, the legs of the bridle can be led from the end of the chain to the port and starboard toe rail (see page 87) or from cleats to the primary winches. A wooden mast might be considered, but the consequences of an alloy mast being crushed are such that the risk is not worth taking. Stem fittings, being designed with ground anchors in mind, are usually the appropriate lead for the parachute line to pass through, but the drop nose pin intended to prevent the anchor chain jumping out may need beefing up. Closed fairleads are usually entirely acceptable as as alternative.

Clearly if a parachute is made part of a vessel's equipment, the means of securing the rode safely must be established before it is ever used.

The rode or parachute line

Because the parachute is effectively a fixed object, the long rope line used for holding the sea anchor – which is usually called a 'rode' in the USA and increasingly in the UK – must have considerable elasticity, not withstanding the model tests carried out on page 80. Only nylon will do. Nylon braid rope (equivalent to multiplait) is best, as this is the most elastic type and is torsionally stable. Hawser-laid nylon rope can put twists in the rigging lines as the load increases and decreases which will reduce the parachute's efficiency. Ropes other than nylon are designed not to stretch, for example those made from polyester, Spectra or Kevlar, and are not suitable.

The rode should have the same breaking strain as is appropriate for the main anchor because the line needs to stretch but not break, even if subject to minor chafe. It should have stainless steel thimbles at both ends, since knots, particularly bowlines, will weaken it. Para·Anchors of Australia used to recommend a minimum length of 120m (394ft) but recently they have found 100m (328ft) adequate and even down to 50m (164ft). Para-Tech stipulates the length of parachute line as ten times boat length with a minimum of 91m (300ft). Daniel Shewmon recommends a minimum of 20 times the expected wave height, or even more because of the unpredictability of the severity of a storm. This requirement could lead to huge lengths of line to cope with, for example, in the 12.2m (40ft) wave heights of the Auckland–Tonga storm of June 1994. There is clearly a disparity in the recommendations, but certainly the need is for the rode to be long enough to stretch enough to accommodate the varying force of the waves, and thick enough to take the maximum credible load. It is suggested that manufacturers' instructions are complied with, but if an opportunity to experiment presents itself, it should be taken.

There is a case for putting a length of chain at one or other end of the parachute line, or half-way along it. This helps to reduce

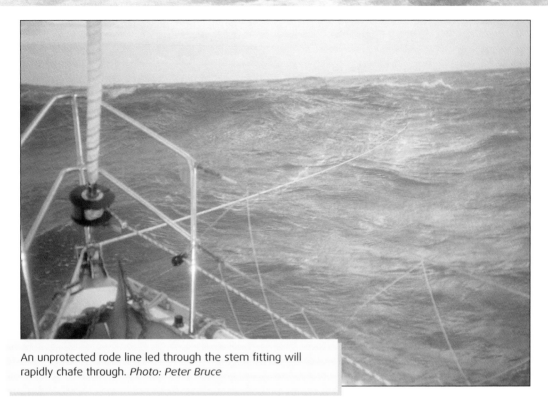

An unprotected rode line led through the stem fitting will rapidly chafe through. *Photo: Peter Bruce*

peak loading, helps the parachute to stay well immersed, clear of flotsam and wave effects, and may allow the use of less line. However in the trials, use of chain seemed to make little difference and when under load the parachute still appeared near the surface. Chain at the outer end or mid-point of the parachute line does make the task of recovery more onerous. Larry Pardey says that he likes to see his Bu-Ord near the surface. He also says that if the parachute inverts this could flip the shroud line to the wrong side of the canopy but he has never known this to happen.

A length of parachute line can be heavy to handle. For example, a 136.5m (448ft) parachute line of 16mm (⅝in) eight-strand weighs 28kg (62lb) when dry, and 39kg (86lb) when wet. In addition to the parachute deployment bag, a purpose-built 'parachute line deployment bag' is recommended to avoid tangles and to save time, which might otherwise be spent in flaking out the line.

Nylon absorbs over four times as much water as polyester and, if the line is allowed

to dry out after use without being thoroughly washed in fresh water, salt crystals will damage the fibres. Ice crystals will have a similar effect.

Chafe

Once deployed, the whole expensive and elaborate parachute anchor system can soon be lost if no proper provision is made for chafe. A bare rope, led through a normal stemhead fitting, is almost bound to chafe through in an hour or two. Anchors over the bow, boomkin stays or foul leads around the forestay will have the same effect. On the basis that one may spend a number of days lying to the parachute, a length of chain leading through the stem fitting is a sure way to give adequate long-term protection, but one should make provision for emergency release as chain cannot be cut. In the USA, double-lined firehose is also often used for the protection of a rope line against chafe, but chain is undoubtedly superior. If plastic hose is to be used, it should be inserted over

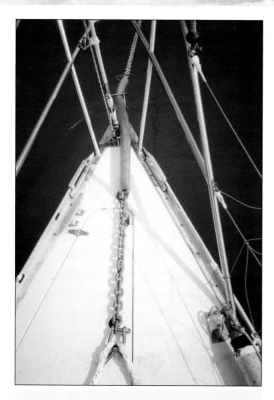

ABOVE A length of 10mm (³⁄₈in) chain enclosed by a length of polythene hose will neither chafe, nor create noise. With this arrangement the load is taken by two legs, secured to the alloy toe rail on each side. *Photo: Peter Bruce*

the line before the thimbles are spliced at each end. Small holes to take a lashing line should be drilled near the ends. Do not cut the tube lengthwise as split tube tends to work away from the point of contact. The practice of parcelling the line with cloth, as is often used for warps, will be better than nothing but probably won't last long.

The float

Parachutes above 3.7m (12ft) diameter need a float line and float secured to the apex of the parachute to ensure that the parachute takes up a suitable depth and not, under no load, a position on the end of the parachute line directly underneath the vessel. If this happens, the effort needed for recovery is tremendous and likely to defeat many crews. In one recorded instance the line was cut by the crew and the parachute lost rather than hauling it all in. Fenders, conveniently, can be used as floats, and the bigger the better as it is useful to be able to spot where the parachute is whenever possible. Of course, white fenders do not show up particularly well when the sea is white with foam.

The float line should be of a length to keep the parachute at a depth of 10–15m (33–49ft), clear of wave effects. Parachutes do tend to come to the surface when the load is especially heavy. Larry Pardey says that he takes comfort from seeing the parachute at work and has never experienced any difficulties

RIGHT Each leg can be shackled to the alloy toe rail. The bolts holding the toe rail pass through the hull-to-deck joint, giving good strength, but can be further backed up to spread the load.
Photo: Peter Bruce

Once a parachute sea anchor is deployed it is in virtual hydraulic lock.
Photo: Richard Clifford

due to the parachute being at the surface. A swivel should be placed at the float end of the float line. If a length of chain is used at the parachute end of the parachute line, a single fender may not provide enough buoyancy.

Trip or recovery line

In addition to the float line, another 30–45m (100–150ft) of 5mm (³/₁₆in) soft buoyant line with a swivel should be used between the float and the recovery buoy, for all but small parachutes. By motoring up to the recovery buoy and hauling it and the float buoy aboard, the parachute can be collapsed using a single shroud line. The trip line buoy should be easily distinguishable from the float buoy for obvious reasons. Trip lines permanently led back to the boat have been tried, but can often become tangled up in the parachute. They are seldom employed more than once, but if one perseveres one may acquire the knack and thus have the advantage of easier recovery. The technique for a 'standing' trip line, is to keep just the right amount of weight on the trip line rather than allow it to become too slack. The standing trip line is recommended in a current, such as the Aghulas or the Gulf Stream, when unusual effects, such as down-going eddies,

may require that the parachute be tripped as a matter of urgency. It should be said that for a quiet life it is much better to deploy the parachute clear of currents.

Swivels and shackles

Parachutes can rotate in use and therefore a swivel, which may turn at times when the parachute becomes less heavily loaded, is recommended by manufacturers; some supply one with the parachute. There is some doubt as to whether a swivel does rotate under load but, if a swivel is used, it must be recognized as a frequent point of failure and needs to be of high quality with a greater breaking load than that of the parachute line. The same applies to shackles used to attach the parts of the system. When it comes to buying shackles and swivels, one can safely verge to the oversize. All shackle pins should, of course, be seized or double seized with Monel wire, seizing wire or a 'cable tie'.

Riding sail

In the trials the long-keeled yacht tended to lie nearly head-to-wind on a parachute sea anchor, but the fin-keeled yachts tended to yaw about, adding to discomfort and possi-

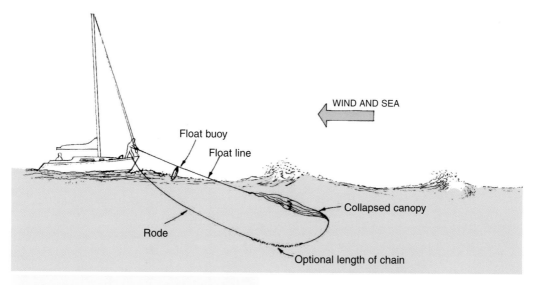

Figure 7.3 (ABOVE) Recovering the parachute.

Figure 7.4 (RIGHT) Hove-to Pardey-style with triple-reefed main and 3m (9ft) diameter parachute anchor made of coarse-weave nylon stretchable fabric, which allows the water to sieve through under strain. Both boat and parachute anchor should be on the wave crest at the same time.

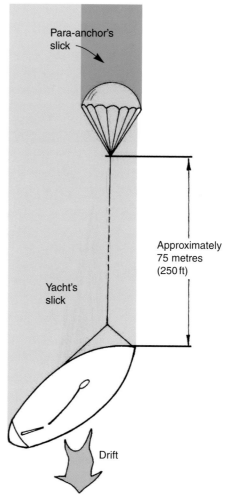

bly hazard. If a yacht yaws about in strong winds at a mooring, possibly because the mast and/or hull generate lift, then she will probably yaw on a parachute sea anchor. The amount of yawing will also depend on whether a yacht has a lot of windage forward or aft. For example, a furled headsail will increase the amount of windage forward.

Yawls should be able to set a suitably small amount of mizzen to prevent yaw. Sloops may need some kind of riding sail rigged on the backstay. A storm jib set on the backstay tends to be too large. Best is a 'spitfire jib' of less than half the area of the storm jib and specially made for the backstay. Motoring slowly astern can also achieve the desired effect.

When riding to a sea anchor a purpose-made riding sail rigged on the backstay can be valuable for yachts with no mizzen.
Photo: Peter Bruce

The Pardey method of deployment

Normal practice is to deploy the parachute straight over the bow, but there is an option to rig a Bu-Ord parachute, with a deep-reefed mainsail or trysail set, so that the boat lies at a 50° angle to wind and wave as described in Lin and Larry Pardey's *Storm Tactics Handbook*. The advantage of the arrangement is that the boat does not swing continuously through the wind, but stays at a more comfortable fixed angle, like being hove-to. In addition, the slick formed by the drift of the boat and the parachute will reduce the likelihood of waves breaking to weather (see Fig 7.4). It is said that the Bu-Ord parachute is most suitable for the Pardey method of deployment, as it is more porous and therefore capable of taking a shock load.

A snatch block is used at the bow to accommodate the angled parachute line. Then a bridle, or pendant line, is taken from another block snatched onto the parachute line and led aft to a cockpit winch, directly or via a leading block – whichever gives the best lead. When the bridle is tensioned (and it may be necessary to veer some parachute line simultaneously to give enough slack to position the bridle block) the boat can be made to slew round to an angle that gives neither ahead nor astern movement.

Some yachts may need their stem fittings adapted to take the bow snatch block so it will lead the parachute line clear of obstructions. Larry Pardey likes to adjust the length of the parachute line so the yacht and parachute crest the waves at the same time.

Storm accounts where the technique has been used, and the trials, showed that there is a huge weight on the bridle line when using the Pardey method and some deck fittings may not be up to it. The loads for yachts above 12.2m (40ft) are massive and may preclude the use of the Pardey method altogether. In some cases larger yachts naturally take up an appropriate angle to the seas on a parachute, in which case the main objective is achieved without the need for a bridle line. The manufacturer of the Para-Tech parachute sea anchor does not recommend that their parachutes are used for the Pardey method of deployment.

It was also found in the trials that the fin-keeled yachts, as opposed to the long-keeled yachts, were prone to tack over the lines in less than force 7. It seems that the longer and deeper the keel the better when using the Pardey method of deployment.

Deploying the sea anchor

The parachute with all its accompanying gear should be carefully laid out on deck. This task is made much easier when deployment bags are used for rode and parachute

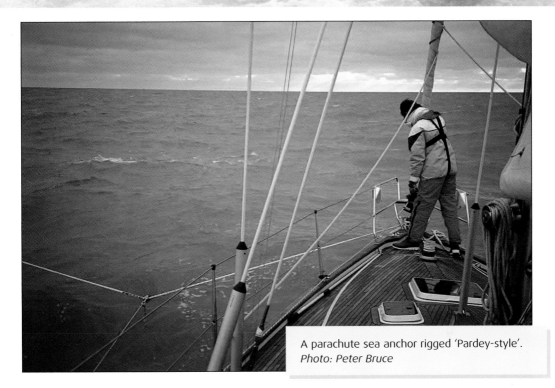

A parachute sea anchor rigged 'Pardey-style'.
Photo: Peter Bruce

and if it is undertaken before rough seas develop. Shackles should be seized and knots should be tight. To allow the gear to float quickly clear of the keel and rudder the boat should be stopped and drifting with sails lowered before the start of operations. The parachute should be thrown over in its deployment bag on the windward side, followed by the floats and float lines. The rode should be paid out as the boat drifts, and it is sensible to snub the rode at an early stage so that the opening of the parachute can be witnessed. On completion the helm should be lashed securely.

Riding to a sea anchor

The parachute sea anchor provides a remarkably secure mooring. Contrary to what one might think there is usually no undue load on rudders, probably no more than would be experienced at a ground anchor in deep and open water. It is recommended that the rudder be lashed amidships. Happily there are few records of rudder trouble while lying to a sea anchor.

Once set up correctly, the parachute needs no tending and therefore allows the crew to rest. This, for an exhausted crew, is a tremendous advantage, though in extreme conditions rest is a relative word as the hull will take a tremendous battering and the movement of the boat will be severely uncomfortable. As the rode stretches and contracts, heavy, quick rolling, yawing and pitching will take place much as could be expected if it was possible to anchor in the open sea. Maximum drift rate is likely to be 1.5 knots, but usually rather less if the parachute is of adequate size.

It should be remembered that the boat, rode and parachute are vulnerable to other craft when a parachute is deployed. The VHF radio should be used to put out a Sécurité message periodically, giving position and circumstances.

Recovery of the parachute

Small parachutes do not need float and trip lines and can be recovered by winching in the parachute line until a shroud line can be

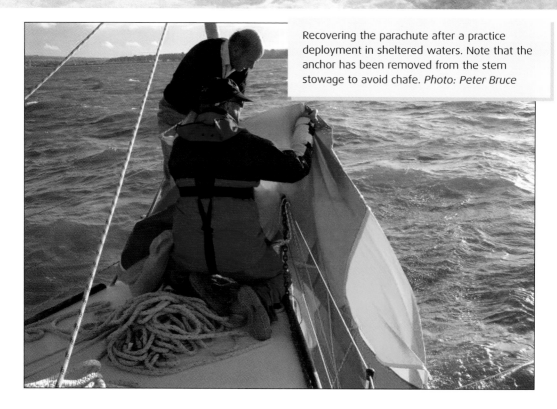

Recovering the parachute after a practice deployment in sheltered waters. Note that the anchor has been removed from the stem stowage to avoid chafe. *Photo: Peter Bruce*

grabbed. Large parachutes (see Fig 7.3) are recovered by motoring gently into the wind, gathering in the rode until most of it is on deck, then heading for the recovery buoy, picking this up and using the tripping line to haul in the deflated parachute. It can be heavy work requiring precise steering. A system of hand signals is advisable to assist the helmsman, who will not be able to see the direction and tension of the line. During the recovery process in rough conditions there is an evident risk of losing a man overboard, or catching the line round the propeller. Even in moderate conditions the task is tricky, and when the wet parachute is finally back on board it will inflate in the wind and be difficult to manage. Some not-so-young cruising couples, sailing on their own in yachts of over 12m (40ft), would probably find the recovery procedure difficult in any conditions. Nevertheless, practised and experienced shorthanded sailors do manage parachutes in severe weather.

Conclusions following sea trials of parachute sea anchors

Accounts of successful deployments of parachutes in extreme weather continue to appear, and they amount to compelling evidence in their favour. After the trials it was clear that parachute sea anchors might be one of the safer means of coping with heavy weather. On the other hand, they are not a comfortable answer and large parachutes are not easy to recover by small crews.

Nevertheless, a parachute, for all the provisos, does meet the claims made. A parachute brings a fresh and welcome option to the seafarer, giving – once deployed – security without any effort on the part of the crew. Clearly a parachute will be worth its weight in gold in the event of a steering gear failure in prolonged rough weather, but as a method of coping with extreme severe heavy weather it may be no less valuable.

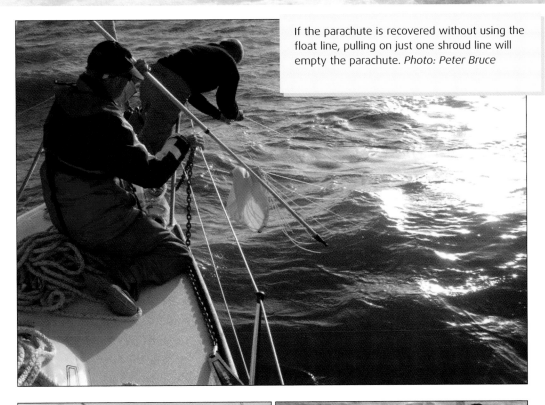

If the parachute is recovered without using the float line, pulling on just one shroud line will empty the parachute. *Photo: Peter Bruce*

LEFT Recovering a parachute single-handed can be a frustrating process. RIGHT Two strong men make the business of parachute recovery easier. *Photos: Peter Bruce*

A selection of drag devices used in the trials. The 135m (448ft) x 16mm ($^5/_8$in) drogue parachute line is in the deployment bag (left). The Bu-Ord parachute is in the centre, and the 5.5m (18ft) diameter Para-Tech parachute is centre right. *Photo: Peter Bruce*

There are convincing accounts in Victor Shane's *Drag Device Data Base* that yachts using a parachute can weather ultimate conditions, and without active participation from their crew which, for cruising couples of retirement age or with young children, is just what is needed. A further welcome benefit of a parachute sea anchor, compared to running with a storm, is that the storm blows through more quickly.

When the direction of wind and sea are markedly different a yacht will lie-to the wind rather than to the sea, and therefore be vulnerable to beam seas. Sea anchors may, and quite often do, become lost or tangled. They can impose heftier loads than their deck fastenings or their structures are able to take. Moreover, though carried, in the event they have not always been used because their deployment could possibly put their users at greater risk than they would otherwise be, especially as many people do not manage a successful deployment at their first attempt.

Circumstances need to be allowed for when it will not be possible to use the sea anchor by treating it as one of several options. Overall success is more certain with fully committed investment, preparation, good seamanship, timely deployment and practice.

If a decision is made to buy a parachute, purchasers are well advised to ensure that the parachute rode and joining shackles are large and strong enough for the job, that their vessel has strong enough fittings to take the load, to make proper provision for chafe, and to try the parachute out for the first time in easy conditions.

Drogues

Trailing objects astern to control speed and improve steering is an old and well-known tactic in heavy weather. Drogues are the purpose-made alternative to improvisation and have several other uses. For example, they have been successfully used as emergency steering devices and as devices for promoting directional stability, especially when entering narrow harbours or crossing bars.

When running before a growing ocean storm the speed generated by a vessel down the fronts of the waves can often be elating. A wise skipper will recognize this to be a time for precautionary action. As wind and wave build up, so maybe does the load on the helm. However, sponginess in the helm can develop through aeration in the sea and, worse on top of a breaking wave, water flow past the rudder may be reversed, leading to loss of control and the probability of broaching. The first step will be to reduce sail but, after that, use of a drogue of some sort may be needed to bring the boat down to a sensible and comfortable speed. Modern yachts seldom have 'balanced ends' and are thus not very directionally stable, so the beneficial

effect of a drogue in maintaining a boat's course can be another large advantage.

Slowing the boat down and pointing the stern directly into the sea may result in more waves breaking over the stern than would otherwise occur. In fact, in stormy conditions it may lead to regular pooping. Accordingly, the aft-facing structure needs to be strongly built and, especially for craft with a stern cockpit, the crew on deck to be well secured.

Using the vessel's anchor and chain over the stern is said to be effective. The weight of the anchor and chain takes the arrangement below surface effects, and the downward angle creates good drag. There are two disadvantages. There could be a disastrous outcome in the unlikely event of an encounter with shallow water, and recovery could prove to be tricky. A compromise might be to use the anchor chain alone. It may be possible to use the windlass for recovery.

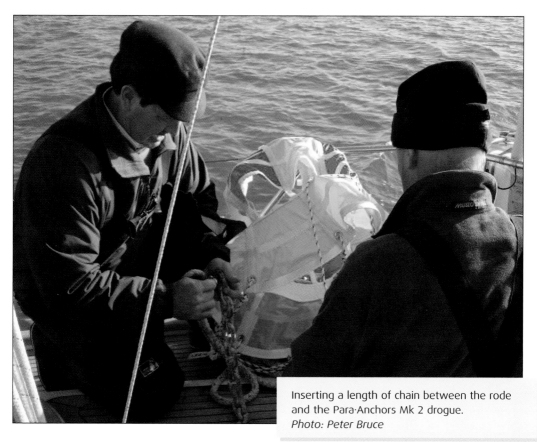

Inserting a length of chain between the rode and the Para-Anchors Mk 2 drogue.
Photo: Peter Bruce

The established method is to use a drogue line of at least 80–100m (236–332ft), possibly plus a weight and drag-producing device on the end. As with the parachute sea anchor, too much line is better than too little, though there are occasions with an unweighted drogue when, surprisingly, short lengths work best. Yet more line will be necessary to span longer ocean wavelengths, possibly built up from warps and spare rope. Some users prefer to secure the drogue line to a bridle so that the load is split between attachment points on each quarter of the boat. The arrangement may allow the boat to lie at a more desirable angle to the waves. The arrangement is set up by tying a rolling hitch to a point at least a boat length short of the end of the drogue line, and securing the bridle line to the opposite stern cleat to the main line. After fastening it, the bridle line is eased out, to middle the two lengths of the 'V' at an angle of 30°, or staggered as necessary to achieve the desired angle to the waves. There are some disadvantages in using a bridle. It is neither so easy to adjust the length of the drogue line nor adjust the nip, ie the first point where the rope is twisted around a cleat and where it will tend to chafe, and the rolling hitch becomes so tight that it may need to be cut out when the arrangement is dismantled.

An essential feature of a drogue system is that the line should remain taut and as evenly loaded as possible. If the line becomes slack, a vessel immediately becomes vulnerable to being rolled, and shock loads on the vessel are likely. To prevent this, experimentation with the line length to bring the drogue into the ideal position relative to the waves is often recommended. It is said that the ideal position is when the drogue is in a trough when the vessel is half-way up the leading side of an overtaking wave. The trouble is that it may not be possible to see where the drogue is and, anyhow, waves are never quite uniform and sometimes not uniform at all. The best way of ensuring a consistent load may sometimes be to have a very long line, and place sufficient weight on the end

of the drogue line to keep it away from the worst of surface effects. When the drogue is deep enough it will neither come out of the water nor be much affected by the orbital motion within a wave. An alternative, better but more complicated method is to deploy two drogues in series, so that if one drogue is carried forward by a breaking wave, another will still provide a braking force.

The slightly controversial Wolfson report recommends a sinker weight between 20–30kg (44–66lb), so that the drogue should operate at 10–15m (33–49ft) below the surface. Solid sinkers are awkward and heavy to move and stow, and have the potential to do serious damage when unsecured, though they do have a dual purpose as an 'angel' or 'chum'. A suitable length of anchor chain or an anchor are often used as sinkers, and if diving equipment is kept on board, diving weights are suitable too. In moderate conditions, should the drag of the drogue slow the boat down too much, a little headsail or engine power may improve the situation. However, many drogue users find that weighted drogues pull the stern down and that their drogues work well with no sinker at all, and are consequently easier to recover. It will pay to experiment.

The load on the drogue line can be very heavy but rather less than that of the parachute. The Wolfson trials showed a peak load of 3.8 tonnes for the 10m (33ft) yacht when struck by a breaking wave. These heavy loads can be dangerous, and care should be taken that the line has an adequately strong fastening point, a fairlead, and that the legs of crew are not in the bight when the drogue is deployed. A cockpit primary winch is the obvious attachment point so long as it is strong enough, and plastic pipe or other antichafe may be necessary at the fairlead.

Towing trials

With the aim of finding a suitable drogue to slow a vessel to a comfortable speed when running before a storm, it was desirable to establish by empirical means the drogue's effectiveness solely at creating drag. It was also desirable to compare commercially available products with makeshift arrangements improvised from whatever happens to be available – for example, to compare the performance of a relatively expensive purpose-made device with sails or an old motor car tyre. It was also useful to find out whether there were benefits in deploying drogues in series.

A towing trial was undertaken using a Najad 391 under power, as one can roughly equate the situation when motoring to running under bare pole. A fixed engine speed short of maximum was chosen, and the hull speed remeasured by the boat's log with the various drogues on tow. The line used was 136.5m (448ft) of 16mm (⁵⁄₈in) eight-strand.

When the drogue was fully weighted, as the Wolfson Unit recommends, hand recovery was heavy work and a single person might need to allow an hour or more for the task. In one recovery in the open sea the line had to be let go when an especially heavy load came on it, a reminder that it is advisable to keep the bitter end secured. In boats under 11m (37ft) it is usually easiest to recover the drogue using a primary sheet winch. In some circumstances in larger craft it may be easier to recover the drogue over the bow using a power-driven capstan.

Trial results

Najad 391	Drag device	Boat speed (kt)	% of set speed
Engine rpm 2820	Nil	6.6	100
	Line alone	6.3	95
	HSD 300 Seabrake	(6.0)	(91)*
	Single car tyre	5.9	89
	No 3 genoa	5.8	88*
	Delta (1.2m/48in)	5.5	83
	Series drogue	(5.3)	(80)*
	Galerider S (0.9m/36in)	5.1	77
	Large single cone	4.6	70
	Para·Anchor Mk 2	4.5	68
	Home-made parachute	4.3	65
	Delta (1.8m/72in)	4.2	64
	Two cones in series	4.0	61
	No 3 genoa	3.8	58*
	Bu-Ord para (3m/10ft)	(1.2)	(18)*

*Results are qualified in the text.

Further trials were undertaken to try to establish the amount of drag obtained by the various methods at low speed. The ideal drogue will cause the vessel to maintain a comfortable speed: neither too fast which might involve a broach, nor too slow, which could bring about loss of steerage way. Clearly it is highly undesirable to be so tethered by a drogue that there is insufficient steerage way to bring the stern round to a breaking wave, thus one is looking for the minimum reduction in drag at low speed. For the purposes of the trial, 'low speed' was chosen to be 2 knots. If a drogue in moderate conditions is over-effective, a headsail can be set to ensure that steerage way is not lost.

Trial results

Najad 391	Drag device	Boat speed (kt)	% of set speed
Engine rpm 800	Nil	2	100
	Line alone	2	100
	No 3 genoa	2	100*
	HSD 300 Seabrake	2	100
	Single car tyre	1.7	85
	Para·Anchor Mk 2	1.6	80
	Galerider S (0.9m/36in)	1.3	65
	Large single cone	1.3	65
	Drag device	1.2	60
	Delta (1.2m/48in)	1.2	60
	Delta (1.8m/72in)	1.0	50
	Series drogue	0.9	45
	Home-made cone	0.8	40
	No 3 genoa	0.7	35*
	Bu-Ord para (3m/10ft)	0	0

*Results are qualified in the text.

The line alone

At one time, trailing warps alone was considered a primary storm tactic. They provided a degree of drag and gave a soothing effect to the waves. My father, Erroll Bruce, successfully ran before hurricane strength winds in the 30ft (9m) *Samuel Pepys* off Bermuda in May 1950, trailing warps. When Sir Robin Knox-Johnston sailed alone round the world in 1969 (the first to do so non-stop and single-handed) he used a long warp in the form of a bight in severe weather. In addition, he used to set his storm jib sheeted amidships for directional stability, and *Suhaili* was so well balanced that, with the tiller lashed, he could retire to his bunk.

The performance of the line is much affected by depth of immersion, ie the deeper the line is immersed, the more even and effective the drag will be. Miles Smeeton, the veteran world-girdler of the 1960s, once remarked that the 110m (360ft) hawser he was streaming astern did not seem to be making much difference, and that he could

occasionally see a big bight of the rope being carried forward on the crest of a wave in storms. Incidentally, he later advocates for his own boat, *Tzu Hang*, that some form of drogue should be attached to the line, but he never got round to doing it.

In the trials, the 136.5m (448ft) of 16mm ($^5/_8$in) eight-strand trailed over the stern on its own made a small but significant difference in drag. Of course, an even longer length of line comes to the same thing as a drogue. The difficulty is that so much rope may be needed to match the performance of a drogue there is insufficient space to stow it, and it may be an all-day job to recover after the storm is through. It made no noticeable difference to the drag whether the line was towed in a bight or straight, and there are arguments for both methods. By allowing the line to stream straight behind it has a better chance of bridging the whole wavelength and therefore may produce a steadier pull. By using it in a bight there is a chance that it may discourage waves breaking astern; it is easier to recover and less likely to be lost. Peter Cook (see Chapter 24) believes that a warp in a bight is more likely to surface. The choice should probably depend upon the length of the line and the wavelength of the seas. A sea anchor line can, of course, double as a drogue line.

Long, heavy wet ropes are awkward to handle. For larger vessels it may be desirable to install a reel on deck from which the rope can be deployed either for a drogue or a sea anchor. A power-driven reel would be ideal. Smaller vessels can best use another 'deployment bag'. This bag contains the entire length of line and has a hole in the centre at the bottom. It can be put in the water enabling the line to run out without fouling anything. The deployment bag should be prevented from being carried down the line into the water as it will seriously upset the operation of the drogue.

The handling difficulties and the expense of very long lines make a good case for using a good drogue or, better, a series of drogues, in conjunction with a suitable length of line.

The series drogue

The beauty of the series drogue (see Fig 7.5) is that the pull is nearly uniform regardless of wave effects – a unique and very desirable feature, given stories of drogues being picked up from astern by a breaking wave and carried forward. Another feature is that series drogues give good directional stability and many craft will maintain a course reasonably stern-on to the waves with the helm lashed amidships. On the other hand, making them is hard work and they are bulky to stow. With its delicate droguelets, the series drogue should not be used for any other purpose.

The series drogue used in the trials was designed for a 8.5m (28ft) yacht and had 110 cones attached to 18mm (³⁄₄in) Multiplat and a 21kg (46.2lb) sinker. A series drogue for the Najad 391 should have 130 cones with a similar weight of sinker.

The series drogue provided a good pull in spite of being undersize. Recovery without a windlass was hard work and, when using a windlass, it was found that it was necessary to fold each individual cone to prevent part of the cone being trapped by the adjoining turn of line which caused the cone to be torn as it came away from the barrel. Putting a line and float, or a floating standing trip line, at the weighted end of the series drogue would aid recovery.

The cones will stand up to normal use but could be damaged in shallow water. Like the parachute anchor line, the 18mm (³⁄₄in) drogue line was very heavy to handle when wet.

The series drogue used for the trials was owned and constructed by Professor Nöel Dilly. As related in the *Drag Device Data*

Figure 7.5 An effective drogue is the Jordan series drogue which uses a multitude of cones attached to a line streamed astern. An anchor at the end weighs the drogue down until the boat accelerates. This causes the drogue to rise and the drag to increase.

Optional float

Sinker

51–85m (167–280ft) of cones spaced 50cm (20in) apart

23m (76ft) leader

Bridle (twice width of transom)

LEFT Part of a series drogue showing the droguelets. RIGHT Deploying a series drogue.
Photos: Peter Bruce

Base, he used it off the Azores, deployed from his Twister in force 10, and was deeply impressed by the beneficial effects of its steady pull. He is not alone. For example, Tony and Coryn Gooch have used a series drogue most successfully on their worldwide cruises to high latitudes in *Taonui*, both in bad weather and in order to rest. *Taonui* is long-keeled and holds her course admirably at 1.5 knots with the series drogue deployed. They use a bridle over the stern that can be adjusted to give the yacht a small angle away from dead downwind, which makes for a more comfortable ride.

Users say that though not the most convenient of drogues to recover, the series drogue is one of the most effective.

The Galerider

The 0.9m (36in) Galerider (see photo on page 101) has good pulling power. It seemed to 'dig in' nicely in calm conditions. The hoop is highly sprung, so take care as it is withdrawn

from its bag to avoid being hit in the face. Attractive features are low drag at low speed, ease of recovery, and the fact that it does not absorb much water. The hoop has to be doubled to fit the Galerider back into its bag and that makes it a little more difficult to handle on board than others. It is advisable to lash the doubled hoop with sail ties before putting it away.

In July 1994 Mary Harper, a solo sailor aged 79, used a Galerider from her LM30 under bare pole in a 'hard gale' in mid-Atlantic. She said she did not think she used the drogue correctly – the line was rather short – as she could not find the instructions; nevertheless, she found that it slowed her boat down to 5 knots and she was 'so happy with the results'. Michael and Doreen Ferguson also used a Galerider during the Queen's Birthday storm with good results once the line had been shortened in to 24–27m (80–90ft).

There are a number of other favourable reports regarding the Galerider.

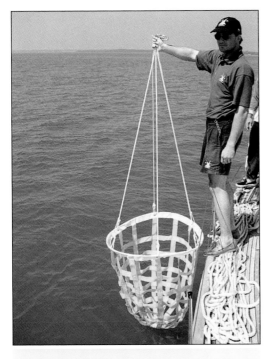

The Galerider has good pulling power, but may need weighting to give a steady pull in extreme conditions. *Photo: Peter Bruce*

Seabrake

Sir Peter Blake used to say that his most worrying time ever at sea was in a wing-masted multihull. This was *Steinlager 1* in the Round Australia Yacht Race. He used a Seabrake to good effect, but at one point the drogue emerged from out of the face of a wave and became airborne. It was also damaged. The remedy was to use the Seabrake with 9m (30ft) of 12mm (½in) chain added to the drogue end. There were no further problems.

The Seabrake used for the trials was the HSD 300 hard version designed for vessels up to 10m (33ft) in length. (The larger fabric version, which takes up less space and is a more appropriate size for the yachts used in the trials was not available at the time. The instructions for the solid Seabrake state that a chain of 5kg (11lb) minimum weight should be used in conjunction with a warp of three times the length of the vessel. Accordingly, 3m (10ft) of 10mm (³/₈in) chain

was used with 40m (133ft) of 16mm (⁵/₈in) nylon rope. Unless you happen to have the right sized shackle it will be necessary to use two shackles to secure the Seabrake to the chain. The instructions also bade one to launch the drogue at very low speed. (It would be nice to be told what very low speed is, as it might not be convenient, or possible, to stop in a rising storm.) Three and a half knots was judged to be slow enough, and on going to the set revolutions the Seabrake gave more drag than its slender body would suggest.

It was tested with the small and short line recommended, and also with the line used for all the other tests, but there was little difference in the results. The HSD 300 version was significantly undersize for the boat, and the results might be thought reasonable for a drogue of only 30cm (12in) diameter and 56cm (22in) length. The Seabrake scores well by having low drag at low speed. However, space is at a premium in small vessels and a solid drogue will not be popular aboard most craft.

The Delta

The 1.8m (6ft) Delta is intended for boats up to 13.7m (45ft) and the 1.2m (4ft) Delta is intended for boats up to 10.7m (35ft). The Deltas are small drogues and therefore stow easily. They are also made of non-absorbent material, a heavy vinyl-coated fabric, and so

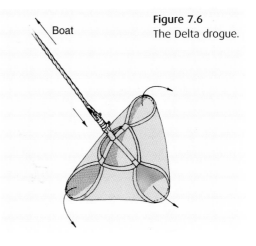

Boat

Figure 7.6
The Delta drogue.

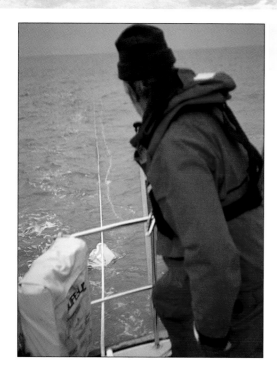

speeds and recovery laborious. On the other hand, sail can be set to overcome the steering problem and the Delta gives a remarkable amount of drag for its size.

The Para·Anchor Drogue Mk 2

The Para·Anchor drogue is a robustly-made nylon double parachute arrangement of 0.5m (1.85ft) diameter, which folds away into a small bag 34cm (13in) long. On test it was entirely stable and produced a good steady drag. Much of the time the drogue was at the surface and produced a distinct wake, but the drag load was unaffected. A further trial took place with a 1.93m (6ft 4in) length of 13mm (0.5in) anchor chain of weight 7kg (15lb) inserted between the drogue and the rode, and with the added weight the drogue did not come to the surface.

No 3 genoa

The use of a small genoa, 11.6 × 11 × 4m (38 × 36 × 13ft), was intended to establish whether satisfactory drag could be achieved without a purpose-made drogue. If a sail joined by pieces of rope from its three corners was to open out like a parachute, one might expect some hefty pulling power. Using rigging lines of about 1.2m (4ft), the drag figure suggests that the sail did not deploy and therefore only provided a very modest degree of usefulness. When longer rigging lines were used – a 4.6m (15ft) line from the head and two 7.6m (25ft) lines from the tack and the clew (to balance the sail approximately round the centre of effort) – it made a marked difference, as the results show. The sail gave colossal drag, probably more than would ever be required, especially

can be simply dried with a wipe. The 1.8m (6ft) Delta impressed with its pulling power. It seemed stable under load and did not break surface in calm conditions but, in Para-Tech's own publicity video, the (presumably) unweighted Delta could be seen breaking surface when towed behind a 8.8m (29ft) yacht in a seaway, and writhing about and breaking surface when towed behind a tug.

The Delta seems to have a possible disadvantage in that it provides a hefty drag at *low speeds*, making steering difficult at low at low speed, and performed more like a parachute sea anchor than a drogue.

Used either way, a disadvantage is that it is not easy to manage a sail on the upper deck in stormy conditions. Though the sail appeared to be stable, its asymmetrical shape could easily give rise to instability. A major advantage, however, is that sails are always on board and one does not have to buy additional equipment, and a minor advantage is that the sail can be dried by hoisting it after use, not that this is always convenient.

Many will prefer to use a proper drogue from a deployment bag rather than use their expensive sails for a purpose for which they were not designed. However, given long enough rigging lines configured so that they bisect the angle of the sail, a small sail will work as a drogue and a large sail will work as a parachute sea anchor. For the latter, a full-size genoa would be more appropriate than the No 3.

The Bu-Ord

Using the 3m (10ft) Bu-Ord parachute as a drogue produced the most dramatic of the results. The yacht's propeller was unable to cope with the parachute at the rpm set for the trial and cavitated severely. It was necessary to reduce rpm from 2820 to 2000 to avoid cavitation when a speed of only 1.2 knots was achieved, indicating very high resistance. Without a float and recovery line attached to the apex, the parachute does tend to sink and then becomes extremely laborious to recover. The Bu-Ord absorbs quite a lot of water, but is small enough to be hung up, allowing it to dry out quite easily. It is soft and takes up very little space. The Bu-Ord provides so much drag at all speeds that it is unlikely that steerage way can be maintained at all times. Depending on the size (bearing in mind that Bu-Ords have a mixed record of strength and reliability), a Bu-Ord is best used as a parachute sea anchor.

Cone drogues

Cone or sleeve drogues (see photo on page 104) are available in chandlers and are easy to make. These are the shapes that gave sea anchors a bad name, but in the small sizes available, if weighted, they seem to be no less effective than other drogues. Two were tested, one proprietary type with a 61cm

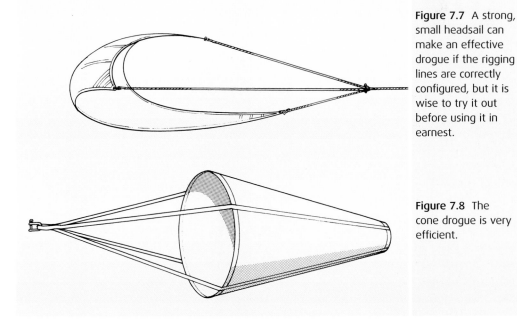

Figure 7.7 A strong, small headsail can make an effective drogue if the rigging lines are correctly configured, but it is wise to try it out before using it in earnest.

Figure 7.8 The cone drogue is very efficient.

A proprietary cone drogue. *Photo: Peter Bruce*

(24in) diameter mouth and 10cm (4in) exit hole, and another of 76cm (30in) diameter and 7.6cm (3in) exit which was home-made in two layers of parachute nylon. They were tried both singly and in series with 15.2m (50ft) between them and were weighted with chain. The results of drag trials were impressive, both as a single drogue and when two were set up in series. The latter arrangement can be expected to give especially good results in a seaway as a single drogue is bound to be disadvantaged by wave effects.

A heavy-duty sewing machine was used to make the homemade drogue. An ordinary sewing machine could not manage.

The car tyre

The tyre seemed to produce a modest but useful amount of drag; it doubled the amount of drag given by the line on its own. It had been expected that the tyre might porpoise or just skid along the surface, but there

was no sign of this in calm conditions, though instances have been reliably reported in a seaway. A car tyre is an awkward, large object to stow and, unless used in conjunction with a fender board, it can mark paintwork. One should drill drain holes in the side of the tyre or remember to sponge out the inside after use. Some will find a dual purpose for a car tyre; for example, a tyre makes a good fender for slimy dock or lock walls, as it does not rotate.

Conclusions following sea trials of drogues

The purpose-made drogues tested were strong, compact, easily handled, and gave an effective amount of drag, though it is thought that few owners of small craft will wish to find space for solid-built drogues. It is tempting to choose a drogue that will perform well without being heavily weighted.

The amount of drag that will be needed will vary with the severity of the weather. Ideally one should have a drogue that will hold the stern of the boat firmly into the seas, slow the boat down to a comfortable speed, yet retain steerage way in the troughs of large waves from force 8 upwards. A most important requirement is that the line should never go slack. To bridge an ocean wavelength, the drogue line may have to be more than 100m (328ft) in length.

Directionally stable yachts using a drogue may be able to maintain a good downwind course using vane steering, an auto helm or with the helm lashed amidships, but many yachts will need to be hand-steered.

Small parachutes, such as Bu-Ords, have been used over the stern of multihulls as drogues as well as over the bow as parachute sea anchors. Generally, monohulls will find the drag of a parachute too much to retain steerage way. At the other end of the scale a single weighted line, similar to the line used in the trials, will provide insufficient drag for most

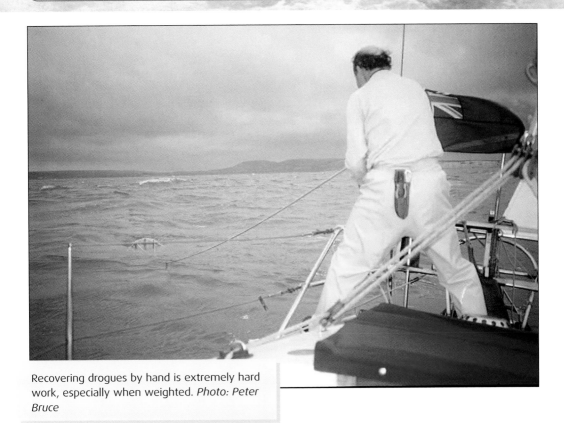

Recovering drogues by hand is extremely hard work, especially when weighted. *Photo: Peter Bruce*

purposes. Makeshift devices are not likely to be very effective either. The car tyre, for example, does not give much drag and can be the least trusted to stay submerged of all drogues.

Given the choice it is best to go for a drogue which is easy to stow and handle and which, by disproportionally reducing the drag, will allow the boat to be steerable at low speed. If one can cope with the added complication, there is a good case for putting two purpose-made drogues in series to obviate the effects of cyclical wave motion.

Though easier to manage, a drogue is not necessarily an alternative to a parachute. Apart from lack of sea room in the unlikely event of conditions becoming so extreme as to cause discontinuous load, for the yacht to be repeatedly pooped, or to become unsteerable, then she is probably better off with her bow facing into the seas, hove-to, under power, or lying to a parachute sea anchor – the decision best made early rather than late.

However, it is generally accepted that all craft are safer 'end-on' to the waves rather than 'broadside-on' when it really comes on to blow. Thus owners of craft that do not heave-to comfortably will be better off having any well-tried drag device, whether deployed over the bow or the stern, rather than nothing at all.

8

The meteorology of heavy weather

RICHARD EBLING

(This is written for the benefit of sailors, not meteorologists, and therefore many of the finer points have been simplified or glossed over.)

THESE DAYS, WITH THE VAST AMOUNT of weather information that is available to the sailor, in theory there is no need to be caught out, but no meteorologist can truthfully put his hand on his heart and always guarantee 100 per cent satisfaction for 24-hour forecast products, let alone those that look ahead for the best part of a week.

Obtaining offshore data

Sailing from a UK port should mean access to services such as the Met Office's dial-up facsimile service. This is a source of not only a text forecast with outlooks for the north Atlantic or Biscay, but charts covering an area between 70°N–40°N and 40°W–15°E for up to four days ahead, all for the cost of a couple of pints of beer. In France, similar services are available (equal to five bottles of the cheapest vin rouge). Australia and many other countries offer dial-up services.

At sea it is no longer necessary to receive actual and 24-hour forecast coded charts by Morse, which then require plotting and

drawing by hand (as it was 40 years ago). For many years radiofax has provided charts for up to six days ahead in some parts of the world, either using a dedicated receiver/printer or, more recently, the ubiquitous laptop plugged into an AF output socket on the ship's radio. But with increased use of onboard computers, the internet is probably the main data source with charts issued up to ten days ahead freely available: free that is apart from the communication hook-up.

Strong winds

Outside the tropics, the two most common causes of heavy weather associated with depressions are either the development of a secondary low, thereby causing the isobars to be squeezed closer together, or the straightforward unexpected deepening of an existing low centre.

With reports in this book coming from many sources, it may be appropriate to comment on wind profiles. Friction reduces wind blowing over the sea to about 80 per cent of the wind speed above the boundary or friction layer, and friction overland reduces the wind to about 40 per cent. In the scale of winds reported by masthead anemometers, however, there are further factors that are worth looking at, especially when you bear

Height in feet above the surface																		
10	20	30	33	40	50	60	70	80	90	100	120	140	160	180	200	250	300	

Factor over the sea																		
0.89	0.95	0.99	1.00	1.02	1.04	1.06	1.08	1.09	1.11	1.12	1.14	1.16	1.17	1.18	1.20	1.22	1.25	

Factor over the land																		
0.74	0.88	0.98	1.00	1.05	1.11	1.16	1.21	1.25	1.29	1.32	1.38	1.44	1.48	1.53	1.57	1.66	1.74	

Variation of windspeed with height relative to 10m (33ft).

in ... ather forecasts are all based on ... of a standard (land-based) ane... om (33ft) above ground level – a height probably chosen as being just above touch-down for aircraft.

For example, if the forecast is for 30 knots (force 7), with an anemometer 15m (50ft) above the waterline, the expected mean speed should be around $30 \times 1.04 = 31.2$ knots, and on a 49m (160ft) lighthouse such as the Fastnet, $30 \times 1.48 = 44.4$ knots could be recorded: a good force 9! I said 'recorded', as reported wind speed observations on meteorological broadcasts *should* always be corrected for both altitude and exposure. They are in the UK, but may not always be elsewhere, especially in some of the more remote corners of the globe.

It is also perhaps worth remembering the 'weight of the air'. In 24 knots the wind exerts a pressure of $11.24kg/m^2$ (2.3lb/sq ft), but a little under half as fast again, a wind of 34 knots, will exert $22.48kg/m^2$ (4.6lb/sq ft), while at 48 knots it exerts $44.96kg/m^2$ (9.2lb/sq ft) (doubling the wind speed means 4 times the pressure). So even for sails of equal area the 'heeling factor' in a given wind relates very much to the height of the sail's centre of pressure. Increased height of the centre of pressure means increased wind speed, and therefore increased pressure multiplied by an increased heeling moment. Changes in temperature, by the way, make little difference to the pressure.

To avoid confusion, unless otherwise stated, all diagrams and meteorological theories refer to the northern hemisphere, ie cyclonic flow is anticlockwise, and anticyclonic flow is clockwise.

Secondary lows

Without access to weather charts, trying to identify conditions leading to the development of a secondary low is next to impossible, as both surface and 'upper air charts' are needed, but these can now be obtained from an onboard Weatherfax receiver or from the internet which is becoming more commonplace. They give access to a reliable source of charts that are big enough and detailed enough to work on. Scouring the weather facsimile schedules (I personally prefer the 'Klingenfuss Facsimile Guide' rather than 'ALRS 3', as worldwide examples are included) will show references to combined 'surface/1000–500hPa/mb' and to '500hPa/mb/1000–500hPa/mb thickness charts'. (Strictly speaking, the correct SI unit for barometric pressure is the hecto Pascal, and documents such as weather charts and radiofax schedules will use hPa. One hPa = 1mb.

The charts that should be of most use will be:
1 Surface analyses, probably labelled ASXX or FSXX (Actual Surface or Forecast Surface)
2 Thickness charts, probably labelled AUXX or FUXX (Actual Upper-air or Forecast Upper-air)

Use of the word 'thickness' should bring home to us that the atmosphere is three-dimensional, and that it is not enough to consider what happens just at the surface. Average atmospheric pressure is 1013mb (hPa), and since pressure decreases with height, the vertical distance between the level at which the pressure is 1000mb (hPa)

Figure 8.1 Variation of pressure with height due to variation in temperature.

Figure 8.2 Where should the missing isobars be drawn?

Figure 8.3 Plan view of met chart with thickness lines. How 3-D information is displayed on 2-D meteorological charts. Vertical section at A–A.

and the level at which the pressure is 500mb (hPa) is known as the 'thickness' of the lower half of the atmosphere, the lowest 5500m (18 000ft) or so which, after all, is where most of the weather is.

Cold air is denser than warm air, therefore if the thickness value is low the air is cold, and if the thickness value is high then the air is warm (see Fig 8.1). Warm sectors with their relatively homogeneous contents will be shown as areas with very little change in thickness value.

Many weatherfax charts or chartlets will have lines omitted for clarity. If we take a surface chart with isobars, which is probably

the most familiar, filling in many of the missing isobars will be reasonably obvious, but in some cases it won't be possible. Fig 8.2 illustrates possible flow across a col. (Because low and high pressure systems can be thought of as valleys and mountain peaks some geographic terms are used, such as ridge or trough. A col or saddle point is a high valley between two mountains, which at the same time is a ridge between the lower ground on either side of the mountains.)

The size of your weatherfax chart will of course depend on the receiver/printer used, but the 500mb (hPa)/1000–500mb (hPa) chart is normally broadcast in the largest format possible and will probably be complete in as much as all the necessary lines will be there, but since it is not a surface chart, it will of course have no isobars or fronts shown; on the other hand, the surface forecast charts may have some thickness lines included so that it may well be necessary to use one chart in order to complete the other. (On combined charts the thickness lines are normally the ones that are dashed or dotted.)

Once it is understood what is being looked for, the practice is straightforward (Fig 8.3). Just as tightly drawn depth contours on a marine chart (a steep gradient) denote rapid shoaling, fronts or more correctly frontal zones are areas of change, where either cold air is being replaced by warmer or vice versa. Whereas warm sectors with their relatively uniform contents contain few thickness lines, in frontal zones the greater the contrast in temperature, the closer the thickness lines will be, and the steeper will be the 'thermal gradient'. At a warm front, cold air is replaced by warmer less dense air, and so the thickness values will rise, falling again at the cold front as the warm air is replaced by cold air once more.

Forecasting development of secondary lows

In an ideal world the surface and upper air features should be closely related, as in Fig 8.4, but unfortunately this is not always

Figure 8.4 Three stages in the development from a frontal wave to an occluded frontal system showing the relationship between isobars, fronts and thickness lines.

the case. Sometimes the thickness lines are bunched along the warm front, or along the cold, and sometimes even cross into the warm sector. Secondary lows tend to form where the thickness lines are bunched together.

In Fig 8.5a the thickness lines are bunching where they run nearly parallel to the cold front for a considerable distance. On the surface, the cold front may be trailing with little if any gradient across it, ie very few isobars crossing the front. In conditions such as these the distance from the point of development of a secondary low – as a cold front wave – from the point of occlusion is likely to be in the region of 1200–1500nm, with the new low moving generally in a direction parallel to the thickness lines or the isobars within the warm sector. This is probably the most common way in which secondary depressions form.

Figure 8.5
Thickness patterns associated with the development of secondary lows and their direction of movement.
a) Secondary low development as a wave on the cold front.
b) Secondary lows on a warm front.
c) Secondary low developing at the triple point.
d) Least common case of a secondary low developing at the triple point.

In Fig 8.5b the secondary low develops as a warm front wave. The bunching of the thickness lines in this case is seen to be just ahead of the warm front with a distinct ridging over the warm sector, with the resulting depression moving along the thickness lines. (Compare this with Fig 8.5d where the bunching is nearer to the triple point.)

The development of a secondary low – as a triple point low – (Fig 8.5c) is perhaps the most common. In this case the thickness lines will no longer be parallel to the cold front. Some will cross the warm sector, while the rest will turn pole-wards (north) just before they reach the occlusion. Again in this case the movement of the secondary low will be in the general direction of the thickness lines or isobars within the warm sector.

In Fig 8.5d, as in 8.5c, some thickness lines cross the warm sector, and bunching is seen to be closer to the triple point than in 8.5b. This case is the least likely to develop into a secondary low.

In all cases, the driving force behind any development of a secondary low is the strongest thermal contrast, which is shown on a chart by the bunching of the thickness lines.

The following questions should be asked:
1 Is the strongest thermal contrast along and parallel to the cold front? If so, watch out for cold front waves.
2 Is the strongest thermal contrast along and parallel to the warm front? If so, watch out for warm front waves.
3 Is the strongest thermal contrast across rather than along the front? If so, expect a triple point low to develop.

Explosive deepening

Development of weather systems is normally fairly well forecast, so if depressions do suddenly deepen unexpectedly, more often than not it is a case of explosive deepening (which is defined as deepening at over 24mb (hPa) in a day). This usually happens during the winter months, and nearly always occurs over the oceans, with the western north Atlantic being one of the world's preferred areas. However, explosive deepening of depressions can occur at any time, even in mid-summer, especially if the tail end of any ex-tropical revolving storm is involved.

If the signs leading up to one of these events have slipped through the professional forecasters' net, it is very unlikely that the yachtsman will have any additional information to guide him except that of a steadily falling barometer. With no other information to go on, a good rule is that falls of 10mb (hPa) in 3 hours will be followed by a gale (force 8). While the falls may not be particularly rapid, to the rear of the depression the pressure rise may be. (In the October 1987 storm, the barometer at Hurn Airport fell some 33mb (hPa) in 18 hours at an average of 5.5mb (hPa)/3hr or 1.8mb (hPa)/hr, but later the barometer rose 50mb (hPa) in 15 hours! It peaked at 12.2mb (hPa) in the hour 0400–0500 UTC. Rises of over 10mb (hPa) in 1 hour covered an area from Lyme Bay and the Isle of Wight to Reading.)

Initially, the strongest winds may very well be contained within the warm sector, but once the explosive deepening gets under way, storm or even hurricane force winds (force 10–12) can occur over a comma-shaped arc (seen shaded in Fig 8.6) in the cold air behind the cold front, as cold dry air from high in the atmosphere is dragged down and swept into the circulation. A narrow jet, tens rather than hundreds of miles across, begins to descend and dry out; then passing through the snow and ice particles contained within the cloud mass, cools further as these crystals evaporate. Now being cooler the jet is denser and descends even more quickly, eventually hitting the surface. The dryness of this entrained air will result in an area with clear skies, as reported during the 1979 Fastnet Race.

However, just because the wind speed is increasing it does not necessarily mean that the associated fronts will also speed up. Pressure falling along a trough line (Fig 8.7), such as a cold front, will sharpen the trough, tightening the pressure gradient each side of

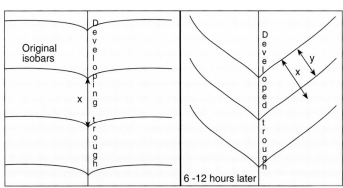

Figure 8.6 Comma-shaped arc of enhanced wind due to the intrusion of subsided air.

Figure 8.7 Isobar spacing along a developing trough may remain constant in spite of closer isobars and strengthening winds. Y = tighter gradient, therefore increased wind speed compared with X.

the front without affecting the gradient measured along the front.

The distance apart of the isobars measured along the trough – in this case, a measurement of 'x' units – remains constant even though the distance apart of the isobars 'y' has now decreased. Very rapid post-frontal pressure rises will of course also have the same net result.

Lee lows

Depressions can also be caused by high ground. Examination of the chart may show a 'hole in the isobars' or wide space in an apparently regular circulation about the main depression, and it is within this empty space that a lee low may form.

As air is forced to rise over a range of mountains, in general the curve of the isobars becomes more anticyclonic. Likewise, on the leeward side of the high ground with descending flow the isobars become more

Figure 8.8 Development of a lee low as an eddy due to the distortion of isobars crossing high ground.

cyclonic. As well as marked troughing to the lee of mountains, lee depressions can also develop. In the same way, water flowing past an obstruction will form eddies that break away to be carried in the stream.

Often the only evidence for drawing a discrete circulation around these centres is gleaned from satellite analysis. In the mid-1950s, with an anticyclone over Greenland and northerly winds over the UK, charts would be drawn with perhaps very little in the way of isobars due to lack of observations to suggest a lee low to the south-east of

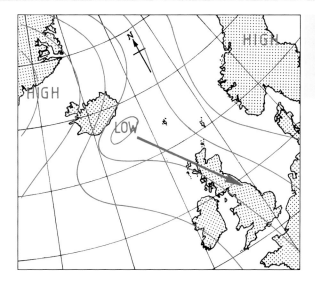

Figure 8.9 Polar low developing as a lee low before breaking away to be carried southwards across Scotland and possibly eastern England.

Iceland. It was perhaps only with the arrival of unexpected prolonged snow in Scotland that we would be aware that one of these eddies had broken away from its source and been carried along embedded within the flow, arriving as a polar low.

High pressure generated winds

Unexpected strong winds may also be caused by anticyclones that fail to move away as expected, with little, if any, indication from an onboard barometer. For example extreme weather south of Iceland occurred that was the result of a complex area of low pressure in mid-Atlantic. On Friday 11 May 1979, a small depression crossed Scotland followed by an area of light winds as a col followed, crossing Rockall early in the day, and then Scotland in the late evening. Meanwhile, the main Atlantic low at around 45°N 40°W appeared to consist of three centres with the lowest pressure around 980mb (hPa). On the Saturday, the lows moved north-east at about 20 knots, with troughing towards Iceland. But the blocking high pressure over the Greenland icecap was, if anything, still building – increasing the pressure gradient (50 knots)

over and to the south of Iceland, leading to the very high wind speeds experienced by the crew of a UFO34 described in the previous edition. On the Sunday, pressure over Greenland was still high, maintaining easterlies of a similar strength over Iceland and over the sea areas to the south and east, as the depression, now a single centre of 987mb (hPa), began to track east-north-east around 60°N. It was not until this stage late on Sunday and into Monday that the Greenland pressures began to fall as the low moved away from Iceland.

The reluctance of an area of high pressure to move was also evident in the 1994 Queen's Birthday storm (Chapter 20) when some 80 yachts were caught out in a storm as they sailed together from New Zealand to winter in the tropical Pacific islands. Again the closest isobars (and strongest winds) were in the quadrant squashed against the anticyclone centred over or close to New Zealand.

Anticyclone winds

The wind circulating around a centre is acted upon by centrifugal forces acting away from the centre. In an anticyclone the pressure gradient force acts outwards as well, so that around high pressure both forces act in the same direction. Around a low the pressure gradient acts towards the centre, in other words, the centrifugal force is acting against the pressure gradient, reducing its strength (Fig 8.10). *Thus around an anticyclone, winds are stronger for a given isobar spacing than around a depression.*

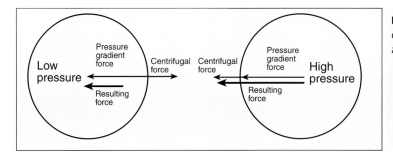

Figure 8.10 Forces acting on air under cyclonic and anticyclonic motion.

Convergence/divergence

When winds meet, either spiralling into a depression or perhaps when a sea breeze blowing inland meets the land breeze, the air has to go somewhere. If the convergence is at the surface the air obviously cannot sink, so it must rise. Convergence also occurs when moving air is slowed down. Obviously air that is rising will expand and cool, and if the air is cooled sufficiently any moisture will condense into clouds. In the same way diver-

gence at the surface can only be satisfied if the air aloft is subsiding – in which case the air will be compressed, warmed, and any moisture particles will evaporate.

With north-east trades in the northern hemisphere blowing towards the south-east trades of the south, there must be a front and a line of convergence separating these two flows. It was once thought that there was convergence along the entire length of this intertropical convergence zone (ITCZ), but it is now accepted that the actual convergence occurs only here and there. Nevertheless, the

Figure 8.11 ABOVE Trade winds converging towards the equator in January and July.

Figure 8.12 Satellite view of the convergence zone on 11 October 2006.

ITCZ is a breeding area for tropical storms – although they may not develop precisely on the ITCZ. Fig 8.12 shows a photo montage of several satellite pictures taken on 11 October. In these the coldest (highest) clouds are brightest.

The bright clouds associated with the ITCZ can be seen over the central Pacific close to the Equator, over Colombia and Guyana, over the east Atlantic, the Gulf of Guinea and Africa's Congo basin, again close to the Equator. Rather more activity is visible over the Indian Ocean and across Sumatra and North Borneo. This shows a series of convergence areas rather than the continuous belt that had been thought to exist.

Tropical revolving storms

1 Charts displaying tracks of tropical revolving storms (TRS) (Fig 8.14) show that formation does not normally occur within 5° north or south of the equator, or in the South Atlantic. In March 2004 the first ever reported TRS in the South Atlantic was observed off the Brazilian coast. Whilst we can be pretty sure that it was the first TRS since satellite observation started in 1966, prior to that lack of reports cannot be taken to mean that they never had occurred. This TRS, called NoName #1, was responsible for three deaths and for 2000 people being rendered homeless. It will present a challenge to research, as sea surface temperatures were only around 24°C, and may only be resolved by running repeated mathematical simulations.

2 High water vapour content is required. In order to supply both the water vapour and a sufficient source of heat for convection, sea temperature in excess of 26°C (79°F) is essential, allowing the air to contain typically 20–25g (0.7–0.9oz) of water per 1kg (2.2lb) of air (2 per cent of the air will in fact be water vapour!). Logically the warmer the better, and the greater depth of warm water the better as well – since rough surface conditions will churn up the sea, mixing the warm surface waters with the deeper colder layers and in so doing can 'kill off' the potential storm. As the moist air within the circulation rises, expands and cools, condensation takes place, releasing large amounts of energy in the form of latent heat.

3 The released latent heat needs to be contained within the vertical column of the circulation and therefore TRS need to be well away from the influence of any jet streams.

Figure 8.13 In a fully developed TRS, the rising air and the cloud generated by its furious ascent will be rather like a factory chimney with the condensing water vapour replacing the bricks and stones, and with the descending central core generating the clear eye of the storm. The base of this 'chimney' may be obscured by low cloud or may start a little above the surface projecting through various layers of cloud; there may be other convective cloud cells embedded within the larger circulation. These embedded convective clouds might well contain active thunderstorms that would be considered severe in their own right.

40,000ft

30,000ft

20,000ft

10,000ft

Tropical revolving storms

Area and local name	Jan	Feb	Mar	Apr	May	Jun	Jul	Aug	Sep	Oct	Nov	Dec	Average No per year	Average of over F11 per year
N Atlantic, W Indies (hurricane)					?	—	—	====	====	====	—	?	10	5
NE Pacific (hurricane)					?	—	====	====	====	—	?		15	7
NW Pacific (typhoon)				?	—	—	====	====	====	—	—	?	25–30	15–20
N Indian Ocean, Bay of Bengal (cyclone)			?	—	====	====	—	—	—	====	====	?	2–5	1–2
N Indian Ocean Arabian Sea (cyclone)			?	—	====	—			?	—	====	?	1–2	1
S Indian Ocean W of 80°E (cyclone)	====	====	==—	—	?						?	—	5–7	2
Australia W, NW, N and Queensland coast (cyclone)	====	====	==—	—							?	—	2–3	1
Fiji, Samoa, New Zealand (N Island) (cyclone)	====	====	====	—	?						?	—	7	2

— main season   ==== period of greatest activity   ? period affected if season is early/late

4 Eventually a small amount of the rising air at the top of the system turns inwards and sinks. This dry air is then responsible for the clear eye of the storm.

The initial track of a TRS is mainly westwards, typically at 10–15 knots, with a slight pole-wards component (Fig 8.14), steered by the tropospheric flow. Somewhere between 20° and 30° away from the equator, depending on the position of the high pressure belt, the track usually curves increasingly pole-wards at 20–30 knots. As the system leaves the tropical circulation, its course will

Figure 8.14 Typical tracks of tropical revolving storms.

60°N

30°N

0°

30°S

60°S

Figure 8.15 Justin's erratic track for some 20 days.

The notorious hurricane Katrina that caused so much damage to New Orleans near its peak strength on 28 August 2005. Maximum sustained wind was 175mph (280km/h). Minimum barometric pressure was 902mb(hPa). Note the clearly formed eye in the centre of the swirling cloud mass. Later in the year came hurricane Rita with maximum wind strength of 180mph/290km/h, and a lowest central pressure of 895mb (hPa).

be governed by the westerly winds of the mid-latitude troposphere.

Not that all TRS do as expected, for example Cyclone Justin, off the northeast coast of Australia, moved just 180nm in 9 days (3–12 March 1997). With dew points and sea temperatures in the mid to high twenties, Justin's slow movement can only have been due to lack of any steering flow throughout the height of the cyclone until around 12 March, when Justin headed north-east towards New Guinea for three or four days before returning to hit the coast near Cairns and then to travel south down the coast towards Mackay.

The moral of this is that although tropical storms *should* curve away from the equator, in reality they are very unpredictable and a close eye on the barometer is required. Within the tropics the diurnal variation of pressure (the atmospheric tide) of perhaps up to 3mb (hPa) may mask early warning of approaching systems. It is normal for tendencies of ±0.5mb (hPa)/hour to occur around 0100 and 0700, 1300 and 1900 local time.

Thunderstorms

On a smaller scale to tropical revolving storms, thunderstorms are also fuelled by convective processes. What is needed is 'conditionally unstable air', allowing a parcel of saturated air to be buoyant and to rise, when an adjacent parcel of dry air does not. (Indeed, were the parcel of dry air to be lifted it would sink again to its starting point.) In the lowest 3000m (10 000ft) of the atmosphere dry air cools with height at around 3°C (5.4°F per 300m (1000ft), and at about half that rate if the air is saturated, due to the release of latent heat as moisture is condensed out. The trigger to start this movement could be heating from below, or cooling from above, or ascent as air is forced to rise over high ground in the case of air mass storms, or is forced to rise as a front approaches. Convergence near a front can give rise to some of the severest storms, but another requirement for severe storms is a marked change of wind velocity with height which tilts the updraft.

The updraft is almost self-perpetuating as it is fuelled by the latent heat released by condensation. The small 'cloud' droplets that originally form have a slow drop speed, and will easily be carried up in the strong updrafts – giving them the chance of growing larger.

Since within a cloud 'the higher the colder', at around −20°C (−4°F) ice crystals develop. Higher in the cloud as temperatures get even lower, more and more of the updraft

consists of ice rather than water, until temperatures reach −40°C (−40°F) by which time the cloud consists only of ice crystals.

As the droplets/ice particles grow they become heavier, and because the updraft is no longer vertical, falling ice/water will leave the saturated updraft and fall into drier air – where evaporation takes place. The latent heat required for this cools the adjacent air – generating negative buoyancy and hence the downdraft. Not only is the downdraft due to the coldness (density) of the air, but the falling precipitation also drags air down with it (due to friction).

When this downdraft hits the surface it rapidly spreads out as a cold pool giving rise not only to a rapid or even violent increase in wind speed, but also changes in direction. As the cold pool and its 'gust front' undercut the surrounding air so conditions become ripe for development of a new up-current of air. In storms with many updrafts, the falling ice/water may enter another updraft and so be carried upwards once more, providing the opportunity for further growth (this process can be repeated many times). For example, examination of large hailstones will show many 'shells', as layers have progressively built up.

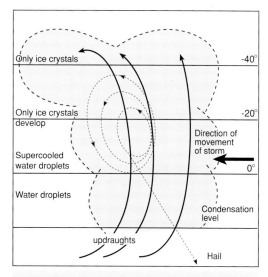

Figure 8.16 Development of hailstones within a cumulonimbus cloud.

A thunderstorm over East Falkland viewed from Pebble Island. Although the main storm was 30–40 miles to the east, on flying some 50 miles south-east to Goose Green, the last 15 miles were through hail. Note the effect of the stronger southerly wind towards the top of the cloud, producing the typical anvil head. *Photo: Richard Ebling*

A thunderstorm can also be considered as a very efficient electrical generator even though the exact electrical mechanism is unknown. Fields of 100kV/m to 400kV/m develop within the storm, a positive charge at the top, a negative charge towards the bottom of the cloud, and an induced positive area on the ground immediately below the cloud. It may well have been this 'build-up' under cloud that affected Bill Cooper aboard his steel ketch just before she was struck by lightning (see Chapter 17).

Once a critical field strength has been generated (1 000 000kV/m), a lightning discharge takes place, temporarily neutralizing the field, but build-up is immediately recom-menced as long as the cell is still active. The lightning stroke can be cloud to cloud, either within the same cloud or to an adjacent cloud; or cloud to ground, ground in this case being either land or sea.

A ground stroke (land or sea) is initiated by a 'stepped leader'. This is a surge of electrons that move downwards at about 50m (164ft) per microsecond, and after a pause of about 50 microseconds, a second step takes place, this sequence being repeated until the leader reaches the ground. A charge will then move rapidly upwards along the path taken by the leader. After about 0.01 seconds another stroke occurs. (Up to 30 or 40 strokes have been observed in the same channel.)

A fleet of yachts at the Grenada Sailing Festival seem to be in the path of a squall. *Photo: Onne van der Wal/Bluegreen*

Cloud to cloud strokes also consist of a stepped leader and a return stroke.

While the strength and direction of local winds generated by air being drawn into a thunderstorm will be a combination of both the in-flowing air and the pre-existing wind, the cold downdraft wind will be blowing out from the storm, arriving as a chilly squall with a sudden increase in speed and change of direction, undercutting the surrounding air in the same manner as a cold front.

Tornadoes and waterspouts

Strong updrafts are also needed for tornadoes; this time the updraft is also rotating, initially at an altitude somewhere between 3000m–6000m (10 000ft–20 000ft). As the rotation increases, the local pressure gradient across the rotating core, and the local centrifugal force about the core, come into balance, and the system is now called a meso-cyclone. By this time most if not all of the flow is drawn in at its lower end, and this in turn extends the rotating core lower and lower until it reaches the surface.

Near the surface, however, friction prevents the balance between the local centrifugal force and the local pressure gradient, and so air streams in towards the centre. The funnel cloud that extends from the cloud base is mainly condensation as a result of cooling due to the decreasing pressure and initially the rotating core may not be visible, but if it extends to near the surface, dust and debris will be swept up over land and spray will be swept up over the sea.

What will not probably be visible from a small boat but has been observed from the air is a 'dark spot' on the surface of the water due to the very localized rotation and ascent of the air. Once the visible funnel reaches from the cloud to the water's surface, waves will develop and as the spout tracks across the water, a wake of small bubbles may be noticed due to gases released by the low pressure.

Strong or violent tornadoes are, thankfully, only found over land, when theoretically a maximum speed of 313 knots is possible but examination of film has led to estimates of up to 165 knots for waterspouts. Weak tornadoes may also form beneath the rapidly growing cloud that develops over a gust front – perhaps around the fringe of a thunderstorm where funnel clouds and waterspouts may occasionally be seen.

In conclusion, if professional forecasters are not 100 per cent accurate, then amateurs with fewer facilities are unlikely to do better. Nevertheless, if information is available, it is good to have the knowledge to be able to interpret such information correctly, and is very satisfying too.

Waterspout off Guadeloupe Island.
Photo: Christian Février/Bluegreen

9

Waves

SHELDON BACON

Wave growth

A YACHT IS FAR FROM LAND, BECALMED on a glassy sea; and then the wind appears. What now happens to the surface of the sea? If the wind were a perfectly steady and uniform airflow and the sea surface were perfectly flat and smooth there would be no waves generated. The friction between air and sea would drive a current in the sea, but some irregularity in the wind is needed to disturb an initially smooth sea surface to begin to generate waves.

The real wind is gusty, blustery and turbulent. There is an atmospheric boundary layer about 100m (330ft) high above the sea surface within which the airflow is directly affected by the presence of the sea surface. This induces turbulence on scales from millimetres to tens of metres (also the air/sea temperature difference can induce circulation in the wind to over 1km (3280ft) above the surface). The turbulence is carried along by the overall flow of the wind, and it is this turbulence that starts up the wave motion on the sea. This is the initial phase of wave growth, and it is relatively slow.

Once there are some waves present, a very rapid (in fact exponential) phase of wave growth takes place. The more waves there are, the rougher the sea surface is, so the more turbulence is generated in the wind,

which produces still more waves, and so on. However, this process cannot continue for ever. For any given wind speed, low or high, a state of saturation is reached when energy input to the waves by the wind is balanced by dissipation of energy from the wavefield, either by waves travelling out of the generation region, or by breaking. The exponential growth phase does not tail off to the steady state however; it gets carried away and, for a short time, energy is pumped into the waves that the waves cannot hold. This is called overshoot, and it can be dangerous for yachts because the wavefield will have to lose energy by waves breaking at a greater rate than during the saturation phase.

Ultimately, the sea state reaches a steady state which will not change until the wind changes its speed and/or direction. If the wind should increase further, the waves will continue to grow; if it decreases, dissipation will remove more energy than the new lower wind speed is injecting, and the waves will become lower. If there is a change in direction, potentially the most dangerous possibility in extreme conditions, a new sea will develop on top of the declining old one, resulting in a cross-sea, and it will develop rapidly since the sea is already rough and the wind turbulent.

With the passing of a wave, water particles travel in nearly circular paths. At the surface, the diameter of the circles is the

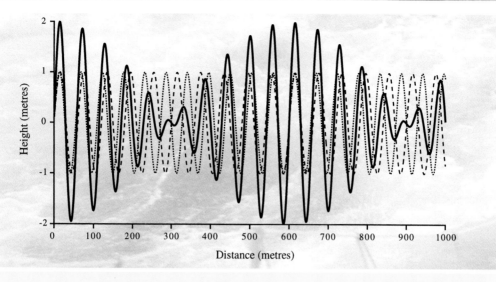

Figure 9.1 This is a demonstration of the formation of wave groups by the addition of similar waves. In this example there are two basic waves, one of length 177ft (54m) crest-to-crest (dotted) and the other 197ft (60m) crest-to-crest (dashed); they are both 7ft (2m) high crest-to-trough. The height of the resulting wave (solid line) varies between 13ft (4m) crest-to-trough and zero. It is made of waves at the average length of the two basic waves 187ft (57m) wrapped in an envelope whose length depends on the difference between the basic waves: the smaller the difference, the longer the groups made by the envelope.

crest-to-trough height of the wave. At the top of the crest, the water is travelling straight forwards; at the bottom of the trough, straight back. At some point on the front and rear faces of the wave, the water travels straight up and straight down. The water is also in motion below the surface, to a depth that depends on the length of the wave. Consider, for example, a 20m (66ft) long wave: at 5m (16ft) depth (25 per cent of the wavelength), the particle speeds are 20 per cent of their surface values, and at 20m (66ft) depth (one wavelength), only 0.1 per cent. This becomes very important in regions of shoal water: if there is seabed in the way at a depth where the wave is trying to influence water motion, the wave can feel the bottom.

There is a unique connection between the length, period and speed of a wave, which can take any height, but for any one length of wave, there is only one possible speed and one possible period. Long waves travel faster than short waves (in deep water), so if many

waves all of different lengths are produced in one place, which occurs during a storm, the longer waves that are generated will travel out of the area of the storm faster than the shorter ones. This is the origin of swell: fast-moving, long waves that may arrive in advance of an approaching storm. Wave shape changes as the wave becomes steeper: long, low swell waves are rounded and vertically symmetrical (sinusoidal), but as steepness increases they become asymmetrical: more peaked at the crest and flat in the trough (trochoidal).

If two waves of similar lengths are added, another important phenomenon arises, that of wave grouping. If the crest of one coincides with the crest of the other (or a trough with a trough), the resulting height is the sum of the two, but if a crest coincides with a trough, the two waves cancel. The single wave resulting from the addition of two looks different: there is now an envelope around the short-wave basic wave train that groups the individual waves into 'packets'. This is illustrated in Fig 9.1, which shows two waves of the same height but slightly (10 per cent) different lengths added. Now the two waves travel at different speeds according to their lengths: the longer one faster than the shorter. This will cause the envelope to travel forwards as the crests and troughs move in and out of phase, so that the envelope has a forward velocity of its own called the group velocity. This is related to the difference in speed between the two waves, so the envelope can move quite slowly forwards while within each resultant group, the individual waves rise at the back, move forwards through the group, and finally disappear at the front of the group. This can be seen happening within ships' wakes, for example.

After presenting some of the basics of wave growth, propagation and decay, the following sections consider wave height prediction, global wave climate and extreme waves.

Wave prediction

Here is a recipe for reasonably accurate prediction of wave height. If a quick estimate is required, skip parts (1) to (5) below and go straight to (6), which will at worst result in an over-estimate.

Wave height depends (among other things) on wind speed, fetch (distance upwind to 'where the wind starts' – either the coast or the far side of an approaching weather system) and duration (length of time the wind has been blowing). If the wind blows at the same speed in the same direction for long enough, the waves will stop growing and will have become fully developed; so we proceed to treat three cases: the growing fetch-limited sea, the growing duration-limited sea, and the fully developed sea.

Accordingly, there are three decision graphs for deciding which case applies, and three prediction graphs for providing the estimate of wave height for the relevant case. This is how they work.

Figure 9.2 First decision graph. Given a known situation described by wind speed, fetch and duration, use this graph to decide whether the case is fetch-limited or duration-limited.

Figure 9.3 Second decision graph. If the first decision graph has shown that fetch-limiting is relevant, use this graph to decide whether the sea is really fetch-limited or actually fully developed.

1   First establish your 'case': decide on the wind speed (in knots), fetch (in nautical miles) and duration (in hours). Call these values W, F and D. Fig 9.2 shows limiting duration as a function of wind speed and fetch, and it provides the answer to the first question: is the

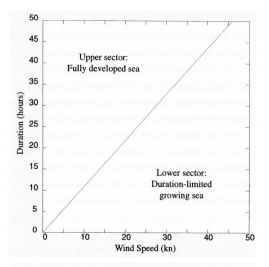

Figure 9.4 Third decision graph. If the first decision graph has shown that duration-limiting is relevant, use this graph to decide whether the sea is really duration-limited or actually fully developed.

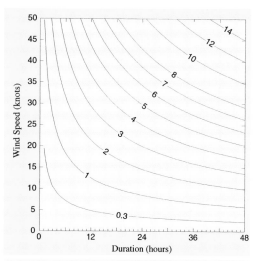

Figure 9.6 Second prediction graph. The decision graphs have led to the conclusion that the sea is duration-limited and growing. Use this graph to predict wave height (Hs, metres) given duration and wind speed.

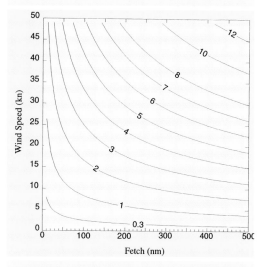

Figure 9.5 First prediction graph. The decision graphs have led to the conclusion that the sea is fetch-limited and growing. Use this graph to predict wave height (Hs, metres) given fetch and wind speed.

Figure 9.7 Third prediction graph. The decision graphs have led to the conclusion that the sea is fully developed. Use this graph to predict wave height (Hs, metres) given wind speed.

case duration-limited or fetch-limited? Find what duration in Fig 9.2 corresponds to W and F. If D is greater than this value, the case is fetch-limited, so go to (2) below. If D is less than this value, the case is duration-limited, so go to (3) below.

2   Is the case really fetch-limited, or is the sea fully developed? Turn to Fig 9.3. Find what sector of the plot wind speed W and fetch F fall into. If the sea is fetch-limited and growing, go to (4) below. If the sea is fully developed, go to (6).

3 Is the case really duration-limited, or is the sea fully developed? Turn to Fig 9.4. Find what sector of the plot wind speed W and duration D fall into. If the sea is duration-limited and growing, go to (5) below. If the sea is fully developed, go to (6).

4 Fetch-limited growing sea: use Fig 9.5 to predict wave height for fetch F and wind speed W.

5 Duration-limited growing sea: use Fig 9.6 to predict wave height for duration D and wind speed W.

6 Fully developed sea: use Fig 9.7 to predict wave height for wind speed W.

Here is a worked example. Say you are in the north Atlantic, 300 miles from the east coast of America, and you anticipate 25 knots of wind from the west to last for 24 hours. The limiting duration from Fig 9.2 is 36 hours. Our case (24 hours) is less than this, so proceed to Fig 9.4, from which we see that 25 knots for 24 hours is in the duration-limited growing sea sector. Finally, looking at Fig 9.6, we get a wave height of about 4m (13ft) for our case.

Of course, this is not the full story. Rates of decay are less easy to compute, if the weather is easing. Shallow water effects come into play when the water depth is less than half the wavelength. For waves of 5–10 second period (typical open-ocean values), meaning 50–150m (165–482ft) wavelength, water depths of 25–75m (82–246ft) and less will begin to affect the behaviour of the waves. They will become steeper until eventually they break, usually in the very shallow water near a beach called the surf zone, but in very severe weather (very high/long waves), they can break over offshore banks. Waves can also be made steeper or less steep by running into or away from a current. This is commonly seen in coastal waters over tidal cycles, but is also relevant for strong offshore currents like the Gulf Stream or the Kuroshio, which are notorious for their steep confused seas whenever the waves run against the current. Swell, which will increase the average wave height just by being around, also slightly increases the growth rate of waves in the presence of wind.

View of a small freshwater loch in Uig, Isle of Lewis, on 8 October 1995. The fetch was 183m (600ft) and the wind was south to south-west, gusting 61–78 knots. *Photo: Murray Macleod*

A global tour

Observation of the waves of the world's oceans by satellite has been underway for a sufficiently long time that a meaningful picture of the global wave climate can be presented. This section will describe the global mean wave climate as measured between 1985 and 1996 by a sequence of satellites. The instrument used is the Satellite Radar Altimeter, which, from a height of 700km (435 miles), is able to measure the sea surface wave height to an accuracy of a few centimetres (an inch), comparable to the best surface-based (ships and buoys) instruments.

The data are shown in Figs 9.8 to 9.11, being the global mean wave height distributions for January, April, July and October. The wave heights are in metres, and the measure actually used is significant wave height, which is a scientific measure close to what an observer would estimate visually. January and July are shown because they are the peaks of summer and winter winds (for both northern and southern hemispheres); the intermediate seasons are seen in the other two figures.

The idealized picture of global atmospheric pressure is: low pressure at the equator (the Doldrums), high pressure about 30° north and south latitude (the Horse Latitudes), low pressure about 60° north and south latitude, and finally the polar highs. Light or variable winds are ascribed to these locations. The strong winds that blow between these alternating belts of high and low pressure are well known: the trades between the equator and 30° (north-east trades in the northern hemisphere, south-east in the southern). Between 30° and 60°, the northern hemisphere experiences south-westerlies and the southern hemisphere north-westerlies (the Roaring Forties); and between 60° and the pole, south-easterlies blow off the Antarctic, and north-easterlies off the Arctic. How do the waves conform in reality to this scheme?

There are some obvious features in these figures. The northern winter appears as rough seas in the north Atlantic and north Pacific from about 35°N in both oceans and continues up past Iceland in the Atlantic. Average wave heights in the northern deep ocean winter are in excess of 5m (16ft), with hardly a trace left in the summer. The southern winter appears as a great belt of rough seas extending from about 35°S to close to the Antarctic continent in about 65–70°S. In great contrast to the northern hemisphere, however, in the southern summer the seas don't reduce nearly so much: from over 5m (16ft) to 3–4m (10–13ft). In further contrast, the equatorial Atlantic and Pacific are relatively placid much of the time. The calms under the Horse Latitudes show up clearly in the north Atlantic, less clearly in the north Pacific, and not at all obviously in the southern hemisphere, where the seasonal advance and retreat of the Roaring Forties sends waves northwards beyond 20°S.

Plainly there is much more to the story beyond the simple 'banded' model, and the most significant missing ingredient is *land*. Land soaks up and gives out heat much faster than the sea, both on time scales of a day and of a year. Where there is no (or little) land, the sea has a moderating effect on the wind regime, so that the degree of variation between summer and winter is smoothed out. This applies in the Southern Ocean wind belt (the Roaring Forties). The great land masses of the northern hemisphere cause the reverse to happen. Changes between seasons are amplified, particularly in that the northern summer is a lot calmer than the southern summer.

Land has other effects on the sea. The figures show the effect of sheltering. Enclosed seas are much calmer on average than the open ocean: look at the Caribbean, the Mediterranean, the Baltic, the seas of the East Indies, and others. As well as the generally short fetch in enclosed seas, they get little or no swell, and the presence of swell promotes wave growth (as well as contributing to the total wave height). There are shadow zones 'behind' Iceland, the Hawaiian islands, New Zealand and, very noticeably, east of southern Argentina over a thick slice of the south Atlantic.

Figure 9.8 Global mean significant wave height (metres) for January.

Figure 9.9 Global mean significant wave height (metres) for April.

Figure 9.10 Global mean significant wave height (metres) for July.

Figure 9.11 Global mean significant wave height (metres) for October.

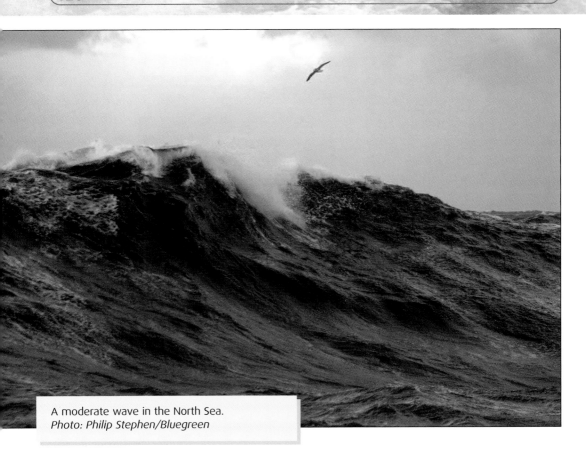

A moderate wave in the North Sea.
Photo: Philip Stephen/Bluegreen

Probably the most significant large-scale effect of land on conditions at sea is the monsoon (the word 'monsoon' derives from the Arabic for season). In the northern summer, the Asian landmass heats up, creating an enormous low-pressure area centred near the Himalayas. Winds blow around it anticlockwise, and it affects most of Asia, from the equatorial Indian Ocean, past the China Sea to the seas around Japan. In the northern winter, everything reverses: the cold generates a continental high (this centred over Mongolia), the winds blow clockwise, etc. On the figures, the waves caused by monsoon winds appear particularly in July in the Arabian Sea, where the south-west monsoon is strong, and in the China Sea east of the Philippines in January, where the north-east monsoon is strong.

Extreme waves

It's useful to think about three sorts of extreme (meaning very high) waves. Firstly, those which crop up in the normal course of events, which we'll call 'normal extremes'; secondly, those caused by rather unusual circumstances which we understand, in principle, and we'll call 'unusual extremes'; and thirdly, those which we might truly call 'freaks', whose existence is shadowy, related through rather terrifying anecdotes but (as yet) not conclusively described or explained scientifically. We'll consider them in order.

Normal extremes

Time is an important factor when thinking about extremes proper. Referring back to Fig 9.8 to 9.11, remember that they show monthly *averages*. In any ordinary month, there is likely to be a day that is double the average. Now, thinking about individual waves rather than averages: for a given significant wave height Hs, in any three-hour period the most likely highest individual wave will be about twice Hs. The longer you look, the higher the likely highest wave. Engineers like to use the 50-year return height as an offshore design parameter. This means the highest Hs seen on average once in 50 years, based on three-hourly estimates of Hs. In an enclosed or semi-enclosed sea like the North Sea, this might be 6 or 8m (20 or 26ft). In the open ocean, the 50-year return value of Hs is over 20m (66ft) (for the North Atlantic), when the highest individual wave would be over 40m (131ft). Extremes, and waves intermediate in height between average and extreme, and waves lower than average, can all occur for a given Hs because of the shifting relationship between all the different component waves of different lengths in any sea state, and all these 'ordinary' statistics are quite well measured and well understood.

These 8m (26ft) waves were found about 1.6nm off the city of Bayona in north-west Spain. They were breaking where the seabed shelves to between 100 to 30m (328–98ft) depth and could possibly capsize a craft of 24m (80ft).
Photo: Hugo Montgomery-Swan

Unusual extremes

Very large waves can result from well-understood combinations of conditions, and some examples follow.

The Agulhas Current region off South Africa seems to be uniquely blessed both in its reputation for high, steep waves and deep troughs ('holes') in damaging and sinking ships, and in the combination of oceanographic, meteorological and even orographic features which combine to produce those conditions. There are the long east-going waves propagating out of the Roaring Forties; they run into the strong Agulhas Current itself (similar in strength and character to the Gulf Stream and Kuroshio, reaching up to 4 or 5 knots) running south-west and west on the east and south coasts of South Africa; coastal lows (see Chapter 8) influenced by the presence of the Karoo plateau (over 1000m high) and the Drakensbergs (over 3000m high) can add more strong winds; and the physical effects of wave trapping and focusing caused by meanders and rings in the Agulhas, on scales of many tens or hundreds of miles, add further to the confusion.

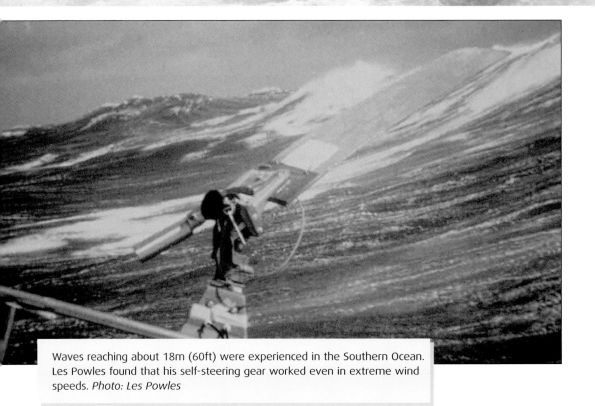

Waves reaching about 18m (60ft) were experienced in the Southern Ocean. Les Powles found that his self-steering gear worked even in extreme wind speeds. *Photo: Les Powles*

Tropical revolving storms (typhoons and hurricanes) cause localized wave conditions rather different from the background average. They originate up to about 30° away from the equator, and if they move more than about 40° from the equator, they turn into 'ordinary' extra-tropical depressions. For example, the West Indies and North Atlantic have about nine per year; the Western North Pacific, including the South China Sea, gets about 30 per year. The worst of the strong winds (above force 8) and resulting high seas tend to be confined to a radius of about 100nm of the centre of the storm.

Within this class of examples, we might also consider tsunamis. The Japanese word *tsunami* was borrowed to replace 'tidal wave' (they have no connection with tides), and it refers to very long, very fast waves produced by marine geological activity: volcanic eruptions, undersea earthquakes, and the like. Tsunami wavelengths are around 100nm, with 10 to 20 minutes between crests; they travel at speeds of hundreds of knots. Some particularly notable examples are the waves produced by the Lisbon earthquake of 1704 and the explosion of Krakatoa in 1883. In the latter case we know that the waves crossed the Pacific Ocean in 12 hours, travelling at 300 knots. More recently, the 2004 Indian Ocean tsunami, caused by the Sumatra-Andaman sub-sea earthquake, was of enormous destructive power. Even so, the open-ocean tsunami wave height was less than 1 metre. It was when the waves came ashore that they reached heights of over 20m (66ft) in places. These waves are hardly noticeable in the open ocean. They acquire their destructive power by steepening and increasing height as they run into shallow water.

Freak waves

We also sometimes hear of 'rogue waves'. These are well-used terms in the popular press and in broadcast media, and it is worth wondering, whenever the term is employed, whether what is *really* meant is simply 'very large waves'. It is also worth emphasizing that, in the strict sense employed here, freak waves are very, very rare. For this reason, once we exclude the classes of extreme waves described previously, not much is left: only anecdotal evidence, scary stories and damaged ships. This does not mean that we're dismissing freak waves, because the anecdotes have a persuasive consistency. However, because they are so rare, they are seldom encountered; they have probably only ever once been measured scientifically (the so-called 'Draupner Wave', measured from a Norwegian oil rig in 1995) and oceanographers are at pains to explain what they might be. Eventually, we'll know how and where to look for them, but for now, explanations are speculative.

The Draupner Wave: Sverre Haver

The Draupner oil rig platform is located between the southern tip of Norway and Scotland in the North Sea. On 1 January 1995 the effect of two lows combined to bring strong northerly winds that brought about a significant wave height of 11.9m (39ft). Within this overall pattern a wave of maximum height 15m (49ft) might be expected, but the possible freak wave shown here had a height of nearly 26m (85ft). This may be compared to the maximum significant wave height in the Fastnet storm of 1979 of 7.8m (25ft) and those of the English Channel in 1987.

10

Seasickness remedies

NOËL DILLY

HOPEFULLY, ONE'S PREPARATIONS FOR heavy weather will have been so appropriate and carried out in such good time that no tremendous exertion will be necessary when it comes on to blow. However, one cannot be sure that this will be so, and it is important that both skipper and crew are at the peak of their physical ability when this is most needed. Seasickness can severely limit physical and intellectual performance; lack of sleep and poor diet can also be significant.

Good clothing, food and leadership ensures a warm, dry, confident sailor. Suitable clothing for heavy weather is problematic. A good set of foul weather gear is effective up to about force 7. On deck when the rigging really starts to howl, water soon works its way into the innermost layers, especially if activity is necessary. In more rigorous conditions, a dry suit is ideal, but the old-fashioned totally waterproof plastic-based gear is surprisingly efficient and cheap. Discomfort and cold are very debilitating and provoke fear that can contribute to seasickness.

When we stop being self-propelled animals, and step aboard some device that moves, we incur the risk of motion sickness. Some cynics have suggested that this was an evolutionary expedient to inhibit travel and so preserve the purity of the local gene pool. Seasickness or naupathia (from the Greek word ship-suffering) is probably the oldest form of motion sickness recognized by man.

From the Argonauts to the astronauts, a surprisingly high number of people have been motion sick. Anyone who has a normal ear is susceptible. This was first discovered when a deaf mute institute took 70 inmates on a cruise and, despite a storm, none of them was seasick.

Although most people adapt rapidly, there are a few who suffer from seasickness all the time that they spend afloat. Children less than two years old are immune, but we are most susceptible between the ages of two and twelve years. It is surprising to learn that excessively fit exercise freaks are very susceptible to seasickness, but not space sickness.

Although individual subjects differ in their degree of susceptibility, there are also sexual and racial differences. Women, especially during menstruation and pregnancy, are 70 per cent more vulnerable than age-matched men. Asian races, especially the Chinese, get sick more quickly. Seasickness is not unique to humans, as many pet owners have found to their discomfort when taking their animals to sea.

While seasickness is generally not life threatening, it markedly reduces the quality of life. It usually culminates in cyclical nausea and vomiting. Although there is a large psychogenic element in seasickness (ie originating in the mind), one does not have to be conscious to be seasick.

In heavy weather, reefing makes severe demands on the crew. In these conditions it is easier to heave-to when reefing the main, when the motion of the boat will become easier. Bashing to windward under the drive of the jib just makes things more difficult. For headsail changes you can avoid foredeck heroics by running before the wind. *Photo: Peter Bruce*

There is no obvious evolutionary explanation for seasickness, so why should the mechanism still exist after millions of years of evolution if it serves no obvious purpose? Motion sickness is the result of activation by an artificial stimulus (unnatural motion) of mechanisms that do have a function (removal of poisons from the stomach). Why should unnatural motion provoke this response? Well, because very tiny doses of poisonous neurotoxins provide just the same disturbance of the signals to the brain from the eyes, the ears and the limbs as does the motion of a boat. The brain interprets these signals as indicating the first signs of an ingested poison, and one vomits to get rid of the poison! The accompanying nausea might also serve as a reminder to the individual to avoid such poisons in the future.

Much research has been done on the causes of seasickness. The most accepted theory is the sensory mismatch hypothesis, which holds that the brain is confused by conflicting information from the eyes, ears and the body's other position indications. The sensory inputs to the brain do not conform to the expected pattern. For example, the eyes looking at the chart are telling the brain that the chart is still, but the ears are telling the brain that the boat is moving about. Ultimately the interactions between the brain, the gut and increasing nausea activates what is loosely described as a vomiting centre in the brain, and afterwards one feels temporarily better until the cycle is repeated.

Fear also plays a role. Many studies have shown that there is increased activity in the 'fight and flight' part of the nervous system associated with vomiting.

Feeling nauseated is often associated with a specific activity like cooking, navigating or getting dressed into foul weather gear. When watching out for the condition in others there are several signs, apart from the victim becoming pale. Sometimes they sweat profusely, yawn and cough. They withdraw from the general activity and become listless and apathetic.

What about treatment?

Strategy – prevention is the aim

The simplest and the most effective approach for the vast majority of sailors is to frequently, but slowly, increase exposure to the motion that produces sickness. While pushing the limits of each exposure there is good evidence to suggest that the best technique is to lie in the supine position (face upwards with only a thin pillow). The head should be lodged still, with other pillows, and the eyes closed. This will

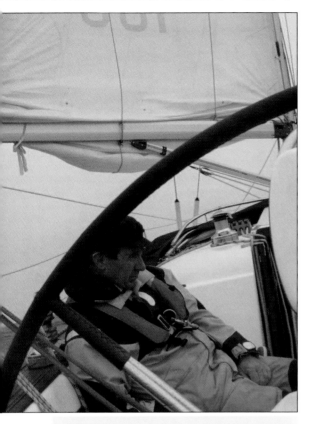

Seasickness sufferers become listless and reluctant to become involved. Motivating them to carry out simple tasks will often help their condition. *Photo: Peter Bruce*

increase the time before the onset of nausea. Before one takes these extreme measures, some people manage to survive by looking at a fixed point on the distant horizon. Keeping the axis of vision at an angle of 45° above the horizon will reduce the receptor stimulation. Reading should be avoided.

A well-ventilated cabin is important, and going out on deck for a breath of fresh air is helpful. It is advisable to avoid alcoholic or dietary excesses before and during adaptation. Small amounts of fluids and simple foods should be taken frequently.

Despite the conventional wisdom of not eating before exposure, there is good scientific evidence that food may suppress seasickness; a light meal comprised mainly of carbohydrates is beneficial to many.

Some habituation can be achieved by spending the first and second nights of a cruise at anchor rather than in a marina. The additional exposure to motion even whilst asleep will accelerate acclimatization.

Heaving-to will often allow people on the brink of sickness to relax enough to avoid suffering. A non stressed visit to the lavatory, some easy deck work, a light snack without having to hang on to the boat, and similar relief of anxiety activities can have a highly effective therapeutic effect.

Non-drug treatment

Ginger

Ginger has been cultivated for so long that the plant is unknown in the wild state. The spice ginger has a very good reputation as a seasickness remedy, and two major scientific studies have found it to be superior to a placebo (pretend pill). It has also been used with success in treating both post-operative nausea and sickness following radiotherapy. But a study of its effectiveness in controlling space sickness in astronauts found no benefits.

The Chinese recommend a dose of about 1g taken at least half an hour before travelling. Some Chinese crews chew little pieces of ginger root continuously until they acclimatize. Western experiments suggest a smaller dose, somewhere between one-third to one-fifth of a teaspoon of dried ginger (up to $\frac{1}{2}$g), is appropriate. At this dosage, six gingersnap biscuits or a pint of ginger ale (not fizzy ginger beer) might just provide an adequate dose. Since ginger has few if any side effects, the dose can be repeated whenever necessary.

Alternative remedies

Alternative treatments such as acupressure bands applied at the wrist over the P6 or Nei Knan acupuncture point seem to work for some people. Although there is a lack of scientific evidence regarding their effectiveness, it has been shown that any treatment is better than nothing. Electronic wristbands have entered the field of seasickness management.

High speeds in heavy seas induce violent, irregular, impact motion in the boat, further exaggerating the effects of the sea state. Simply slowing the boat or changing its orientation to the sea will often achieve a surprisingly large increase in comfort. *Photo: Safehaven Marine*

They apparently work by emitting low level electrical impulses on acupuncture points on the wrist; this seemingly can relieve the feeling of nausea in some individuals. The bands are not always fully waterproof, moreover they tend to slip from the acupressure point when the wearer is active.

Other simple remedies, such as sugary sports drinks (Gatorade, Lucozade) and warm tea, can be remarkably effective.

Drug treatment

Motion sickness is more easily prevented than cured. Whatever drug is chosen, the timing of the doses is a key factor in the efficacy of the treatment. Starting the treatment 8 to 12 hours before sailing produces a more successful outcome than starting once the symptoms begin.

There are a bewildering array of remedies on the market, suggesting that no single drug works for everybody, and that once one has found one that works one should not bother to change. The table on page 136 lists some common ones. The drugs can basically be divided into two groups: first, the short-acting ones such as hyoscine, therefore the drug of choice for a Channel dash; and second, the longer-acting ones such as meclozine and promethazine, which are suitable for cruises requiring several consecutive days at sea. Before starting a cruise, longer-acting drugs have to be taken earlier than the short-acting alternatives.

If your particular favourite is not on this list, do not worry. If it works, stick with it. We know that the actual act of *treating* seasickness will cure 30 per cent of sufferers even if the treatment itself is apparently useless. Whatever drug is used it is important not to exceed the stated doses and to tell someone what you are taking. If you have worked through most of this list without success, then it is probably worthwhile trying one of the sedating antihistamines like Phenergan.

Non-proprietary name	Proprietary name (amount of drug in each tablet)	Oral dose (No of doses per day)	Remarks
Meclozine	Ancolan (Australia) Bonamine (Canada and Germany) Sea Legs (UK) (25mg)	50mg (1)	Low incidence of side effects. May cause sleepiness, good for prolonged treatment. You can even start taking it the night before you set off.
Promethazine hydrochloride	Phenergan (universal name) (25mg)	25mg (1–3)	Best taken in evening. Sleepiness fairly common. The 'knockout drop' also comes as a sugar-free syrup, very useful for children. It is also available for injection for treatment of the long-term hopelessly seasick.
Diphenhydramine	Benadryl (UK) (25mg)	50–100mg (3)	May cause sleepiness and more effective as an antihistamine than when used for motion sickness.
Cyclizine	Marzine (France, Italy and Germany, Marezine in USA) (50mg)	50mg (3)	Low incidence of side effects. Good for prolonged treatment. No longer obtainable in UK due to hallucinatory properties.
Hyoscine (hyoscine hydrobromide)	Hyoscine is universal name but also Kwells (UK and Australia) Sereen tabs (UK) Travacalm (with antihistamine mixed in; Boots, UK) (0.3mg)	0.6mg (3)	Useful in single doses for short journeys. Side effects too troublesome for prolonged use. Its great advantage is that it starts working within half an hour and will be absorbed if sucked. Skin patches are also available (Scopoderm). Reports are appearing of hallucinations and blurred vision persisting for several days or weeks.
Cinnarizine	Stugeron (universal name) (15 mg)	30mg (3)	Medium action. Pleasant tasting and may be sucked or chewed. Many people find it very effective. Beware when buying tablets abroad, they usually contain 75mg whereas in the UK, over the counter tablets contain 25mg. More is not better.

If your seasickness remedy causes drowsiness it is possible to counter this by taking (pseudoepinephrine) Sudafed (15–30mg) every 4–6 hours. Contra-indicated in high blood pressure and heart disease sufferers.

A Jeanneau Sun Liberty 34 close reaching off Les Sables d'Olonne in fresh conditions with as much sail as can be carried. The motion in such conditions can be testing. Much could be done to ameliorate their effects. Heaving-to or reducing sail would help. Perhaps the skipper was seasick and finding it difficult to manage his boat efficiently. Most of us cruise for enjoyment not unnecessary discomfort. Notice the reefed genoa beginning to 'bag up'.
Photo: Christian Février/Bluegreen

The most effective (in controlled trials) over-the-counter medication is the antihistamine Dramamine (dimenhydrinate).

Experiments suggest that the most effective treatment is a combined therapy using scopolamine (hyoscine) plus dexamphetamine, or the antihistamine promethazine plus ephedrine. However, since some of these drugs have been abused, prescriptions for these combinations are almost impossible to obtain.

Of the easily available drugs, scopolamine, which has been used for treating motion sickness since the 1940s and as a hallucinogen for centuries, is likely to be the best choice. The active ingredient is hyoscine. The major disadvantage of this drug is its side effects. In lower doses they include drowsiness and dry mouth, and higher doses produce profound side effects, such as hallucinations. It also has some unpleasant interactions with alcohol.

For the really determined sufferer it is often effective to use a sedative such as diazepam as an adjunct to the seasickness remedy. In the USA, some people advocate Prozac!

After nausea has begun

The 'skin patch' preparation of hyoscine 'Scopoderm' forms the mainstay of treatment after the symptoms have started. They are the ideal means of delivering a quick-acting remedy to vomiting sufferers. The drug acts rapidly. It is absorbed through the skin and is an easy alternative to taking the drugs by mouth. Absorption of hyoscine via the skin is unreliable and subject to many factors. Wet skin increases absorption and can induce overdosing in slightly-built people resulting in disturbing hallucinations.

The other potential treatments are with suppositories or, more elaborately, by injection, neither of which are attractive, but do work in emergency situations. After two or three days, an attempt should be made to stop any medication by slowly reducing the frequency and amount of the drug taken. Most drugs of prevention have side effects, which include the hazards of sleepiness, blurred vision and a dry mouth.

Managing a seasick crew

A seasick person on deck must be wearing a harness and be clipped on. The greatest danger of seasickness is falling overboard while vomiting.

Management really has two phases. Managing someone who feels nauseous, and then managing someone who has vomited.

If the victims are just feeling queasy, they can often still be valuable members of the crew, and the age-old, but extremely effective, treatment of getting them to take the helm works. When these people go off watch, try to place them in an amidships berth. Although many sufferers will object and be macho, it is a good idea to help them take off their foulies and assist them into the berth, doing things like fixing the lee cloths and making the berth narrower so that they don't roll about.

Those who have vomited usually fall into two groups: the remarkable-recovery lot, and the moribund. The rapid recoverers can be treated like the first group. However, the low self-esteem, loss of morale and near-suicidal feelings of the major sufferer have to be experienced to be believed. They cannot just be left in the cockpit. The risks of falling overboard, hypothermia, dehydration and other serious problems make it essential that they are taken below.

You will have to undress them, zip them into a warm sleeping bag, give them a bucket, a handful of tissues, and a bottle of water. Better than plain water during seasickness or dehydration recovery is an isotonic solution. This fluid mimics the salinity of the human body and is therefore more rapidly absorbed. For example, the World Health Organization produces a sachet which, when mixed with water, is called a 'WHO solution'. Many other brands are available such as Dioralyte in the UK, Gastrolyte in Australia.

It is suggested that sufferers lie flat with their eyes closed. A child's spill-proof mug is an effective way of serving drinks. However, one has to look at the overall picture when treating these people. They need to be cosseted and protected, but they are useless. Remember that someone must sail the yacht, and useless seasick crew should not monopolize the best berths. The hard workers need these berths to maintain optimum rest off watch.

If during a long passage you do become acclimatized, do not gloat just yet. There is a form of seasickness associated with returning to the land after a long voyage – mal de débarquement. Treatment is identical, and a quick cure is to go back to sea.

One should remember that recovery takes place rapidly on arrival in harbour. Several children owe their existence to seasickness having brought about the removal of several doses of the contraceptive pill!

Seasickness can spoil the pleasure of seagoing, and render the sufferer incapable. It is much better to experiment with different antidotes until a satisfactory remedy is found.

11

Taking refuge in heavy weather

RICHARD CLIFFORD

THE OLD LANDLUBBER'S CRY 'ANY PORT in a storm' is questionable from a seaman's point of view. Whilst the thought of being in port may sound attractive when being bashed around at sea during a gale, remaining at sea, or even putting to sea, may be both the safest and most comfortable option. It is probably true to say that more leisure craft come to harm in bad weather when in harbour rather than at sea.

There are a number of things that must be considered prior to heading for port in heavy weather, particularly if the geography is unfamiliar. Alternatively, a yacht may already be in port with a dirty forecast, or even with the wind already howling, possibly in an unsuitable anchorage, and there is a need to find a safe haven or even 'hurricane hole' that is more secure. Deciding whether to stay put in an unsatisfactory location or whether to risk putting to sea in the hope of better shelter elsewhere is a complex choice dependent on local circumstances, the type of vessel and the strength and experience of the crew.

In this chapter it is assumed that the yacht has suitable gear and deck fittings for anchoring, lying to a mooring or lying alongside, and these much-debated matters will not be covered in detail. However, it bears repeating that there is no substitute for weight of ground tackle, carefully designed and strong stem fittings and deck cleats

when taking refuge in storm conditions. Moreover, whether at sea or in port, it is chafe and other small vessels that probably present the greatest hazards. Another general point is that heavy weather can be a test of communications between the steering position and foredeck. All systems should depend upon hand or torch signals rather than voice messages, which are the first to fail when it comes on to blow.

When a forecast of bad weather occurs or the weather deteriorates, the decision needs to be made whether to ride out the bad weather at sea, or to run for shelter. As with moving berth, much will depend on the strength of the crew and the ability of the yacht, the expectation of the duration and strength of the storm and the proximity to land. A look at the chart will show whether there is a suitable port that is within reach in the current conditions. Staying at sea can often be the uncomfortable but safest option, using one of the tactics described elsewhere. Occasionally it is better to leave shelter and deliberately go to sea. The 10m (32ft) South African yacht *Gypsy Girl* went to sea on hearing that hurricane Ivan was approaching Grenada in 2004. Whilst Ivan caused havoc ashore, the crew had an uncomfortable few days at sea, but they had plenty of sea room and suffered no damage. Factors such as having to be in a particular place at a particular time, for example to catch a flight, must

The 10m (33ft) *Gypsy Girl*. Photo: Morten,
Yacht Blaartur

remain secondary. The safety of yacht and crew should be pre-eminent.

When selecting a refuge, the primary consideration should be shelter from the seas, protection from the wind generally being a secondary consideration. I once spent two and a half days at anchor on the west side of the causeway joining Tarifa Island to the shore in a strong Levanter easterly (50–60 knots) and, although the wind was too strong to risk launching the dinghy, the sea was flat calm. Whereas in mountainous areas, gusts can make life unpleasant and possibly even dangerous on the *lee side* of high land. For example, at the mountainous Island of Rum on the west coast of Scotland, if the wind is force 7 from the west on the west side of the island, there may be over 50 knots in the gusts at Loch Scresort on the east side. This effect can also occur off high volcanic tropical islands, particularly when the trade winds are strong, so generally it is better to find shelter behind low-lying land, given the choice.

Preparation is the key to making a safe harbour entry in adverse conditions. The off-shore geography of the port should be studied, especially if there is a bar, or such depth that could cause breakers. Allowance should be made for poor visibility, which is common in storm conditions, and every detail noted to make the entrance easier to find. The chances are that others will have heard the same forecast, and it may be possible to find out if there is room in the harbour in advance by radio, or whether the conditions in the harbour approaches are acceptable, and where to berth. It is often useful to make a list of marks and courses or draw a chartlet, beforehand, since conditions are unlikely to allow detailed consultation of pilot books or charts during entry.

Though preparations are important, there may be times when, for safety reasons, planning for the options on arrival may be all that is possible or sensible until shelter is gained. If leaving the cockpit, in particular to go on the foredeck, a lifejacket is advisable. Just in case things do not turn out quite as expected, preparations should include ensuring that the anchor is at immediate readiness for letting go, even if your first choice is to go alongside or pick up a mooring. If the plan is to anchor, it is wise to prepare the second anchor and other anchoring devices such as anti-snubbing gear or a chum/sentinel in advance. Clearly, if it is intended to go alongside, then lines and fenders need to be made ready.

Once at anchor with storm or hurricane force winds in prospect, decks should be cleared of gear that will fly around, cause more windage, or be lost overboard. This includes dinghies, windsurfers, horseshoe lifebelts, sails, biminis, sprayhoods, cockpit dodgers and so on. A furled headsail is prone to unroll, and a flogging headsail makes a fearful noise as it tears itself to pieces. If it is thought that the sail may be needed at short notice it may be better secured by wrapping it with the sheets and spare halyards. Alternatively, lower, fold it and stow it below. When at anchor during a storm it will be wise to run a watchkeeping system for the duration.

At lunch time on 5 July 2003 a Hallberg Rassy 42 tried to enter Victoria Harbour, Dunbar, on the east Scottish coast, under power on passage from Anstruther. It was an hour before low water when there was possibly only 0.8m in the harbour. There was a 2m (6ft) swell running from the north, and this was rounding the harbour mouth and running up the entrance. The yacht struck the bottom in the harbour mouth, and was driven by the surge up to the Castle cliff to the right of the entrance. Both crew were rescued by hauling them up the cliff face. The yacht was a total loss. *Photos: Alastair Punton*

Once safe in port it should not be forgotten to let next of kin and the Coastguard know where the vessel is, if this is appropriate.

Anchoring

Anchoring is usually the best course of action, should space and holding conditions permit, as the boat is free to swing into the wind and there is no need to rely on the integrity of some unknown mooring. A single anchor may be insufficient to provide the required holding power in strong conditions and two anchors are often considered to be standard practice for heavy weather. For vessels under 12m (40ft) the most usual arrangement is to use two anchors off the bow with about 45° separation, so that they share the load and prevent the yacht from shearing about. Positioning the anchors should take into account any expected change in wind direction as well as the proximity of other boats, and dangers such as shoals.

Using two anchors *in tandem* on the same length of chain is not my preference for my 10.7m (35ft) yacht, though there are sailors with larger yachts who may prefer this method if they do not have dual anchor rollers and a capstan that will hoist two anchors separately. If using anchors in tandem, swinging is not reduced as it is with an anchor chain over each side of the bow, and using the tandem method means that if the main anchor chain breaks, no second anchor will be in place to provide back up. However, without a dual anchoring system the great weight of metal of a larger boat's gear can make recovery of the second anchor difficult when two anchors are laid at 45°. If the tandem method is used instead it is important to make the distance between the two anchors less than the depth of water to ensure that, by the time the first anchor is housed at the stem fitting, the second anchor will have broken out of the seabed. If a line has been attached between the two anchors before anchoring, this line can be used for

hoisting the second anchor, using a convenient winch. Some yachts have a windlass winch barrel that can be operated independently from the gypsy. This feature enables tandem mooring to be undertaken with relative ease, and users of this tandem anchor method describe themselves as being 'bolted' to the seabed.

Offshore cruising yachts should carry three anchors and associated gear, and some even carry four. Lying to three anchors at once is not advocated, but the third anchor can be useful in very strong winds when it may be necessary to use it to take the weight whilst weighing and repositioning one of the other anchors. Anchors should be laid out in good time. Rowing, or outboard motoring, anchors out by dinghy in gale or storm conditions is hard and dangerous work even using a robust solid dinghy. When taking out a second or third anchor, the anchor and its chain should be taken in the dinghy with a long line attached to the yacht. This is an occasion when a lighter Fortress type anchor will be most valuable. The line and chain should be paid out from the dinghy, not the yacht. It may be preferable to lay second and third anchors from the yacht by letting out additional scope on the main anchor and motoring over to the drop position for the new anchor. When this has been accomplished the anchor cables should be adjusted to spread the weight appropriately.

The amount of chain required depends on the depth, bottom and available room to swing. Rope or line has its place as an anti-snubbing line but not as a main anchor rode. Apart from lack of weight, rope is particularly unsuitable in rocky anchorages or when coral is present because of chafe. However, few yachts carry sufficient chain to allow full chain lengths on more than one anchor and it is likely that the second (and third) anchor will be on a combination of chain and rope. In shallow water, say around 5m (16ft), one should have at least five times the depth in gale or storm conditions or even more, as the chain catenary will tend to be quite flat and consequently does not allow much damping action before becoming bar taut as the yacht comes up to the end of the scope. This results in heavy snatch loads in the chain and a good anti-snubbing device is essential in these conditions. One, or even two, snub lines attached to the chain just short of the seabed can work well provided they are led through adequately strong and chafe-free bow rollers. Hawser laid line with stretch, such as nylon, is best and a diameter that would be used as an anchor rode. The addition of a rubber shock absorber may also ease snubbing. The anti-snubbing line needs to be attached to the anchor chain with either a chain hook or rolling hitch. Though a rolling hitch will have to be almost certainly cut off after use, it is the more reliable of the two methods, as chain hooks have been known to become detached when the load is slack. To obtain a fair lead it is usually preferable to rig the anti-snub line, or lines, through the stem head fitting using reinforced plastic pipe to reduce chafe.

Laying out more chain will also increase holding power and help damp swooping movements, as it is difficult to drag chain round an arc on the seabed. A good supply of nylon snubbing line is necessary, as when more cable is veered, the old snubbing lines will need to be tied to the cable and new ones attached; besides the fact that snubbing lines become shorter every time they are cut to remove the solid rolling hitch. In addition, redundant snubbing lines may suffer chafe on the seabed when more cable is veered out.

In the Cape Verde Islands I had ten times the depth during a vicious 50 knot blow and still broke the 14mm ($\frac{1}{2}$in) anti-snubbing line. In deep water there may not be enough chain on board for five times the depth so compromise may be necessary. For example, a heavy warp can be added to the chain to obtain the required scope, or the weight of chain can be backed up with a chum. A chum, angel, sentinel or anchor weight increases the holding potential of the anchor if it is looped onto the anchor chain and slid down to near the seabed. Two or three 20lb (9kg) weights are easier to handle than one

of 40lb (18kg) or 60lb (27kg). When anchoring on coral and using a rope extension, it may be worth putting a small fender or float at the join between rope and chain to float the rope clear of abrasive coral.

It is easy to underestimate the forces and the amount of movement, should a sea develop. Consequently it is important to use a pin or a similar contrivance to ensure that the cable cannot jump out of the stem head fitting as the yacht shears and dips her bows to the seas. Stem head fittings have even been known to break off in extreme conditions so it is wise to examine the stem head fabrication before departure to judge whether it needs to be beefed up and whether the working surfaces need to be made more fair. Anchoring fore-and-aft in storm conditions is inadvisable. In particular, if the wind changes and blows strongly on the beam this will put considerably more weight onto the chain and deck fittings and may trip one or both anchors. It is much better to let the boat face the wind, except when it is necessary to face an ocean swell coming from a different direction from the wind. In this case comfort may dictate anchoring fore-and-aft but a contingency plan is necessary. If there is requirement to limit swing, two carefully positioned bow anchors can be employed.

In wind-against-tide conditions, a nasty chop may develop within an anchorage; moreover if the tidal stream is sufficiently strong, the yacht may lie across the wind. This may not place undue extra force on the anchor (or anchors) but it will be necessary to watch the anchor carefully through the turn of the tide to ensure that it resets properly. Of course neighbouring vessels may lie differently and should also be watched.

Once it is believed that the anchor is holding, transits should be chosen and regular checks made to ensure that the anchor is still firmly set. Transits that will remain distinguishable in unexpected weather and in darkness are best. The 'anchor watch' facility fitted to many GPS sets can be used for this purpose, as can bearings and distances taken by radar, which can also be useful both day and night to detect other vessels dragging. It may do so in sufficient time to take avoiding action.

If the anchor starts dragging, there are several options. These include letting out more scope of anchor line, adding a chum weight to the chain, laying a second anchor if not already done. Running the engine ahead will take some of the weight off the anchor and reduce shearing about. It is necessary to keep the bow into the wind while running the engine, which requires considerable concentration, and will be exhausting if carried out all night. Laying out a second anchor from the dinghy may be unacceptably hazardous, but may be possible from the yacht. Once the anchor has broken out it may not reset properly if it has caught a clump of weed and generally should be hoisted to check for weed or other encumbrances before laying once again.

It is best to take steps that reduce the chances of dragging in the first place. When positioning the anchors, ensure that they are well dug in and on an appropriate scope before the bad weather hits, and make sure that account is taken of any expected change in wind or tide direction. When possible, it is worth diving on the anchors to ensure that each one is properly dug in, especially when anchored in the tropics on poor holding ground.

Shock loads caused by snubbing or shearing are the most common causes of anchors breaking out. Anti-snubbing measures and an appropriate scope are clearly important. If the yacht has a tendency to sail around her anchor it is often helpful to encourage her to remain on one tack either by lashing the helm to one side or leading the anchor rode slightly off centre. Another scheme is to set a very small jib, made for the purpose, on the backstay. lying to two appropriately positioned anchors also helps to reduce scope of the swing and hence the force available to break out the anchors. It should be remembered that a yacht sailing about her anchors in bad weather is employing much the same

tactic that is used when trying to break out a stubborn anchor from the seabed.

The most dangerous aspects of anchoring in strong winds are other yachts dragging, and debris flying around the anchorage. Both dangers seem to be more prevalent at night! So when selecting the anchoring spot, be aware of these hazards and also of the fact that different yachts will respond differently to the conditions. It may be worth choosing a spot close to yachts of similar design, and there is clearly an advantage in being the windward yacht. What seems to be a reasonable distance apart in daylight becomes too close when careering around in the dark. It is obviously seamanlike to have an anchor light turned on at night in case other yachts choose to manoeuvre, though it is difficult to judge distance from a masthead anchor light, particularly in a crowded anchorage, unless spreader lights are turned on.

There are parts of the world where a yacht can fit snugly into a tight anchorage with rocks, ice or mangrove on three sides. As well as lying to one or more anchors it may be necessary to take lines ashore. It is debatable whether to go bows or stern-in. Stern-in is easiest from the point of view of handling anchors, but, should the vessel drag, the rudder will probably be the first point to touch. Tying lines to old or dead trees should be avoided. The 17m (56ft) yacht *Toucan* pulled down such a tree in Chile, albeit in 50 or 60 knot winds, and grounded on her rudder, fortunately without much harm. Using chain or slinging strops around rocks will prevent chafe, and fenders should be used to float lines clear of rocks or coral.

If the seabed is sand or mud, deliberately running the vessel aground can be considered in severe conditions, particularly to be clear of other vessels. Allowance may need to be made for the tide and storm surge. On one occasion my yacht *Shamaal* ran ashore and experienced 100 knot winds without damage. If it is necessary to back up the anchor, mangrove swamps provide good shelter in tropical revolving storms and have plenty of points to tie up to.

When it is considered that the yacht has been made snug, it might be thought that it will be safer for her crew to be ashore. If conditions have already deteriorated this temptation should be resisted, as the dinghy trip may be rather more hazardous than remaining on board. Some people will always believe that one should stay with the vessel.

Lying-to a mooring

Having endured bad weather at sea, using a mooring with known good credentials can be a great relief. But to go onto a strange mooring, particularly when cruising away from western Europe, is potentially disastrous. People often say 'it looks a big mooring buoy, so it must be strong enough for big vessels!' In many parts of the world, diving to survey a strange mooring should be considered obligatory. This option may not be feasible when entering a strange harbour in bad weather. A dive may reveal that the condition of many apparently serviceable moorings in developing countries is quite horrifying. The sinker is often a lump of concrete with a riser line of dubious worth.

Rarely is a swivel attached to it, so the riser is often all twisted up. If the riser is made of rope it will, of course, chafe. Furthermore, concrete is not a good material for a mooring sinker, as it needs to be very large to overcome its relatively low density.

In many parts of western Europe, where visitors' moorings are provided, and anchoring is either prohibited or strongly discouraged, taking a mooring may be the only option. Such moorings are likely to be in the prime location so that there is no space to anchor safely, and it is reasonable to assume that they will have been at least moderately well maintained. If possible, make enquiries to ensure that the selected mooring is of suitable strength. Assuming that harbour authorities describe the mooring as sound and there is only a ring on the top, the biggest problem of securing to it will be chafe. It is worth carrying a short length of chain for these circumstances; otherwise some form of protection against chafe will be required. In Europe most visitors' buoys are provided with a rope riding strop, but even in Europe it is wise to check the rope and back it up if necessary.

When riding out bad weather on a mooring it is prudent to have the yacht's main

Boats at moorings in a force 12 storm at Ringhaddy Sound, N Ireland at 1430 on 16 January 1984. Three yachts broke free from their moorings and went ashore, six inflatable dinghies came adrift, danced up the beach and over the hill. *Photo: Sir Dennis Faulkner*

anchor ready to let go at short notice should the mooring part or begin to drag. In some cases it may be appropriate to drop the anchor underfoot with, of course, a tripping line.

Lying alongside

Going alongside in a gale or storm is fraught with problems. A wall with a lee may provide the necessary shelter, but will the wind push the vessel off on the final approach? Is there space? Can lines be attached ashore or onto the pontoon or wall, before being blown off? Is there anyone with sufficient experience on the wall to take lines? If it is a lee wall or pontoon, is it safe to come alongside? Are there waves, which will bounce the boat around at the wrong moment? Even more than when manoeuvring in an anchorage, bold and decisive boat handling will be necessary. The decision may not be perfectly correct, but indecision is more likely to cause

embarrassment and damage to all the yachts concerned.

Once alongside, problems may not end. The greatest danger associated with lying alongside in gale or storm conditions is probably being crushed against the wall or pontoon, either by the force of wind and waves, or as a result of the weight of boats that may have moored outboard. There is also the potential hazard of vessels that may have broken free from other parts of the harbour. Clearly it is preferable to seek a berth in which the yacht will be blown off, rather than on. If this is not possible, it may be necessary to find a way of holding the yacht off. This could involve stringing lines across a harbour or to the windward side of a finger berth in a marina, or laying an anchor to windward to hold the yacht off. It also should be appreciated that pontoons in marinas are not always as sturdy as they look. Some will remember the chaos in Concarneau marina after the severe storm of October 1987 when finger pontoons were

The photo below shows the 13m (43ft) yacht *Ocean Grace* sheltering alongside a jetty at Kópasker in northeast Iceland on 2 September 2002 following extreme bad weather on the previous night. The crew had to wait until afternoon before it was safe to land and take this photograph.
The boat had been secured with every rope available, happily there was plenty on board, and the anchor had been dropped underfoot in case the ropes failed. Warps were adjusted to come taut simultaneously, and were well wrapped with anti-chafe material. There was not much more than a metre's range of tide at Kópasker but the ropes had to be carefully adjusted to allow for the swell.
Photo: Sarah Watson

ABOVE AND BELOW The views forward and aft from *Ocean Grace* taken before the storm. Both the yacht's deck and the adjacent part of the quay had been cleared of anything that might fly.

As the storm developed, the wind increased from the south-east, blowing the boat onto the large tyres attached to the quay wall, compounded by a significant sea. At this point *Ocean Grace*'s fender boards took some heavy punishment and were of great value in preventing serious damage to the topsides. The strongest winds, force 9 or 10, occurred as the barometer began to rise from a low of 968mb (hPa), after falling by 32mb (hPa) in ten hours. By this time the wind had veered around to the west and *Ocean Grace* was being blown off the quay, held by her numerous lines and strong deck fittings. It was a wild, noisy and uncomfortable night, shared with a large paddling of eider ducks that had come into the harbour the previous evening to shelter. When inspecting the lines in the night the anchor watch wore safety harnesses, and they could feel and hear waves coming over the outer breakwater. By morning the decks were covered in debris but, apart from the tail end of the burgee in tatters and the new fender boards now looking well used, the boat and her lines were unharmed; all credit to her skipper and crew. *Photos: Alaistair Punton*

broken up into fragments. The ideal solution is probably to four-point moor so that the yacht is held in a cocoon of lines and cannot make contact with either the pontoons or harbour walls. This is the mooring system often used for yachts wintering in exposed locations such as the west coast of Scotland.

Ample fendering is crucial if there is any chance that the yacht will lie against a wall or pontoon. In strong winds the weight of a yacht may be sufficient to burst her fenders. However, the biggest danger is generally associated with fenders either popping out, either through riding up or becoming trapped as the yacht moves around in her berth. It may be worth attaching the fenders to the wall or pontoon to ensure that the yacht is protected from protrusions, no matter how the yacht moves. If lying against a rough wall, then fender boards or a plank are invaluable.

It is crucial to minimize chafe on mooring lines used to secure the yacht, and time should be spent in working out the leads. Account should be taken of the expected rise and fall of tide, storm surge when tidal range may increase by up to 5m (16ft), the likely direction of the sea, and the forecast changes in wind direction. The strength of cleats and rings and their fastenings should be considered carefully before deciding to secure to them. Chafe points on the warps should be protected. Rubber shock absorbers or similar devices are likely to be valuable, and it is worth using short lengths of chain around rough cleats or bollards that otherwise might chafe the lines. Weight should be distributed as evenly as possible over the various breast lines and springs and, as far as is possible, one rope per mooring line should be used so that each line can be adjusted independently.

Finally, the danger of flying debris should be anticipated. Flying galvanized iron roofing has been known to cut telegraph poles in two, and fish boxes form dangerous projectiles once airborne.

In conclusion, the hazards of entering or remaining in harbour in heavy weather should not be underestimated, and adherence to the suggestions given will make a safe and restful period in harbour more likely.

Remaining at sea in stormy seas off Chile.
Photo: Onne van der Wal/Bluegreen

12

Storm tactics in RIBs

HUGO MONTGOMERY-SWAN

Hugo Montgomery-Swan relates his experience of helming a Rigid Inflatable Boat (RIB) in stormy weather on an occasion when he and a flotilla of 15 other RIBs embarked on the 2002 circumnavigation of Ireland.

THE FORECAST WAS NOT GOOD FOR leaving Newport, County Mayo – an initially 'on the nose' northwesterly, with a wind strength of force 7, increasing later. After some consideration, we decided to set out with the intention of reaching Killybegs, some 80 nautical miles to the north, but on the understanding that we would return to port if the conditions became too hazardous.

The Severn Class lifeboat that led the RIB flotilla out of Newport and down the waterway to the entrance of Achill Sound dwarfed our little 'ships' as we plunged along behind. The wind was fairly whipping off the land now, and the spray from the agitated waters of the lifeboat's wake flew horizontally across our craft. Even here, in sheltered waters, the scene about us was already menacing and did not bode well for the day ahead.

Soon the lifeboat cox radioed his goodbyes and set course for home at Clew Bay, and we were left to our own devices. We made our way along the winding sound before joining the rest of the fleet waiting with idling engines in the inshore waters of Blacksod Bay. It was touch and go for the big boats to clear

under the road bridge, but this tricky inshore route cut off a good 20 miles of potentially difficult and exposed waters around Achill Head and we were all very grateful for the pilotage provided by our RNLI friends.

Now all safely mustered on the seaward side of the bridge, everyone busily set about ensuring their kit was fit, lashed down and ready for sea. It would be our last chance, for once out into the open ocean, the likelihood of being able to stop to secure gear would be remote.

We all tried to stay together as a group in the rough conditions that we encountered in the exposed fetch beyond the bridge and I was amazed at just how well my little 6.5m (21ft) Redbay Stormforce RIB was coping. Some RIBs of this size would have been throwing their heads wildly in such close-coupled, steep seas, but not mine. She ran astonishingly level and, because of this, maintained a speed that justified leading the flotilla.

As we met the waters between the heads of Inishbiggle Island and nearby Bunacurry on Achill Island, we faced the true effects of the north-westerly fetch running directly in from the northern Atlantic. Adding to this was the concentration of tidal stream through the narrow passages that caused unusually high seas to pile in relentlessly at both Annagh and Inishbiggle. We powered on to meet the first of the big seas. It is always difficult to judge the height of waves in these situations, but suffice to say they were easily able to accommodate the full length of the 10m (32ft) RIB running off our starboard side, as she climbed to their summits.

Icy spray smacked against our screen, running in torrents down the glass and momentarily obscuring any clear forward vision. Screen wipers would have helped but we were still very glad of the cuddy cabin, as our weather side was taking a real hammering from the driving rain and spray. To add to the difficulties of forward vision, I had to crouch over the wheel and crane my neck to get a proper view of each sea as we began to climb the face. Applying the correct amount of power was vital in order to maintain good steerage, and to ensure that we negotiated the crests of these waves comfortably. Of course, the bigger the wave the bigger the trough on the other side – the slide down into some of these chasms was sometimes nothing short of breathtaking. By now the size of the seas frequently required the use of reverse power to slow our descent, though many expert RIB-drivers might be amazed to hear this. Surfing too wildly would be sure to result in the boat suffering an unwelcome 'stuffing', ie she could smack the bow into the wave beyond the trough so firmly that a wall of green water would come over the bow and the boat would stop and lose steerage way. Such an incident would immediately compromise our own boat's security and also the safety of any other members of the flotilla who might come to provide assistance. All 16 RIBs had to keep moving.

We pushed on out to the open sea beyond the complicated area of tide and overfalls. Mind you, we didn't really have a choice; turning round was not a good option – it would have put all the boats at a very real risk of capsize.

Running as a pack, the flotilla continued to remain tightly grouped all the way out to the land west of Belmullet. Every now and then I would glance astern, much to the annoyance of my navigator, Jan Falkowski, who quite rightly reminded me that it was my job to look ahead. 'Never mind what's going on behind, we'll take care of that', he shouted. He was right, of course, for just a momentary lapse of concentration could result in a breaking sea catching the boat unawares. As it happened, moments after he shouted at me, I failed to steer square to a very steep sea and as we ran up its face the crest curled and burst down from above on the starboard side of the cabin – streaming down the canopy and onto the rear deck in a cascade of freezing water. Thankfully, due to our RIB's extraordinary lateral stability, we suffered no harm – but it was a tense moment nonetheless. Thomas, my teenage son and third crew member aboard our RIB, remained cool amidst the commotion, though I could tell by the hard-done-by look on his face that he really wanted to be behind the wheel! We pushed on as we had to although, as later weather reports confirmed, the wind in our region was by now touching force 8.

With the seas now on our quarter we were able to push along at a surprisingly good 17 knots. One moment we would be climbing dark grey ramparts of water that occasionally replaced our view of the sky ahead before surfing at even greater speed down their long sides into the deep troughs below. But as we edged further offshore to maintain our course, the seas began to lengthen to a more typical ocean type swell. This sea state was less dangerous and, although maintaining visual contact with our buddy boats continued to be difficult, it was apparent that many of the RIBs were now getting into their stride.

All the boats and engine systems fared remarkably well that day, with no breakdowns. When talking to the crews and watching with interest how the RIBs performed in these sea states, one thing became obvious; the smaller boats very often had the advantage with their high degree of manoeuvrability and quick acceleration proving very successful in the prevailing conditions. The big RIBs, especially those fitted with turbocharged diesel engines, were disadvantaged by the throttle response times and proved

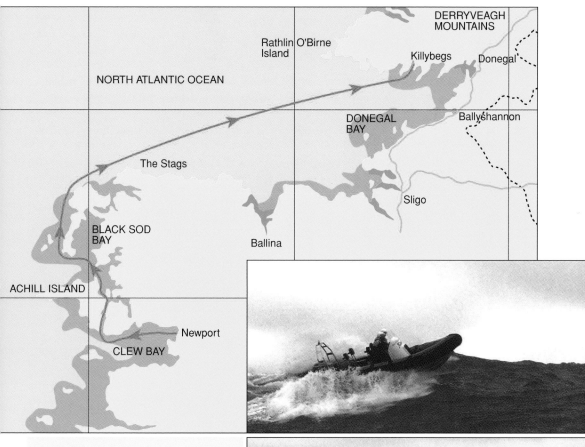

DERRYVEAGH
MOUNTAINS

Rathlin O'Birne
Island

Killybegs

Donegal

NORTH ATLANTIC OCEAN

DONEGAL
BAY

Ballyshannon

The Stags

Sligo

BLACK SOD
BAY

Ballina

ACHILL ISLAND

Newport

CLEW BAY

ABOVE Chart extract: Clew Bay to Killybegs.

RIGHT, TOP The small, outboard-powered RIBs often fared better than their larger diesel-powered counterparts. This is a Ribcraft 5.85m (19ft).

CENTRE With the Stag Rocks in the background, a big sea sweeps across the path of one of the RIBs as it crests a wave.

BOTTOM This Tornado outboard RIB with crew of five shows its immense stability, amidst the heavy seas. Note the relaxed nature of this RNLI crew taking part in the event.

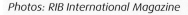

Photos: RIB International Magazine

more difficult 'to place' in the difficult seas. The little RIBs were nippy, weaved a safe course and proved nimble enough to dodge the big 'curlers'.

Most of the Round Ireland RIBs were open craft, and we were jolly glad of the protection the soft-top cabin our RIB gave us. Without it, the amount of flying water would have been difficult to deal with, so the protection that it gave was a major safety factor as well as reducing fatigue.

Report analysis

Driving and design

All the crews taking part in this leg of the Round Ireland Challenge learnt an important lesson: sheer overall length was not necessarily an advantage in these heavy sea states. In fact, the smaller RIBs with their high power-to-weight ratio seemed to fare better than their larger counterparts.

Whilst the larger craft at between 8.5 and 12m (28ft and 39ft) were more able to take a sea broadside, or even a breaking wave thanks to their greater tonnage, they invariably featured turbo-charged diesels, which caused them to suffer from 'turbo lag'. This mechanically-delayed throttle response meant that the helmsmen of these larger craft were unable to respond quickly enough to the more dangerous seas that confronted them; they lacked the powerboat's greatest attribute – immediate power. Once the force/power advantage is reduced to the point that it is not available in sufficient measure, even a RIB with its low central point of gravity can be compromised in certain sea states. The smaller RIBs rarely came close to being compromised thanks to their nimbleness.

Nearly all the RIBs between 5.8 and 7.5m (19 and 25ft) were outboard powered, with horsepower ranging from 150 to 250hp. Agility is the RIB's trademark and with a responsive throttle, a well-found RIB should be able to both dodge and run from a dan-gerous sea, even when the cox is on passage and steering to a compass course. A policy of yield and adjust should be adopted under such circumstances.

Contrary to many people's imagination, seas move very quickly in heavy weather, and often in more than one direction, so reaction time on the part of the helmsman and the motor he is controlling is absolutely paramount. But one word of caution: rapid helm adjustments, particularly in short steep seas, can encourage the propeller to cavitate – or spin in its own pocket of vapour. The correct choice of propeller is essential when it comes to operating in adverse sea states. In most rough water instances, a slightly lesser pitched prop is required to ensure quick throttle response, but also the number and type of blades the propeller features is important too. One of my favourite rough water propellers is stainless steel and five-bladed. The stainless steel construction ensures near zero flexing, and coupled to the shape and number of blades it features, results in a propeller that is almost immune to cavitation – the enemy of quick throttle helming.

A good helmsman or powerboat cox will use his engine's power to great advantage – one moment hitting the throttle to the stops, the next, snapping the engine into neutral to let a dangerous sea pass by. He will also need to gently feather the throttle to nurse his craft over a crest to prevent it from flying wildly off the top of the wave – before then powering up again to lift the vessel's bow in readiness for the next sea directly ahead. The use of trim requires a skilful understanding of the boat and the sea state it is operating in. Correct use of trim will allow the boat to operate to its optimum and thus even affect fuel consumption – which may be a matter of concern on a long haul in worsening weather. But in adverse seas it is quite possible that the cox will be constantly adjusting the angle of trim; trimming the nose right down in an effort to literally pin it to the water's surface as a steep sea is climbed, before quickly trimming out again on the downhill slide into the trough, in order to raise the bow of the vessel before it negotiates the sea ahead.

Ballast tanks are often employed in larger RIBs. These allow water to be collected into a holding tank within the vessel's bow which can then be dumped by means of a release system controlled at the helm. This form of trim device, as in the case of trim tabs, is useful because, unlike trimming-in the leg of an engine with its spinning propeller, the craft can be trimmed or balanced without the unwanted effects of prop torque. Very often, a powered craft will heel horribly to port, landing on the flat of its chine when fully trimmed via engine leg alone. Even if a boat does not possess ballast tanks and the like, a great deal can be achieved by giving careful attention to where and how ancillary kit and items such as dry bags are stowed. In head seas, strap as much down as possible in the forepeak, or alternatively when running in following seas, transfer this kit into the stern. It really does make a difference.

Whether due to poor use of trim or some other misjudgement, if a cox does get it wrong with the result that the RIB flies off the crest in an ungainly fashion, the advantage of a RIB with its inflatable sponson design is that its high degree of lateral stability is more than capable of saving the day. RIBs are very forgiving beasts and in general the golden rule is often 'when in doubt power on'. Further to this, if a sea is negotiated with too much speed and the boat does fly, once again, try to re-enter water with some power on, in order not to land with a sudden stop, with all the accompanying dangers to crew. So, if it is judged that the boat has really taken off, a quick shut down of the throttle in mid air will help negate an overrevving of the engines before opening the throttle wide once more just prior to the prop re-entering the water again. Of course, as we have already said, successful helming takes skill and, in the instance just described, split second timing as well.

In a previous experience of running before a gale in a 7.5m (25ft) RIB off Cape Wrath, in order to prevent the boat surfing at too great a speed down into the deep trough of a following sea (where she might well stuff her bow), it was necessary for us to put the throttle hard astern in order to brake the RIB's descent. Such tactics can be employed with great effect as long as one has plenty of power/acceleration response at one's fingertips, though the loads on the transmission are colossal. Without acceleration, the sea quickly begins to get the mastery over a powered craft and there is no greater feeling of despair than when one realizes, perhaps all too late, that the sea is quickly gaining the upper hand. In addition to the use of throttle in the manner described, in very large seas where one is running before a gale, or even when crossing a dangerous bar, a wise and safe tactic can be to literally sit on the back of a wave, positioning the boat just behind the crest. When the sea breaks or dissipates, its force is released forward or downwards well clear of the RIB. When this occurs the cox should simply advance to ride piggyback onto the next sea in front and repeat the procedure all over again. I will just say that whilst this tactic can be most effective in making good speed in dangerous seas, it is nonetheless imperative to keep a strict watch astern to ensure the following sea, which no doubt is being destabilized by the boat's wake, does not itself break and overtake the boat.

Still on the matter of engines, if it has been decided that the right form of power for a RIB is an inboard diesel installation, it is really important to ensure that it is properly installed, protected and the structure of the hull is strong enough to take it. On one occasion, when running off La Corbière in a 8m (26ft) Italian-built RIB on Jersey's west coast in a force 6 head sea/wind against tide, one of the engine mounts suddenly broke. Not surprisingly, the diesel engine started to suffer and very quickly the crew had to adapt their helming to lessen the likelihood of yet further damage. This was difficult given the conditions, as much power was needed to climb the curling seas. Poor installation caused this gear failure and led to the crew being endangered. It also resulted in a wrecked engine by the time a safe haven was found.

Another great failing common to inboard powered RIBs relates to the design of many engine housings. It is imperative that an engine housing is designed in such a way as to ensure that no water can pass inside, even if the vessel is swamped from tube to tube. If a big sea sweeps right over the boat, or if the boat buries its nose in the foot of a trough at speed, the weight of water charging down the length of the craft will easily amount to several tons. The force of this can take out screens, smash consoles and even lift the crew clean out of their jockey seats. In one instance, when ribbing solo, 35 miles offshore, the entire boat suddenly disappeared beneath the water's surface. The RIB, a 4.8m (15ft), with a 50hp engine – a craft in which we successfully circumnavigated the British Isles – stuffed itself very badly indeed in a following sea. I can remember looking up and seeing the top of the helm console beneath the water and the sun shining down through its surface!

I have never found any modern outboard to suffer adversely from a swamping such as the one I experienced in this mid-Channel incident. The RNLI of course not only immersion-proof the outboards on their RIB fleet for normal work, but also to protect them in the case of a capsize. Today's marine outboard technology is highly suited to the environment in which it is designed to operate. Being immensely reliable, robust and efficient, these modern engine systems, both 4-stroke and 2-stroke, have changed beyond all recognition in the last ten years. This is why so many commercial and offshore operators often favour outboard power over the inboard alternative.

In cases where the boat is diesel powered, it is vital that the engine compartment is watertight and secure, and that all breathers are located well above the top edge of the tubes, so even if the boat is swamped, the engine will remain unaffected. Frequently 'water-tight' hatches are not as watertight as they should be, so it is worth checking them out. And, remember, however watertight the

hatch might be, it is vital in adverse conditions to ensure all external hatches remain firmly closed. Cabins should also have watertight doors and adequate drains leading to bilge pumps, as should cockpits on all RIBs designed for offshore use.

However, if the worst happens and total power is lost through engine malfunction, as long as the vessel's essential components such as battery and electrics are not earthed by sea water then, in extreme conditions, it has been known for steps to be taken to actually encourage the swamping or flooding of a deck on an open RIB. The intention being to reduce the central point of gravity yet further and cause the boat to sit even lower in the water. As powered craft of this type tend to lie with their stern quarter to the seas, the more they wallow with reduced windage, greater weight and lowered central gravity, the less likely they are to be capsized in very steep seas. A small parachute sea anchor with the line over the bow can work very well, so well that the engine usually can be worked upon if necessary. In terms of RIBs, a drogue would rarely be deployed over the stern in the instance of crossing a bar because, once again, a RIB's main line of defence lies in the use of its throttle. Powering up onto the back of a wave is a much better option than a device that holds the boat's stern true to the waves at the expense of it being pooped.

Fit out

Though one may not associate a vessel's fit out with the all-important factors of weight and balance, it is nonetheless crucial to consider the effects that every item has upon the vessel's trim and seaworthiness. The position of the RIB's batteries can be critical for trim and must be well secured in a fully watertight position. How much offset should be given to the helm console and to the engine, especially in an effort to counteract propulsion torque? Where is the optimum location for under-deck fuel tanks? Where should the reserve engine be located – up in the fore-

LEFT Deploying a small parachute anchor, a Bu-Ord 9ft (3m), over the bow of a RIB. RIGHT A RIB lying quietly head-to-wind in the open sea. Wind 20 knots, 1 metre swell. The white float buoy can just be seen in line with the bow. *Photos: Peter Bruce*

peak above the anchor locker or strapped to the arch-mast on the transom's inside face? Such decisions, when correct, will not only enhance a boat's performance but may make the difference between a boat that is sure-footed in all sea states and one that struggles when the going gets tough.

On the Round Ireland event, aboard our 6.5m (21ft) soft-top cabin RIB, it was clear that the additional weight of the cabin structure and the extra large helm console balanced the boat to just the right angle of trim to allow it to perform superbly in high head seas. Furthermore, when climbing up the face of a wave, just before breaking through the crest, we were able to use the boat's forward weight to our advantage. This was achieved by half closing the throttle abruptly just at the point of break through, and allowing the boat's inertia to let it fall forward so the bow punched *through* the wave crest as opposed to 'skimming' up and over it. If the RIB had suffered from being bow light, such a technique would never have been possible. Thanks to the high bow sheer and good forward buoyancy/lift in her hull, she was also able to recover very ably in the deep troughs.

When considering the fit out of a RIB, it is imperative to consider the likely ultimate use to which it will be put. Offshore ribbing requires large through-transom deck scuppers, for example. Water entering the deck must be able to drain quickly back through these scupper points by the simple application of forward power. If water cannot be ejected quickly and efficiently, then the resulting payload of trapped seawater on deck will burden the boat to the point of it being as manoeuvrable as a holed battleship! Whilst electric bilge pumps are a useful addition, they should never replace a natural means of draining off water through scuppers. Many commercial craft, such as the RNLI's Atlantic Class, have open transoms and a deck that is sufficiently above the waterline to not require fixed scuppering.

Offshore venturers should also consider as great a duplication of systems as possible. It is good practice to carry hand-held electronic equipment and a good supply of batteries to back up the fixed radio and GPS. Whilst on the subject of fixed equipment, remember that the seas always do their utmost to un-fix it! Fixings for offshore use need to be some-

Meticulous attention to every detail is essential when preparing a RIB for use in rough sea states. Seen here, an 8m (26ft) Delta in storm swells off the Isle of Lewis. *Photo: Murray Macleod of Seatrek*

what better than those on a RIB whose only use will be on fine Sunday afternoon jaunts round the bay with the family. Some mariners will further secure brackets with gaffer tape to stop gradual loosening.

The ergonomics relating to such items as the console screen in an open RIB which, without a stainless steel grab rail to guard its leading edge, can be as lethal as a knife at one's throat. Also the positioning of the throttle in relation to the helm seat and the wheel, are important factors to consider. Good positioning is not only highly relevant to comfort of course, but also enables one to drive the boat to its optimum. Furthermore GPS brackets, VHF antennas and lashing cleats are all vulnerable items that invariably fail in adverse sea states, and though relatively small bits of kit, they all have the potential to divert a helmsman's attention away from the job in hand, which is to judge the speed and direction to take the next sea!

Giving attention to detail when fitting out and maintaining a craft will pay dividends out at sea. Preventative maintenance is essential but should be undertaken in conjunction with trial runs of emergency equipment. For example, it would be easier to have a rehearsed drill for rigging an auxiliary engine rather than doing it for the first time in a heavy sea when things have already gone badly wrong.

If *all* these factors are considered in advance and the skills relating to their use are developed progressively at sea, then, when foul and angry seas are met with, it will be all the more possible to yield and adjust, to keep a level head and maintain an advantage over the sea.

A final thought for RIB drivers is that the helmsman should drive in a sympathetic manner, which reflects consideration, not only for the well being of the vessel but also the crew. Even in rough conditions, little will be gained if the helmsman has the attitude that the sea needs to be *fought*. It is better to try to accommodate the angry moods of the sea. Whilst positive helming is necessary, too heavy a hand on the throttle will most likely lead to gear or component failure and cause possible injury to the crew. At the very least, the latter will become fatigued and even unnerved. As extreme sea state 'supremo' Hamish McDonald once told me: 'soft hands belong to a good throttleman'. A good cox, therefore, will constantly seek to reassure his crew both by the manner in which he drives as well as by conversing with them, and enquiring how they are feeling from time to time, throughout the passage.

13

Storm tactics in powerboats

DAG PIKE

THE SHAPE OF POWERBOAT HULLS IS generally very different from that of sailboats and apart from a few notable examples they tend to be less seaworthy. This means that in rough sea conditions a powerboat will have to be nursed much more carefully and the speed of progress can be quite critical to survival. Initially methods of handling displacement craft at speeds of below 10 knots will be covered. Whilst the displacement hull is primarily built to operate at these speeds, in a planing boat low-speed operation tends to be a secondary consideration, so the particular problems of handling planing vessels at slow speeds in stormy seas will be covered in a later section.

Rough seas are considered to be those in which the throttles cannot be left set and the boat left to take its course. Instead, speed has to be reduced or throttles operated continuously to negotiate the boat through the waves. Much depends on the size and construction of the vessel as to what will constitute rough seas, but in general these will be seas generated by winds of force 6 and upwards.

Displacement craft

Head seas

When operating in a head sea the main thing to do with a displacement hull is to find a speed at which the boat runs comfortably. Provided the boat is strongly built it is possible to find a speed even in quite rough seas where the boat will lift over the wave and drop down the other side without too much discomfort to the craft or the crew. Matching the speed to the conditions is the secret of operating in head seas, provided the waves have a normal gradient and a wavelength that allows the boat to operate without any undue change in attitude.

When a displacement boat is driven hard into a head sea, the bow will lift to the wave and then become unsupported as the wave crest passes aft. In this situation, the bow will drop to restore equilibrium before lifting once more to the next wave. The problems start in a short, steep sea when the bow may not have time to lift to the next wave, particularly as the stern will still be raised under the influence of the wave that has just passed. Reducing speed will give the boat more time to adjust to the changing wave profile and will thus help to make the motion easier.

If the vessel is driven too hard in a head sea, then there is a real danger of a wave breaking on board as the bow is forced through, rather than over, a wave. Water has surprising weight, and with solid water breaking on board in this way there is a risk of structural damage. In this situation, the most vulnerable parts of the boat are the wheelhouse windows. Although I have never

157

experienced them breaking, despite seeing tons of water crashing down on many occasions. In a boat with a fine bow there is a greater risk of the bow burying into a head sea because it has less buoyancy.

When trying to find a comfortable speed for operating in particular conditions, it is important to ensure that sufficient speed is maintained to give steerage way. At a slow speed the response of the helm will be slower and the bow could fall quite a way off course before the corrective action on the rudder starts to take effect. If, at this time, a wave should rise and strike against the weather bow, then the slow rudder response could mean that the boat will be knocked round, beam-on to the sea, before the corrective action is effective. In this situation, opening the throttles is one way to get a fairly immediate improvement in control, and this can bring the boat back on course quickly without any rapid increase in momentum. The safe minimum speed to maintain steerage way will vary from boat to boat, and with wavelength, height and steepness, but it is unlikely to be less than 3 knots and will be more with craft that have small rudders. The risk of being knocked off course is greatest with a breaking wave where the water is actually travelling towards the boat as this exerts a considerable force on the bow.

If the sea conditions reach the point where the boat has to be forced hard in order to maintain steerage way in deteriorating conditions, then the time has come to start nursing the boat over the waves. This is when the throttle can be used to good effect. By opening the throttle as the wave approaches, the bow of the boat will lift and a burst of engine power will also improve the steering effect. As the bow lifts to the wave, the throttle should be eased off before the bow punches through the crest. Easing the throttle will cause the bow to drop slightly, thus reducing the tendency for it to fall heavily into the trough. As the next wave approaches one has to be ready to open the throttle again.

By using this throttling technique, reasonably comfortable progress can be made to windward. There will be better control of the boat and if a larger-than-normal wave comes along, the person at the helm will be better prepared. However, this type of operation does require considerable concentration because there is always the risk of being caught out of step by the irregularity of the waves and, of course, for that larger-than-normal wave.

Beam seas

Going with the wind and sea on the beam in moderate seas has the disadvantage of discomfort, due to the heavy rolling that is likely to occur. In these conditions, full speed can generally be used on a displacement boat without any real problems arising because the boat is lifting bodily on the waves, and the bow and stern have little movement in relation to each other. However, occasionally the boat drops off the edge of a fairly steep wave front and that can be both uncomfortable and a little frightening so, as the beam seas start to get rougher, more care has to be taken.

Keeping the sea on the beam exposes a large area of boat to the approaching waves and in stormy seas this can make the craft vulnerable. The transition from what is an uncomfortable beam sea to a dangerous one will depend a great deal on the type and characteristics of the craft, but once the waves have started to break then, again, more care has to be taken.

There are two main problems with beam seas. First, as the waves become steeper, the boat will try to adjust to the tilted surface of the sea and, consequently, will heel to quite a large angle. This in itself is not too serious, provided the range of stability of the boat is adequate, but it has to be remembered that the wind will also be pressing on the windward side of the boat, tending to increase the angle of the heel. The second problem is more serious and occurs when breaking waves are encountered. When the surface of the water is moving bodily to leeward it can exert very

The throttle setting is the key to heading straight into the sea. Find a comfortable level, which is tolerable for the crew, and then keep clear of the breakers. The photographs in this chapter were taken at the entrance to Cork Harbour in a southeasterly gale. All the craft shown in this series were built by Safehaven Marine and were designed by Frank Kowalski who, in many cases, was at the wheel. *Photo: Safehaven Marine*

great pressures on the windward side of the vessel. The pressures are resisted by the still water on the lee side of the hull which produces a heeling moment that could develop to the point where the boat will capsize. In these conditions there is the risk of seas breaking on board, because many displacement boats have reduced freeboard amidships. These breaking seas could fill a cockpit or other deck openings which makes the predicament worse, so that there will come a time when operating in a beam sea is not the optimum way to go. These conditions can be very tiring and the right level of concentration can only be maintained for around an hour or so.

Fortunately, a wave rarely breaks along a long front, but tends to do so in patches so that, with anticipation, it is possible to avoid breaking waves in beam seas. This means watching the sea ahead carefully and anticipating which part of the wave crest is going to break. It is then necessary to reduce speed to let the wave break in front of the boat, or turning into or away from the wind so that the boat passes either behind or in front of the breaking crest. Even in moderate breaking seas, life can be made a lot more comfortable on board by this method of avoiding the largest of the waves and steering round the less friendly-looking crests. In moderate seas there is not too much to worry about if things go wrong, but once the seas start to break then the stakes become higher and it is necessary to be much more cautious.

If, in a beam sea, a situation occurs where a wave that is about to break is bearing down on the boat and it is too late to reduce speed, then there are three options. The course can be maintained, hoping that the boat will cope, one can head into the wave, or steer away from it. A lot will depend on the type and capabilities of the boat, but the best action would normally be to turn away from the wave, because this has the advantage of buying time and it will also reduce the impact of the wave on the boat which is then moving away from it. The breaking crest often rolls only a limited way to leeward and one can escape the breaking water altogether

by this action. If it is decided to turn away from a breaking wave in this fashion, then the throttles should be opened wide, both to get the maximum steering effect and to keep the distance from the breaking crest as large as possible. If the opposite course of action is chosen and one heads into the wave, then reducing speed will probably be necessary to reduce the impact of the wave.

A point to notice when running in a beam sea is that a wave will often be seen on the quarter starting to break. It may seem lucky to be always in front of these breaking crests, but they are, in fact, caused by the wash of the boat combining with the approaching wave to create an unstable wave which consequently breaks when otherwise it would not have done so. Such seas seem to have little force in them.

Following seas

Running before a heavy following sea has the reputation of being the seaman's nightmare, conjuring up visions of broaching, capsizing or being swamped. Much of this fear stems from sailing boats, where running before a sea may be the only option left under extreme conditions. There is no doubt that running before a following sea has its dangers, but provided they are recognized, they can be compensated for and the dangers can be minimized.

At first glance, it would appear that running before a sea and travelling in the same direction as the wind and sea would be a far safer course to take than battling against the waves. However, a boat is controlled by the rudder and it needs a good flow of water to be effective. If the water flow is reduced or even reversed because of an overtaking breaking wave, then there will be much less control of the craft, or control could be lost altogether, and it is this factor that presents the major hazard in a following sea. An average open sea wave will be travelling at somewhere between two and three times the speed of the average displacement craft, so it will take some time to pass the boat.

At near displacement speeds it is necessary to keep the bow up as a wave approaches using a burst of high engine power. This will also improve steering control. *Photo: Safehaven Marine*

When the crest of the wave is approaching the stern, this face of the wave is the steepest part and the bow will be pointing downwards towards the trough. In this position, gravity will exert a downward pull on the boat, combining with the thrust from the propeller leading to an increased forward motion down the wave slope. Similarly, when the boat is on the back of the wave with the bow pointing upwards, it is, to all intents and purposes, going uphill and the speed will be correspondingly reduced. These involuntary increases and decreases in speed can be controlled to a degree by opening and closing the throttle as the circumstances dictate, and unless the waves are breaking it should be possible to retain adequate control over the boat. But beware of closing the throttle completely as steering control can be lost.

In a breaking wave, the surface water is moving forwards in the direction of travel of the wave at a speed slightly in excess of the speed of the wave. This forward movement

of the breaking crest is transient, starting as the wave crest becomes unstable and ending when the wave has reached stability again and stopped breaking. The behaviour of a boat in a breaking following sea will depend, to a certain extent, on the position of the boat in relation to the crest as it breaks and on the design of the vessel itself. If the wave rises up and starts to break immediately astern of the boat, then there is a real danger that the breaking crest will fall onto the craft. This is more likely to be a problem with the type of heavy breaking wave found when a current or tidal stream opposes the waves.

One thing in favour of the boat at this stage is that the downward angle of the boat on the forward surface of the wave will help to increase the speed of the craft, and might even enable it to accelerate away sufficiently to escape the breaking crest. If not, the crest, in falling, will accelerate and take the boat with it, which will also help to increase the momentum, particularly if the boat has a large transom stern which faces the oncoming rush of water. With a double-ended boat, also known as canoe stern, the theory is that the pointed stern divides the oncoming water and allows it to pass safely along each side of the boat.

A craft that is accelerating under the combined influences of the rush of breaking water at the stern and the downward slope of the face of the wave would probably be all right if the boat could just keep accelerating in this way. However, as the stern is lifted by the rush of water the time comes when the bow of the boat starts to bury into the next wave ahead. This means that the bow starts to act as a pivot and also starts to put up considerable resistance to the forward rush. It is at this point that the risk of broaching occurs, with the bow trying to stop and the stern trying to swing to one side or the other under the influence of the rush of water. This strong turning effect can turn the boat broadside on in the classical broaching situation. Once broadside on the sea, the turning moment reduces, but is then replaced by a capsizing moment similar to that of a beam sea. Even if the boat escapes this particular situation, it could well find itself vulnerable to the next wave that comes along, because it is unlikely that it will have recovered in time and achieved the steerage way necessary to cope with the situation.

A deep-draft vessel with its rudder well immersed should still retain steerage control in this following breaking sea situation, whereas the shallow-draft boat could be much more vulnerable. Apart from shallow-water breaking waves, the actual depth of the breaking crest can be quite shallow, rarely more than a metre, so the deep rudder will be in more stable water below and remain effective. The hull design of the boat also has a bearing on its behaviour, and a boat with a sharply angled forefoot is likely to create a pivot point more readily than one with a cut-away forefoot. A transom stern also makes the boat more vulnerable.

Found in this situation with a breaking wave approaching at the stern, there is not a great deal that can be done, other than try to keep the boat absolutely square on to the sea for as long as possible. This will demand concentration and hard work with the steering wheel, although the rudder could become virtually ineffective in these conditions. As a general rule, the throttle should be opened as wide as possible to try to run from the breaking wave or at least reduce its impact, and to retain steerage control for as long as possible. This will also have the effect of lifting the bow to a certain extent and it will also help to reduce the impact of the wave at the stern.

When the breaking wave crest is overtaking the boat, the water flow past the boat will be reversed. In theory this means that the rudder on a shallow draft boat should work in reverse but I have never had the courage to try this in rough following seas because the consequences of getting it wrong could be severe. When running before a following sea that may be large, but is not breaking, full throttle should be used to maintain steering control. Try to keep pace with the waves as far as possible, although on a displacement boat the waves will be overtaking. In these conditions it may be noticed that the waves astern are starting to break, but this is again usually the influence of the wash of the boat combining with the crest which causes it to break. This can be a significant problem when crossing a harbour bar in a following sea, and I have seen quite harmless-looking waves suddenly rear up astern in this situation. It seems that the extra disturbance caused by the progress of the boat is enough to turn the waves into an unstable form. In theory these breaking waves that are assisted by the wash should not cause any problems, even though they may present a frightening picture when looking astern.

When running in front of a moderate following sea that is not breaking, there can still be a considerable change in the trim of the craft as a wave passes underneath. In this case the change in angle is more noticeable than in a head sea because the wave takes longer to pass under the vessel, giving it longer to adapt to the angles of the different faces of the waves. When the crest of the wave is passing underneath, the boat suddenly feels rather unstable. This is due to the fact that because the boat is only supported amidships, rather than over its whole length, her stability is considerably reduced at this point. This is a fairly transient situation and stability is rapidly restored as the wave passes, but if running at a speed close to that of the wave, this period of instability could last for longer, and it might be sensible to consider reducing speed to allow the wave crest to pass more quickly and thus reduce the periods of instability.

One problem found on many boats when operating in a following sea is that the visibility astern is not as good as it might be. It helps a great deal to have a good view astern and on each quarter as well, but many boats lack this facility.

With a well-found vessel, running before a heavy following sea can be a very exciting experience. I have travelled down the Irish Sea in a 14.5m (48ft) lifeboat on a wild night when the wind was blowing up to force 10. The first hour or two were quite frightening while we became used to the conditions, but once we had gained confidence that the boat was adequate for the job, we could revel in the excitement of rushing like an express train down the face of a wave, or so it seemed, and then watching out through the windows in the top of the wheelhouse, for the next wave approaching from astern. I think an unnecessary dread of following seas has been built up among the small-boat fraternity, but one needs a sound boat before taking chances in a following sea, or indeed in any rough sea, and concentration is vital.

In conditions where the sea is starting to become rough when running before it, a quite dangerous situation can build up because one is unaware of just how bad things are getting and because, to a certain extent, the boat is running in harmony with the sea. The lack of impact of the waves in a following sea can lull one into a false sense of security. Thus it is a sensible precaution to stop every now and again, turn round, and head into the sea, just to see what conditions are really like. It might be frightening to realize just how the waves are building up, but it is better to be frightened in this way than to be caught out unawares.

Planing boats

If operating a planing boat at displacement speed, then you can be more vulnerable than if you are in a displacement boat in the same conditions. There are two reasons for this. First, if you are at the point where you need to slow down to displacement speeds in a planing vessel, then conditions are probably becoming quite bad anyway and, second, a planing boat is not running at its optimum at displacement speeds, both in terms of hull shape and of control.

In terms of hull shape, planing boats tend to have fine bows and full sterns, which is not necessarily a happy combination in rough seas. At the bow there can be a lack of freeboard when off the plane if the boat has a reverse deck sheer. This, combined with a fine bow, gives a lack of buoyancy in this area which can mean that the bow buries readily into both a head sea and a following sea. The craft is also much lighter and probably more affected by wind, so that it may be more difficult to maintain steerage way at low speeds in a planing boat because the bow will tend to fly off to one side or the other. This situation will be exaggerated because the rudders are always smaller and are therefore less effective at slow speeds. On vessels fitted with outboards or stern drives, where the propeller thrust is used for steering, good steering can usually be maintained at low speeds.

A delicate hand will be needed on the throttles at displacement speeds because a small movement of the throttle can produce quite a large variation in the speed. However, this can be used to good effect when it is necessary to nurse the boat through the waves.

The throttle will need to be used a lot more on planing boats in rough seas with a short burst being used to help maintain heading and to help lift the bow to approaching waves. A marked lifting and dropping of the bow can be noticed when the throttle is opened or closed.

The tactics of operating a planing boat in rough conditions can often mean that rather than reducing speed when operating in a head sea, one should look for an alternative heading for the boat on which it can still be operated at higher speeds. For instance, whereas a planing vessel may well have to slow right down in a head sea, it can still maintain good speed in beam seas or in following seas particularly, and this could well be a safer course to take, rather than running the boat at displacement speeds on the original course. Much will depend on the destination and what the options are, but high speed in a following sea will often be safer than for a displacement boat operating in the same conditions because the high speed allows the helmsman to dictate his position with respect to the waves.

Most long-distance cruisers are of the displacement type because this is where fuel economy for long distances is achieved. However, an increasing number of semi-displacement long-distance cruisers are appearing. Most of them are trawler yachts of one type or another, but some planing, deep-V boats are able to achieve respectable ranges for cruising. The big difference between these types and displacement hulls is the influence of the dynamic stability on the performance. The dynamic stability created by the forward motion helps to stabilize the hull at speed, but a much greater response to the throttle will be noticed, not only in the speed of the hull, but also in its trim angle. This change in trim angle can be used to good effect to help progress in rough seas and it can even be effective at quite low speeds, down to those found on displacement hulls.

Indeed, it would be fair to say that the primary means of control in semi-displacement

and planing hulls is the throttle. By varying the propeller thrust with the throttle you have the ability to raise or lower the bow, but the throttle also has a vital role to play in the speed at which one impacts with approaching waves. This speed of approach, to a certain extent, determines whether the boat will fly off the top of a wave or not. Although it looks photographically spectacular when a boat does this, it is not an efficient means of progress. Every time the boat flies or even partially flies off a wave, the propeller is losing effect but, more importantly, it puts an enormous stress on the boat, the machinery and the crew. When we were setting a record round Britain a few years ago in a 15m (50ft) deep-V, we made it a rule that the hull should never leave the water. In this way we felt we might be able to cope with standing up in a fast boat for 44 hours.

Few cruising yachts are likely to attempt such heroics, but the same rule applies. If you do hit bad weather, particularly head seas, then careful throttle control is vital to give the boat as gentle a ride as possible, but this doesn't necessarily mean that one has to come down to displacement speeds. In many cases the bow should be kept up to reduce the chance of water coming over the foredeck, and you can use the change of trim that usually occurs at around 12–15 knots, when the hull tries to climb over its own bow wave, to keep the bow up.

Unless the sea gets too rough, it is possible with a deep-V hull to get it up and running so that it stays virtually at a level trim despite the impact of the waves which try to upset the trim. Much will depend on the wave size, but if the boat is trimmed properly it can run virtually across the top of the waves with the control of the attitude of the boat being exercised solely by the use of the throttle. The biggest problem with this is actually getting the vessel up into this situation, and it does mean that several waves have to be negotiated rather uncomfortably as the boat builds up speed; it then levels out at high speed.

Getting a craft trimmed in this way is a real joy and the boat really sings as she flies

ABOVE It should be possible to turn and accelerate away from breaking waves in a planing boat. *Photo: Safehaven Marine*

BELOW Much concentration is required when steering through beam seas to find the flat water between breaking crests. *Photo: Safehaven Marine* along. It requires careful setting up, using the power trim, the flaps and then, finally, the throttle to keep the balance, as passing waves have varying influences on the hull. When the boat is up and running in this way, it is possible to make very rapid progress to windward even though the waves can be quite large. It does require some degree of courage to take the bull by the horns and get the boat up into a situation where one can take advantage of this, but this is not just a technique for use on smaller sports cruisers.

When I was delivering the world's first large deep-V hull from Britain to Greece we managed to get it up and running in this way when the Mistral started to kick up a nasty sea in the Mediterranean. The boat was an 26m (85ft) patrol boat for the Greek Navy, and the choices were to wallow at displacement speeds for a long night at sea, or try the high-speed technique to make harbour in a couple of hours in the rapidly freshening wind. This is probably a technique to use when running for shelter rather than when general cruising. It needs a strong boat and it is not likely to be effective on semi-displacement craft.

When running like this, concentration is needed because there is always the risk that a bigger wave than normal will come along and upset the delicate balance of the boat. A good throttleman will read the waves and concentrate very closely on each one as it approaches, adjusting the throttle almost by instinct as the craft meets the wave, so that the bow slices through the top without the wave imparting too much lift, allowing the boat to continue on an almost even keel. With the Greek boat it took a fair amount of courage to wind the boat up and open the throttles, and we suffered a few nasty bangs as we hit the first two or three waves, but soon after the boat really got up on top and, with the flaps down, away we went, travelling at close to 30 knots in conditions where I would never have thought it possible for a boat of this size.

One of the major ingredients when running a planing boat in rough seas is to use the throttle very delicately. The tendency, when a larger wave is seen approaching, is to bring the throttle right back to reduce the impact between wave and boat. But this will bring the boat off the plane, the bow will drop, and there is every chance that the larger wave will come curling down the deck as the bow buries in it, rather than the boat riding over it. In most cases only a slight reduction of the throttle setting will be needed to adjust to the approaching wave. This will not change the trim of the boat too dramatically, and it will be found that much better progress can be made. This is one of the reasons why I favour throttle controls separate from the gear lever, because then you have a much wider range of movement which allows for the more sensitive control necessary for this type of driving.

Head seas

We have already covered most of the aspects of head sea handling when using the throttle. Getting the boat up and running on the tops of the waves may have limited application, and those with a cruising boat, which tend to be less well designed to cope with the heavy impact which can result if things get out of hand, are not likely to take the risk. It is also unlikely on a cruising craft that the necessary level of concentration can be maintained for any length of time, and very often the visibility from the steering position is not good enough for the waves to be easily read. Reflections in the windscreen, and even the windscreen itself (if it has been sprayed with water), can greatly reduce the ability to read the waves ahead.

In these conditions, you are more likely to find a throttle setting at which the boat runs comfortably and let the boat do the work. In moderate seas good progress can often be made in this way, and certainly if you are on a long passage, this takes a lot of the tension out of driving and makes for a more comfortable life. In moderate conditions it may be possible to set the autopilot and have a relatively gentle cruise, but always in a planing boat it pays to remember the wide variety of shapes and sizes of waves that can be met at sea. If the throttle is set in this way, then the speed at which the boat is travelling must leave an adequate margin for the boat to ride comfortably over larger than normal waves, without danger or too much discomfort.

If conditions start to deteriorate there will be an instinctive tendency to ease back on the throttle, because the motion of the boat will soon indicate that things are being pushed too hard. Fortunately, with most modern fast cruising craft, the weak point in the boat (and the one that generally starts to complain first) is the crew, and this is a good safety factor. If the motion starts to get uncomfortable for the crew, then the boat is probably being pushed too hard and by easing back the throttle a more comfortable speed should be achieved.

When conditions get to the point where it is difficult to find a comfortable speed and still keep the boat on the plane, then there are two options. The first is to ease back and come off the plane and operate the boat in the displacement mode, but the low freeboard at the bow of most planing boats does not always make this a comfortable option. Nevertheless, if there are any doubts about driving or concentration capabilities, then this is probably the wise course of action to adopt. The main secret of fast-boat driving into a head sea is to match the speed of the craft to the conditions, and the throttle is the main control to work with. Obviously, there will be a benefit from adjusting the flaps to help keep the bow down when on the plane and normally if a reduced speed has been chosen, it will almost certainly be necessary to bring in the power trim if it is fitted, which will also help to balance the boat to the conditions.

The other option open is to alter course. Even a 20° alteration can make a significant difference to the way the boat behaves. Altering course off the wind may take the boat away from the direct course to the destination but it will have the effect of extending the wavelength, which in turn reduces the wave gradient, which in turn will give a more comfortable ride. Experimentation will be necessary to find the best amount to alter course. There may be times when it is necessary to turn up into a big wave and reduce speed, or turn away and open the throttles to escape from the section of a wave, which is breaking. But 'tacking' in this way can be a very effective tactic in rough conditions.

Beam seas

A planing craft in beam seas can be quite an exhilarating ride, but if rapid progress is required in waves on the beam then again much concentration will be needed. Even in beam seas it is necessary to read the waves ahead all the time, otherwise there will be some unpleasant moments. If the waves came in a regular pattern, then it would simply be a question of the boat lifting over the wave as it passed underneath and dropping down into the trough in a nice rhythmical way. However, waves are far from regular and when in a beam sea this becomes most apparent. It can happen that a wave suddenly presents what appears to be a near vertical face as the boat approaches, and then equally quickly that wave seems to disappear and the boat drops into a trough. The boat can suffer some quite heavy impacts dropping off waves in this way, but much of this can be avoided if the steering and throttle controls are used to good effect.

Watch the waves in a beam sea and it will be noticed that some are considerably higher than others, some having gentle gradients, others having steep gradients and with varying peaks and troughs. Very rarely is there a long wave front. It is quite easy to see where the flatter areas of sea are and by using the throttle and steering one can often steer around the worst of the waves, which tend to form in localized peaks. It is surprising how comfortable a ride can be achieved if the boat is driven in this way but it does require a lot of concentration and a sensitive hand on the throttle and steering. It is often difficult to get good steering control in these

A comfortable ride is achieved in beam seas by steering round the wave peaks. *Photo: Safehaven Marine*

conditions because only one hand is available on the steering wheel. And it can pay to concentrate on just one of these controls, normally the steering wheel, so that this can be really used to good effect, leaving the throttle setting at a speed that is comfortable for the conditions.

In taking evasive action from threatening wave crests with the wind on the beam, the boat will steer off the wind much more easily than trying to alter course towards it, so turning away downwind will be the normal course. Having said that, when steering off the wind, the waves are still effectively coming from ahead, so it may be necessary to steer further off to actually miss a particular wave. By steering into the wind, on the other hand, one will get a better chance to let the wave pass across the bow and run into the smoother water behind. Every wave is different and a quick assessment is required for each one. A point to remember here, as far as navigation is concerned, is that if frequently turning off course in the same direction, the course made good can be a long way off from the intended course.

Even when the wind is not exactly on the beam, and a course of 30–40° from the wind

is steered, the same technique of driving the boat across or round the lower parts of the wave can be adopted to make good progress. These are tactics that can be adopted even in quite rough seas, but as the seas get rougher the consequences of making a mistake become greater and concentration needs to be yet harder. It can be a very exhilarating ride, but it is necessary to be aware of the risks that are being taken and the consequences of getting out of step with the waves.

Mention needs to be made of the way in which fast boats, particularly those of the deep-V type, lean into the wind under the influence of the rudders. This is most pronounced when the wind is on the beam. Obviously, if there are flaps fitted to the vessel, then the boat can be levelled up so that it runs true. But even then, if steering to avoid the worst of the seas, whichever way you turn will cause the boat to lean. This is one of the primary causes of an uncomfortable ride in a beam sea because the hull may land on the flat of the V of the hull rather than the apex. The only way to avoid this is to use the steering gently so that the effect on the transverse trim is minimized.

Following seas

Running before a following sea in a power-boat can be equally exciting. Not only is it possible sometimes to employ full throttle in this situation, but also it may be felt that it can be done with comparative safety, because the speed of encounter with the waves is much slower than with a head sea. The speed at which the waves travel is determined by their wavelength, so that smaller waves will be travelling at 12–15 knots and the larger waves, perhaps those generated by a force 5–6 wind, may be travelling at between 15 and 20 knots. In coastal waters waves travelling at more than 20 knots are unlikely to be found unless, of course, there are swells where the wavelength can be considerably longer and the wave travels faster accordingly. But these waves tend to have a very gentle gradient, which is unlikely to impinge on progress. With a moderate-speed planing boat, there should be the potential to overtake following sea waves, possibly even

travelling at twice the speed of the waves, so that the period of encounter allows the boat to recover from each wave in turn without any dramatic change of attitude of trim.

With boats capable of speeds up to around 30 knots, it is often possible to simply set the throttle and let the boat take its course whilst still making rapid speed downwind. Much will depend on the size of the waves and their speed of travel. One of the problems is that, as the craft climbs up the back of the wave, it tends to lose speed because it is, in effect, climbing uphill. Then when it gets to the crest it tends to sit there for a moment until enough of the bow projects over the steeper leeward face of the wave to cause it to drop with a quite sudden change of trim. This all tends to happen in slow motion. Relatively speaking, with the boat on the crest of the wave travelling little faster than the wave itself, there is a marked change in attitude as the boat drops down the leeward face of the wave, and at the same

A quartering sea can be comfortable at high speed in a planing hull, but watch that the bows do not bury themselves in the wave ahead. *Photo: Safehaven Marine*

time suddenly accelerates. This acceleration is under the impetus of the throttle and of gravity. In rough conditions, and depending a great deal on the speed and type of the boat and the speed of the waves, the bow of the vessel can be found to be burying quite heavily into the next wave in front as it rushes down the downhill slope. Certainly, with a boat with a full bow, the impact of the boat into the wave can be quite harsh, giving a very uncomfortable motion.

There are two remedies in this situation if it becomes uncomfortable, which is likely if the wind and waves start to increase. First, if there is the power to increase speed, this will have the effect of reducing the time that the boat spends on the crest of the wave, thus reducing the dramatic change of trim at the crest. Second, if there is not the potential to increase speed, it can be reduced so that the boat will tend to ride with the bow on the upward slope of the wave virtually keeping pace with the wave. If the wave, should disappear in front or break, then the throttles can be opened and the boat will accelerate over it. This will give a slower and more comfortable ride, and is the tactic to adopt if the sea conditions start to rise to the point where it is felt that the boat ought to be nursed. Sitting on the back of the wave in this fashion also requires a fair degree of concentration and a bigger wave may come up behind which could well be travelling faster than the boat. In this case there is the potential to have a broaching situation, unless the problem is recognized and action taken to accelerate away.

In rough conditions, say force 7 or upwards, running in a following sea in a planing boat can be one of the safest means of progress, provided of course that the vessel underneath is reliable and sound. Rapid progress can still be made in this direction, at least travelling roughly at the speed of the waves, simply by sitting on the back of a wave and waiting for that wave to collapse or break before driving onwards. It is not really a wise tactic to adopt if there is a long way to travel because the person at the helm will soon get tired and lose concentration. As

already stated several times, concentration is the name of the game because in rough seas the safety margins get smaller and mistakes can soon cause trouble.

The same technique can be used when entering harbour where there is breaking surf on the bar and the boat has to be driven in through this with the wind and sea astern. In many situations, such as a harbour entrance, it could prove dangerous for a displacement boat because of the risk of broaching and losing control as the waves overtake. In a planing boat there is more freedom to dictate position in relation to the waves, and here the boat can be kept riding on the back of a wave while heading in. If the wave breaks, then it should be driven over to place the boat on the back of the next wave in front and so on until you are through the area of breaking waves. It requires nerve, concentration, good visibility and this is not the time when one can afford to have anything go wrong with the boat, but it is a feasible way of running an inlet.

In following seas one problem that can be encountered is a certain loss of stability, particularly when travelling at lower planing speeds, say around 18 or 20 knots. Here the dynamic stability of the hull, generated by the boat moving through the water, will be much less and it will be further reduced if the boat is in breaking waves where the water is moving ahead. This loss of stability will be most noticeable when the boat passes through the crest of a wave where the inherent stability of the hull is also reduced. It can cause the boat to lean over, so that if the boat does fly off a wave it could land very heavily on the flat of the V of the hull. Whilst such a loss of stability is not likely to be dangerous to the point of capsize, it can make handling the boat more difficult. If this sort of instability is felt to be developing, once again it is a question of using the throttles at the right time to increase the dynamic response to get the bow up as one comes through the crest of the wave. Instability will be apparent by the rolling of the boat and by sloppiness in the steering. As so often with a high-speed craft, when this situation seems to be occurring, the solution is to put on more power rather than to close the throttles.

At slower speeds in following seas the flaps will generally want to be kept up in order to give the bow as much lift as possible so that the bow doesn't drop off as the waves are overtaken. At these slower speeds the power trim should be brought in, if it is fitted, for the same reason. Both of these controls have less effect at slower speeds anyway.

In planing and semi-displacement boats, it is not possible to relax in rough seas in the way that one might with a displacement boat. The boats tend to be more lightly built so that they are less resistant to wave impact. Even by slowing down to displacement speed the best solution will not always be found, particularly if the bow drops in a trough at the same time, as will certainly happen with a fully planing hull. Semi-displacement hulls tend to be better because they have a fuller bow.

The need for concentration has been constantly mentioned in faster boats but this can become a problem at night when it can be difficult to see what the waves are doing. This is the time to set the boat on the most comfortable and least demanding course, irrespective of destination. Again a lot will depend on the conditions, but somewhere with the sea about 30–45° on the bow is likely to give the best ride running at reduced speed, with the reserve to cope with those larger than average waves when they are spotted.

Coping with extremes

When conditions turn really bad, the best place to be is in harbour. However it can sometimes be more dangerous to try to enter harbour than to stay out at sea. Some of the worst sea conditions can be found in harbour entrances, so the first decision that has to be made when bad weather arrives is whether to stay out at sea or whether to make for harbour. It is never an easy decision because the thought of harbour always seems so attractive, but before heading for harbour consider the conditions in the entrance, particularly if the harbour lies downwind and is wide open to the wind and sea. With thoughts of being snug in harbour, the worst conditions of the voyage can appear just on arrival.

Speed is the first thing to consider when out at sea. Speed, comfort and stress are directly related and a slower speed can solve many problems when bad weather is encountered. However speed should not be reduced to the point that steerage way is lost, otherwise the boat becomes vulnerable to breaking waves. Unless steering control is maintained, the desired heading will be lost and that could bring as much trouble as going too fast. If the sea builds up to the point where the situation is worrying then it is time to look at what resources there are to cope. When things get really bad then it is time to go into a survival mode with the object of weathering the storm until things improve.

There are no magic solutions in these situations and the decisions will be based to a large degree on the type of vessel, the nature of the conditions, personal experience and your ability to cope. In these extreme conditions, lifeboats are expected to cope and to have something left to help others in trouble. A lesson can be taken from lifeboats and the way they operate, but it has to be remembered that much of the safety of lifeboats in rough seas is determined long before they actually put to sea. The boats are strongly built, their equipment is sound and the crews are well trained and fit. These are all prerequisites for survival in bad conditions. But there is always the risk of being caught out, and the prudent sailor will make some mental as well as practical preparations for this by ensuring that both he and his craft are in good condition before putting to sea.

When caught out in worsening conditions, the first thing to do is to make an assessment of the situation. What are the weak points in the boat and its equipment? Is the crew fit for the task ahead? Where is the nearest shelter and safety? The first concern should be with the boat and where the weak and vulnerable points might lie. If there are large areas of glass in the bridge windows it is wise not to push the boat into a head sea. If there is a deep rear cockpit, the risk of a sea breaking over the stem in a following sea should be avoided.

On the machinery side, there could be concerns about the amount of fuel remaining and the reliability of the engines, and auxiliary systems such as the electrics. In rough seas it only needs a small failure which, in itself, may not be too serious but which can start off a chain reaction of events that can lead to disaster. I remember coming across a boat at sea which was on fire in rough conditions, a pretty serious situation that had started because of a steering failure! The steering was a wire and pulley system and the wire frayed and then finally broke. Given time, such a condition would not have been too difficult to fix, but without steering the boat turned broadside on and was rolling very heavily. This made it difficult to effect the repair but, much more seriously, the rolling set the poorly secured battery sliding about, which eventually broke the main battery cable. The short circuit that resulted started a fire and the single occupant was lucky to get out alive. This may be an exceptional case, but any failure in the boat or its systems can escalate or add to the worries. When assessing the situation it is important to take all factors into account, and if unhappy with any of them then it is time to go into survival mode.

Methods of heaving-to in a powerboat tend to require the boat to be driven, which means that long hours have to be spent at the controls. There are alternatives, and one is simply to close the boat down and leave it to its own devices. I don't think this would be my choice, but I know of several cases where powerboats left to drift have come through unscathed. The problem is that we tend to hear about the ones that made it rather than those that simply disappeared without trace.

Even when very tired, keeping some semblance of control is better than just letting the boat drift. With nothing to do, there is a tendency to give up mentally and that is not a good state of mind for survival. It might be possible to get away with it in a strong displacement vessel, but in a light planing boat the chances would not be so good.

One solution is to drive the boat on a course that seems sympathetic to the boat and the sea, but the good skipper tries to keep something up his sleeve. There are the traditional methods of coping with rough seas, such as using drogues, sea anchors and oil. The use of this equipment may often be talked about, but few modern motorboat skippers have the experience of using this equipment and fewer still have used them for survival. They are certainly not the solution to all the problems as often portrayed, but they are worthy of consideration if only to know when to reject them.

The universally proclaimed panacea for all desperate situations at sea is that of spreading oil on troubled waters. There is no doubt that the correct type of oil used under certain circumstances can have a beneficial effect, but this is limited and miracles must not be expected. The recommended oil is unrefined fish oil, normally supplied as 'storm oil'. It is rare to find a boat carrying oil for the specific purpose of spreading it on the water, so that when the need for it arises, the only oil likely to be available is either lubricating oil or diesel oil. Diesel oil is almost useless, but lubricating oil will have some effect. It is less viscous than the optimum and it will spread readily on the water, but its effect in reducing the breaking of waves will be less than the recommended fish oil. On balance, though, I do not think much of the idea of using oil mainly because everything will get coated in the oil and that can increase the risk of personal injury, something you can do without in this survival situation.

Drogues, sea anchors and oil can be some of the weapons available to help cope with extreme conditions, but the best weapon of all is a fit crew who think about what they are doing and how they are doing it. In a slow displacement boat, the best approach is

Going downwind is the most comfortable direction for a planing hull, but dynamic stability can be lost on the wave crests. *Photo: Safehaven Marine*

to drive the boat at slow speed, probably head to the sea or just off the bow. In a planing boat the best solution may be running before the waves provided that the boat has enough speed to travel faster than the waves. Failing this, turn and point the strongest part of the boat, the bow, into or close into the waves and *just* maintain steerageway to reduce the stresses as much as possible. Preparation is another important weapon, but there is not much to be done about that at sea except batten down and make sure everything is well secured.

Survival in extreme conditions will be a mental as much as a physical challenge so it is necessary to guard against tiredness and stress. Once tired everything seems to be too much trouble and there is a tendency to let things take their course. Having crew who can alternate routines and take charge is a huge bonus in these situations, and getting what rest is possible will help survival. There is no magic formula here, and most reactions will be guided by instinct. The most important thing to guard against in survival conditions is a failure in the boat. Failures can tend to escalate in a way that puts a boat on the road to disaster. Preventing failures is something that is best done before leaving harbour and a well maintained boat is the best protection when survival conditions are encountered in a powerboat.

14

Multihull tactics in heavy weather

MARK ORR

AT THE TIME THAT THE FIRST EDITION of *Heavy Weather Sailing* was published in 1967, multihulls were on the fringe of the sport, at an experimental stage in their development, with designers and adventurers pushing the boundaries of what multihulls could do. James Wharram's transatlantic voyage in 1956 and Derek Kelsall's transatlantic in 1964 and Round Britain adventures in 1966 gave significant examples of early progress, but multihulls breaking up or capsizing gave the impression of a concept still in the early stages of development.

Since those days, materials, technology, computers, experience and passion have transformed multihulls to a position where they are a respected and reliable option for anyone who might be looking to race, cruise or embark on a long distance voyage.

There are so many different types of multihull available, with such a wide range of uses, that it would be hard to prescribe for the handling of all types in heavy weather. Not surprisingly, the handling of a lightweight racing trimaran will differ considerably to that of a heavier cruising catamaran. However, there are common features that apply to all multihulls: they are generally lightweight, their stability is provided by their beam, and they have shallow draft, though some will have small unballasted stub keels that provide directional stability and protect rudders and propellers.

In heavy weather their motion will vary depending on their design, however their beam gives them great stability so there is minimal rolling. There is likely to be more pitching when going to windward than a comparable monohull as relatively little mass and their buoyant bows cause multihulls to go over, rather than through, the waves. At a given speed, generally speaking, a multihull ride will be the more comfortable. However, due to their relative light weight, generous sail areas and windage, multihulls can be hard to slow down when sailing off the wind or downwind.

On catamarans there are generally large working areas, whereas on a trimaran, unless also fitted with trampolines, the working areas can be limited to the central hull and are therefore equivalent to that of a similar sized monohull.

In heavy weather a multihull's speed, light weight and stability are key factors that can be used to advantage. However, there are actions that consistently threaten survivability in heavy weather.

Structure

Multihulls have increased in popularity as reliability has improved. Designers and builders have successfully taken what has worked on the race course, and engineered it

174

into cruising structures. Even the most modest cruising multihull will usually be designed to accept high point and torsional loads. The structure will be light but strong. Its engineering will include a high safety margin. Modifications, however, such as cutting holes in bulkheads to fit heating, or removing structure to modify interior accommodation, can compromise strength. Folding trimarans sometimes rely on the rigging for structural integrity and thus, if the rig fails, the beams may fail. This arrangement may not be suitable for ocean passages.

Modern materials may seem reasonably easy to repair but often require professional support to do so effectively. Damage must be properly repaired to ensure long-term reliability. For example, a high-tech composite craft will require high-tech composite repairs.

All multihulls, whether racing or cruising, undertaking offshore or ocean voyaging should be fitted with escape hatches. They should be fitted in either the hull sides or the bridgedeck. They must be large enough to allow a fully clothed crew member to go through, and be able to be opened from both sides. A robust deck hatch is often used but the escape hatch must be sited away from areas of wave impact such as the hull sides forward of the bridgedeck. They must be sited in a position that is above the inverted waterline so opening the hatch does not allow water to flood into the boat. Lifelines should also be securely attached to the underside of the boat so that the crew can clip on to the relative security of the upturned hulls. Painting the bridgedeck, rudders and daggerboards in high visibility paint is a sensible precaution.

Overloading

The space available on any cruising catamaran tempts owners to overload them. Loading should not exceed the designers' or manufacturer's recommendation, but a useful guide is that loading should not exceed one-third of the weight when the craft was built (ie when empty). Overloading affects speed, places additional load on the structure and reduces the height between the bridgedeck/beams and the waves, thus increasing pounding and the likelihood of damage through wave impact.

Weight should always be kept out of the ends of the hulls to reduce pitching and to ensure that the bows and sterns lift easily over waves. Thus weight should be concentrated around the centre of the boat, and, in a catamaran, balanced between the two hulls.

In extreme conditions multihulls rely on being able to side slip when hit by a big sea. The more weight a multihull carries the greater the inertia to be overcome by the wave and therefore the greater the likelihood of damage.

Windage

Whilst most trimarans are designed for speed, many catamarans, even of modest length, boast full standing headroom on the bridgedeck. Either lowering the bridgedeck floor or increasing roof height achieves this, but a compromise between the two is usually the result. The consequence is increased windage and the possibility of increased wave pounding. In heavy weather the greater the windage, the less the windward performance. Multihull owners have a tendency to add biminis, sail covers, dinghies on davits which all increase windage unless they are stowed away when at sea.

Maintenance

Multihulls generally have more equipment than the equivalent monohull. If not properly maintained then there is more to go wrong. Poor maintenance of engine and electrical systems will usually ensure that when an item is needed most, it will let you down. Rigging and sails will be tested most in heavy weather, so highly loaded components, such as halyards, rigging, furling systems and sails, should be routinely checked or replaced, eg standing rigging should be changed every ten years.

Preparation for heavy weather

Weather information

All skippers of craft sailing offshore or ocean voyaging must have a reliable source of weather information and be aware of how to analyse it. The onset of heavy weather should rarely be a surprise. The prudent sailor will analyse the weather information available and plan accordingly. With sufficient warning, a multihull should have time to use its speed to sail away from the worst of the weather in an approaching depression and, if sea room permits, position itself to receive least risk from lee shores, rocks, shoals, shipping lanes and suchlike.

Deck preparation

There is much that a crew can do to prevent damage from breaking waves and to reduce windage. All moveable deck gear should be stripped off and stowed securely below. Biminis and spray hoods should be removed, dinghies deflated and stowed in lockers. Sail covers and stack packs removed or lashed down, windsurfers stowed or stored flat, etc.

Consideration should be given to crew movement around the boat. Nowadays, multihull cockpits are large and should have some rope lifelines set up at the mid point, for example, to prevent crew being thrown too far by the sudden motion of the boat. On deck, in addition to lifelines to which safety harness strops can be attached, there should be jackstays to enable movement from side decks to the mast, or forward onto the trampolines or foredeck.

The blocks and ropes for sea anchors or drogues should be set up for immediate use.

The drag devices should be checked and stowed in deck lockers for easy access.

All ocean voyaging multihulls should have storm boards for large saloon windows and smaller boards for port lights or hatches in the hulls. These are usually 6mm ($\frac{1}{4}$in) plywood with a strongback and butterfly nuts to enable the plywood to cover a damaged window or port light. With the plywood placed over the outside of the damaged saloon window or portlight the strongback should be tightened against the boat's structure with the butterfly nut. Waterproofing can be improved with thick neoprene, perhaps from an old wetsuit, being placed between the plywood and the hole it is sealing. The trend towards vertical saloon windows and large hull portlights makes the carriage of storm boards more critical.

Storm sails

Compared to trimarans, catamarans rarely have a particularly tight forestay due to lack of bow structure. Consequently forestay sag is likely to increase as the wind builds, and in turn windward performance will deteriorate, particularly if the part-furled headsail has a poor shape. In both cases a backstay may not be fitted because the roach of the mainsail is too large and the forestay can only be made taut by tensioning the mainsheet. Generally foresails have a reasonably high centre of effort that often increases as the sail is reduced, which is exactly the opposite of what is needed.

Two options exist. The first is to replace the working headsail, before the storm is evident, with a flatter-cut storm sail, which can be reduced in area without furling by having slab reefs. As the wind increases, the slabs are taken in, reducing sail area while keeping the centre of effort low.

The second option is to have an inner forestay attached to a separate strong point, or alternatively a high load lashing around the front beam, which can be tensioned using a bottle screw or Highfield lever. The storm sail is attached with hanks.

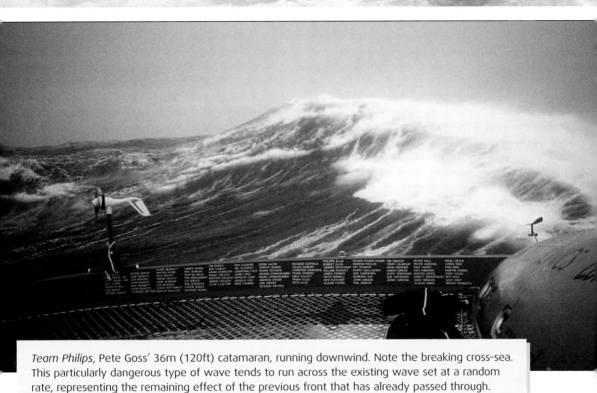

Team Philips, Pete Goss' 36m (120ft) catamaran, running downwind. Note the breaking cross-sea. This particularly dangerous type of wave tends to run across the existing wave set at a random rate, representing the remaining effect of the previous front that has already passed through. *Photo: Phil Aikenhead*

Few multihulls carry storm trysails, usually relying on a deep fourth reef. This is acceptable provided that the reef is truly deep, and equivalent in area to that of a storm trysail by being no more than 15 per cent of the total mainsail area. The reefing line must be rigged as part of storm preparation and a strop used to ensure that the reef tack can be brought down to the gooseneck when required.

Multihull storm sails needs to be very strongly built, as with little heel to dissipate the load, the head, clew and tack have to absorb the impact of a gust. Moreover, sails have to withstand the flogging that often occurs in heavy weather. It is essential to have a rope lashing (earring) between the clew of the mainsail and the boom to help the reefing line absorb some of the load, and to back it up in case of failure through chafe. If not fitted with a rigid boom vang, or other means of supporting the boom, the topping lift can be attached to the head of the main-

sail to provide back up in the event of chafe causing the main halyard to fail. If at some point the mainsail is not required, the boom should, if possible, be lowered to the deck, supported with fenders, and well lashed down. The reduction in windage will be significant. The redundant main halyard and topping lift can then be used to support the mast should one of the cap shrouds fail.

Crew preparation

It is essential that crew eat, drink and sleep to maintain their alertness and, happily, the stability of a multihull means that the weather will have to be exceptionally bad to prevent preparation of food and drink. A multihull with a bridgedeck cabin is the ideal place in which to rest, as it is light and airy, close to the helmsman, and reasonably stable. It is very important to keep crew briefed and active so that they know what is going on and feel that they are playing their part.

Sailing to windward in heavy weather

There are times when a lee shore, proximity to a shipping lane, or the avoidance of even heavier weather makes sailing to windward necessary. Sailing to windward in heavy weather is wet, uncomfortable and can be testing for the helmsperson and the crew. Good waterproof clothing is essential. Progress will be greatly influenced by the wave height and sea state. A general rule is to point up as the crest of the wave is approached and to bear away once the crest has passed. This technique should enable reasonable progress to be made to windward under shortened sail, but it is important to have sufficient sail power to drive over waves and not be pushed aside by them. If this means carrying more sail than would be prudent, then running the engine(s), usually at slow speed, is the best tactic. In the case of catamarans, the leeward engine or, if necessary, both will serve to ensure that progress is maintained. Engine power can be varied with the wave conditions.

When you need to tack there should be no hesitation in backing the headsail to ensure that the boat comes round. It will be necessary to bear away, whilst sheeting in, to build boat speed before coming back onto the wind. If there are doubts about the ability to tack in the prevailing wave conditions, the engine should be used to drive the boat through the wind. If the boat is without an engine, a moment has to be found between large waves to gybe round. The gybe should be done quickly with the mainsail sheet manned by a crew member who can ensure that the boat is not overpowered in the gybe by releasing the main sheet as needed.

A boat with daggerboards should only keep the windward board down. Use of the leeward board may provide too much lateral resistance and will prevent the boat slipping sideways should the boat be hit by a large wave, which could expose the boat to the risk of wave damage or even capsizing.

When sailing to windward the load on the windward shrouds will be large whilst the leeward shrouds may become loose enough to shake around as the boat rises over the waves. Shock cord should be used to restrict this movement and avoid fatigue with the risk of a failure when the shroud becomes loaded.

In strong winds, sails need to be sheeted as flat as possible and it is important to ensure that the slot between the headsail and the mainsail is even. This can be hard to achieve with a furling headsail whose poor furled shape, combined with forestay sag, may cause a lot of twist in the sail and decrease the sheeting angle. It may therefore be necessary to use a barber hauler on the headsail sheet to pull the clew to windward to flatten the sail and reduce the sheeting angle as much as possible. Conversely if sailing slightly freer, the barber hauler will enable a better slot to be created as shown in the photographs (right).

Sailing to windward places a lot of load on equipment so it is necessary to conduct frequent visual inspections to ensure that gear remains in the right place, rigging is secure, shackle pins are in place and that chafe is being managed. A checklist will remove the need for a tired crew member to have to remember everything. The checklist also engenders confidence that all that can be done is being done. This, along with regular briefing, feeding and sleeping, will keep a crew efficient and their morale high.

Sailing on a reach

Sailing free but not downwind can be exhilarating in a fresh breeze with even the most modest cruiser. These are the most favourable conditions for multihulls. However, wave height and shape will dictate the safe speed at which to sail. The more confused the sea, and the steeper the waves, the greater the restraint required. On this point of sail a greater safety margin is required, as an increase in wind or a change

LEFT A headsail without barber hauler
Photo: Woods Designs

ABOVE Headsail fitted with barber hauler
Photo: Woods Designs

in sea state can turn being 'under control' to being on the 'edge of control'. A good rule is to only sail downwind with the amount of sail area that is appropriate for making to windward in the same conditions.

When sailing free there is always the option to bear away or to point up a little to avoid a large or breaking wave. Indeed with speed available, a good helmsman will be able to pick the easiest path through the waves.

At night, unless there is plenty of phosphorescence, it is much harder to steer through the waves, and the prudent option is to slow down by reefing. It is also psychologically more comfortable. Sailing free in a fresh wind will mean rapid progress but it is usually noisy below deck and wet and uncomfortable above deck. The boat will be hit by waves, sometimes going through wave tops, so that deck hatches, windows and portlights will be vulnerable. Crew morale will need to be maintained through frequent rotation of helmsman, making sure that ample food is eaten regularly, plenty of fluid is drunk and rest is taken whenever possible.

Sailing downwind

There may come a time when reaching is no longer safe as wave fronts have become too steep, or the sea conditions have become too confused. The decision may be taken to sail downwind if sea room allows it. Indeed it may suit the destination. Downwind a multihull will have plenty of stability and can sail quickly and reasonably comfortably, usually with the wind over the quarter, but rarely completely downwind, as there is a great speed advantage to have both headsail and mainsail filled on the same side.

Downwind sailing can be exciting, as multihulls, being light, will tend to surf in the right conditions. There is therefore a balance to be struck between exhilaration and safety. At speed, particularly when surfing, the rudders may cavitate and control can be lost. The only remedy is to slow down.

Small increases in the apparent wind can mask significant increases in true wind and an unwary or tired helmsman may not appreciate the significance. If, for whatever reason, the boat stops, it is then exposed to the true wind. If it has to go upwind, perhaps to reduce sail, the boat will be sailing in the true wind plus boat speed. In either case the crew will now find themselves with too much sail area for the conditions, and the stability of the boat will be tested unless immediate action is taken to reduce sail. Consequently when sailing downwind, set sail for the true wind, and the speed of the gusts, not the lulls.

In these conditions, when it is essential to reef, prior fitting of reefing downhauls, attached to the tack of each reefing point, enables the halyard winch to be used to pull the tack of each reef down to the gooseneck. If the mainsail slides 'stick' against the mast track under batten load then pump the mainsail to momentarily relieve the batten load.

If wave conditions increase, then the boat may start 'running over' waves, which will increase the pounding on the bridgedeck. In some cases this may require the boat to slow down. Indeed in one race I have been in, this has caused an escape hatch to burst with the obvious dangers. If reducing sail does not slow the boat then other tactics need to be employed.

Slowing when sailing downwind

There are many means of slowing down and their effectiveness needs to be practised by the crew prior to their use in a real situation. It is often very difficult to control the speed of downwind sailing in heavy weather as the stability of a multihull encourages the crew to keep too much sail area, and windage alone can drive the boat fast downwind. The main cause of a capsize is digging in a hull or a float as an indirect result of having too much sail up. In these conditions moving weight aft and to windward will help prevent the bows driving into the sea, but usually prior to this point being reached, the crew need to slow the boat by reefing and, when no sail is left, by towing warps or a drogue. This will also apply when it is

Figure 14.1 Typical plastic drogue – the vanes choke the water movement through the drogue, increasing the drag. It should always be used with a length of chain to ensure it stays beneath the surface of the water.

necessary to reduce progress towards a lee shore or to allow crew to rest.

The simplest method is to tow long ropes, for example mooring warps. These can be as many as there are ropes available. Efficiency can be increased by knotting ropes together and by weighing them down with anchor chain. Indeed anchors can be towed at the end of the rope to increase drag. However, the more drag created, the greater the load on the attachment point and the harder it is to recover all the gear.

Efficiency can be improved by creating a large loop with both ends of the rope attached to the boat. However, if sailing quickly downwind, the rope will need to be weighted to prevent the acceleration of the boat pulling the rope out of the water and the rope bouncing on the top of the waves until the boat slows down again – quite the opposite of what it was deployed to do.

A more efficient means of slowing progress will be a purpose-built drogue. These are canvas or solid plastic devices often attached to between 5 and 10m (16 and 32ft) of chain, specifically designed for slowing vessels. They work by choking the rate at which water flows through the cone, or a series of vanes, or a large number of droguelets in the case of a series drogue, and are more fully described in Chapter 7 which covers drogues and parachute sea anchors. The load induced

Figure 14.2 The drogue should sit about 1.5 waves behind the boat, because as sea conditions change it is important to lengthen or reduce the rode.

is considerable and drogues are an effective means of slowing a boat's rate of progress downwind. In particular they keep the stern and the rudders immersed, and prevent a multihull sailing so fast that severe cavitation at the rudders causes loss of control.

It is important to adjust the rode length as wave conditions change. The drogue needs to sit at least one and a half waves behind the boat, so that it sits in a trough as the towing craft sits on the top of a wave. A steady pull is essential so if the wavelength changes and the drogue starts to sit on a crest, it will be necessary to adjust the length to prevent the rapid acceleration of the boat forcing the drogue out of the water to bounce down the wave front.

If the drogue fails to slow the boat sufficiently then it will need to be supplemented with warps. If that is not sufficient then it will be necessary to find a means to stop.

Whatever the method, the critical manoeuvre will always be when turning to head

Stopping

towards the wind to enable the boat to take any seas over the bow. Sailing to windward must be done with regard to the sea conditions using minimal sail area to ensure

sufficient speed for control. In most cases a quick turn between waves is better than taking too long. Use of the engine to make the turn is recommended.

There are three recognized methods of stopping: parachute sea anchors, heaving-to and lying a'hull.

Parachute sea anchors

These are described at length in Chapter 7. As a rule a multihull requires a sea anchor suitable for a monohull of 1.5 times its overall length, so a 12m (40ft) multihull will require one appropriate for a 18m (60ft) monohull. This is to allow for the additional windage and snatch loads that a multihull will place upon it. Once deployed, the 'parachute' opens and the boat is anchored to the ocean and should drift with the tides or currents. Downwind drift is significantly reduced, and in all but the most severe of conditions, multihulls will lie comfortably to a sea anchor.

To provide directional stability and to help spread the load, the sea anchor rode should be attached to a bridle mounted on the outer hulls of a catamaran or trimaran (see Fig 14.3). The length of the bridle lines needs to be adjustable, so it is preferable to lead the lines back to mooring cleats perhaps using spinnaker sheet blocks to feed the

(If using a drogue the bridle arrangement will be set through the stern spinnaker sheet blocks tied to the rode)

Parachute sea anchor

Swivel

Rode length: 20 x wave height

Swivel

Rolling hitch

Led through spinnaker guy blocks

Rode led to anchor windlass or anchor cleat

Led through spinnaker sheet blocks

Spinnaker or genoa sheet winches

Figure 14.3 The ideal bridle arrangement using spinnaker sheet and guy blocks to lead the bridle lines back to cockpit sheet winches, enabling adjustments to the bridle to be more easily and safely made.

bridle lines cleanly onto them. Alternatively lead the bridle lines back to the cockpit genoa or spinnaker sheet winches so that the bridle can be easily adjusted without extreme manual effort or having to go forward. The bridle lines should be tied onto the rode with a rolling hitch and the rode led through the anchor roller to the anchor windlass, if fitted, or to the anchor cleat as a back up. It is possible that some multihulls will lie comfortably with their rode attached to just one hull. Of course the boat's structure has to be up to the force of waves striking the forward outer hull.

The sea anchor requires a substantial rode – as a guide, the same diameter as anchor warp, ideally attached to a swivelling shackle at the end of the bridle. A lot of warp is required, approximately 20 times the height of the waves.

A multiplait rope is ideal as a rode as it resists the twisting loads that the sea anchor will place on it. For this reason, cheaper hawser-laid warp is not recommended, as it tends to tie itself into knots as the sea anchor twists under load. Most cruisers will combine anchor warps and their chain with spinnaker sheets to ensure sufficient length. The chain is useful as it provides additional load absorption, relieving snatch loads on

Float buoy

10m

x 20 = 200m

Figure 14.4 The sea anchor must be deployed two wavelengths from the boat with the boat and sea anchor moving together up and down the wave. As a guide, the rode length needs to be 20 times the height of the wave.

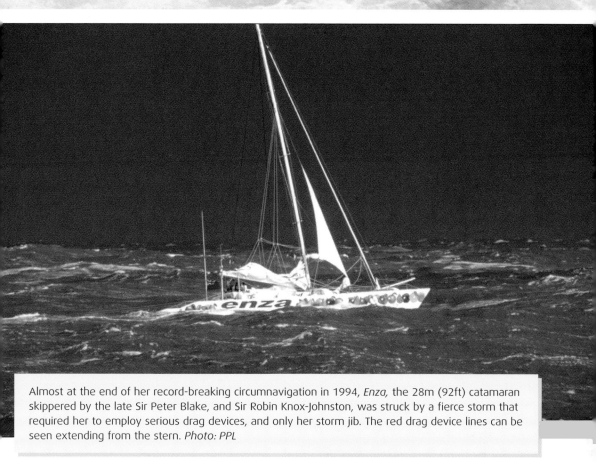

Almost at the end of her record-breaking circumnavigation in 1994, *Enza*, the 28m (92ft) catamaran skippered by the late Sir Peter Blake, and Sir Robin Knox-Johnston, was struck by a fierce storm that required her to employ serious drag devices, and only her storm jib. The red drag device lines can be seen extending from the stern. *Photo: PPL*

the boat. This should be mid length as placing it too close to the sea anchor could pull the sea anchor down too deep which in turn will pull the boat's bow down. The sea anchor float, which is attached to the crown of the sea anchor, has to be large (much larger than a typical fender) if it is going to have any effect on lifting the parachute, and is important for keeping the sea anchor at a set depth beneath the water.

Launching the parachute sea anchor or drogue

Unless kept in a deployment bag, the parachute sea anchor should be wetted before deployment to prevent it inflating in the wind before it is put in the water. The yacht should be rounded up close to the wind, and the sea anchor deployed over the windward bow to allow the multihull to drift

back without fouling the sea anchor. As the multihull drifts downwind, the rode should be paid out under control, and use of a winch is advisable as the loads can be significant. Steady paying out of the rode is essential as the tension created helps to deploy the parachute, whereas surges of warp will cause the parachute to collapse and possibly tangle.

The object is to have the sea anchor deployed in the water beneath the crest, two wavelengths away from the boat. Once deployed, attach the bridle to the rode using a rolling hitch, and check that the parachute has pulled the bows around into the sea; if not, then adjust the bridle. Relieve all possible chafe points.

Once everything has been checked, if the boat has daggerboards, these should now be lowered as they will provide directional stability and stop the boat yawing around the bridle. Rudders should be rigidly and strongly locked on the centreline or lifted to prevent damage.

Launching a sea anchor is not the end of the story. Loads on the structure will be considerable and all lines and equipment must be frequently checked to ensure that chafe is prevented. With the boat 'anchored', waves may now break against the boat with an awful surging noise that preludes a wave strike. Crew need to be briefed that this is normal and survivable, but storm boards should be fitted if waves start to hit the saloon windows hard. Generally waves will tend to roll under the bridgedeck with little more than spray hitting saloon windows. If wave strikes are too powerful or the snatch loads too great, more rode should be let out if it is available. If this is still not enough, then lower a weight down the rode. On one occasion I deployed a padlocked toolbox down the warp as everything else, including the anchor, had been used.

Once the sea conditions allow the crew to start sailing again, it will be necessary to recover the sea anchor so that it can be used again. A trip line and float (an anchor tripping line and hi-vis buoy is ideal) should have been fitted to the crown of the anchor to hold the parachute at a suitable depth. It enables the crew to see where the parachute is and adjust the length of the rode to ensure the sea anchor is two wavelengths away.

Recover the rode while motoring gently towards the float. As the sea anchor is approached, slow down, and take care that the sea anchor does not go under the boat. Retrieve the tripping line, and then recover the sea anchor using one of its shrouds, which will cause the anchor to collapse. Wash the sea anchor in fresh water at the next opportunity, to prevent the salt crystals rotting it. It is better to keep the sea anchor wet rather than allow it to dry out prior to being rinsed in fresh water.

It can be difficult to recover a sea anchor, and a number of cases have occurred when the crew has decided to cut the parachute and its rode adrift with their consequent loss.

Heaving-to

Heaving-to is a commonly used tactic, popular with the older multihulls, which have less windage than current production designs. Heaving-to means that the helm is lashed so that the boat is trying to round up into the wind. As the foresail is aback (sheeted on the wrong side) and the mainsail is set normally, the boat cannot tack. Most multihulls will alternate between sailing on a reach, then accelerate, be driven by the rudder angle to sail to windward, stall and then drift slowly back to sailing on a reach. They make slow progress upwind and therefore do not drift downwind. This is a good tactic as the boat is continually moving, is not losing ground downwind and is not tethered to the ocean and therefore not resisting breaking waves. However, it is not advisable in extreme conditions as the boat can be pushed downwind by a breaking wave, at which point the mainsail and headsail will fill and accelerate. A compromise is to lower the mainsail and set a small headsail and adjust the helm so it is turning the boat to windward so that the same effect applies. Even if knocked well off the wind, the helm will always drive the boat quickly upwind.

This tactic is generally effective in most heavy weather conditions. However, if the boat is frequently being pushed astern either as a result of a wave strike or a steep wave front, then the load placed on the rudders can be considerable and damage is likely. The crew should try more sail area, or use the engine, to increase forward motion, or if this is not feasible then turn downwind or lie-to a sea anchor.

Lying a'hull

This means lowering all sails and drifting under bare poles at the mercy of the wind and the waves. A multihull will generally sit beam onto the seas, where it will be uncomfortable, as waves will break against the structure, forcing the boat downwind. In exceptional circumstances waves will lift the windward hull and the crest breaks beneath the bridgedeck and against the leeward hull, forcing the boat to surf beam on until the trough is

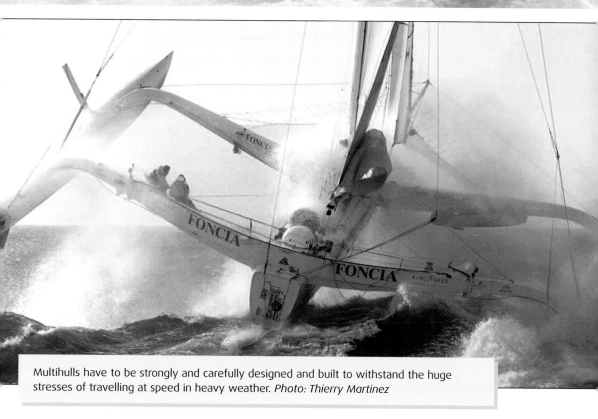

Multihulls have to be strongly and carefully designed and built to withstand the huge stresses of travelling at speed in heavy weather. *Photo: Thierry Martinez*

reached when the same cycle may start again. Not a happy situation. A particular danger is that with no forward motion or sea anchor to hold the bows into the sea, a breaking wave may force the multihull to surf backwards. This places a huge load on the rudders, possibly causing damage to them but may also force the leeward stern to dig into the water prompting a diagonal capsize.

Lighter craft, with daggerboards and rudders raised, fare better when lying a'hull as they present little lateral resistance, indeed they may sail downwind at between 45 and 60° to the sea. In this case the motion, though still uncomfortable, is much kinder as the waves are taken along the length of the boat whereas heavier craft will be lying broadside on, giving the feeling of being at the mercy of the sea. If sea room allows and the breaking waves are infrequent, this can be a useful tactic, even though the downwind drift will be considerable. Lying a'hull is ideal for temporary repairs but has many disadvantages over long periods.

Capsize

The worst that can happen in heavy weather is capsizing, usually as a result of sailing too fast through using too much sail. It is a terrible event but should not result in the loss of the crew or the yacht, provided that escape hatches are fitted, and the crew are trained for this situation. For example: automatic emergency floor lighting should be fitted which, of course, becomes overhead lighting after the capsize. Flares, handheld radio, and a telephone should be stored in a waterproof container that is accessible whichever way up the boat lies. There should be places where the crew can lie that will be out of the water when capsized, and clothes should be stowed in dry containers above the internal water level. Handholds should be provided on the hull to assist crew in climbing onto the upturned hull and there should be a facility to lock daggerboards in a position outside the hull, so they can be clung to. Multihulls

An inverted trimaran. Note that the foils are painted red to show up in this situation. *Photo: Royal Air Force Nimrod/PPL*

without a safety hatch should have an area marked on the underside of the hull, perhaps in a different colour of anti fouling, where the hull can be best cut into to rescue the occupants. The capsized multihull should become a stable raft in which the crew can survive inside the hulls or, at worst, survive between or on the upturned hulls.

With buoyancy compartments in the bows and sterns and no fixed ballast, multihulls will sit high in the water, and, provided the hull is not punctured, the safest place for the crew is inside the upturned hull, sheltered from the wind and the waves. There are many reports of an inventive and resourceful crew living for extended periods in their upturned hulls until rescue arrives. The upturned multihull will be more easily spotted by emergency services than a fragile and vulnerable liferaft, which should only be used as the very last resort.

Conclusion

Heavy weather should be expected and prepared for. It should be approached with confidence gained through prior preparation and knowledge of the options available. Multihulls do require different handling to monohulls in heavy weather, though many of the matters discussed elsewhere in this book are relevant to whatever hull form is chosen. Their inherent advantages of speed, light weight, stability and shallow draft are advantages that dictate the tactics deployed by the crew in preparing for and handling their boats through heavy weather. Regrettably overloading can compromise much of this.

Unless a crew on their own boat has tested out the equipment required to tackle heavy weather, the equipment will be of little use. A well prepared boat and crew will usually survive all that the weather can throw at them.

15

Monohull storm tactics

PETER BRUCE

MILITARY OFFICERS ARE FOND OF saying that few plans survive first contact with the enemy, and the same may be said for the plans of the crew of a small vessel encountering heavy weather for the first time. Any plans have to be flexible. Unexpected events are likely to occur, the weather forecast is often a simplified overview, and people's behaviour may be unpredictable after prolonged exposure to blinding spray, fear, cold temperature, wearying noise and violent motion. One can be fairly sure, however, that crews, boats and equipment that have done well in previous storms will do so again.

Regardless of the expected wind strength, there are courses of action that can be taken before the weather takes control that can much reduce the chances of disaster. Vessels should be placed to avoid lee shores, shoal water, currents, tidal races, headlands and areas marked on charts as having overfalls. Once the storm has struck, while a vessel is still afloat, however cold and uncomfortable the conditions, her crew should neither seek nor accept offers of rescue, nor take to the liferaft without very good reason, for to do so may incur graver risks than enduring the storm. One should be very cautious about taking a tow in a seaway, too. Few modern craft have adequate strong points for towing even when the master of the towing vessel has the patience and skill to maintain a low enough speed.

Apart from these recommendations there is no universally applicable advice to be offered: there is no one simple remedy. If only there was. Every skipper should plan suitable tactics, carefully taking into account the characteristics of his boat, and be prepared to adopt them in good time. Some courses of action are, of course, heavily committing, and once decided upon are hard to change. In this concluding chapter of Part 1 an attempt will be made to summarize the various tactics available to the skipper of a monohulled sailing boat in heavy weather.

Drag devices, both parachutes and drogues, have established their worth and can be counted as important additional options for coping with heavy weather, but are not the only option. The tactics that are described in this chapter have been employed in one or more of the accounts of heavy weather in this book and their effectiveness in actual circumstances can best be judged by referring to them. It is not possible to specify the exact wind strength when the various options can be recommended due to the number of variables involved. Obviously, the size of the craft is of considerable relevance and, in storms, big is beautiful. But other factors count heavily too, such as the nature of the seas, the design and strength of boat, and the size and strength of the crew. In broad terms, this chapter covers courses of action to consider when the wind speed exceeds force 9, to force 10 and above.

This is a most unusual and amazing photograph, as Jérôme was not to know, as he took it, whether his boat was to be capsized through 360°, and whether he would be able to continue to cling on to the rigging as his boat was knocked over by the breaking wave. As it is, the boat has been flung about 75° onto her starboard side. *Photo: Jérôme Poncet*

It is evident from Adlard Coles' own modest accounts that he was skilful at choosing the moment to shorten sail. As he advocates, this should be undertaken in advance of immediate necessity, despite a natural reluctance to do so in the hope that the weather may show an improvement. He was of the opinion that, when cruising in bad weather, it will be prudent to adjust sail area for the squalls and gusts rather than for the mean force. He was also a believer in running with no more sail than can be carried if close-hauled, thereby avoiding the need for frenzied reefing action in the event of a man overboard, or a bad landfall. Obviously, the longer sail reduction is deferred, the harder it is to carry out, and the greater the risk of damage meantime. Incidentally this applies to all heavy weather tactics, in that bold and resolute decisions are best made before a situation becomes desperate. Likewise, serious problems are often best dealt with as soon as they occur.

When bad weather is approaching, most people, very sensibly, make for a safe harbour. But once caught out in a storm there is

much to be said for enduring it rather than continuing to run for shelter, as breaking waves in shallow water can be far more of a hazard than the open sea. Besides, if entry into harbour becomes unwise or impossible, the loss of sea room is irrevocable.

When beset by a storm, the human objective is to remain as safe and as comfortable as possible. As far as the boat is concerned, the aim is to avoid sinking, being rolled over, pitchpoled or otherwise suffering damage to hull, rig and sails. As Adlard Coles says, the wind dictates the amount of sail that can be carried and can also cause loss of sails, rigging or mast; but it is the breaking seas that do the more dangerous damage to hull and superstructure. There is great energy bound up within a wave, and major forces are at work when a breaking sea strikes a boat. A boat can also be picked up by a breaking sea and accelerated to an alarming speed. A moment later the boat may be flung into the still water in the trough of the wave where she will stop almost instantly. It is at this point that serious damage to crew and boat is likely to occur. Clearly, it is desirable to avoid breaking waves but, if this is not possible, then

Bernard Stamm and crew broad reaching off the Lizard in February 2001. The determination of top single-minded racing sailors is borne out by this photograph, which shows his yacht carrying maximum sensible sail in a winter storm.
Photo: Thierry Martinez

the waves should be taken within 20° of either the bow or the stern. Before the days of self-draining cockpits, being pooped, ie a wave breaking over the stern, was a major hazard to yachtsmen. It is now less of a problem, but remains a danger to motorboats open at the stern, to yachts with unusually large cockpits, or with low bridgedecks that require wash-boards or doors in place to prevent a sea sweeping down below.

Pressing on

As increasingly severe weather overtakes a craft, a seaman's instinct encourages him to continue to maintain his approximate course while reducing sail appropriately. When the destination is to windward and the crew has the determination to press on, perhaps under storm jib or trysail alone, despite the uncomfortable motion, this is commendable and, incidentally, is a policy that has won many races. The helmsman's technique is to close-reach across the troughs, then head up into

the waves, and bear away hard on the top to avoid a slam. Likewise, when reaching, the helmsman will luff into the wave crests and bear away in the troughs. Every wave may need different treatment: a steep wave about to break will need to be taken head on followed by bearing away hard to re-gather speed and to avoid a slam, while a gentle-sloped wave will need no change of course at all. A certain amount of judgement is needed as on the one hand there is a danger of capsize should the boat be caught at an angle to a breaking sea, whereas on the other hand the boat can be stopped by heading straight into a breaking sea and then thrown backwards onto her rudder. Light craft are more likely to suffer the latter fate but are also most responsive. In this case, keeping speed on can best be achieved by giving a last minute luff into an awkward wave.

The crew will be heartened by continuing in the desired direction, and hand steering – unlike heaving-to or lying a'hull – provides an opportunity to avoid breaking waves. As a storm tactic, this type of action has its merits only when the crew is strong

enough to persevere and while it is still possible to make progress under storm sails.
For example, it was a tactic adopted by Ed
Psaltis, skipper of the overall winner of the
stormy 1998 Sydney–Hobart Race (see
Chapter 3), under storm jib alone, and is
particularly appropriate in daylight for
beamy IMS racing yachts with low underwater lateral area and low range of stability.
To paraphrase Ed Psaltis, 'Having speed and
acceleration gives manoeuvrability to steer
through big and confused seas. It is possible
to position the yacht best for each wave as it
comes, or steer around it. Without speed,
acceleration and manoeuvrability a boat is a
sitting duck to large waves.' It is significant
that the majority of the yachts in this race
reported that they fared best when sailing
15° off close hauled.

As conditions deteriorate further, any size
of sail set, however small, can become over-
powering. At first the helmsman will luff to
reduce the angle of heel, but the flogging sail
will cause the whole boat to shake violently.
On the other hand, when the helmsman
reaches off to gather speed, the boat will be
thrown on her beam-ends across the seas. At
first some middle ground will be found
between these extremes, but as wind and
wave increase there comes a point when it
may be necessary to consider other options,
especially if the helmsman's difficulties are
about to be increased by darkness.

Heaving-to

Sabre, a 10.4m (34ft) steel cutter with a crew
of two, was one of the few centre-stage
yachts that survived the June 1994 Pacific
storm virtually undamaged. She sailed
through the eye of the storm and undoubtedly experienced as bad conditions as any
without any rolls or knockdowns. Her crew
commented afterwards: 'Our boat is prepared with very rough conditions in mind
and, lying hove-to, has proved herself on several occasions.'

When it comes on to blow it is better to
heave-to early rather than late, and indications that the time is ripe usually come from
the helm. If control is becoming difficult or
the helm is feeling spongy as a result of
water aeration, it is time to heave-to. If waves
are breaking, plan to round up between the
waves that are about to break. One can often
find a good area of water just behind a wave
that has recently broken. At night, breaking
waves can be heard and sometimes the phosphorescence can be seen.

One can heave-to either by backing the
headsail or by tacking and leaving the jib sheet
made up, accompanied by a mainsail appropriately reefed for the conditions, or a trysail.
The helm should be secured with heavy shock-
cord or rope so as to hold the boat's bow
towards the wind, and adjustments then made
to the sheets and the helm until the boat is at
her most comfortable. At this point she will
probably be moving gently forward at a knot
or two and about as fast to leeward.

In the right design of boat the increase in
comfort that can be derived from heaving-to
in a seaway has to be experienced to be
believed. Noise and motion are promptly
much reduced and there is no longer a need
for a helmsman, though it is important to
check for chafe. Thus heaving-to is a good
expedient to adopt, not only in heavy
weather but also for having a meal in comfort or when an uncertain pilotage situation
demands time for thought. Incidentally, it is
wise not to try to back an overlapping headsail in order to heave-to, as there is a high
chance of bursting the sail on the spreaders.

Storm jibs, deep-reefed mainsails or trysails are sometimes employed on their own
and in these instances it is more likely that a
helmsman will be necessary. Given the
choice, it is better to set a deep-reefed mainsail or trysail on its own rather than a storm
jib set on its own (see Sydney–Hobart Race of
1998, Chapter 3).

It is relevant to quote Alan Webb who
used to have a 13.7m (45ft) heavy displacement steel yacht called *Supertramp*. He now
owns a quicker, much lighter and more lively

Bernard Stamm, now single-handed, hove-to whilst adjustments are made to the steering system. *Photo: Thierry Martinez*

cold moulded 10.7m (35ft) yacht called *Supertramp II* designed by Laurie Davidson with a fin keel and a skeg-hung rudder. She draws 1.78m (5ft 10in) and weighs only 5 tons. Incidentally she has a separate track for her trysail. Alan Webb writes:

In heavy weather sailing these two yachts responded very differently. With the heavy displacement *Supertramp*, the tactic in extreme conditions was to run under bare pole as long as sea conditions allowed and as a last resort to lay a'hull and take the pounding. In the lighter boat I found the only strategy in survival storms is to turn up into the wind with the trysail sheeted on hard and the helm lashed to bring the boat to windward. The yacht then travels up the waves and lies on the peak of the wave so that her forward momentum carries her through the breaking crest and prevents her from being knocked down heavily. In this lighter vessel, to continue to run in heavy conditions would surely mean a pitch pole or a capsize. Initially I tried this tactic in the first 40 knot easterly I encountered in the lighter vessel to test the theory of John Sanders, the famous West Australian sailor who completed three non-stop solo circumnavigations. I found it worked well then but I never anticipated risking this strategy in survival conditions. Yet as luck would have it, I was already hove-to under trysail when I was hit by what I believe was a hurricane. This, the strongest storm I encountered, was at only 34° 35' South–3° 32' East, in the South Atlantic en route from Recife, Brazil to Cape Town, South Africa on 1 November 2005. It happened so fast that I had no choice but to leave the trysail in place, and anyway it was working well in these extreme conditions when the violence of the squalls was comparable to the williwaws I had experienced in the Cape Horn region.

The wind was ESE 25–30 knots to start off with. I was pounding into it getting nowhere, except being pushed too far north, so I hove-to under trysail. I slept for two hours and awoke just before dawn to find the barometer had plummeted. At 0730 the wind backed northeast 45–50 knots with violent squalls. I stayed hove-to under trysail. At 1000 the wind went south-west like a hurricane. I estimated it was blowing 80 knots with torrential rain. The sea was a total white out. I couldn't see anything for the blizzard of rain and spray. The yacht under try-sail was laid over to 60° with water streaming over the decks. This lasted two hours when the storm moderated to 60 knots increasing to 70–80 knots in the squalls. The waves reached 9m (30ft) with the top four feet being torn-off white spume. The yacht was pointing high, climb-ing the waves, making 3 knots to windward. These conditions prevailed until 0100 when the wind decreased to 40 knots with stronger squalls.

I am certain that to attempt to run in those conditions in a light boat of five tons would have meant certain capsize due to the violence of the squalls and the state of the seas. The wind was so strong it stretched the trysail, and I had to have it re-cut in Cape Town.

Alan Webb's experience is of much interest to owners of light yachts that, as a rule, are dif-ficult to stabilize in stormy conditions. It is noteworthy that the trysail was sheeted flat and that *Supertramp II* has a skeg-hung rud-der. With the helm lashed to bring her up to windward she would come up to 25° off the wind in very strong gusts of 70 knots plus, but then would fall off again to about 40°. She never once tacked.

A deeply reefed mainsail works as well as a trysail but should not be considered an unqualified alternative to a trysail, as main-sails can easily be torn, and cannot work efficiently if the boom has broken. Thus a try-sail should always be carried as it can be used with or without the boom though, if working to windward, use of the boom will make life easier and more comfortable. On the other hand, if reaching or fetching, the sail will work well without the boom, and, if it is not used, the boom will be less of a hazard to the crew. If it is necessary to run dead before the wind, twin headsails will be preferable.

Traditional remedies best suit traditional boats. When hove-to, a yacht should lie about 50° to the wind, but unfortunately not all fin-keeled yachts will heave-to untended in a sea, probably because they lack underwater lat-eral area. In particular, light-displacement yachts with slim high-aspect ratio keels may not stay at a constant angle to the wind and can dance about while making great speed to leeward. The problem with such boats is that when it seems advisable to slow right down,

they won't. Heaving-to is a time-honoured and seamanlike tactic to employ in moderate to severe conditions, and owners of many craft may need no other. However, owners of some modern yachts (though clearly not *Supertramp II*) will find that heaving-to can become neither comfortable nor safe, and there is always the chance that any yacht lying hove-to can be caught heavily beam-on by a large breaking wave.

Lying a'hull

If heaving-to seems no longer sensible it may be tempting to resort to lying a'hull, ie taking off all sail, lashing the helm – usually slightly to leeward – closing all hatches securely, and letting nature take her course. The ease with which types of yacht will lie a'hull is variable. Broadly speaking, old-fashioned narrow-beam heavy-displacement yachts often lie a'hull well, while light-displacement beamy yachts often do not. Nevertheless, lying a'hull was the most popular survival tactic in the gener-ally light-displacement 1979 Fastnet fleet. Harry Whale lay a'hull off Ushant aboard *Muddle Thru* in the great English Channel storm of 1987. It is a tactic employed by many yachtsmen – and not always of dire necessity. In a sufficient force of wind the windage of the mast alone provides stability, like a steady-ing sail, and the turbulence caused by the yacht's drift may reduce the chances of waves breaking to windward. As an illustration of a vessel's ability to look after herself during a storm, one may recall that most of the vessels abandoned in the Fastnet Race were later found bobbing about in the swell with hatches left wide open.

Unfortunately, while lying a'hull may seem relatively comfortable, often more so than other tactics, it gives a false sense of security. The problem, of course, is that the boat is vulnerable to breaking waves from broadside on and, to paraphrase Andrew Claughton in Chapter 2, 'breaking waves do not have to be very big to roll any sort of small craft right over, whatever her hull features'. The consequences of a roll-over can be most dramatic down below – more so than one might imagine – and the chances of the mast being lost are high. This occurrence, apart from the obvious effect on mobility, can lead to all kinds of immediate problems – not the least of these is that the lack of damping effect of the mast, without which a yacht's roll inertia is halved, results in quicker and more unpleasant motion with a much-increased chance of being rolled again.

While on the melancholy subject of capsize, it may be significant that several yachts have been rolled over just as a storm seems to have abated. Examples are Bill King in *Galway Blazer* in 1968, *Sayula II* in the first Whitbread Round the World Race in 1973, Michael Richey in *Jester* in 1986, and the Swan 46 at sea in the October 1987 storm, described in Chapter 18. This is a phenomenon called 'over-shoot', for which Sheldon Bacon provides the explanation in Chapter 9. Another contributory factor may be the shift of wind direction as a front goes through, when the effect of two wave trains crossing at an angle is known to produce regions of extreme wave height where the seas may break heavily.

Having pointed out the dangers of lying a'hull, to try to put matters into perspective it should be mentioned that world girdlers such as Alec Rose, Nicholas Davies and Alan and Kathy Webb, albeit with heavy-displacement boats, have found the practice of lying a'hull entirely satisfactory for weathering the gales of a normal world circumnavigation. For such solidly built vessels it is quite a rare event to encounter the sort of weather that does not allow lying a'hull without a high risk of capsize, but there are enough examples in this book of yachts being rolled over while lying a'hull to show that the tactic, sooner or later, may lead to being rolled through 360°. For this to happen a craft has to be caught broadside on just as a wave breaks, so luck plays a strong part.

Use of engine

Nowadays the diesel engine is a generally reliable item of equipment that can be used to good effect when managing under sail would be difficult, such as entering and leaving a berth. The old-fashioned view that 'to use an engine is unseamanlike' may have been based upon more than just prejudice, for early auxiliary engines were not always dependable while running, nor easy to start, and it was wise not to encourage over-reliance on them. Moreover, the high chance of catching a rope round the propeller in a stressful situation is well known.

Nevertheless, the competent use of an engine was demonstrated by Alain Catherineau's celebrated rescue feat in the 1979 Fastnet. One is not likely to be able to make directly into the sea under auxiliary engine or tack through the wind in storm conditions but, bearing in mind that even a bare pole will provide some aerodynamic lift, it may be possible to make across the seas to windward. There may often be circumstances when it will be safer to 'heave-to under engine' rather than lie a'hull, especially when running before a storm is not possible due to a lee shore. In this case the use of an engine, either in combination with sails or without, may be highly desirable, though lubrication of some engines will not work at a large angle of heel. It should not be forgotten that skippers of power craft have no option but to 'heave-to under engine'.

When running before the sea it may be significant that the old-fashioned British lifeboat with a speed of 8 knots could not always be handled confidently without the use of a drogue in combination with the engines. Coxswains of modern lifeboats, with a speed of 18 knots, find they have no such trouble as they can power their way clear of breaking seas. Bearing in mind the opening sentence of this chapter, which suggests that flexibility may be necessary when facing severe weather, yachtsmen should regard the use of an engine as another string to their bow, and be ready to use it when the situation justifies, after carefully checking for ropes over the side. Having started the engine it should be checked from time to time.

Running before the seas

There is nothing new about the tactic of letting a vessel run freely before the sea, when sea room permits. Apparent wind is reduced, motion is more comfortable, and the risk of being rolled becomes less likely than when lying a'hull. When considering extreme conditions, running with full directional control is vitally important to avoid the breakers and keep the stern at the optimum angle to the waves to avoid broaching. This is not easy, especially at night, though experienced planing dinghy helmsmen and surfers may have an advantage. In a confused sea, waves can come unexpectedly from odd quarters, necessitating a quick response from the helmsman and boat. Clearly the speed of the boat has to lie within a range necessary to achieve good control. If speed is too slow, the boat does not respond quickly enough, and if too fast, especially in darkness, the helmsman may not be able to react in time to avoid pitch-poling or a broach, both of which can have very serious repercussions.

Some craft undoubtedly handle better than others when running before the seas, and it might be easy to assume that displacement is the controlling factor. The situation is not so clear cut, with a combination of design factors such as the degree of balance of the ends affecting the issue, as described by Olin Stephens in Chapter 1. In any case an overly low-geared wheel is a considerable disadvantage. The corollary is that in the case of a high-geared wheel, or a tiller, some degree of physical strength is likely to be needed on the helm. It is worth mentioning that vane self-steering can usually work in any amount of wind, and can be invaluable for shorthanded crews in heavy weather. As described by Alex Whitworth in Chapter 25, *Berrimilla* ran under a bare pole and her vane self-steering through a storm where the wind speed peaked at 84 knots.

The tough professional crews of yachts in the Volvo Round the World Race find exhilaration in the downwind 'sleigh-rides' through the southern oceans under as much sail as they can carry. Their technique is to luff across the trough to maintain speed, then to bear away almost square to the wave, just as the crest arrives, to encourage the boat to surf down the wave. It is similar to methods used by dinghy sailors and Malibu board surfers and requires some skill, strength and a great deal of concentration, especially when carrying full sail. Such crews will have perhaps six or eight expert racing helmsmen to share the steering task, whereas the average cruising boat may not have more than one, for whom the task of steering may become extremely wearisome after not many hours. Thus the average cruising yacht should only run before the seas while it is clearly safe and comfortable to do so. Many vessels have come to grief by pursuing this tactic too long.

Running with warps

As already mentioned, it is important to try to find an appropriate speed for good steering when running before a storm. Towing warps as a means of keeping the stern to the seas, while flattening the breakers behind and helping to reduce the yacht's speed to a

After two severe knockdowns while lying a'hull, Ernest and Val Haigh tied together 183m (600ft) of heavy line and trailed it astern. The improvement was immediate. *Photo: Ernest and Val Haigh*

desirable level, may sound archaic to some, but it is a technique still used by experienced seamen, particularly in shorthanded situations. First, warps, having more than one use, are usually available, easy to stow, and uncomplicated. Furthermore, one can control the length of rope paid out to ensure a steady pull. Too short a warp and breaking crests can carry it forward so that there is no retarding force at all. A long warp, unlike a single drogue, can span a whole wavelength, so making the pull more constant. Warps intended for securing alongside will not be long enough for spanning an ocean wave.

Thus for ocean passages one should be looking at a length of 122m (400ft) or more. Even experienced warp-users such as Sir Robin Knox-Johnston relate the ease with which warps can tangle when being paid out in the sort of conditions when they can help; thus preparation and skill are necessary in their deployment.

When Sir Robin Knox-Johnston encountered heavy weather in the southern oceans he put out 183m (600ft) of 5cm (2in) circumference warp in the form of a bight, lashed the helm tightly amidships, and went to sleep. He says:

The warp held the heavily built *Suhaili* firmly stern-to the waves. She lay very comfortably, regardless of the wave height, in forces of at least 12 on the Beaufort scale when the sea was white with spindrift. *Suhaili* drifted downwind at an average of about 2 knots in big stuff and strong blows with only a storm jib set right forward, sheeted tight amidships. If she tended to yaw, the force on the jib increased the more she came round, tending to push her back downwind. *Suhaili* has a canoe-type stern, or Norwegian type if you prefer, and this meant that there was no great resistance to the waves as they rolled past, they were just divided. The warp stretched quite a lot in surges, but that was to be expected. Had I been able to get the warps out in 1989, I am sure that we would have been all right, and I am intending to make a couple of rope reels, which I shall hang from the deckhead in the fo'c'sle, so in future I can lead the warps directly over the stern if I need them in a hurry.

Bernard Moitessier's experience with warps during a survival storm in the South Pacific in 1965–6 is often quoted. The 12.2m (40ft) yacht *Joshua* was towing 'five long hawsers varying in length from 30.5m (100ft) to 91.4m (300ft), with iron ballast attached and supplemented by a heavy net used for loading ships'. At the onset of the storm it seems possible that this arrangement was successful, but once the wave height and length reached a certain point, the yacht failed to respond to the wheel, and the warps did not prevent her from surfing down the crests. Not finding these circumstances satisfactory, eventually Moitessier cut the warps, whereupon he found himself in a much more comfortable situation.

Interestingly, Dr David Lewis, returning from the USA after the 1960 single-handed Transatlantic Race, recounts a similar experience. He had been running under staysail alone, but after the sheet fairlead had pulled out of the deck with the increasing wind strength, he lowered the sail and streamed 36.6m (120ft) of warp in a bight. At once, he says, his boat became unmanageable, and even when he did succeed in steering down the seas, the breaking waves would carry the warp alongside. Similar difficulties were experienced in the 1979 Fastnet Race.

Tony Marchaj explains the apparent anomaly regarding use of warps to some extent in his book entitled *Seaworthiness: The Forgotten Factor* (published by Adlard Coles Nautical). He believes that, in a fast-growing sea, wave height increases more quickly than wavelength, producing especially steep seas. As waves develop in size there will be a time when their wavelength is twice a given boat's length. At this point the bow will arrive in the trough just as the stern is at the top of the crest. With steep enough seas as a result of the fast-growing effect, one can see that there may be a tendency for the boat in this attitude to topple, ie pitch-pole or broach, especially as the water particles driven by the orbital action within a wave will be moving forward at the crest of the wave, reducing the effectiveness of the rudder.

When a boat has been designed with the rudder placed well aft, the control situation may be further aggravated as a result of 'ventilation', a term used to describe the situation when the rudder may be lifted partly out of the water or its efficiency reduced by aeration. Moreover, if a yacht is overtaken by a breaking wave the water flow upon which the rudder relies can be reversed.

In very short steep seas, when a boat could topple and when the rudder may be less effective than usual, many yachtsmen have felt that they would benefit from the use of some drag device to prevent their vessel broaching or pitch-poling.

Tony Marchaj suggests that when the wavelength has had time to develop further there will be a need for less drag and more speed to evade breaking crests and awkward cross-seas in the troughs, hence a need to discard the use of warps as the wave system matures. Nevertheless, this does not explain why those such as David Lewis and Bernard Moitessier had control difficulties with warps streamed after seas had had ample time to grow, and others did not.

The explanation seems to lie in the length and height of waves compared with the length of warp used. If Bernard Moitessier used warps, as he says, of up to only 91.4m (300ft) in seas of wavelength 152–171m (500–560ft), one could expect, through the orbital movement within a wave, his warps to be ineffective at times. Likewise, allowing for the bight, David Lewis' warp only extended 18.3m (60ft) in waves that he estimated to be 46m (150ft) in length.

After disposing of his warps Moitessier found that it was an advantage to luff a little at the arrival of each wave crest to take the sea 15–20° on the quarter. He was now in the same situation as the Webbs in *Supertramp* (Chapter 17) and using the same tactics. These two are not alone in preferring to run free with the seas slightly on the quarter. Not only does it reduce the chances of pitch-poling, but also – like a surfer – by steering across the waves one may be able to avoid the worst of the breaking crests. When the face of the

A view of the Southern Ocean by Les Powles. He estimates the wave height to have been 18.3m (60ft). *Photo: Les Powles*

wave is exceptionally steep there will be a very fine balance between pitch-poling and broaching, and in this case the helmsman may have to weave his boat down the wave to optimize the situation.

The experience of Bernard Moitessier and others leads one to the view that to avoid being pitch-poled, rolled over or being pooped, boat speed must be kept at a level to give directional stability at all times. Of course, once huge seas have had the time to develop, it is usually in the troughs of the waves that problems occur. Here the boat's speed is no longer being helped by gravity, and the shelter of the adjacent wave crest may reduce wind strength. Nonetheless, in the trough of a wave, the need for directional stability remains as vital as elsewhere. Thus warp drag has to be adjusted, or enough sail has to be set, to take the craft

safely through the troughs, accepting that at other times even with warps streamed, this may mean that a boat could be surfing at what may seem to be an unnatural rate. Some boats, like *Suhaili*, may be directionally stable when towing warps with helm lashed; others may demand competent helmsmanship, but probably to a lesser degree than when running completely free.

An auxiliary engine can possibly provide the additional drive needed to achieve good steering control in the troughs. To illustrate this point there follows an extract from an account by Richard Clifford when cruising off Ireland in his Warrior 35, *Warrior Shamaal*, in August 1979. As luck would have it, he found himself alone at sea in the midst of the infamous Fastnet storm of 1979. It may be of note that it was not his first storm.

I dropped off my crew in Glengariff on 13 August and sailed gently down Bantry Bay, then headed south-west out into the Atlantic. At 0400 the next morning the wind was too much for the storm jib, so I handed it and lay a'hull. Very soon afterwards *Warrior Shamaal* was knocked flat by a large breaking wave. I grabbed a bucket and bailed, found the bilge pump and pumped, and fought my way to the wheel to try to get the boat to run downwind, but she would not come round. The next extra large wave again filled the cockpit and the saloon to just above the cabin sole. When we came back on an even keel I noticed that the liferaft was floating in its container beside the boat, the bilge pump handle had gone and the anchor had come out of its well on the foredeck. The immediate problem was to stay afloat, so I rushed below, got the heads bilge pump handle, and put the washboards in position. Still *Warrior Shamaal* would not run down-wind and yet another wave bowled the boat over, filling the cockpit and pouring water below. By this time the liferaft had inflated itself and broken adrift.

I was not prepared to set my 9.1sq m (98sq ft) storm jib as it would have been too big: my 15.2sq m (50sq ft) spitfire jib was in my garage! So I started my 15hp auxiliary engine and with this ticking over in gear I was able to keep the stern into the wind with an occasional burst of full throttle after my concentration had lapsed.

Suddenly we were at the top of an extra big wave. *Warrior Shamaal* hung at the top then plunged forward in a horrifying nose-down attitude. Her bows plunged into the trough and I fully expected to continue on down, or the stern to flip over, pitch-poling the yacht. With a shudder we pulled out of the dive and rushed on with the next mountainous wave.

Tactics had to be changed again, so between waves I passed a mooring line from one cockpit winch aft around the self-steering, and back into the cockpit. My 91m (300ft) warp is coiled and seized with sailmaker's twine every 18.3–21m (60–70ft) to avoid tangles. I attached the end of this onto the mooring line and paid out each coil until the whole bight of rope was more or less floating astern. Still running ahead on the engine and towing the bight, I experienced no further problems.

In this account we not only have an engine being used to good effect, but we again see that lying a'hull may not be a satisfactory tactic in extreme conditions. Furthermore, we see that warps were thought to be necessary to avoid broaching or pitch-poling during the period when the seas were developing rapidly in height and steepness.

On balance it appears that warps streamed astern on their own can work well in extreme storms so long as the warp arrangement is long enough to span a whole wavelength of the seas. The shorter the warps are in relation to the wavelength, the lower the proportion of time when the warps are providing effective drag. Consequently a collection of short warps may slow a boat down below the speed necessary to steer, or for the boat to steer herself, yet they may provide insufficient drag to prevent wild surfing when the orbital movement within the wave is moving in the same direction as the boat.

Having established that a long length of warp would seem one form of desirable equipment for heavy weather, it is worth quoting from Michael Richey's experiences in July 1981. He was returning to the UK from Bermuda in his famous 7.6m (25ft) Folkboat *Jester* when he was overtaken by a fierce storm from the south-south-west. He writes:

How to handle a boat in extreme conditions is a matter for judgement and much will depend upon one's knowledge of how the boat behaves. Perhaps there are no hard and fast rules. In *Jester* I have never felt the need to tow warps, although I have often run before gales. Now, under self-steering, we were surfing down the slopes of heavy seas and the tops were beginning to fall off. My fear was that she might bury her head and pitch-pole. It seemed essential to slow the boat down. I carried on board a 5kg (11lb) Bruce anchor as a kedge, and since the Bruce is reputed to be hydrodynamically stable I reckoned it should tow like a paravane. Accordingly I streamed the anchor over the starboard quarter, on some 23m (75ft) of line, taking the end – with some difficulty, as one must crawl out to it – to the cleat. This immediately slowed the boat down to about half her speed and kept the stern nicely into the seas, preventing her from slewing about. So we spent the night of 9–10 July, the storm rising in violence and with a general situation of discomfort, but *Jester* well under control.

This report encourages an alternative to the use of very long warps during a storm.

Using drogues

Warps have several disadvantages. The warp, or series of warps knotted together, may need to be very long to provide enough drag and also to bridge a whole wavelength. Not every yacht carries enough line and, even if it does, the crew may not have the will and patience to handle a long length of rope in bad weather, and when the storm is over there is the dreary task of bringing the line back on board.

Much the same effect as that of a warp can be achieved by using a line in conjunction with a weighted drogue. A good drogue will provide the same drag as hundreds of feet of rope but, better still, it will provide strong resistance when the boat is tending to go too fast and disproportionately less when the boat slows down and is in danger of losing steerage way. Additionally, a suitably weighted drogue will operate clear of surface effects. Given the choice, a drogue is much more efficient, but allows less scope for fine-tuning and is more committing, as it is even more difficult to heave in than a long warp. Fuller details are in Chapter 7.

The disadvantage of any form of effective drogue is that it will hold the stern aggressively into the seas, increasing the chances of the boat being pooped. Centre-cockpit vessels are to be preferred when using drogues. It may be necessary to steer when using a drogue, but some vessels will be steered by an autopilot and a few others, particularly long-keeled yachts, will steer themselves with the helm lashed. As in the case of warps, there may come a point as waves mature when a drogue will give more hindrance than help and the boat is better off without. Alternatively, waves may develop so much that there is a risk that the yacht may pitch-pole, as happened to *Silver Shadow* in the Queen's Birthday storm of 1994 (Chapter

20). If the boat is of a type that does not heave-to comfortably, and there is a danger of pitch-poling, the options are to motor into the sea or deploy a parachute sea anchor.

Using parachute sea anchors

If running before a storm, perhaps using a drogue or warps, a point may be anticipated when the vessel is in danger of being pitch-poled, a lee shore is becoming an issue, or the crew is too exhausted to continue to steer. A remedy in these circumstances is to deploy a parachute sea anchor, and for some yachtsmen this tactic is now their first line of defence. The advantage of a correctly deployed parachute is that it will hold a yacht bows-on to the seas, and when struck by a breaking wave she will not be rolled or pitch-poled, however large that wave may be.

Of course it is not necessary for the situation to become desperate before deploying a parachute sea anchor, and it will be much easier to set it up before the storm breaks. There are plenty of recorded instances to be found in yachting magazines and in the *Drag Device Data Base* when a parachute sea anchor has proved to be an advantage. The parachute sea anchor has come of age, but for success a number of conditions have to be met. The parachute has to be the correct size and strong enough, and the parachute line has to be the right length and of the correct diameter. Moreover, all the components of the system including the securing points on the boat have to be solid enough to take the considerable load. Many people do not achieve a good deployment at their first attempt, and recovery can be difficult.

There are no half measures in the use of a parachute, but there are growing numbers of yachtsmen who, having successfully used a parachute, would not now be without one, in spite of the uncomfortable motion when the parachute is deployed. One variation, developed by the remarkable couple Lin and

Larry Pardey on lying head-to-wind and -sea on a parachute sea anchor, is to set up the parachute line at an angle using a snatch block on a pendant line led from aft. With a trysail or deep-reefed mainsail set, a boat can be much more comfortable than when the parachute is directly over the bow. Several accounts suggest that this method may take time to perfect and the technique appears to be most suitable for long-keeled yachts under 12.2m (40ft), such as the Pardeys' own yacht *Taleisin*. More information is to be found in Chapters 7, 19, and 21.

Using oil

There has never been any doubt that oil on troubled waters provides a calming influence. Some scientists attribute the mechanism to something called the 'Marangoni Effect'. A rider of probably academic interest is that a film of vegetable oil, which has a high elasticity, is said to work better than a film of mineral oil. However, there are precious few recent records of small craft using oil of any sort to their benefit during severe weather. It may be significant that whereas British lifeboats were fitted with a small tank of 'wave subduing oil' – a vegetable oil called Garnet 46 – the oil was seldom used, and modern lifeboats no longer carry it. We have the instance of HMS *Birmingham* using oil in the 1987 English Channel storm to assist a vessel in distress (Chapter 18). The captain had good reason to use it and the opportunity to study its effectiveness; in this case the oil could be seen to be working, but the problem was to position it so as to be useful. There is no doubt that oil can be a lifesaver in the right place.

A feature of many storm experiences is that crews are often forced to work through a variety of tactics as conditions worsen beyond previous experience, and it becomes obvious that something different has to be done. Instinct and improvisation come to one's aid, but we can be sure that the people who deserve to come off best are those who have the resolve to keep on top of the situation, who have chosen and thoroughly prepared their vessels and crews for heavy weather and, when necessary, have alternative measures in mind.

This book illustrates that there is no one answer to survival in heavy weather, yet there is a great deal that can be done to optimize one's chances. At the same time one must not forget Adlard Coles' words: 'No yacht, however sound, and no crew, however experienced, is immune from the dangers of the sea.'

STORM
EXPERIENCES

16

Santander Race storm

ADLARD COLES

OUR FIRST EXPERIENCE OF BEING caught out in *Cohoe* in open water in a severe gale occurred in the Santander Race gale of 1948. The last time I had been properly caught out was as far back as 1925, which goes to show that a real gale in summer time is a rare bird indeed.

Of British ocean races, the Santander is one of the most genuine. From the starting point at Brixham only once does one approach land, and that is when rounding Ushant, the most westerly point of France and an island of ill repute because of its strong tidal streams and off-lying reefs and rocks and the frequency of fog. For the rest, some 300 miles across the Bay, if the wind is westerly, one is for all intents and purposes racing in the Atlantic, in soundings of well over 2,000 fathoms (3656m).

As usual, *Cohoe* had a crew of three in total. Geoff Budden, a schoolmaster, came as astro-navigator, having learnt his craft as an instructor during the war. He was then new to offshore racing yachts, but settled down quickly, as he was an experienced dinghy sailor. As mate and cook I had my son, Ross, also a dinghy sailor, who had sailed with me in several previous ocean races. Watches were arranged in the usual manner, but in practice, with so small a crew, the duties and responsibilities overlap and we raced as a team, each ready to take over anything needed. There was precious little sleep for any of us.

In the three days before the race we were kept pretty busy as there were many things to see to, including provisioning. A small yacht may not make good more than an average of 100 miles a day, and less if she meets prolonged calms or gales. I reckoned we needed rations which could be stretched out to cover ten days in the event of the yacht being disabled or dismasted. Allowing half a gallon of water a day per man, we required about 68 litres (15 gallons). The main tank held 50 litres (11 gallons) and we had a 16-litre ($3\frac{1}{2}$-gallon) portable tank made to fit under the cabin sole.

The race was to start from the line of the Brixham Yacht Club at 1530 on Friday, 6 August. Thirty-one yachts were entered, including many of the well-known ocean racers. The morning's weather report was not good. A depression was moving in from the west and there was a southerly gale in the Bay of Biscay. Strong winds were probable, so nobody was under any illusions as to what might be expected.

The wind was light at the start, but soon freshened. For the first 24 hours the racing fleet beat westwards off the English coast. The night was thundery and squally. Several yachts retired, reporting 'Friday's gale', but if it was a gale it must have been very local, as we experienced nothing over force 6, but at 0300 on Saturday morning 7 August it was blowing hard. *Cohoe* was going like a train

202

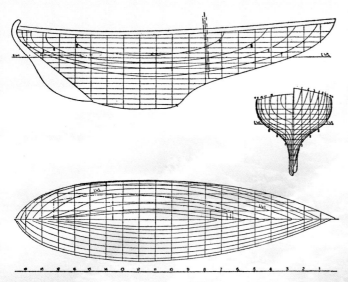

Cohoe. Lines and accommodation. LOA 32.1ft (9.78m), LWL 24.4ft (7.74m), Draft 5.2ft (1.58m) Displacement 3.5 tons (3556kg), sail area 362 ft² (33.6m²) Note the narrow beam and the balanced ends.

RIGHT *Cohoe 1*, 32ft (10m) light displacement, large Tumlare designed by Knud Reimers, winner of the Transatlantic Race, 1950. She is seen here with her 'false nose', the bow having been lengthened to qualify for the Bermuda Race. *Cohoe's* normal racing crew was three.
Photo: Morris Rosenfeld

ABOVE *Mehalah* hove-to after the Santander Race storm. The blow is over but the swell remains.

LEFT The stanchion of *Cohoe* uprooted in the Santander storm, and the jury runner.

BELOW The barograph trace from *Golden Dragon*. Notice the remarkably rapid fall in barometric pressure, which at about 8mb (hPa) per hour equals the extraordinary rate of increase in pressure during the Channel storm of 1987.

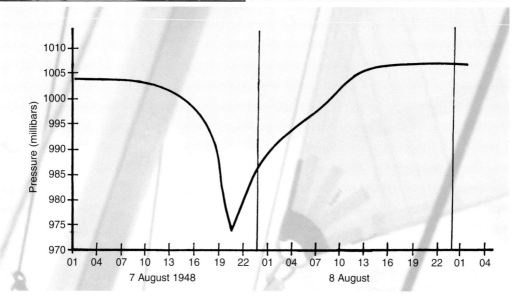

under genoa only, surprisingly carrying weather helm under this single sail. However, by 0730 the wind had moderated temporarily and we were once more under full sail. Later in the morning the wind backed and I noted the barometer had fallen 7 millibars since the start of the race. We stood close-hauled on the port tack and the best course we could lay was about south-west, which would take us some 30 miles west of Ushant.

During Saturday afternoon the wind freshened again. In view of the forecast and the long swell which was building up, I set about reefing again. At 1500 I double-reefed the main and at 1600 set the working staysail in place of the genoa. A little later the small jib was hoisted in place of the staysail and the storm jib hanked on the spare forestay and halyard. At 1730 we lowered the main-sail, ran it off its groove and lashed it down, and set the storm trysail and storm jib. At this time the wind was about force 6 and a fairly rough sea was running. The reefing and shifting of sails had been precautionary and in anticipation of events to come.

It is of interest here to look at the baro-graph readings of *Golden Dragon*, which are reproduced by courtesy of her owner, the late Mr H J Rouse. *Cohoe* was far astern of the Class II *Golden Dragon*, so the depression would have reached *Cohoe* an hour or two later. It will be seen that the slope steepens rapidly, 10 millibars in three hours, followed by an almost vertical 17 millibars within 2 hours. A secondary depression had formed northeast of Spain in the morning and had deepened and moved rapidly across the Bay of Biscay, though we were not to know it at the time.

It was shortly before 1800 that the wind increased to well above force 6, and this, cou-pled with the falling glass, the driving rain and the menacing conditions, decided me on reefing the trysail and bringing *Cohoe* down to storm canvas. At this time Geoff was at the helm, while Ross was below off watch. I was stand-by, and I pulled down the forward ear-ring of the trysail and made fast. Then in order to take the strain off the clew pendant I checked off the main sheet. Then I returned to the cabin top to swig in the after reefing tackle.

The next moment I found myself over-board. Fortunately as I fell I held onto the reefing tackle. I suddenly realized that Geoff was overboard, too, for I saw him floating aft, but hanging onto something. Meanwhile the yacht was well balanced between her storm jib and the trysail, which was checked right off. She was sailing herself on a 5-knot reach to the west.

At that instant, it being the 1800 change of watch, Ross had put his head on deck. His appearance was providential, for he was in time to haul aboard Geoff – whose position was precarious, as he had fallen in head first, and his head was being towed under water by the speed of the yacht. In some miracu-lous way he retained his grip on a lifeline which, with a stanchion, had gone over the side and was trailing in the water.

My circumstances were less pressing. I had managed to get a foot aboard and wedged it into some wire rope, presumably the runner. But, suspended between the reef-ing tackle at the outer end of the boom, which was checked off, and my foot at the other, my body was in the water and I was unable to extricate myself. Instead of putting my foot aboard I ought to have pulled myself forward along the tackle to the inboard end of the boom, but one does not think of these niceties at the time – so I was glad when I was pulled on deck again.

It had been a narrow shave, for both Geoff and I were wearing heavy oilskins. If we had lost our hold, there would have been but a slim chance of survival, as with the trysail half-reefed it is doubtful whether Ross could have manoeuvred single-handed in such a sea to find and pick up survivors (not wear-ing lifejackets). It is easy to make light of such incidents after all is over, but it was something little short of a miracle that there was no casualty. The incident resulted from an extra large sea catapulting both Geoff and me against the lifelines simultaneously. These collapsed under the impact of our combined weight as the after securing eye was torn from the deck, and one stanchion rooted out, taking with it part of the toerail.

All in all the damage was light. Geoff had lost his glasses and for some while he feared he had broken a bone in his hand. I had some nasty-looking scratches on my shin and ankle, which bled a bit. Ross probably came off worst, as it must have been a shock to come on deck and find he was alone with not a single man left on board, and a second shock when he saw us both in the water.

Once aboard I finished reefing the trysail (apart from the reef points which were not urgent) and then went below with Geoff to change into dry things, and to bandage my foot, leaving Ross at the helm, for it was now his watch. It is easy enough to talk of dry clothes, but after racing for 24 hours to windward there is often precious little left that is dry. Geoff had run out of clothes, but fortunately I had a reserve kitbag forward and Ross had a few spare dry garments. I donned winter pyjamas (what warm, comfortable things these are at sea), sailing clothes on top and oilskins over that. I felt like the well-known Mr Michelin of the inflated tyres.

Meanwhile the barometer was starting on its spectacular plunge and the wind increasing all the time. I decided to prepare for the worst and went back to join Ross on deck. We lowered the reefed trysail and storm jib and secured them.

For this race I had brought a sea anchor. To be of real value at sea one wants a sea anchor of very large dimensions, too cumbersome for stowage, but Cohoe's was a small one. It was sufficient only to satisfy the qualms of those who thought that Cohoe was too small to look after herself. However, I decided to experiment with it. To the sea anchor we bent 55m (30 fathoms) of nylon, and at the inboard end we parcelled the rope with cloth where it would lead through the fairlead before belaying it to a cleat and also to the mast for extra security.

First we experimented with the anchor in the conventional position forward. Here it did no good. The yacht continued to lie broadside

to the seas and the anchor lay away on the windward quarter. So we passed the nylon warp aft and made it fast. At the stern it had much the same result as is achieved by towing warps. It seemed to have a steadying effect, and the yacht lay with the seas broad on her quarter. She was perfectly happy, just like a cork, though, of course, the motion without steadying sails was wild in the extreme. At this time there was violent rain and hail. Then we went below, for there was nothing more we could do but reserve our energy for the race, when the gale had blown itself out.

Not long afterwards a Blue Funnel liner approached us closely, evidently desiring to offer assistance. Boats such as Cohoe are small from the point of view of a liner, and when lying under bare poles are often the object of investigation. During Cohoe's first two seasons, ships stood by on four different occasions, and, although their assistance was not required, the courtesy of the sea was appreciated. The liner steamed off, and soon Cohoe was alone again on the wind-swept seas. I looked at the barometer. It was falling faster than ever.

At nightfall I was confronted by the problem of lights. My big fisherman's oil light had been smashed in the Dinard Race, and it had not been returned from repair by the makers in time for the Santander Race. In any case I doubt whether it would have kept alight under such conditions. The same reasoning applied to the small anchor light I had brought as a reserve. It might not blow out, but, as I have pointed out before, oil lights rarely stand up to the shaking of a gale; it is the vibration rather than the wind which extinguishes them. Besides this I had a small electric all-round light. This I put up, but in the dense rain and spray I felt it was not enough, so I switched on the navigation lights as well, and exhibited a Powerlite electric lamp over the stern. The chances of being run down were small, for the English Channel approaches comprise a large area and ships tend to keep to the north or south.

I have often been asked what it is like in the cabin of a small yacht in a gale. I say

The Santander Race course took *Cohoe* past Ushant, where this photograph was taken, and the seas may have been similar to those that *Cohoe* experienced. Note the distant breaking sea to be seen on the left hand side of the horizon and the distant island of Ushant to the right of the ship.
Photo: Christian Février/Bluegreen

unhesitatingly that it is beastly. It is an experience nobody desires, but from time to time is unavoidable. To some extent it is frightening, for a severe gale is such a very violent thing that there is an instinctive apprehension. On the other hand, a yacht's cabin is an extraordinary haven of peace in hard weather compared with what it is like in the cockpit. The cabin lights swing in their gimbals, flooding the little compartment with light and warmth. One has companions to talk to.

When Geoff came off watch he expected to be stand-by for two hours and had taken the quarter berth so as to be within call from the cockpit. Quarter berths are the wettest in the ship, so Ross and I were lucky to have the cabin berths, one on each side of the saloon. The canvas leeboards were lashed up, so we could not be thrown out. Our principal discomfort was damp. Geoff had got wet again in the quarter berth when the companion door was opened and I went on deck to deal with the lamps. Ross and I got soaked when lowering the sails, and no more dry clothes were available. The cabin was wet, too, not from leaks, but from the water carried below by our clothes when Geoff and I changed after being thrown overboard, and from general condensation. Forward there was an occasional deluge of spray through the fore-

hatch, despite its canvas storm cover. Our cumbersome clothes added to the discomfort, especially the oilskins which we had to wear in case we should suddenly be needed on deck. Ventilation was not good either, as both ventilator cowls had been caught, lifted off the Dorade boxes, and flung overboard by the flogging jib sheets when tacking. We were, however, able to keep a lee porthole open, while the companion hatch was also kept ajar until the head of another sea descended upon the protesting Geoff.

The glass was still falling. It had fallen 34 millibars since we left Brixham, and the barograph record, which I was shown after the race was over, indicated a fall of over 22 millibars in 3 hours. At midnight the greatest fury of the gale fell on us. The wind and rain flattened the sea. The yacht heeled as though under full sail. On the deck above our heads blasts of rain hammered fiercely. I think then the wind shifted. How heavy the sea was I do not know, for the sea cannot be seen at night except for the flashing white phosphorescent crests. It was certainly violent and large. One exceptional wave woke us up later as it threw the yacht almost on her beam ends. Some said afterwards that the seas ran 'mountains high'. But as for the wind; it was the highest I had known up to then. If the reader examines the barograph readings he can judge for himself. With a gradient so steep as this, winds far exceeding gale force 8 are inevitable and the gusts may be anything.

In all this *Cohoe* behaved very well. The yacht was lifted bodily great heights in the air and then down she would go. Down, down and one tensed oneself for the crash, but at the bottom she never slammed, but gently came to rest before rising once more to the next. No seas broke over the coachroof or came aboard solid, but Ross said the self-emptying cockpit was often a foot or two underwater from heads of seas and driving spray.

By dawn on Sunday (8 August) the wind had moderated, but in *Cohoe*'s cabin conditions did not seem much quieter. For a while after a gale the sea is often more truculent than during its height. The yacht is no longer steadied by the wind and the motion is worse in consequence. At 0700 I got up. I felt amazingly well and refreshed, for I had had a good deal of sleep – more than we got at any other time in the race. I went forward through the cabin and tried the radio, as we wanted a weather report. It would not work. I tried various ways, but the only thing to do was take it into the cabin for drying out and testing. I unscrewed it and carried it aft. At that moment I suddenly began to feel seasick.

I handed the radio to Ross and lay down, feeling fit again at once. Ross played with its innards and inserted a new valve, but after sitting up he, too, suddenly felt ill. All of us were fit when lying down, but each felt seedy the moment we sat up and tried to do anything. Ross, however, dealt with the radio, alternately working on it and lying down when he felt sick. I decided not to make sail again until we got the 0800 weather report. The glass was rising, with a jump which might presage more bad weather. By 0800 Ross got the report, though feebly, having to press his ears to the instrument. The report was fair, but the past 24 hours was described as a 'vigorous depression with severe local gales in Biscay and the West Channel'. A severe gale is force 9, with a mean wind velocity from 41 to 44 knots.

Once the weather report had been received we immediately made sail. Geoff and Ross got *Cohoe* under way. The two of them heaved on the long warp leading to the sea anchor. Aware of the great strain imposed by a sea anchor without a tripping line, they heaved hard, and with remarkable success, for they got the nylon rope in hand-over-hand as if nothing were at its end. With the final heave they discovered the truth: there *was* nothing at its end. The sea anchor had gone in the night, and no one noticed any difference.

Before we had been long under way we sighted a sail. At one moment it would appear high in the sky and at the next it would be lost in a trough. The sea had gone down, but a lumpy swell was still running. As *Cohoe* drew near we fetched cameras and as we passed close under the yacht's stern we exchanged photographs; she was *Mehalah*, a Class III rival. Unfortunately, our arrival on the scene was the sign for feverish sail-making in *Mehalah* and she was quickly after us. We responded by setting more sail. As the morning drew on the wind softened and eventually *Cohoe* was under full sail again.

Meteorological conclusions

Let us now assess the gale. A depression was moving west towards Ireland and a vigorous secondary established itself in the early hours of Saturday morning north-west of Spain and crossed the Bay of Biscay, arriving off Brest at 1800, and continued across the English Channel approaches towards Plymouth. The centre of the low (which had deepened to 976 millibars) thus passed a little to the northward of the leaders of the ocean-racing fleet and directly across those in mid Channel, which included *Cohoe*, *Mehalah* and others hove-to near by.

In the Bay of Biscay, a number of fishing vessels were lost when running for shelter and there were casualties along the coast of Brittany. The gale was reported as one of the worst known in the Channel Islands. The *Isle*

Mountainous waves are not a problem as long as they do not break. *Photo: Lin and Larry Pardey*

of Sark, with 750 passengers, took shelter at St Peter Port, where even in the harbour six pleasure vessels broke from their moorings and were sunk. On the English coast many yachts and other vessels were in distress. Cross-Channel steamers reported their worst crossing of the year. As I have remarked, a severe gale is always recorded in the newspapers, but this particular gale featured as the leader on the front page of the *Daily Telegraph*, which devoted three columns to it, so great was the damage and loss.

The gale was reported in the newspapers as a 70 mph (61 knot) gale. Mr J S A Rendell (a former officer in the Clan Line) in a letter to *Yachting Monthly* in September 1966, stated that he had passed the yachts during the gale in MV *Stirlingshire* when homeward bound from Australia. If he remembered correctly, it was logged at force 11 (56–63 knots) at one stage.

I thought perhaps there might be an error in the recollection of the *Stirlingshire*'s log or that the entry related to gusts, but Alan Watts, a meteorologist, commented that 'it seems inevitable that the report of force 11 from the Clan liner was correct, even though … such wind strength could not have been sustained for long', and he gives barometric graphs in support of his opinion. The only evidence in the ocean-racing fleet came from *Theodora*, who recorded gusts of 60 knots on her anemometer, which were not necessarily the highest and were probably taken at deck-level, which gives a lower reading than 33ft (10m) aloft, which is the correct position for judging the wind on the Beaufort scale.

The only records that I have received from the Meteorological Office show hourly values of force 8 at Portland Bill and force 9 at Guernsey. These are coastal stations where winds are usually lower than at sea, and what is more, they were not in the direct track of the centre of the low.

Looking at the tight isobars on the synoptic charts, I think a fair assessment of the gale when it passed over the yachts was possibly force 10 (48–55 knots) or even force 11 during squalls. If this is true, the gusts might have been about hurricane force. I write with caution, because I frankly admit that I cannot judge wind strengths over force 8 or 9, as they are so few and far between, and in the general hubbub it is difficult to guess the mean speed on the Beaufort scale or to distinguish between gusts of 65, 60 or 55 knots. The latter is quite enough for me.

17

Short accounts of weather phenomena, 1983–1997

PETER BRUCE

WHEN ADLARD COLES STARTED TO write *Heavy Weather Sailing* in the 1960s he drew mainly from his own experiences because there were not many recorded accounts from small craft caught out in very severe weather at that time and the number of ocean going yachts then was tiny compared with today. Besides, when small craft were overtaken by extremely rough weather, there was often a scarcity of information from which comparisons could be made.

Corroborative weather information was not easily available and accurate anemometers were seldom fitted in yachts; so good information was probably lost through sailors not having enough solid facts on which to hang their account. Adlard Coles' collection of storm stories, based on corroborative information, gave the background to the thinking of 40 years ago or more. Knowledge of meteorology has moved on and so has instrumentation, so it is now much easier to quantify heavy weather in terms of wind speed and wave height than it was 40 years ago.

Continuing with Adlard Coles' own practice, a collection of brief accounts of heavy weather is given in this chapter, together with occurrences such as the effects of thunderstorms and waterspouts. These latter events, which are often short-lived, can be as life threatening as any normal storm.

Bill Cooper has an account of an extraordinary experience in the Bermuda triangle aboard his 58ft (17.7m) steel ketch *Fare Well* in June 1982. He, his disabled wife Laurel and a lady friend Nora had sailed from Bermuda heading for New England when they heard on the radio that Hurricane Alberta was coming their way. The forecast gave conditions in which 'elderly gentlefolk should not be at sea' but they had nowhere else to go. Having made relatively light work of the hurricane, happily quite distant, something totally unexpected and sinister then took place.

By the evening of 19 June we were hove-to under storm jib and very close-reefed mainsail. Our wind was averaging 40 knots with the gusts going well off the clock. I think the seas were about 15ft (4.6m). These conditions persisted all night; the average wind not rising much but the seas built up a bit, and I estimated 20ft (6m) in the morning watch. Each broadside wave shot a little jet of cold water through the perished rubber sealing of the deckhouse window onto the protesting form of Laurel in the stand-by berth. Otherwise all was dry and sound below. The yacht was behaving very well indeed. The decks were awash most of the time, but the high poop had only spray, and the cockpit, which is really a sheltered area at deck level, had received no green sea, but enough itinerant slosh to justify one storm board in the hatchway.

The storm centre was then reported to be in position 41°N, 66°W, some 170 miles away to the northwest, and probably the closest we came to it. Our position was based on DR, of course, for we had seen no sunshine for some time.

A feature of these violent and fast moving storms is that the advanced semi-circle has strong winds over a much greater radius. Behind the storm the radius was only 50 miles and conditions soon started to improve. The sea was slow to give up, but the wind moderated quite quickly. We tacked when reasonably sure the storm had passed, and headed 290°T, leaving our reduced sail up for the night.

When I took over the watch at 0400 on 20 June the wind had eased to force 4, but the seas were still considerable, though not dangerous. We rolled badly, and the main was not filling properly. I furled it, and decided to set the genoa and mizzen to get some way and stability. It was very dark, and raining heavily. There had been a couple of thunderstorms during the night producing moderate squalls: there was thunder about at that time, but nothing exciting.

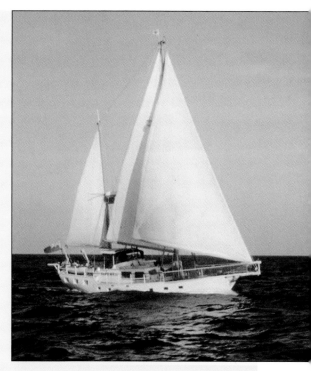

Bill and Laurel Cooper's *Fare Well*, which was thought to have encountered a waterspout at night. *Photo: Bill Cooper*

I had got the mizzen half-way up when I heard, rather than saw, what looked like a wall of very heavy rain approaching. In a second or two it arrived, rain of unbelievable intensity. I had been glad of our cockpit shelter, but it was of no help against this sort of rain, when even the splashes wet everything. Then the wind arrived before I had time even to move. It came across the few yards of water I could see, blowing the waves flat. It hit us an almost solid blow, and we were flung over to starboard; how far I cannot say for there was no point of reference, but certainly more than 90°, and I fell onto the starboard bench at the limit of my lifeline. While we were over, a sea broke and swept us, wresting the boom from the gallows, parting lashing and gaskets.

I scrambled up as the ship righted. The mizzen blew out. The main boom shook like a slipper in a puppy's mouth and, with a loud report, the 14oz (397g) main split and blew to shreds. The genoa, which had been rolled up, stretched in the wind and, without the core turning, allowed a few feet to unroll; the clew then blew out. My oilskin was ripped open; all buttons gone and the zip pulled apart.

As I tried to gather myself to deal with matters, I felt all the power to move leave me. I stood holding the leather-covered wheel feeling strangely euphoric as if being drawn steadily upward off my feet. The feeling went on and on as if time had stopped, and I could not breathe, though my lungs were full. I could not move at all.

Then the lightning struck. Instantly, tension disappeared. The whole space around the yacht seemed to be glowing but I had absolutely no sense of time. I was aware of Nora appearing in the hatch followed by Laurel, looking very white. Both had been rudely propelled from their bunks when the gust had heeled us over, and all the above had taken place as they scrambled to the deck, say 20 or 30 seconds. Laurel describes me as standing motionless at the wheel, mouth wide open, with water streaming down me as if I were standing under a waterfall. I had to be roused to move. Presumably I was in a state of shock.

The ladies turned to, and gradually I joined in, largely doing as I was told. Together we tamed the main boom, which had broken its gooseneck. When it was safely in the gallows we bundled together the collection of streamers that had been a mainsail. The mizzen was grappled in. The genoa was more of a problem. The sheets had slackened as the clew pulled out, and had tied themselves into a spaghetti knot so tight we could neither furl the sail, nor get it down its extrusion core. I did not fancy my chances half-way up the forestay at that time so we let it go.

There was big trouble in the engine room, and compass deviation went from zero to 90°W then slowly to 25°W, which only came to light through logging the direction of the swell. But what was it, apart from the lightning that struck the ketch at 0430 that morning? Bill Cooper now thinks that he encountered a waterspout. Presumably, it would have been the lightning strike that caused the magnetic anomaly. Details of the mechanism of tornados/waterspouts will be found in Chapter 8. Whilst it is too simplistic to describe a waterspout as a tornado at sea, there are many similarities.

A yacht race off Australia in 1983 will long be remembered for the loss of four yachtsmen who were drowned when their yachts sank. This was the JOG Tasman Cup on 15 April 1983 with a 44-mile overnight course from Sydney Harbour, south along the exposed coastline to a buoy off Port Hacking, and back. The forecast was for 20–30 knot south to south-west winds as well as southeasterly swell, giving a beat down to Port Hacking. It seems that the wind that materialized was much as forecast, but it created a secondary swell across the one from the southeast. In addition, there was a south-going current running offshore – locally known as the 'set' – and the whole combination created steep breaking waves.

The first yacht to run into trouble was the *Montego Bay*, a Hood 23 production boat with an experienced crew. After falling heavily off several waves she was found to be making water. The crew decided to abandon the race but, in spite of some spirited work with a bucket, the boat sank rather quickly. Just before this happened, they had succeeded in firing two flares but had obtained no acknowledgement from their Mayday transmission and were too late to reach their lifejackets in the cockpit locker. There seems to have been some confusion in the crew of the two boats of the fleet that saw the flares, as to whether there was a genuine emergency, and it was not until three hours later that a yacht returning to Sydney after abandoning the race happened to find two of *Montego Bay*'s crew in the water, and raised the alarm. Two more of the crew were picked up half an hour later, but a fifth man was never found.

Meanwhile another yacht of the same size, the Farr 727 *Waikikamukau* with a crew of four, had also sunk. She had been capsized by a particularly large breaking wave, and with no washboards in place, she had filled rapidly through her main companionway. The crew was attached to the boat with their safety harnesses, and one of them was unable to detach his safety harness before the stern of the yacht submerged and he was drowned. Another crewman had great difficulty in kicking off his sea boots which were hampering his ability to swim. None of the crew was wearing lifejackets, and the horseshoe lifebuoy stowed in the stern sheets of *Waikikamukau* had gone down with her. The three remaining crew quickly separated in the heavy seas and darkness.

In the end, there was only one survivor, who had to swim for ten hours before being picked up by a passing fishing boat. He reported that both helicopters and rescue craft, who were still looking for the fifth man from the *Montego Bay*, had repeatedly passed close by him, but had failed to spot him or hear his cries. He was spotted by someone who was leaning over the side of a fishing boat being seasick.

But for the warmth of the water, no one would ever have known what had happened to the two yachts and their crews, and there were several hard lessons to be learnt from the tragedy. The importance of lifejackets is clearly one of them. Another is the necessity of having washboards (or storm boards) in place in the main hatchway in big, breaking seas. Compliance with current regulations would probably have saved the lives of some or all of those lost. The ISAF regulations for category 3 races stipulate, for example, that lifejackets must have a light, and be worn between sunset and sunrise; safety lines must have a snaphook at each end.

There are dramatic local changes in the weather from good to bad that are seldom forecast, and sometimes are over so quickly that those who were not there often doubt their severity. They could account for a number of losses of vessels without trace in what seemed to have been benign conditions. For example, the British barque *Marques* was racing from Bermuda to Nova Scotia in 1984. At about 0800 she was 80 miles north of Bermuda in moderate weather when a hurricane force wind hit the ship 'out of the blue'.

She capsized and only those on deck survived, the remainder being trapped below. One of the explanations was that she was hit by a microburst, a localized down draught associated with a thunderstorm that struck at an angle of 45°. Thunderstorms were about that morning, though the *Marques* was apparently not particularly close.

A less distressing event took place in the South Pacific in February 1985 when an experienced Australian couple, Alan and Kathy Webb, with their 16-year-old daughter, Portia, were overtaken by a survival storm. Their heavily built 13.7m (45ft) steel cutter *Supertramp*, in which her owners had great confidence, had been designed for world cruising with a moderate fin keel, a skeg hung rudder and immense strength.

They arrived in the Roaring Forties with Easter Island 450 miles to the west and Chile some 1400 miles to the east (40° 20' S, 101° 37' W) to be confronted by a plummeting barometer and 80-knot winds that continued for 36 hours. The self-steering soon broke and Alan Webb was left to steer for the duration as *Supertramp* ran under bare pole in winds they estimated at force 12. Huge breaking seas developed, aggravated and confused by squalls. The Webbs make a practice of lying a'hull with the wheel lashed to windward in gales but in this instance Kathy Webb says it would have been impossible to heave-to as they would certainly have been capsized. Alan comments:

When running down waves of this extreme height, *Supertramp* developed too much speed, but by surfing down them at an angle, I found I could remain high on the crest and also take speed off the yacht. It was vital to keep her on top of the first tier, high upon the shoulder of the wave, by steering about 20° across its face rather than let the boat slip into the trough. We still stood a chance of being rolled over, but a slow roll-over would do much less damage than being pitch-poled at speed.

The Webbs have since wondered if they might have used their storm jib in the lulls to give steerageway, but conclude that their bare pole speed seldom dropped below four knots; for the rest of the time any sail would

have been too much. Perhaps a drogue/engine combination may have helped?

Several other interesting points came from the experience. Firstly, Alan Webb felt his beach surfing experience was helpful in negotiating the breaking seas. He was also assisted by the fact that *Supertramp* was extremely controllable under bare pole, and could even be gybed when lying a'hull. Another good feature of the boat was her centre cockpit with 10in (25cm) coamings and large diameter drain holes. Alan Webb

now has a smaller light displacement yacht and his comparisons with the two contrasting types can be found in Chapter 15.

Harry Franks had a slightly similar tornado cum waterspout experience to Bill Cooper in 1997 off Ushant in the 38ft (11.6m) Morgan Giles wooden sloop *Matawa*:

We were coming to the end of our summer cruise in *Matawa*, celebrating her 50th birthday that year. After a quiet night a little way up the river Elorn attached to a convenient buoy, we had taken the ebb out of the Rade du Brest and were heading for Ushant.

The wind was light and on our beam from the north and we were intermittently sailing and motoring, wanting to make Ushant in good time for a run ashore that evening. A few showers were threatened and there was some thunder about, but it looked like an uneventful sail as we passed Pierres Noir South Cardinal and headed for Pierres Vertes buoy. I was on the helm and the rest of the crew were variously loitering below, navigating, sleeping, reading etc. We had the engine on to help us to windward as the land breeze that had helped us out of the Rade had given way to the forecast northerly. To starboard the rather jagged rocks of Les Pierres Noir were coming and going in the poor visibility but we were well clear of them and to leeward.

I was idly wondering what the likelihood of a lightning strike on our metal mast was as

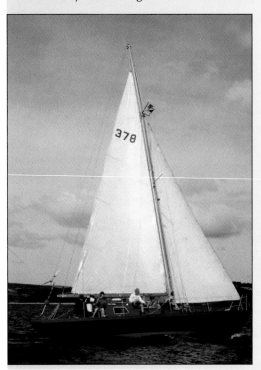

Matawa is a traditional 38ft x 9ft x 6ft (11.6m x 2.7m x 1.8m) yacht designed by Morgan Giles and built of plywood by Cardnell Bros in 1947. *Photo: Peter Bruce.*

the thunder rolled around us when suddenly 'BANG', over we went as a massive gust hit us. For a moment I had that frightening feeling, remembered from dinghy sailing in times past, that we were going to go right over as I hung on desperately to avoid being pitched over the lee rail. Thankfully, *Matawa* did the right thing and slowly came into the wind, giving me the chance to check sheets. Down below, Henry on the windward bunk had been thrown across onto Michael junior on the leeward one and Tim, in the forepeak, was sure we were going to capsize. With the wind came torrential rain and much reduced visibility and we were now, it seemed to me, being driven towards the rocks.

Fortunately Mike senior had recovered from the initial shock quickly, thrown oilskins on and was soon on deck. The first priority was to lower the foresail and this we soon managed though, as I checked away the foresheet, I had a glimpse of the comprehensive shredding of the sail, fortunately not a new one. We were still out of control and the wind seemed to be turning us around like a top, the sea flat but stirred by

Thundery squall. White breaking sea can be seen under the right hand cloud indicating that the squall has much wind as well as rain. The presence of a strong wind in a squall is rarely so obvious. *Photo: Christian Février/Bluegreen*

driven wavelets. By this time Tim was also on deck and we had hands to lower the main; those rocks looming in the mind closer by the second as we were driven onwards. Down came the main and I finally began to feel that I had some control, thankful that the engine was still on. I steered due south as gradually the wind subsided and the rain eased off from its frantic pelting. Soon, and with much relief, the rocks appeared still to north of us – I half expected us to have been driven past them! Fifteen minutes later we had the main up again, soon after that the number 2 genoa, and we were able to get back on our old course.

One hour later we were at anchor in Lampaul. We did however notice that one or two other boats had their oilskins out to dry which reassured us that we had not been hallucinating. The whole episode had only lasted half an hour at the most.

In retrospect, I suspect that we had experienced a tornado-cum-waterspout. This is surely why I had the impression of being driven at will through all points of the compass while we reduced sail. What warning had we had of such an 'event'? The navigator says that he had noticed the sky going dark; but obviously not dramatically enough to mention it to me. I suspect that I had not noticed it because I was wearing dark glasses. More important was our mind set; we had had two weeks of calms and light airs and, perhaps out of ignorance, associated thunderstorms with drenching rain and calm wind. I shall know better for the future. Fortunately, the only damage was to the sail, because that sort of experience really tests the seaworthiness of a yacht, not only the rigging but how well things have been secured above and below decks after weeks when the most extreme motion we had experienced was the wash of passing trawlers.

This alarming experience is again notable for the sudden arrival in thundery weather of storm force wind, accompanied by unusually heavy rain. It was noteworthy that *Matawa* was out of control and being turned by the wind like a top.

Sandy Gilbert, with *Magnum Opus* in the Mediterranean, sailing between Majorca and Minorca, tells a story of how, with a distant thunderstorm in sight, his boat was hit by a squall of tremendous violence, later accompanied by hail, which ripped to shreds the only sail that was left set. The boat would not respond to the helm and was circling. A catamaran's crew in the same situation not far away reported that they had also spun round and round. In one yacht nearby, a man went overboard, and in another the main sheet would not release under its load and the fabric of the mainsail had to be cut to prevent a capsize. Of quite a large number of yachts in the area, almost all reported an initial severe knockdown.

The event is similar to Harry Franks' tornado cum waterspout, in that the wind arrived with remarkable suddenness and strength, boats were spun round, and it was all over in half an hour. The forecast of easterly force 4 would not have accounted for such strong winds, estimated to have been force 12, and the explanation seems to have been that the thunderstorm brought about a precipitation down draught, a microburst, which turned into a tornado.

Finally there is another account of a large US cruising yacht in the Bahamas torn from her berth when hit by a waterspout, breaking off two marina piles in the process. The owner, who said the noise was like an underground train at speed, saw a motor bicycle lifted into the air from the jetty, and when last seen it was ascending at an angle of 45°. His steel foredeck ventilator weighing 91kg (200lb) was found half a mile away.

Accounts of vessels being hit by waterspouts, which can be between 15–46m (50–150ft) in diameter, are rare, though waterspouts are known to have caused great damage when they have come ashore. It is rare but not unknown for a waterspout to form in the early morning as happened to *Fare Well*.

Clearly thunderstorms (even when distant), tornadoes and waterspouts at sea can be dangerous and should be avoided if possible. The noise of thunder, anvil-shaped clouds combined with dark low-level cloud or an actual waterspout may be as much warning as one may ever have. The good seaman should adopt practices that will withstand sudden adverse weather and be ready for an intense squall whenever thunder is about.

The events described in this chapter, in most cases, were not expected and the crews were operating from their normal level of preparation.

The harrowing story of the JOG Tasman Cup is, perhaps, the most instructive. The yachts that sank were close to land, close to other yachts, and experiencing rather less heavy weather than in most of the accounts in this book. Chances to save the situation were missed. Accidents often result when insufficiently strong action is taken in the early stages of an adverse situation. We need to remember Admiral Nimitz's words about precautions at the beginning of Chapter 6, 'The time for taking all measures for a ship's safety is while able to do so'. We need to ask ourselves whether we can be sure that, in the same circumstances, our own standards of seamanship would have prevented loss of life. For example, why was it that other yachts did not respond to the distress flares from the *Montego Bay*? Aboard *Montego Bay*, in the rush of activity, would we have had the presence of mind to say firmly 'it's time to put on lifejackets, boys' before it was too late? Would we, in *Waikikamukau*, have insisted upon washboards being fitted in the companionway?

Assuming some fundamental error has occurred, will our remedies that are required as a result do the job? As Chay Blyth so rightly says: 'Hope for the best: but prepare for the worst'.

A waterspout 3 miles out of Newport Harbour, California. It formed after a tremendous thundery storm front had passed. *Photo: Blake Dragonlord*

18

Channel storm of 1987

PETER BRUCE

THERE WERE SEVERAL SMALL VESSELS at sea during the great storm of October 1987, but with massive destruction ashore, both on the north coast of France and the south coast of Britain, little has been heard about them. The intense small depression brought winds of over 100 knots to the English Channel area, and though the wind speed was of hurricane strength, it is wrong to describe the event as a hurricane. It was a storm, albeit a truly violent one, but not a tropical revolving storm.

October is late in the year for leisure sailing, but the sea water temperature is still warm; so there are still a few sailors who go out for pleasure at this time. Moreover, delivery trips continue all through the year, and the Joint Service Sailing Centre yachts, based at Gosport, have a long season. Thus, with manageable conditions during the day, and without a warning of ultra-severe weather made manifest, it was not surprising that several yachts were still out at sea on the night of Thursday 15 October. A small fleet of warships from Portland naval base were also at sea for the opposite reason. In very strong winds, ships at anchor can drag onto the shore even in Portland Harbour, and as a result of a timely warning from the senior meterological officer there, Lieutenant Commander Peter Braley, who had made his own interpretation of the impending weather, the Portland fleet was ordered to sea.

Five descriptions from the sailing vessels at sea in the storm are related in this chapter, to give a wide cross-section of experiences; but before the accounts from the sea, there follows a meteorological report by Peter Braley.

Meteorology

As early as the weekend of 10–11 October 1987, the Meteorological Office at Bracknell had been forecasting severe weather on the following Thursday and Friday.

At midnight on Tuesday 13 October, the depression in question was centred near 50°N 47°W, off Newfoundland, tracking east. It was expected to deepen progressively by midnight on Thursday 15 October, after which explosive deepening was predicted, with storm force winds expected in the South Western Approaches during Thursday, and moving up Channel and into the North Sea overnight. The prediction was reinforced and updated at 1545 on Wednesday 14 October, when the low had begun to move rapidly east. The storm warning suggested that the centre could be expected to be 150nm north-west of Cape Finisterre by 0600 on

Thursday 15 October, with winds in its southern quadrant expected to reach storm force 10 up to 200nm from the centre. The low was then predicted to curve north-north-east to bring south-west storm force winds to the east Channel and southern North Sea areas late on 15 October.

The development became noticeable to meteorological authorities throughout Western Europe after midnight on 14–15 October. At that time, an elongated trough was located over a distance of some 500nm westwards from Cape Finisterre with two apparently distinct depression centres – one 983mb (hPa) just north-west of Coruña, the other about 986mb (hPa) near 43°N 19°W, some 450nm farther west. A strong pressure gradient existed on the warm southern side of the frontal trough, but with a slack gradient on the cold side. Noticeable potential temperature differences across this front were apparent from the few available observations, suggesting a sharp differential between the polar maritime and tropical maritime air masses. By midday on 15 October this broad surface trough lay from Brittany across Finisterre, and pressure in the trough was falling markedly. By 1800 the axis of the surface and upper troughs had extended north-east, bringing the frontal feature across the Channel and into southern England. The two centres were still apparent, one over Ushant, and the other now more vigorous centre of 963mb (hPa) near 45.5°N 8.5°W. Surface pressure continued to fall within the trough but, more significantly, marked rises in pressure had occurred over the previous six hours both south-west of the main centre and astern of the cold front, with corresponding increases in wind speed. At about 2100, a signal was received at Portland from the forecaster in RFA *Engadine* in the north Biscay area, drawing attention to the sudden falls in pressure in his vicinity, thus suggesting explosive deepening of the Biscay centre. The signal also remarked upon the pronounced cross-sea and swell conditions. Soon afterwards the centre passed close to *Engadine* and winds rose rapidly in strength, occasionally to exceed 90 knots.

Thus by 2100 the depression centre had tightened considerably and begun to move rapidly north-east at about 40 knots to deepen to about 960mb (hPa) in the extreme south of sea area Plymouth. The trend continued towards midnight when a centre was indicated just south of the Eddystone with a central pressure nearing 952mb (hPa). Notably, this feature was now a single, definable centre. A clear and fairly accurate track became discernible, making short-term forecasting and timing somewhat simpler and more certain. These, together with surface analyses, demonstrated the exceptional pressure gradients now developing in a narrow swath to the south and east of the centre, with surface gusts exceeding 100 knots in exposed locations.

During the next six hours the centre of the depression moved in a north-easterly direction across England after crossing the coast between Charmouth and Lyme Regis at about 0215. By 0500 on 16 October it had reached Lincolnshire and the occlusion had swung rapidly across southern England. Very marked rising pressure tendencies were widespread in the three hours from 0300 to 0600 as the depression filled: for example, +25.5mb (hPa) at Portland. This later rise has now been established, by a comfortable margin, as the greatest three-hourly pressure change ever to be recorded in the UK.

Retrospective examination of meteorological records has been extensive, but it may be of interest to draw attention to a few facts:

1 The band of strongest gusts, with isolated maxima over 100 knots, extended across the Channel areas from north-west France in a band some 90 miles wide, parallel to the track of the depression centre.

2 Gusts of 70 knots or more were reported for a period of three to four consecutive hours, during which time the wind veered from 180° to 230°.

3 A double-peaked wind speed region apparently occurred over central southern England and the adjacent Channel coast. The first was associated with winds from 170° and 190°; the latter from a direction of around 230° – the peaks being at around 0200 and 0500 respectively.

4   A separate area of strong northerly winds affected Cornwall and North Devon from 2300 on 15 October until about 0200 on 16 October.

5   The strongest gust over the UK was recorded at Gorleston (Norfolk): 106 knots at 0424. Over 20 other gusts in excess of 90 knots were recorded between 0400 and 0715. A higher gust was estimated at 119 knots at a station near Quimper on the Biscay coast, while a gust measuring 117 knots occurred at 0030 at Granville on the south-west corner of the Cherbourg peninsula.

6   The passage of the cold front heralded the onset of the really strong winds at the surface. It was the strength of mean wind speeds that was noteworthy, rather than individual gusts.

7   The pressure falls ahead of the advancing depression were large but not remarkable, yet the subsequent rises in pressure appear to have been exceptional. Large areas of south England experienced rises in excess of 8mb (hPa) per hour.

8   While very marked, short and steep seas built up in the Channel, recorders show that no remarkable storm surge followed and no pronounced swell developed due to the short duration and small size of the maximum windfield.

Figure 18.1 The charts show two months of wave data recorded at the Channel lightvessel in 1987. This includes the very severe storm of October, and also the one in March of the same year. Though the intense, fast-moving system of October 1987 caused havoc on land, it was not around long enough to create exceptionally high waves, unlike the very large depression of the March storm.

A Sadler 34 off Ushant

The first sea account comes from a new shoal-draft Sadler 34 called *Muddle Thru*. She had been bought by a Canadian, Allan McLaughlan, who had come over to Poole in Dorset, England, from Ontario with two other Canadians, Harry Whale and Bill Bedell, both of long sailing experience, to take delivery of his boat and sail for the Caribbean.

They set out on 13 October 1987, but progress towards Ushant was very slow due to strong head winds, and the boat was 'caught out' 60 miles to the north of Ushant in the 100–120 knot winds of 15–16 October.

The persistence of *Muddle Thru*'s crew was enhanced by the fear that VAT might have to be paid on the boat if she was to return to the UK. After the great storm, another gale came, and this time the boat was rolled through 360°. The effects of the capsize, which included a broken lower shroud, caused Harry Whale, the skipper, to head back to Falmouth, where, incidentally, HM Customs took a benevolent VAT view in the circumstances. Harry Whale kept a log of events by speaking into a tape recorder, and it is his account of the storm that follows:

Winds increased to force 9 from the west-south-west during 14 October; and though close-hauled and carrying only a deep triple reefed mainsail, we made fairly good progress in almost the right direction. To keep a proper lookout was difficult because one could never be sure in the dark if we were looking towards the horizon or merely into yet another big wave. Certainly we did see many ships and made every effort to stay well clear, believing that under the prevailing conditions we were probably invisible, despite the radar reflector on the mast.

By about 0300 on 15 October the wind had abated enough for us to add some foresail to the sailplan and, after experimenting with the furling genoa, we rigged the detachable head-stay and hanked on a small flat jib. The rest of the day was spent in heavy rain, crashing along into force 7 wind, heading south-west by south. In the afternoon the wind ceased quite suddenly and, after an hour or so, came in from the opposite direction, north-east. It then rapidly built up to force 7 again. Under jib only we were soon making splendid time directly towards our destination with a following wind, but meeting the waves that were still coming from south-west. Some waves we seemed to jump over and others we went through; nevertheless, it was good finally to be able to make our course at a respectable speed. Suddenly the turn at Ushant didn't seem so far away.

The run continued until 2100 when the wind died completely for half an hour. It then came in from the south, quickly built up, and veered to the south-west. By midnight we had taken off all sail and were lying a'hull. On the tape I said 'we are in a shocking blow'. Having experimented with the helm and the wind vane steering, I finally came to the conclusion that the boat took the best attitude to wind and waves when left to its own devices with the wheel lashed amidships and the wind vane disconnected. I feel sure this was largely due to the spray-hood and its considerable windage, which had the effect of keeping the bow into the weather.

Having seen several east-bound ships I was concerned about traffic in the area. We had heard the traffic controller at Ushant speaking to another vessel on VHF radio. I called to inform him that we were lying a'hull and virtually at the mercy of wind and sea, so suggested a *securité* call to vessels in the vicinity. This he did very obligingly, giving our position, estimated drift and course. He also told me that his wind gauge indicated wind speed ranging from 100 to 120, and that he was concerned for the safety of his radar. I did not think to ask if the wind speed given was in nautical miles, statute miles or kilometres per hour. It seems now that they were knots. Psychologically I think all of us on board felt better for the exchange, especially when he called an hour or so later for an update on our position. I provided this, and mentioned that we had noticed two or three west-bound ships passing to the north of us. I was impressed by the fact that he wanted to know how our position was obtained. By now we were starting to hear parts of one-sided conversations on the VHF and realized that something pretty major was going on by the number of distress calls, including a Mayday from a yacht in a French port. Two other conversations I remember involved one vessel that had been driven hard aground, and another that had lost its steering.

Generally, our little boat seemed to be handling things very well, although the noise of the wind and the waves breaking over the vessel was extreme and the motion quite erratic. Occasionally the boat would seem to get temporarily turned broadside onto the waves and a great thumping one would hit her full on the beam. The furling jib was tightly wound about its stay, the small hank-on jib tightly lashed to the toe rail, and the mainsail lashed to the boom. A small part of the mainsail got free and proceeded to thrash so wildly that I felt sure the sail would end in tatters, and possibly even strain the rigging. Having determined that the loose part of the sail was below the second reefing point and therefore most of the sail should survive, I decided to let it flog rather than risk a man or two overboard trying to retie it to the boom, which would involve working around the sprayhood where the holding was least secure. As it turned out, the sail fared well, though the battens were lost.

The three of us remained fully dressed in foul weather gear and harnesses; we spent our time below with just a brief check on deck every 15 to 20 minutes. With so much water constantly coming onboard the boat, one had to be careful about the timing when opening and closing the main hatch.

Eventually, at about 0730 on 16 October, the wind abated sufficiently to start sailing again. We had gingerly worked our way up to a double-reefed main and small jib by 1400, and even had glorious sunshine for three hours. We were visited by some dolphins, and though still on a dead beat, we generally felt very fortunate to be in such good overall conditions as we listened to the radio telling of the damage done during the night both at sea and ashore. At 1600 more gale warnings were broadcast – force 8 going to force 9 from the south-west. For the next 13 hours we made good course of west-north-west at an average speed of $3\frac{1}{4}$ knots.

During 17 October the wind direction varied from south-west to west-south-west and we tacked accordingly, always mindful of giving Ushant a wide berth. By 2200 we were again down to bare pole in a raging gale, this time with mainsail lashed very tightly to the boom and the outboard end of the boom lowered and lashed to the toe rail. Once again I experimented with the wind vane steering and various positions of the helm, but came to the same conclusion as before – to lash the wheel amidships and allow the boat to take care of itself. From our perspective the main wave pattern was from the south-west; however, we seemed to be constantly under attack from quite unpredictable waves from the south-east and north-west. Some of these seemed to be not so much waves as just great eruptions of water, happening without rhyme or reason.

As before, we huddled below fully dressed in foul weather gear and harness trying to cat-nap, with a check on deck every 15 to 20 minutes. I suppose this continued for three or four hours. I was lying down in the starboard bunk and had dozed off nicely when suddenly I realized I was airborne and on my way across the cabin, easily clearing the lee cloth and table en route. I came up short against the other side of the boat on top of Bill. As I scrambled around trying to extricate myself I remember enquiring after Al, who had been using the quarter berth. He spoke up from underneath me saying that he was OK. He had given up the quarter berth and rigged himself an accommodation on top of some cans of water we had lashed into place in the U of the dinette settee and was wedged between Bill and the folding table. About this time I heard 'we're upside down, boys' from Bill in a quite conversational voice – indeed, almost a mumble.

By use of the two full-height teak pillars that the Sadler has in the vicinity of the galley and chart table, I was able to heave myself over the galley sink and, by the time the boat was completely inverted, I was standing on the deckhead holding onto a pillar with each hand, facing forward, with my back to the engine compartment and the main hatch boards.

The exact sequence of events and time involved is of course very uncertain, but I do have a vivid recollection of standing there and being aware that the noise and motion had ceased, other than the sound of water rushing in through various small openings; I was expecting at any moment to be struck from behind by the hatch boards collapsing inwards under the pressure. It was as well that Bill had insisted that the cockpit locker lids be well secured.

As the boat continued its roll-over I remained clinging to the pillars, negotiating them rather like climbing a large two-rung ladder that is being rotated. As the boat resumed its normal upright position several impressions struck me; one was the resumption of the old noise and motion, another was the additional sound of water sloshing back and forth; and the most disturbing was what I can only describe as a 'wobbly' feeling about the boat. Several explanations flashed through my mind, the first being that maybe we had sustained some sort of a longitudinal hull fracture – yet there didn't seem to be much water coming in. Then I wondered if the keel had loosened, but discounted this thought on the grounds that surely it would have gone entirely or not at all, and since we seemed to be remaining right way up, the keel must still be in place. The only possibility was that the hull was being wrenched around by a loose rig.

My first resolve was to try the diesel engine. This would enable us to run the electric bilge and shower pumps, and also provide motive power should we need it. When we tried the switches we got the whistle of the Calor gas alarm. We waited for some time and it didn't stop. Because the alarm had acted strangely on another occasion, and because we had always been careful to turn off the supply, I felt sure this was a false alarm, at least as far as the Calor gas was concerned. We turned off the alarm and gave the engine a try. It started. Now to check the rig.

Getting on deck to investigate was no easy matter. The sprayhood, with its stainless steel framework, was crushed down over the main sliding hatch and the hatch boards. Eventually Bill and I both got through, and discovered with the help of a small torch that the port lower shroud was loose. Bill bravely went forward and took a jib halyard one turn around the mast and attached it to a stanchion base near the chain plate. He then did the same within the main halyard so that we now had the two halyards running from the spreader roots to the stanchion base. From the cockpit we did our best to sweat up these halyards, no easy matter without winch handles, which had left their pockets during the roll-over. Having thus more or less stabilized the rig, we proceeded to haul inboard sheets, halyards, and other odds and ends all hanging over the port side of the cockpit.

Below, Al had been doing his best to assist the bailing process by trying to pour water into the sink with a saucepan. The outlet was not very big and sometimes, because the motion was so violent, the water was flung back at him before it had a chance to drain away. However, we certainly seemed to be holding our own because the water level was not much above the cabin sole. Bearing in mind that a large part of the volume of the bilge was taken up by canned food and built-in flotation material, the actual volume of water aboard could not have been great.

We found that the shower pump was not operating, and only one of the interior lights was working. All of the electronics except the satnav had ceased to function, ie radios, windspeed and direction, log, speedometer and depth sounder. Our spectacles, charts, dividers, hand compass, torches and spare winch handles seemed to have vanished into the heap of sodden mattresses, tools, clothing and sundry other items.

Figure 18.2 The approximate track of *Muddle Thru,* October 1987.

I decided that the prudent course of action was to make for Falmouth. I thought of Moitessier and Vito Dumas, who advocated that the best way to survive in heavy breaking waves was to sail with them at good speed.

Because I had stared at the chart for so many hours before the incident, I knew the course was about 050°. Before shoving the gear shift into forward I tied a huge knot in the furling line of the jib, gauged to stop at the fairlead. Thus about 1.8m (6ft) of it and no more could be let out in a hurry by one man, should the engine stall and force us into taking a chance on the rig.

We were off on the wildest sleigh ride of my entire sailing career. In the cockpit it was impossible to hear the engine over the roar of the wind and water, and there were no gauges of any kind to indicate rpm or boat speed. The main compass seemed to be working, though a little sluggishly. It was strictly seat of the pants stuff, aided sometimes by the vibration of the engine and propeller through the soles of the feet. The boat was completely overwhelmed on several occasions, leaving the helmsman spluttering and gasping for breath. It was the blackest of nights, and I remember thinking it would be so much better once daylight arrived.

When daylight did finally arrive I wished it had remained dark. It was an impressive scene, huge steep breaking waves everywhere and the air filled with water, either rain or spume. At one point some dolphins came along to join in the fun. Like young skiers on a mogul run they cavorted and frolicked around us, frequently leaping right out of the advancing face of the waves. Never did I feel so out of my element as I cowered at the wheel, tired and afraid, while admiring their wonderful performance. About the time I was beginning to worry about fatigue and hypothermia, Bill squeezed his way out of the hatch and offered to take over. This was a great relief to me, first, because I needed the break, and second, it meant that Bill was now endorsing my strategy of heading for Falmouth, albeit tacitly. I am sure he was originally not in favour.

Later, Al also came up to be initiated and join the watch roster. Time and again it would seem she was about to broach, and be rolled over in a breaking crest; yet at the last minute a little extra power would straighten her out and away we'd go, surfing down yet another huge wave, only immediately to worry that the bow could bury and cause a pitch-pole. Bill was to tell me much later that, at one point when he was steering, the boat did a complete 360° turn (horizontally this time); she seemed, he said, to sail close around a great pinnacle of water, with a cliff face on one side of the boat and a precipice on the other.

About 1900 in the failing light, the loom of the Lizard light showed 10 miles to the north-north-west. The satnav had done a splendid job for us. Now, without tidal information or depth sounder, came the task of piloting our way the remaining 20 or so miles to the harbour. As it turned out, everything went well: and the wind and waves even abated a little as we came into the lee of Manacle Point and the Manacle rocks. The limited information we had on board showed the harbour entrance and not much else. We shot through the entrance, did a sharp left turn, and suddenly all was tranquil, relatively speaking anyway.

This Bay of Biscay roller is to be reckoned with if approaching anywhere near this long lee shore. As it was in the October 1987 storm, waves, though high, never had time to develop to extremes. *Photo: Yvan Zedda/Bluegreen*

A Swan 46 in the Bay of Biscay

Had *Muddle Thru* made Ushant and into the Bay of Biscay, she would not have had a much easier time, as can be appreciated from another drama going on 215 miles south-south-west of Ushant. On the morning of 15 October a Swan 46 fitted with a Scheel keel, on passage to Spain, hove-to in wind speeds shown on the yacht's Brookes & Gatehouse anemometer of, at times, over 85 knots. Apart from periodic lookouts, the crew of four remained below, where it was dry. At 1800, without warning, the boat rolled quickly to port through 360°. Floorboards, and everything stored under them, flew through the boat. The yacht's owner, who was standing in the main cabin after returning from a lookout on deck, broke a shoulder. The mast broke at deck level, probably due to a lower shroud failure.

The mast remained attached to the boat by her intact rigging and, without suitable cutting devices on board to cope with rod rigging, the crew were unable to cut it free.

Around 2000 the mast broke at two other points and started to pound against the hull. At this juncture the owner decided to ask for outside assistance, and an EPIRB was activated. The Swan 46 was 'localized' in 45 minutes, and a Japanese freighter appeared on the scene at 0100 in the morning of 16 October. The freighter launched a boat, but this soon capsized; so the yacht, with her engine still working, was asked to go alongside. While the crew were disembarking, the yacht was smashed several times against the freighter's hull, and at one point she surfed down a wave and struck the freighter at full speed with her bow. Though the EPIRB was heard for an hour afterwards and hatches were left closed, the yacht was never found.

A significant point in this episode was the difficulty experienced in detaching the mast. Bolt croppers will not cope with heavy rod rigging: only hydraulic cutters or other special tools will do the job.

Rescue seen from a destroyer bridge off Portland Bill

But for the seamanship of the rescuers, another craft might have been lost that night. The story is a little bizarre, and is best told by the captain of HMS *Birmingham*:

Cdr Roy Clare (now Admiral) a most experienced yachtsman. The vessel was a modern gas-turbine powered destroyer, carrying a Lynx helicopter on board:

HMS *Birmingham* was operating 7 miles south-west of Portland Bill, turning endless circles on the calibration range. At about 1800 on 15 October my navigator showed me the latest Mufax weather chart, with isobars tightly packed over the Brest peninsula. I commented that I was glad we weren't farther south, and forgot about the weather. We did not see Michael Fish, the weather forecaster, on TV that evening.

At about 0115 I was nearly thrown out of my bunk by an unusually heavy roll. I called the officer of the watch on the intercom to find out what he was up to; he answered at once, saying that the weather had suddenly freshened and that he had just heard a call on VHF for help from a yacht ... would I come to the bridge?

I quickly established that the yacht was in touch with Portland Coastguard. Her position was some 18 miles south of me, about 24 miles from the Bill. Our weather conditions were wind: south-south-west force 8–9; visibility 6 miles, less in drizzle. We set off on a course of about 200° at 22 knots; this was the maximum we could do in the prevailing conditions.

We pitched heavily in the steep seas, but there was only a modest swell and we did not thump at all.

Meanwhile the yacht transmitted frequently on VHF, using Channel 67, as directed by the Coastguard. I put an experienced yachtsman on the circuit to give an informed point of contact. We started an incident log book, told the naval operations room we were proceeding to assist, kept in touch with the Coastguard, established that the Royal Fleet Auxiliary tanker *Black Rover* was also in the area, and made basic preparations on board for search and rescue. Flying was out of the question; the sea state was worsening rapidly and the wind limits for helicopter operations would have been exceeded unless we had been heading out of the wind at some speed. This was clearly undesirable; in any case, the ship's Lynx helicopter was not equipped for night search and rescue over a small object like a yacht, so it would only have been able to aid the search, not the rescue. Ashore, the coastguards decided that the Weymouth lifeboat should be called out. I do not know whether the shore-based search and rescue helicopter was considered; in my view, it would have been of very marginal value in those conditions. In the event, search was not necessary; location was straightforward, aided by a reasonable position report in the first instance, and by continuous VHF transmissions from the yacht, which were DF'd by the Coastguard stations at Portland Bill and Berry Head to give a cross bearing fix.

By 0150 we had established that the yacht was a cruising multihull of 12m (40ft) length. The vessel was in no immediate danger of foundering, had sustained no damage, and was managing to make way across the wind at about 4 knots on a westerly course apparently bound for Ushant. The crew sounded terrified; they were pleading to be taken off their craft, urging rescuers to hurry before dire things happened. It seemed that there had been a difference of opinion as to whether to continue or turn back. The yacht was said to be shaking violently in the gusts and the voice was convinced that each moment was to be his last. In the background of each transmission, it had to be admitted, there was a fearful noise of wind in rigging and crashing waves. We did our best to reassure and console the yacht, keeping the crew informed of our progress.

By 0215 we were down to about 15 knots. The sea state was rising high, the wind gusting 75 knots. Visibility was down to a mile or two. *Black Rover* and *Birmingham* arrived on the scene at about the same time – 0245 approximately. Between us we manoeuvred to windward of the yacht, whose lights were clearly visible in the driving spray.

Black Rover kept pace with the catamaran and provided a solid breakwater; I manoeuvred *Birmingham* between the two, pumping light oil from my bilges to take the edge off the sea. The yacht crew reported that our combined efforts gave them an easier ride; how much of this was due to oil and how much simply to our lee I don't know. Derek Sergeant, the lifeboat coxswain, said he thought the oil helped, but none of us felt it was a conclusively valuable contribution. I believe that the yacht was moving too fast to make maximum use of my slick; with hindsight it might have been more effective if laid to leeward and ahead of the yacht, to allow the craft to pass through the relative calm. That the oil calmed the water was not in doubt as we could see its effectiveness in the searchlight beams: placing it where the yacht (and, subsequently, the lifeboat) could benefit was more tricky.

The craft continued to make progress to the west-north-west as the wind increased to 90 knots. My anemometer would not register above this speed, but it was clear from the roar in my own masts and aerials that the wind was still rising. There were long periods, while I lay virtually a'hull, rolling violently, keeping pace with the yacht, when the anemometer needle lay hard against the stops, and the note in the wind continued to rise steadily and unbelievably higher. On the bridge of *Birmingham* I think most of us were too busy to

Figure 18.3 The barograph trace from HMS *Birmingham* recorded during the October 1987 storm while standing by a distressed multihull some miles south of Portland Bill. Note the rising pressure, which at +25.5mb in three hours, comfortably exceeded any UK pressure change over the same period ever to be recorded.

marvel at the strength of the storm. The ship rolled nearly 45° at times, her stabilizers unable to operate as designed at these very low speeds. I used the bridge throttle controls myself as if they were Morse controls on a speed boat, using high power on each shaft, alternately ahead and astern, keeping the ship close – but not too close – to the yacht. This seamanship was as nothing compared with that in *Black Rover*; she had a single shaft, variable pitch screw, and has a generally heavier and more ponderous hull. Yet she stayed in position and coped very well indeed.

Shortly after 0320, with no warning whatsoever, the wind swung from 180–190°, 95 knots plus, to 270–280°, 95 knots plus. This was remarkable for all sorts of reasons, not least of which was that the sea flattened out for a while. 'Confused' is too elementary a word; the sea was gob-smacked, as one of my sailors put it! The catamaran at this point began to head north-north-east, maintaining a beam wind and a speed of about 4 knots. The crew of the yacht continued to plead periodically with me to take them off. I pointed out that since they were in no immediate danger they were better off where they were. I was about 4800 tons of crushing death if I closed with them in those conditions, and I was not about to put my rigid-hulled inflatable in the water in those seas.

Meanwhile, the Weymouth lifeboat approached steadily from the north-north-east. They had a heavy time of it, and it was to their undying credit that they arrived so quickly, at about 0420, to set about rescuing the crew of the catamaran. For the ensuing hour we in *Birmingham* had the privilege to be spectators as the Arun class vessel manoeuvred repeatedly alongside the yacht. We closed in to about 183m (200yd) from the scene to provide the best lee. The sea was beginning to build steadily from the west. The dramatic wind shift was followed by two hours of unabated fury: the sea became very angry indeed by 0530 when the lifeboat completed her last approach, with, incidentally, no damage on either side. By then the wind was 260°, 80–100 knots, with possibly stronger gusts. The seas were confused and steep with a very heavy Atlantic swell. The female member of the yacht crew had been invited to cross to the Arun first, but she was in fact the last to go, showing some courage. The skipper elected to stay on board and drove his yacht to shelter in Weymouth with resolution, though nearly coming to grief on the Shambles in the process. Once in the lee of Portland Bill, at about 0800, I used the rigid-hulled inflatable to transfer an experienced yachtsman to assist the yacht into harbour.

A Contessa 32 in the Solent

Meanwhile, not far away, a Joint Services Sailing Centre Contessa 32 called *Explorer* was on passage from Poole, Dorset, to Gosport in Hampshire on the last day of an RYA coastal skippers' course. The instructor and skipper was Ray Williams, but the story is told by one of the crew, Martin Bowdler, due to take his examination the next day:

We intended to make this a lazy passage, adding a few night hours to our week's trip. Therefore when we heard the shipping forecast at 1750, we knew we would have a lively sail. The general synopsis gave gale warnings for most sea areas, and for Wight it was cyclonic, becoming west to south-west force 7 to the severe gale force 9, decreasing to 6 later.

We cast off from the Town Quay at Poole around 1845. Our course had already been planned and plotted on the charts. All the sails were sorted out for quick access, in case the conditions strengthened. Anything that could crash around was secured or put away and our harnesses were fitted once more. Though in the week we had many a soaking, we all still had at least one dry shirt at the ready to don if we were to have another wet trip. All other clothes were stowed away. One important aspect that we did not remember was to fill our thermos and make lots of sandwiches for the passage.

When we cast off, the sea and sky gave no indication of the waves and wind to come. The sky was watery; dark – yes; forbidding – no. The course planned was a very simple one: from Poole Fairway across Christchurch Bay to Bridge Buoy, through the Needles Channel to the Solent and thence to Gosport.

At Poole fairway we had one slab in the main and the No 1 genoa set. The weather sharpened to force 6 from the west-south-west, and a well-rehearsed sail change to the working jib was executed. Our thoughts of this passage had not been to push ourselves, therefore our sail changes were always one step ahead.

By the time we were crossing Christchurch Ledge this routine was overtaken by events. The wind picked up to what we imagined to be around force 8 or more, which caused the crests of the waves to froth up and turn into heavy spume. By then we had three slabs in the main and the storm jib set. We were surprised how suddenly it had become very dark; this was not your average cloudy sky at night. The wind continued to pick up; and as a result the sea was gathering strength and height. We had been able to pick out the lights of Bournemouth and Highcliffe continuously, but this became more difficult with the spume and the deepening of the troughs.

Our navigation became an increasingly odious task. As the seas increased, so too did the emergence of a pattern of rogue waves. These would hit us on our quarter and happily break on the cockpit and coachroof. Every so often, one of these would be much larger than the others. We had the hatch shut and the washboards in except for the top one, but these larger rogues had enough force to slide the hatch forward and completely drench the navigator and chart table. I had just finished my stint at the helm and, as part of the rotation of crewing, found myself down below navigating. At last I had a chance to change my sodden shirt. This done, I felt so much better. However, the first of the larger rogues swamped the boat. I know this because much of it came down my drier and warmer neck and the chart table was awash. As I appeared in the hatch this caused much amusement to the crew, who had already taken the brunt of the wave.

We found that we could be prepared for the normal series of waves by continually weaving along them to avoid the breaking crests. We could feel the normal pattern, as the boat began to lift, and whoever was at the helm would play the waves, riding through them as they broke at their crests. A Contessa may be a most forgiving boat, but in these waters we had to play her firmly, constantly dumping and tightening the main. The motion gave us the overall effect of cork-screwing through the water.

However, the rogues were different, in so much as we could not see them coming until the last possible moment – too late. One of the crew, armed with a torch, was detailed to watch for these rogues. Not a very satisfactory task as he would be certain for a head-on soaking. This was one of the jobs no one really enjoyed, but certainly amused the rest of the crew.

Our crew rotation proved valuable in these conditions, due to the various physical tasks on the boat. No one person could continue on a particular job for a long stretch, as certain jobs required more exertion or concentration than others.

The most spectacular seas were off the Shingles where the large waves piled up on meeting the shallows. White waves resulting from this could be made out, although the visibility was limited, while the crashing noise was almost deafening. We had the impression that we were much nearer to the Shingles than we actually were. The seas around us were very steep, broken, erratic and white. This made steering difficult, as our rudder would be as much out of the water as in. We did notice we were being blown down towards the Shingles, and had to harden up to allow for our considerable leeway. For about the next hour the heel of the boat was such that her cabin windows were almost constantly under water. When we bore away there was a moment when *Explorer* would drunkenly come upright, only to fall over again in the next gust. One of the crew found it all a bit overwhelming and he had to retire to the cabin, where he spent the rest of the trip. I cannot say that we were all scared, because there was so much to check on. Having said that, we were apprehensive off the Shingles.

The sails and rigging were being put under a great deal of strain, so the general appearance of the sails, hanks, reefing lines and sheets had to be checked so as to pre-empt any sort of accident. This was a hazardous job, but one that was enjoyable.

Explorer was fairly bucking around and very wet at the bow. But with a lifeline to prevent one being lost overboard, the job felt like a fairground ride.

By the time we had passed Hurst Castle, the wind became increasingly local under the lee shore of the island. The seas had lessened, so while navigating I tried to take the opportunity to make a sandwich for the crew. However, odd omnidirectional gusts threw *Explorer* around; the same can be said of my attempts below – but we were all grateful for something to eat, even if crude, wet and very salty. Past Yarmouth this freak condition lessened. The wind had not yet reached its full force, even though it was screaming through the rigging. The barometer was still falling at an extraordinary rate.

People have often asked why we did not make for shelter to somewhere like Yarmouth; the simple answer being that we seemed to be safer on the water than making for land, and we had our appointment with the examiners the next day at Gosport. However, passing close by Cowes, we did have a small twinge as we could see all the various lights on. The thought of a whisky in the warm, talking about the storm, was not lost upon me.

Past Prince Consort buoy we put our final slab in the main. This did little to affect our speed, some $6^{1}/_{2}$ knots. At just before midnight we came out of the lee of the island and were once again in the full force of the storm. This was an interesting experience as the change of conditions was so quick. From the very loud wind we had experienced in the lee of the island, the wind now roared. *Explorer* could be felt groaning under the strain, while rapid easing of all the sheets did little to improve the slamming of the boat. We fairly hurtled towards Gilkicker Point.

The 0030 shipping forecast was now nearer the mark. Wight was 'south-westerly gale force 8 to storm force 10, decreasing force 6 to gale force 8'. The storm force 10 surprised us, but accounted for the noise and strong conditions.

Normally we might have taken the inshore small boat channel between Gilkicker Point and Portsmouth, but to give a greater margin for error we took the Swashway route. When the moment came to turn towards the harbour entrance we tacked rather than gybed as far to windward as possible. On the new course our angle of heel was markedly increased, such that the cabin windows were constantly awash, and we noticed that we were making a good deal of leeway towards the beach. We were able to make a large allowance in our course for the leeway and, thankfully, no extra tacks were needed to get inside the harbour entrance.

Once we came within the protection of Fort Blockhouse, *Explorer* immediately came upright and we seemed to stop. Our handkerchief representation of sails was dropped and secured. It was just after 0100 and we had made our destination in good time, though, ironically, when day dawned our examiners had to call off the tests due to the weather, being blocked in their homes by fallen trees.

A Hallberg Rassy 42 in the North Sea

At much the same time some more heavy weather sailing was being experienced in the North Sea. In this case the account is by Jeff Taylor who, with two crew, was delivering a new Hallberg Rassy 42 from her builders in Sweden to Southampton. This was a trip he had done many times before in all weather conditions:

After a trouble-free trip across the North Sea, we called into Lowestoft on the morning of Thursday 15 October to fill up with diesel. With a forecast of south to south-west force 4–5 for Thames and Dover, but a wind from the east to south-east of 5 to 10 knots, we departed at approximately 1400 and made good progress motorsailing at 7 knots for the first three to four hours. The 1750 shipping forecast was the first indication that there might be a strong south or south-west wind on the way. At this time we were just north of east from Harwich, with a light south-east wind, making good progress motorsailing with full sail. I looked at all the options and decided to carry on, with the intention of going in to Ramsgate should the wind pick up later, as forecast. After all, even if the wind should increase to force 8 from the south-south-west, it was nothing that we could not cope with, as we were in a well-found boat in which I had utmost confidence.

The wind gradually increased from the south and by midnight was approximately 20 to 25 knots. We were by now motorsailing with no genoa and one reef in the main. Our position at the time was 8 miles west-south-west of the Galloper light buoy and the tide was about to turn with us. The sea was starting to build up from the south. I heard a gale warning on the VHF just before midnight; the forecast was for gale force 9 from the south-west, imminent. I was firming up my plans to make for Ramsgate as we were only 21 miles away, and obviously something was going to happen. The wind steadily increased up to south-west 30 to 35 knots, with the sea becoming quite rough and uncomfortable. It was enhanced by the now south-going tide. There was a lot of water over the decks at this stage, and our boat speed was down to 4 knots.

At about 0130 on Friday morning I was on watch when George popped his head out of the hatch; he told me there had just been a storm force 10 given for Thames and Dover. By this time I was starting to get nervous about the situation, so I asked George to make sure everything down below was well stowed and to prepare for some very heavy weather. The next gale warning came at about 0330 and forecast south-west violent storm 11, imminent.

The wind was still only 35 knots and we were making about 4 knots towards Ramsgate;

but it was obvious that we were not going to arrive before the gale.

At 0430 the wind suddenly increased to 60 knots. I decided to heave-to on the starboard tack and stand out to sea. This presented me with a bit of a problem as we had no storm jib or trysail on board. In the end I found that with no sail up, the helm lashed to weather and the engine running ahead at about 1200rpm, the yacht lay with the wind about 60° off the starboard bow and was reasonably comfortable in the circumstances. We were 12 miles north-east of Ramsgate at this stage. The seas were getting very big with breaking crests and spray everywhere; we started to get laid over on our beam ends as the boat rose up the face of the waves and over the tops. Visibility was down to about half a mile.

At 0500 the wind had increased further and we were approximately 14 miles north-east from Ramsgate.

Figure 18.4 The track chart of the Hallberg Rassy 42 during the October 1987 storm.

Our radar, which worked well throughout, showed a lot of shipping in the vicinity; so I was very keen to get outside the North Falls banks, and decided to run off into deeper water. We were running downwind in generally a north-easterly direction, using our faithful Decca for navigation. The sea continued to rise and became very steep, with every crest breaking. Flying spume filled the air, reducing visibility to nil.

It became increasingly difficult to steer, due to our speed; but it was essential to keep the boat dead down the face of the waves in order to avoid a broach. I felt we really should have had a sea anchor out, but we had nothing suitable on board to rig one with, and I thought it too dangerous to let anyone out of the cockpit.

We suffered our first knockdown at approximately 0830. As we surfed down a very steep wave the boat started shearing off to port, and I was unable to correct this. The wave then broke on top of us, knocking the boat down to about 90°. The boat righted herself very quickly, and the only problem left was a cockpit full of water; but this drained away quickly. The seas were continuing to get worse. I had sailed in winds as high as we were experiencing, but I had never encountered seas as severe and dangerous. Previously I had always been in very deep water which made the seas long, unlike these very steep short waves that were being caused by the shallow waters of the North Sea.

The storm was at its peak around 1030, which was when we suffered our second knockdown. This happened in the same way as the first one, but was far more severe. We were covered by a solid wall of water that seemed to pin us down below the horizontal with a suddenness that was quite alarming. When we came upright we noticed the liferaft, complete with its stainless steel cradle which had been attached to the deck, had been washed over the side. The liferaft, having by now inflated itself, was being towed astern by the painter. Our sprayhood had been turned inside out and the lifebuoy washed over the side. The water in the cockpit had seeped through the sides of the washboards, soaking the VHF radio and rendering it inoperable. Then the liferaft broke adrift and I started to feel very vulnerable, as without a liferaft or VHF radio, I realized that we were very much alone.

The storm started to abate around midday when the average wind speed dropped to approximately 40 knots; but there was still a very fierce sea running. In comparison to the average wind speed of 70 knots that we had sustained over a period of about half an hour, with gusts up to 95 knots (as recorded on the Brookes & Gatehouse equipment), it was relatively quiet. The sea had died down enough by 1530 for us to set some sail and confidently turn the boat beam-on to the seas. We headed in a westerly direction for Lowestoft, from whence we had come. We were approximately 25 miles east of the port, and arrived at 1900 where three very tired and relieved yachtsmen were glad to get ashore.

As a professional delivery skipper, sailing approximately 15 000 miles a year offshore, it is easy to become complacent. I felt that I had a lot of experience interpreting the UK shipping forecasts, with the time delays that one normally gets prior to a severe gale.

In this case I was wrong about the weather, and perhaps could have got some shelter in Harwich. In retrospect, this may not have been a good idea, as there was much damage to yachts in this part of England. Certainly I feel that when we turned and ran, this was the only and correct decision to make.

An experience such as we had brings home the fact that we are all human and that one must always have utmost respect for the sea. There was no doubt in my mind that if I had been in a less seaworthy boat we could have been in serious trouble.

Comment

Peter Braley modestly describes the meteorology of the Great Channel storm of October 1987 as seen from the old naval base at Portland. As a result of his recommendation to the Portland Admiral (which put his professional reputation at risk, as his view was not supported in other meteorological quarters, cf Michael Fish), the Portland naval fleet was ordered to sea. This must have been an unpopular action just before the weekend, but evidently the Admiral did not ignore the bringer of bad news. No doubt he found Peter Braley's case logical, and consequently made a tough, but – as it turned out – correct decision. In this case a potential disaster was averted.

Muddle Thru's brave story provides much interest. First, one has to say that mid-October is getting rather late in the sailing season to embark upon Atlantic crossings via the Bay of Biscay. Having elected to go, one would urge caution to those planning to leave in strong head winds. One should try to look beyond the pressure of tight schedules when making a decision to sail in unsettled weather.

In the worst part of the storm, *Muddle Thru* was left to lie a'hull with the windage of her sprayhood pushing her bow into the wind. We can be sure that the wind speed was over 100 knots, and yet she survived. Only later was she rolled through 360° while lying a'hull in the next gale. Apparently the sprayhood was not enough to keep her bow to wind. Of course it is not the high wind speed, as such, that is dangerous to yachts that lie a'hull, it is the breaking waves that develop as a result. Sooner or later, it seems, a yacht lying a'hull in breaking seas will be inverted.

The wisdom of keeping cockpit locker lids firmly closed is apparent from this account. Should one open when a yacht is badly knocked down, she will fill and sink rapidly.

The matter of the lost winch handles bears comment. Both cockpit winch handles were lost when *Muddle Thru* capsized, and in case of this eventuality, spares should always be kept below.

With *Muddle Thru*'s mast damaged by the roll, it was necessary to use the engine, and it was noteworthy that by increasing power, and therefore the water flow over the rudder blade, broaching was avoided.

The Swan 46 story shows that 360° rolls are not confined to yachts of under 12m (40ft). The Swan is described as having been hove-to, but it is not known what sails she had hoisted and at what angle she was lying to the wind. It seems possible that she was caught beam-on, or nearly so, just as a wave broke. The situation was aggravated by a severe injury to the skipper and the fact that the floorboards were not secured and everything stored under them 'flew through the boat'. It is a time-honoured practice to stow tins of food under the cabin sole, but owners of ocean-going yachts have to weigh the consequences should their boat be unlucky enough to be rolled. The solution may be to assemble groups of tins that constitute a meal, tape them together and mark them, make a stowage plan so that each meal's whereabouts is known, and screw down the floorboards or use special fastenings, so that the floorboards will stay in place in an inversion, yet can easily be removed.

The rescue by the Japanese container ship sounds most alarming, and underlines the difficulty that ships experience when trying to rescue yacht crews.

The catamaran rescue is more revealing of human qualities than anything. The skipper was clearly a determined man and may have been right in considering his multihull to be in little danger. However, when the wind increased to hurricane strength he must have had some special reason for not choosing to go to a safe refuge, especially when Weymouth was at hand. Heavy weather is something a crew should work up to by going out in successively stronger winds and bigger waves. Whatever was going on in this case, it does not look as if the crew was familiar enough with rough conditions to warrant an overnight passage in October in fierce storm conditions.

The story of the bold participants of the coastal skipper's course in their Contessa 32 reinforces the reputation that this design has for good sea-keeping qualities. To have navigated the dangerous Needles Passage at night in such conditions calls for a good deal of luck and skill. Generally it seems that the crew was keen, strong and cheerful. With such a crew, a good skipper can work miracles. Some would say that Ray Williams did just that, though perhaps the seas had not had time to build up to be really dangerous, when the Needles Passage could have become impassable.

Jeff Taylor's courageous account of his delivery trip with a new Hallberg Rassy 42 is an example of how quickly conditions can change. It must have been difficult to imagine in a light south-easterly that the wind would be blowing like fury in the opposite direction in a few hours. As luck would have it, his chosen port of refuge was to windward, ie the worst case.

At least Jeff Taylor had a sound engine and did not have to make to windward to avoid a lee shore. Without a trysail, storm jib and then VHF, he would have been in worse trouble. He does not say whether he was carrying flares.

Regarding his liferaft, this is yet one more instance of a raft lost overboard from its deck stowage, as frequently seems to happen. It has taken too long for designers to plan for integral storage of liferafts. There may be an occasional eventuality when a deck-stowed liferaft is an advantage, as for example in Chapter 6, but more often than not it may suffer from exposure and not inflate when required or, as happened in this case, be driven overboard by the force of a breaking wave. On balance, it does seem best to stow liferafts in a dry dedicated cockpit storage, or below.

19

Storm winds, storm lessons

LIN AND LARRY PARDEY

'WAS IT AS ROUGH AS YOU IMAGINED IT would be?' people ask about our east to west rounding of Cape Horn. Yes, it was rough. But on reflection, though *Taleisin*, our 9m (29ft 7in) cutter encountered headwinds topping 60 knots near the Straits of LeMaire and even stronger when we reached the Pacific and battled the Roaring Forties, with seas topping 15m (50ft), the situation felt less threatening than the out-of-season storm which caught us unexpectedly near Australia's Great Barrier Reef. The severity of the seas we encountered, driven into stunning steepness by storm force winds blowing against two to three knots of current plus the threat of coral reefs less than 100 miles to leeward, made heaving-to, assisted by a parachute anchor, our only option. This storm forced the closure of all ports along the eastern coast of Australia from Sydney to Brisbane for three days and also caused the loss of three lives, five fishing boats and two yachts. Two fully laden container ships each lay within sight of us for over 13 hours, held by their engines at slow, facing the tumbling breaking seas effectively hove-to, just as we were. We have never before, nor since, seen ships lying hove-to.

For three days we beat to windward, using every wind shift, as we tried to complete the last leg of our fight south towards the Tasman Sea and clear of Australia's Great Barrier Reef. We had just spent the southern hemisphere winter of 1988 exploring as far north as Townsville. For a month we had been working south through the islands, hoping to catch the light northerly winds shown on the pilot charts for the month of October. Fair winds had failed to materialize. Instead we had fresh headwinds and frustrating sailing. Anchorages that should have offered pleasant havens were rolly and uncomfortable. It was 3 November by the time we reached Rosslyn Bay, just south of Yeppoon and 150 miles from the open sea. We were concerned about getting clear of the tropics before the beginning of the cyclone season[1]; we had to short tack along a shoal and island studded route using navigation aids designed for motorized vessels, which tend to stick to the centre of the main channels.

Three days after reaching Rosslyn Bay we woke to a forecast of 10 to 15 knot north-easterlies for 72 hours followed by a south-easterly shift ahead of a frontal system with squalls to 25 knots; winds were due to shift to the northeast following the passage of the front. We backed up the coastal weather report with a phone call to Brisbane

---

[1] The Australian Bureau of Meteorology statistics show the majority of cyclones affect this area between mid December and early April, but show occasional tropical depressions reaching the Barrier Reef area as early as mid November.

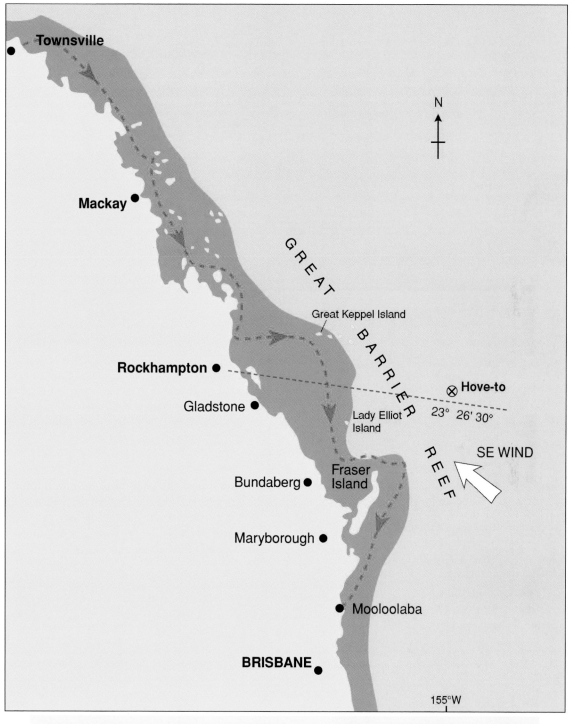

Taleisin's route from Townsville to Mooloolaba showing the area where she was hove-to off the Great Barrier Reef.

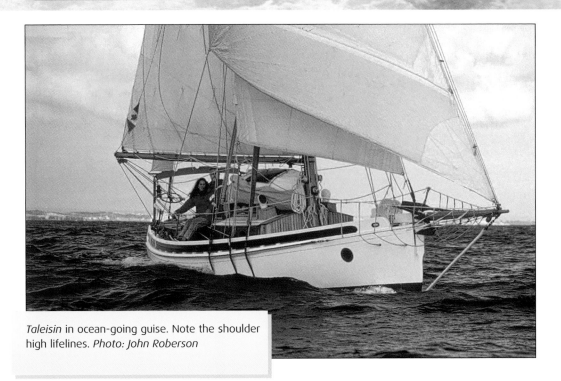

Taleisin in ocean-going guise. Note the shoulder high lifelines. *Photo: John Roberson*

Airport. Mike S, meteorological officer for air traffic control, warned me the forecast squalls might reach 35 knots for a short while. 'Haven't had a cyclone form in the Tasman before the middle of December in the ten years I've been in this job,' Mike added. 'Let's set sail,' said Larry, 'It's only 250 miles to Mooloolaba, and with this forecast we should get in before the front. If not, 35 knots of wind isn't the end of the world.'

Only a few hours of northerly winds materialized. Then the headwinds returned. But our determination to reach our New Zealand Christmas rendezvous, plus unsettled conditions in each of the potential anchorages we checked along our route, kept us doggedly sailing onward instead of diverting to Bundaberg, the only all-weather anchorage in the area. After 65 hours of beating, we were clear of the Great Barrier Reef, beam-reaching with a fresh northerly and I was already picturing the next evening in port at Mooloolaba, now only 100 miles south of us. The most recent forecast did agree with Mike, that within the next few hours we could expect south-easterly gusts to

35, possibly 40 knots as the front passed by our position.

At 0330 light rain, occasional flashes of lightning plus a sudden increase in the wind that shifted quickly to the south, encouraged me to lower the big jib and secure it in the jib net. Just for comfort, I reefed the mainsail, set the staysail and kept *Taleisin* sailing close-hauled on the offshore tack, though we could have lain southeast towards Mooloolaba. Why not err on the side of prudence and gain more sea-room? Two hours later we were becalmed 50 miles off the coast. Flashes of lightning showed a low, cigar-shaped band of clouds rolling towards us. That's when I decided to remove the jib from the forestay. The sea was almost flat with a low undulating swell as the first hint of daylight highlighted the approaching front. I was wearing nothing but my foul-weather jacket as I sat on the cabin-top enjoying the play of lightning behind the approaching clouds. Enjoyment faded quickly with the first gust of the frontal system.

Taleisin heeled until her cabin portlights were awash. For the first time ever, as I crawled forward to pull down first the stay-

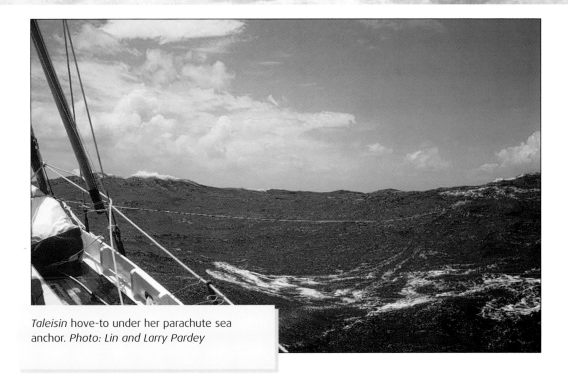

Taleisin hove-to under her parachute sea anchor. *Photo: Lin and Larry Pardey*

sail and then the reefed mainsail, I found I had to hold my breath and, like a swimmer, turn to leeward to gulp in air free of wind-driven rain and salt spray. Hailstones felt like buckshot as they hit my bare bottom. With both sails lashed down securely the boat still lay heeled about 15°, beam-on to the wind. I was just starting to pull the storm trysail up when I felt Larry alongside me. 'Want me to do that?' he yelled. 'I'm okay, get the wind-vane cover[2] down before it blows apart,' I answered. 'Get down below, you're soaked,' Larry called when I came into the cockpit to sheet the trysail in to hold *Taleisin* closer to the wind so she lay hove-to. 'I can take over. This is a hell of a lot more than 35 or 40 knots of wind.'

I gratefully went below, shaking with cold but also eager to catch the updated 0600 weather report. It wasn't what I wanted to hear – a storm-warning effective immedi-ately, small vessels were advised to return to port. A ridge of high pressure lying just off the Queensland coast. An area of low pres-sure intensifying and remaining stationary in the Coral Sea. Reports were of gusts to 85 knots, sustained winds to 65 knots. Wind decreasing to 45 knots by noon.

Soon after, Larry climbed through the hatch in a cascade of rain and spray; he offered to wipe down my back and broke out laughing. 'You should see your bum; it's full of red polka dots, looks like you've been peppered by buckshot,' Larry said. Then he asked me to dig out the components of the combination hatch protector cum sprayhood we use when we head offshore and I realized we'd screwed up. With the favourable fore-cast, the relatively short and coastal nature of our voyage, we hadn't bothered to set the boat up for going to sea. A pile of books and tumble of bedding lay on the cabin sole, unrestrained by their seagoing lee cloth. The hatch protector/sprayhood and other parts of our heavy weather offshore gear were in their in-port storage area right forward next to the chain locker. Preparations that took about half an hour in port would now be a

---

[2] The vane on *Taleisin*'s self-steering gear is a lightweight wooden structure with a removable Dacron cover.

ABOVE, LEFT TO RIGHT: Weather charts from 6, 7 and 8 November 1988.

time-consuming struggle that left us feeling less organized, less competent, less prepared.

Larry stayed on deck once he finally got the dodger and storm gear[3] in place, watching the way *Taleisin* lay, adjusting the shock cords restraining her tiller and estimating her drift. Over the next hour the seas began to build. Heavy spray began pelting the cabin sides on a regular basis. Then Larry called down, 'How many miles between us and the nearest reefs?'

'Nearest one is about 90 miles north of us, but the Aussie current is going south. It should help counter any drift. Now the front is past us the wind should ease in three or four hours.'

'F....ing forecasts haven't been right in months. I want to slow down her drift just in case this wind has slowed down the current,' Larry yelled. 'Seas are damn steep and her head's falling off in between the gusts. I think it's time to get out the para-anchor.' I stuck my head outside for the first time in an hour as I passed him the gear. The rain had stopped but the situation was definitely not improving. How high were the seas? They definitely were not as high as those we encountered near Cape Horn, but never have I seen steeper nor more closely spaced seas, driven by wind-against-current into pipeline-like breakers through which we could see the green colour more usually associated with waves along a sandy shore. The most awe-inspiring aspect of these tumbling breaking seas was the way they seemed to crumble as they hit the slick that *Taleisin* was forming as she slid slowly to leeward. Port and starboard of the slick, the crests broke into roaring cascades that could have poured tons of green water onto us.

---

[3] This includes the hatch protector/spray hood; shoulder high lifelines, extra rope handrails on the cabin-top, plus covers for the forward hawse pipe.

We worked together setting the para-anchor, a 3.6m (12ft) diameter surplus military Bureau of Ordinance parachute (a Bu-Ord). Larry led the spare anchor rode through a 5cm (2in) diameter snatch block secured to *Taleisin*'s bow fitting back over the lifelines to where I held the para-anchor. He attached it to the para-anchor's swivel then put another 5cm (2in) diameter snatch block onto the rode and rigged a bridle line which he led through the windward, amidships fairlead in *Taleisin*'s bulwark and back to the sheet winch, leaving the line just long enough so the bridle block was near the forward shroud. Together we slid the parachute itself down the windward side of the hull.

As soon as it was about 15m (50ft) from the hull, the chute filled. Larry gradually let out more scope until we could see the chute lying two crests to windward of us. The effect was immediate. *Taleisin* lay with her bow about 50° from the wind, all signs of forward motion gone and a swirling slick

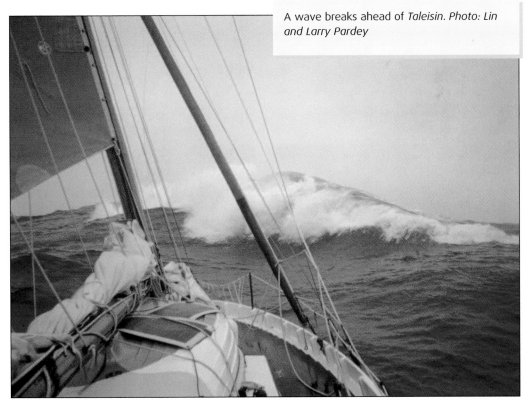

A wave breaks ahead of *Taleisin*. Photo: Lin and Larry Pardey

forming to windward of her, her leeward motion cut to less than a knot through the water. Because we'd been lying hove-to, steadied by the trysail while we worked, it was not extremely difficult to work on deck, though having to fight to keep from sliding around, and effectively help Larry, had been tiring. I went below to heat soup for Larry while he added chafing gear to each line and also jammed cockpit cushions between the tiller and taffrail knees to absorb some of the shock loading on the rudder. It was soon after this that Larry yelled down, 'Take a look out here; this is something I have never seen before!' Just to starboard of us, within a mile, lay two container ships, heading into the wind, hove-to, battling the storm just as we were. They stayed in sight for all that day and into the long night that followed.

Over the next hours, seasickness kept me in the leeward bunk most of the time. I did not have the will to clean up the fallen gear that cluttered the cabin sole. Instead I shoved each new escapee in with the rest of the mess in the forward cabin. This mess, plus the reports I began hearing on the radio, did nothing to make the situation seem better. Within 100 miles of us, a massive air search was on for three fishermen we had come to know in Rosslyn Bay. They had headed off when we did, to work near Kepple Island. Now they had sent a Mayday from a position that put them only 40 miles upwind of the maze of the reefs lying to the north. Within 10 hours of the first blasts of that front, another search effort was being reported: *Marymuffin*, a 22m (72ft) maxi that had been a well-known racer under the name of *Ragamuffin*, had called for assistance. Her skipper had tried to outrun the front and reach the anchorage inside the ring of coral that is Lady Elliott Reef. There is a narrow

entrance through the coral. But we later learned the anchorage turned into a hellhole for the five boats seeking refuge there when the waves went right over the windward side of the reef. Unfortunately for *Marymuffin*, the storm force winds set her 15 miles north of her route. To clear the edge of the reef, she headed closer to the wind only to suffer a knockdown with the mast in the water, which left crew and boat injured, engine non-functioning and mainsail slides jammed in the track so the crew could neither reef nor take down the sail. Now she was in danger of foundering on the very reef her skipper had tried to reach for protection.[4]

When Larry did not come below promptly after his latest hourly gear check I dragged myself out of the bunk and found him lying over the taffrail cursing. Another oversight had been escalated by the storm into a gear-threatening situation. When we first hove-to earlier in the day, Larry had pulled in the taffrail log spinner and its 15m (50ft) of braided 5mm ($\frac{3}{16}$in) line and tucked it behind the windward cockpit combing. Now the occasional wave, rolling along the deck, had washed the spinner and line overboard. The bucking of the boat had crocheted the line into an ever tightening web which had almost immobilized the trim tab. Larry was worried that the strain could damage the self-steering vane. It took us over an hour to finally cut away the last bits of our taffrail log spinner line to free the trim tab.

Each six-hourly update of the forecast added hours to the expected length of the storm. The reported wind speed for Fraser Island Lighthouse, approximately 55 miles from our position, was 60 knots. By dark we'd almost come to accept the motion, the roar of cresting seas to port and starboard of our slick, the splats of foam against the

---

[4] Radio reports over the next hours added to the drama of the storm as we followed the rescue efforts. A large ferry was able to reach *Marymuffin* in time to tow her clear of the reef and escort her into Bundaburg.

The air search for the crew of the sunken fishing boat went on for almost two days. Their overturned aluminium tin tender was spotted, surrounded by large sharks, dozens of miles from the Mayday position. Only one of the crew managed to survive, by clinging to the tender.

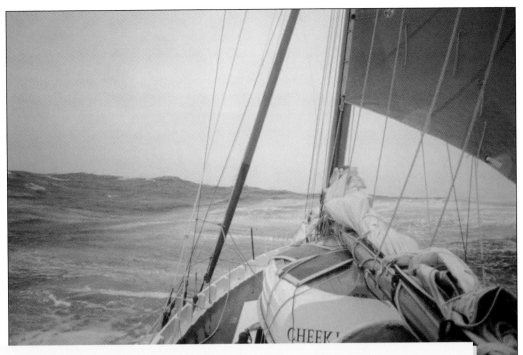

Taleisin lying a'try before the parachute sea anchor was deployed. Though waves break immediately ahead and astern, the turbulent water created by her hull and keel making leeway prevents waves breaking to windward most effectively. *Photo: Lin and Larry Pardey*

topsides. Larry and I stayed prone most of the time, taking turns to doze off and also taking turns going on deck every hour to ease the main para-anchor rode about a foot (about 0.35m).

Just before midnight, an exceptionally loud snap woke Larry. The permanent preventer line attached to the rudder, which keeps the rudder from going over far enough to endanger the pintles, had chafed through. There was no way to rig new preventer lines. To ease some of the shock-loading, Larry added two extra lengths of heavy-duty shock cord to the inboard end of the tiller. He sounded pretty discouraged as he listed the toll that the past 18 hours had taken on our gear. His most careful use of anti-chafing gear had not prevented wear on the 16mm ($^5/_8$in) anchor rode holding the para-anchor. The shock cords holding the tiller were wearing through the woven coverings at the rate of one shock cord every three hours. 'We've got a spare anchor rode and if this doesn't

start to let up by morning I want to use it,' he commented. 'Lin, why don't you put up the lee cloth just in case.'

He was using the windward pilot berth and lee cloth. I did not see a reason to put my lee cloth up since I was in the leeward berth lying against the pillow-padded hull. Besides, I am a bit claustrophobic and hate the closed in feeling it gives. Just before dawn another screaming squall line roared down on us. Larry was quickly suited up and on deck. I remember dozing off. Then I was levitating, grabbing desperately for anything to hold as I heard the snapping rattle of the storm trysail, the loud roar of a breaking wave crest. I flew clear of the bunk as *Taleisin* tacked through the eye of the wind to come to a sudden halt, heeled sharply to starboard. All the breath flew out of me as my chest hit the bronze table support stanchion, then I hit the cabin sole, my teeth slammed against the ice chest so hard I was sure they would be knocked loose. As I slowly pulled my face clear of the woodwork, *Taleisin* lurched sharply one more time, I felt something hit my head with a sharp but not terribly painful blow and warm liquid began running through my hair and across my face. I couldn't restrain the tears as I gingerly felt my head. I did not feel any sense of relief when I realized the liquid was coffee not blood; instead I was downright angry.

My hair was now covered in coffee grounds from the pot I had meant to secure more tightly the last time I had been on watch. To make matters worse, as I sat up and gingerly touched ribs that were badly bruised if not broken, I noticed the deep gouge the flying coffee pot had cut into the otherwise perfect varnished teak of the ice box facing. Just inches from that gash were a second set of dents, the exact shape of my front teeth. By now I had time to realize that no water had found its way into the boat and Larry had not called for urgent assistance, so that meant *Taleisin* was still riding safely. But I could hear him winching and working with the lines that held the para-anchor. Chagrined and guilty at having ignored Larry's warning to use the lee cloth, I had most of the coffee grounds out of my hair before he opened the hatch and said, 'Everything okay down there? I think the damn parachute is too big. We came up over a big wave, *Taleisin* headed close to the wind. The chute didn't seem to give at all and pulled us over onto port tack. The rode is under the bobstay and if we don't get her back on the starboard tack it's going to chafe through.'

The hardest part of the task was getting into my foul weather gear. By the time I got on deck Larry had eased the bridle line and *Taleisin* lay head-to-wind, ranging first 10 or 15° onto port tack, then tacking through the eye of the wind onto starboard. I got into position at the sheet winch in the cockpit. Larry waited until *Taleisin* tacked over onto starboard, then he quickly paid out about 6 or 9m (20 or 30ft) of rode and as quickly as I could, I winched in the slack of the bridle line. *Taleisin*'s head paid off as soon as the

full strain came back onto the rode and bridle and she again lay on starboard tack.

After two days of lying to the para-anchor, the wind eased below storm force, the seas began to crumble instead of breaking, and sprays of spindrift no longer swept the deck. Only then did I show Larry the bands of bruises crossing my abdomen and lower chest. In a way I wish I'd waited. Now he wanted to get underway immediately and begin beating south towards medical attention. But I convinced him the motion of sailing onward in these conditions would be more uncomfortable for me than the motion we were experiencing as we lay hove-to. By late afternoon the winds had dropped to gale force, the seas had lengthened and, with the latest forecast predicting another frontal system crossing our area within the next 36 hours, Larry and I prepared to retrieve the para-anchor.

I gingerly worked with him, for by this time I wanted more than anything to be in port, on an unmoving boat with a long hot shower, medical assistance and lots of time to rest. We use a barebones para-anchor set up, no floats, no trip line, no weights. We also have no engine to let us motor towards the chute and ease the strain on the anchor rode. But retrieval, though it took two hours to accomplish, was relatively easy in spite of the strong winds. Larry removed the pennant line and block and *Taleisin* immediately laid head-to-wind. Just after each wave crest passed, the strain on the rode eased. Then Larry was able to winch in about 6ft (1.8m) of rode. I sat on the deck box next to the mast tailing the line and each time *Taleisin* began rising on the next wave I put two turns on a mast cleat to hold the strain. Six feet at a time, we got closer to the parachute. When the swivel for the chute lay just at our bow, Larry snagged one of the shroud lines with the boathook. Then he began pulling the shroud line in by hand. The water spilled out, within two or three minutes the chute collapsed, and he had it on board. As he secured the mass of the anchor rode against the windward bulwark we found almost 3m

(10ft) of the anchor rode, the portion that had been riding in the snatch block at the bow, was chafed with almost 10 per cent of its diameter chewed away.

I was too exhausted to sail onward that evening so we lay hove-to under just the trysail until daybreak. Then we began close reaching towards the coast, storm trysail and staysail set in 35 to 45 knot winds while I lay on the pillow-padded cabin sole. Our landfall confirmed Larry's concerns, and the sights he'd taken the afternoon before. The storm had caused the south-going current to stall. We had been set 30 miles north during the 2½ days we lay hove-to and only 60 miles had separated us from the almost certain destruction of those just submerged coral reefs.

The lessons we learned or which were reinforced during that storm:

1 Seeking refuge by running back to a marginal anchorage can be far less safe than getting sea room and staying at sea.

2 We knew we would be out in the open ocean for 100 miles. If we had prepared the boat for an offshore passage, nothing would have got loose inside or on deck.

3 Lee cloths are not just for keeping someone in the windward bunk, they are there to keep all crew safe in all bunks.

4 Heaving-to, assisted by a para-anchor, cuts down drift. (In our case our drift was reduced to less than a knot once the chute was set, compared to 1.3 to 1.5 knots with just the trysail.)

5 The motion while lying in the hove-to position 50° off the wind with the trysail steadying us was far more comfortable than lying directly to the wind as we did while Larry prepared to retrieve the para-anchor.

6 Having too large a para-anchor can be a mistake. Compared to the 2.4m (8ft) chute we'd always used previously on 7.4m (24ft 4in) 5-ton *Seraffyn*, the 3.6m (12ft) diameter chute on *Taleisin* held

more than twice the volume of water and exerted tremendous pressure on the rode, the fairleads and blocks. The larger loads meant more stretching, more shock loads, more chafe. Unfortunately, deciding what size parachute to use as a sea-anchor is not something that can be done with any mathematical or engineering certainty. But from this experience and from discussions with many sailors who have used similar gear, we have come to feel that manufacturers are leading sailors to err on the large size.

We used those lessons well as we voyaged onward: downsizing to a smaller 2.4m (8ft) diameter para-anchor, upsizing to a 10cm (4in) diameter snatch block to help reduce chafe on the main rode, making our sea-going heavy weather gear easier to get to, improving and strengthening our rudder stop system, adding extra heavy weather hand holds below and above decks, and using weather forecasts and pilot chart information as guidelines instead of gospel. Probably just as important, I came to trust *Taleisin* and myself to competently handle heavy weather, which let us eventually choose to sail from the Atlantic to the Pacific by way of Cape Horn with better preparations and far more confidence.

Comment

This honestly told tale of an unexpected storm by one of the most respected sailing couples the world has ever known is most instructional. Lin and Larry Pardey find themselves in a situation where bad weather was much more severe and prolonged than expected, and they deal with it using their well-tried methods.

One can only but admire them.

20

The Queen's Birthday
storm of 1994

PETER BRUCE

EVERY YEAR BETWEEN NOVEMBER AND April some 500 cruising boats avoid the south-west Pacific cyclone season by sailing to New Zealand for the summer. As it is customary to return to the tropical Pacific islands from New Zealand after the cyclone season, and before the New Zealand winter, the Island Cruising Association organizes a cruise in company starting around the end of May, an event called the Auckland–Tonga Regatta.

It was widely believed that the date finally selected in 1994 coincided with a perfect weather window. About 80 yachts were heading happily north-east at this time, either as part of the regatta, or on independent passages with a similar strategy in mind.

After the bulk of the fleet had left, a number of late starters were caught in the path of an unexpected storm of extraordinary ferocity and duration. Large breaking seas overwhelmed many of these yachts. One yacht was lost with her crew of three, two people aboard other yachts received severe injuries, and seven yachts were abandoned. Another yacht suffered a fire when electrical circuits shorted after a knockdown.

This storm is often called the Queen's Birthday storm, as it started during the annual New Zealand holiday to mark this event. Alternatively it is also called the June 'Bomb' in recognition of the meteorological term used to describe the explosive manner in which some

depressions can develop. It has some parallels with another fierce storm that had occurred at the same time of year in 1983, when some yachts were returning to Auckland after a race to Suva. On that occasion eight lives were lost. The situation was also similar in some respects to the 1979 Fastnet Race in that a group of yachts was caught out in unforecast hurricane force winds, although the 1994 Pacific storm lasted rather longer. A notable difference was that in the Fastnet the fleet was composed of racing yachts with racing crews, whereas in the Pacific storm the fleet was mainly cruising yachts with cruising crews and, in some cases, children.

The rescues have been well recorded and make dramatic reading. Much can be learnt from Kim Taylor's *1994 Pacific Storm Survey*; from Tony Farrington's *Rogue Storm*; from Commander Larry Robbins' report as seen from the bridge of the principal rescue ship, HMNZS *Monowai*; from a television documentary; and from the New Zealand Maritime Safety Authority's report. An especially valuable feature of Kim Taylor's *Pacific Storm Survey* was his inclusion of the yachts that were in the direct path of the storm, but which did not seek outside assistance. Media attention leans heavily towards casualties, yet we can probably learn more from those who did not need help.

The fact that a number of different craft were caught out in the same storm has allowed comparisons to be made that might not otherwise be so reliable, and this chapter endeavours to recount the strengths and weaknesses exposed by the storm and any lessons that can be gleaned. The emphasis in *Heavy Weather Sailing* is on prevention rather than cure, and little attempt will be made to comment upon rescue or matters of legislation that arose as a result of the storm.

The aim is to identify those actions that will give justifiable confidence to a crew, rather than have them look to making a Mayday call on the SSB radio or the activation of the EPIRB, notwithstanding that these appliances are well worth their place aboard as a last resort.

The yachts, in the order mentioned in the text, are as follows:

Silver Shadow	12.8m	(42ft)	Craddock-designed sloop, 4 crew
Pilot	9.8m	(32ft)	Colin Archer cutter, 2 crew
Arosa	9.8m	(32ft)	Lotus sloop, 4 crew
Sabre	10.4m	(34ft)	Ganley steel cutter, 2 crew
Destiny	13.7m	(45ft)	Norseman 447, 2 crew
Ramtha	11.6m	(38ft)	Simpson catamaran sloop, 2 crew
St Leger	12.5m	(41ft)	GRP cutter, 2 crew
Sophia	9.8m	(32ft)	Thistle cutter, 2 crew
Quartermaster	12.2m	(40ft)	Paul Whiting sloop, 3 crew
Mary T	12.2m	(40ft)	Cheoy Lee yawl, 4 crew
Waikiwi II	12.2m	(40ft)	Les Rolfe sloop, 4 crew
Heartlight	12.2m	(40ft)	Catalac catamaran sloop, 4 crew
Sula II	13.7m	(45ft)	Clark-designed cutter, 5 crew
Por Vida	13.1m	(43ft)	Westsail ketch, 2 crew
Hippo's Camp	13.1m	(43ft)	Morgan cutter, 2 crew, 2 children
Kiwi Dream	10.7m	(35ft)	Ganley sloop, 2 crew
Swanhaven	14.6m	(48ft)	Roberts ketch

Preparation

This storm showed that there is no substitute for knowing how one's boat will react in really bad weather when using a variety of tactics. For example, one owner said that 'he lacked familiarity with how to heave the boat to. That's the one area where I don't know whether I did her justice.' If an owner knows that his boat will lie comfortably hove-to, he will save a lot of energy by having found this out beforehand. Alternatively, if an owner knows that his boat always takes on volumes of water from somewhere or other in rough weather then although there would be no reduction in pumping, there will be significant reduction in *stress*. However, a survival storm is not the time to experiment with heavy weather tactics. It is too dangerous, exhausting and stressful.

When *Silver Shadow* had the misfortune to be knocked down and then rolled, her crew was able to note that few items had broken loose. They attributed this to the double latches that they had fitted to lockers and the care with which everything had been stowed before leaving harbour. The instrument sensor plug that was blown out of its tube into the inside of the boat illustrates the force in the wave that caused their first knockdown. When she came to be rolled through 360°, her floorboards and floor locker tops came out, but that was a lot less than might have happened. When the rescue aircraft asked how serious their predicament was on a scale of 1 to 5, the answer was 2. Overall, one gains the impression of a well-prepared boat, and a competent, courageous and resourceful crew.

It has to be said that not all the yachts that suffered heavy knockdowns or rolls gave the impression of being as well secured for sea as *Silver Shadow*. In particular, the frozen contents of freezers were a common hazard. Being struck by 'aerobatic frozen chickens' rather than the 'aerobatic batteries' encountered in the 1979 Fastnet might be regarded as an improvement, but this too may probably be avoided by spending 20 minutes putting a sliding bolt, or whatever, on the freezer door. There was a 24 volt battery in one yacht that came loose, releasing battery acid and breaking a portlight. The same boat, which had been prepared for a five-year cruise, also had to contend with the spillage of diesel fuel and a two-year supply of flour. One yacht suffered from flying pot plants. When one's boat is one's home, it is understandable that such items come on board, but it might be suggested that if they are to come to sea such items as pot plants must have a proper sea stowage made for them – for example, a bracket within a locker with a restraining arrangement to prevent the plant escaping from the pot even if the boat is inverted. The same applies to another yacht's vagrant sewing machine.

Chaos resulting from a 360° roll is dramatically reduced if a yacht has been systematically prepared for this eventuality before departure. The Royal Navy and other navies make a religion of 'securing for sea', the practice of fastening or enclosing every object that could possibly break loose in a heavy sea before leaving harbour. However, those who have been brought up properly in this respect may agree that teaching a crew, especially those who operate the galley, to secure for sea is difficult without the heavy hand of naval discipline. Nor does the average human seem to learn quickly by experience, especially the slightly reluctant sailor.

Few yachts are built with 360° rolls in mind. It must be appreciated that standard production craft are seldom, if ever, 'ocean-passage' seaworthy when new. For example, positive locking arrangements are required for horizontal locker doors, chart table lids and floorboards; in short, anything kept in place by the force of gravity. It behoves owners contemplating ocean voyages to spend considerable resources in preparing a vessel properly in order to warrant the expression 'roll-over ready'. As it is time-consuming to make proper brackets for pot plants, sewing machines and all other potentially hazardous items of equipment, one should take advantage of any suitable purpose-made brackets.

Seasickness was a problem for some, though with all the high drama not much about it was reported. One yacht's crew tried seasickness pills in the Queen's Birthday storm for the first time. The pills apparently caused an adverse reaction worse than the seasickness, suggesting that the best time to try out new remedies is in less demanding times.

Crew experience

There has been no suggestion that difficulties arose because crews lacked seagoing experience. Very severe storms are, thankfully, rare in the sailing seasons, which raises the question as to whether the crews who requested help were experienced enough to cope in such conditions – a different matter to sailing even 50 000 miles in normal weather. One skipper who lost his yacht said, 'We certainly had enough experience on board for normal sailing, but we didn't have experienced people for those extreme storm conditions; if we'd had three people who could steer in 14m (46ft) seas, maybe it would be a different story now.' There is little information on this question, and anyhow a survey on this matter would be hard to quantify. It could be argued that those who have great skills in avoiding bad weather may sometimes be the least prepared for it if caught out.

Some crews comprised simply a couple, and others had six or seven on board. There

Figure 20.1 The path of the Queen's Birthday storm cut across the route of yachts taking part in the Auckland–Tonga Regatta, and forecasts were not entirely helpful as to both the strength of wind and the direction the storm was to take. The predicted 40–50 knots became 75 knots in the event, and instead of taking the anticipated south-easterly course, the storm first veered to the south.

were examples of tremendous feats of endurance, as in the 1979 Fastnet, when boats had only one helmsperson confident and strong enough for the conditions. In this particular storm it would have needed super-human endurance to carry on steering for two or three days. The skipper of *Pilot* said, 'If we'd had just one other strong healthy crew member, I don't think that we would have abandoned.' One of the yachts that came through the storm unscathed, but not without difficulty, the 10.7m (35ft) Lotus sloop *Arosa*, was steered by hand for the duration. *Arosa* was one of the smaller and lighter yachts in the storm, so she could be expected to be lively. Such yachts do not tend to heave-to comfortably, and clearly the owners felt that four capable crew were essential for them to cope with drogues and, no doubt, steering in heavy weather. Aboard one boat the crew had never hand steered at sea, and had to learn when their autopilot gave up. Thus, bearing in mind that autopilots and self-steering gear often become unequal to the task sooner or later, one may conclude that one should have a crew strong enough to continue to hand steer a boat competently in all weather conditions, unless one has been able to prove that the vessel can be left in some way so that she will look after herself.

Ideally one should have a second-in-command on board who is ready, willing and experienced enough to take over should the skipper be incapacitated, as happened to *Destiny*. When the crew consists of only a man and his wife they should exchange roles from time to time so both are familiar with all aspects of handling the boat. Practising for 'man overboard' is more important than for 'woman overboard' as, generally speaking, a man is the more likely to fall over the side and a woman is less practised in recovery.

Crew endurance

Fatigue is one of the biggest enemies of the small-boat sailor. Thus one of the fundamentals of coping with storms is the conservation of energy. There is little doubt that some of the yachts were abandoned simply because their crews were over-stressed and utterly exhausted. After the first 24 hours of storm conditions, few of these crews, understandably, were able to do much to help themselves. Yet the 10.4m (34ft) Ganley steel cutter *Sabre*, with a crew of only two on board, encountered as severe weather as any, and passed through the eye of the storm without any serious problems, hove-to under deep-reefed main. Comments made by the crew after the storm, drawn from Kim Taylor's report, are illuminating: 'The confidence of previous heavy weather experience tended to reduce stress. Practise well beforehand to identify any weakness. We lay on the floor and attempted to rest. Consumption of liquids and high-energy foods is important. Our small opening ports are modified to take an outside storm window. Our boat is prepared with very rough weather conditions in mind and, lying hove-to, has proved herself on many occasions.' One has the impression of sailors who were mentally and physically prepared for whatever the sea could do. They did not need to experiment to try to find the most comfortable way to ride the storm and, owing to confidence in their preparations and their robust craft, they could conserve their energy and cope for as long as was necessary.

Less confident and less heavy-weather conditioned crews may have used up energy dealing with matters that should have been dealt with before going to sea. It is important to make a careful selection of priorities. Certain irritating things should have been dealt with at another time. They were not, and everyone has to force their minds to ignore them. It can be more important to avoid the risk of injury and husband one's strength for life-threatening situations that usually have to be dealt with straightaway. Not only does the workload sometimes have to be kept to essentials for survival, it also may have to be spread evenly, rather than have one over-motivated person do it all.

Even when all the crew are in their bunks, for example, a crew should stay in watches if possible, so they take it in turns to worry about what might be going on up top. In dire straits, notwithstanding collision risks, a skipper should be prepared to order his crew to stay in their bunks with as much force as he may use on other occasions to have them leave their bunks.

Design issues

A fundamental of coping with heavy weather might be thought to be the size and design of the craft. In this respect, all the hulls stood up pretty well. One catamaran suffered a cracked hull and there were broken windows of all sizes; otherwise, there were very few structural problems. In terms of length, beam, stability and displacement there did not seem to be any particular reason why some boats were rolled and others not. Factors such as a vessel's aspect to the breaking waves and luck seemed to be more relevant. Yachts that were lying a'hull were prone to join the '360° Club' as one might expect, but not in the case of the Robert Perry-designed 13.7m (45ft) Norseman 447 cutter *Destiny*. She seemed to have been overtaken by an extreme wave that pitchpoled her, and it is hard to see what her crew could have done to avoid their predicament. Likewise *Pilot*, a 9.8m (32ft) Colin Archer cutter, was running under control with bare pole when she was pooped by a wave that carried away her heavy-section mast. One can only pity the plight of the crews of the dismasted yachts. Without the windage of mast and rigging it was found that the boats simply did not lie to drag devices, rigged either from the bow or stern, and thus they adopted disastrous beam-on-to-the-seas attitudes. Only aboard *Pilot* was the broken mast cleared away and then the boat steered by hand down the seas. Again, without a mast this could be done only with difficulty, but she experienced no knockdowns, and running before the seas seemed infinitely preferable to lying a'hull. One must not forget, though, that yachts seldom seem to sink if left to their own devices. Of the eight or nine yachts abandoned, four (*Destiny, Ramtha, Silver Shadow* and *Sophia*) were found later either afloat or aground somewhere.

Only one vessel appears to have sunk as a direct result of the storm, and her family crew was tragically lost too. This was

Ramtha and her crew before the rescue. Wind speed at this time was 55 knots average, gusting to 70 or more according to HMNZS *Monowai*'s instruments. Significant wave height was 10m (33ft). *Photo: Lindsay Turvey (RNZN)*

Quartermaster, a 12.2m (40ft) Paul Whiting sloop, advertised as being designed for serious cruising, but of lighter displacement than most offshore cruising yachts of her size. During the onset of the storm the owner had been in regular contact with the Kerikeri shore radio station, and from just before midnight on 4 June he reported the first of a series of bad knockdowns and the fact that his wife had been injured. Two hours and 18 minutes later the third 'hard knockdown' was reported. The boat and her crew appeared to be in serious trouble, though no flooding was mentioned. This was the last call that was heard. *Quartermaster*'s EPIRB was activated another two hours and 36 minutes after that, and at 1745 on 6 June, a day and a half later, *Quartermaster*'s transmitting EPIRB was found lashed to her eight-man liferaft. Examination showed that the liferaft canister had been smashed, probably by the mast, and some or all of the crew had been aboard the liferaft until a wave had, presumably, washed

the occupants out. One can only speculate what might have happened after the owner's last radio message. *Quartermaster* could, for example, just possibly have been sunk by a whale-strike, or collision with a semi-submerged container; however, the most likely explanation is that she was sunk by breaking waves.

Apart from this awful and harrowing misfortune, no other yacht was abandoned because she was actually sinking. One of the yachts, thought by her crew to be in immediate danger of foundering due to the battering of the hull by a section of her broken mast, was spotted afloat some months later and then found after yet more months high and dry on a distant reef. In all cases, with the possible exception of *Quartermaster*, the boats' hulls appeared to withstand the conditions better than the crew.

Standing rigging did not break, but mast tubes did not usually withstand a full 360° roll, as they also had not in the 1979 Fastnet.

There is a case for looking again at the derided 'tree trunks' of the past, bearing in mind that mast failure is catastrophic for a sailing boat. Apart from the additional strength, a heavier mast section will bring about an increase in inertia that will reduce the chances of being rolled in the first place.

Steering arrangements were another weak point, as they were in the 1979 Fastnet. *Ramtha*, a 11.6m (38ft) sloop-rigged catamaran designed by Roger Simpson, had a steering failure before the storm and again during the storm. Her crew was not new to stormy weather but, apart from severe discomfort, they were having control problems, as well as near-capsizes. With the survey ship HMNZS *Monowai* close by, they had talked about being taken off, but when their steering failed again at the height of the storm the decision was made to abandon ship. *Mary T*, a 12.2m (40ft) Cheoy Lee offshore yawl, also reported steering problems at one time, and the 12.8m (42ft) Craddock-designed sloop *Silver Shadow* was found to have an uncontrollable rudder when the crew tried to motor her. In the 1979 Fastnet the numbers of steering failures were increased by the fact that many rudders from a particular designer had been changed to an inadequate carbon-fibre construction. Others failed by simply not being strong enough. One has the feeling that, owing to the additional complication of having two rudders to operate from one wheel, catamarans' steering systems need to be particularly well engineered. This seems obvious, but one does not know the extent to which, in order to keep prices competitive, the person in control of the specification has thought in terms of the average yacht that, arguably, will never encounter a survival storm. It may not be relevant to say so here, but there are brilliant naval architects who are not such good engineers. Design and construction of the steering gear of ocean-going yachts should allow generous safety margins.

A notable similarity with the Fastnet was leakage from cockpit locker hatches after the cockpit had been filled. At one point *Mary T*'s crew found that water was coming in faster than it could be pumped out. It was some time before it was realized that the leak was from the cockpit locker lids. Builders seldom fit watertight seals to cockpit locker lids; indeed, sometimes glassfibre mouldings are constructed so that making a watertight seal can be very difficult. Nonetheless, as cockpits can be filled frequently in heavy weather and remain filled owing to small-diameter drains, it is important that locker lids can be positively clipped in the closed position and adapted, as necessary, to make a watertight seal when closed. Undersized cockpit drains were a problem for *Destiny* as well as for *Mary T*. Pumps also gave problems in at least two yachts. *Mary T* had three pumps operable from on deck, but her crew regretted that they did not have a manual pump that could be worked from down below.

Cabin windows are often a risk to watertight integrity and, through breakage or deformation, became matters of concern in this particular storm. The leeward windows of the 13.4m (44ft) Les Rolfe-designed sloop *Waikiwi II* did not have storm boards and were broken. Big windows, such as those of many catamarans, caused big worries. An anonymous catamaran owner cited his big windows as the principal danger during the storm. To make a series of large windows requires much of the sides of the coachroof to be cut out. This can normally be expected to reduce the strength of the coachroof and hence its ability to withstand a plunging wave. It may be relevant to note that *Quartermaster*, built as a dedicated cruising yacht, had four comparatively large windows on each side of the coachroof, and her skipper had registered concern about them before contact was lost, though there is no evidence that they caused the loss of the yacht. *Ramtha*, a 11.6m (38ft) sloop-rigged catamaran designed by Roger Simpson, sensibly had storm covers for her large windows. So did *Heartlight*, a 12.5m (41ft) Catalac sloop-rigged catamaran designed by Tom Lack, but one of them was ripped off by a wave. Moreover, the smaller portlight windows let in water when they flexed.

It is significant that none of the three cata-marans in the storm area capsized, even though two of them lay a'hull for periods. However, two of the catamaran crews aban-doned their vessels. Their accounts did not lend much confidence to the seaworthiness of catamarans, as opposed to monohulls, in the extreme conditions they experienced. One catamaran crew was at one moment standing on the side windows. Capsize, with its dire consequences for non-self-righting craft, came very close to both *Ramtha* and *Heartlight*.

A serious problem, and not a new one, was injuries sustained when crew were flung out of their bunks. Coming out of one's bunk in this Pacific storm, either intentionally or unintentionally, increased the risk of bodily injury acutely. For example, Peter O'Neil, owner of *Silver Shadow*, was brewing up at the galley when his shoulder was broken. In *Mary T*, sailbags were brought into the saloon and successfully used as buffers. Thus for one not importantly occupied, a bunk is a very sensible place to be and good lee cloths become of tremendous consequence.

Of all the interior appurtenances ever sup-plied to a yacht, few need as much careful thought as the lee cloths. *Destiny*'s lee cloths failed before she was pitch-poled, and one therefore assumes they were not strong enough. If the maximum possible forces at work in a storm are taken into account it will probably be found that few standard lee cloths are strong enough for the job. When told that people fell out of their bunks, one is curious to know how strong and deep the lee cloths were – probably not strong enough or deep enough. It is possible to design a lee cloth that is held down at the outboard side of the bunk, which is next to impossible to come out of unintentionally. In so doing it may be necessary to provide additional handholds around the bunk, a quick release system for the upper body end, and greater material strength than the norm. The skipper of *Sula II* suggested that strongpoints should be fitted down below and safety harnesses worn in bunks.

Tactics

Regarding tactics and drag devices, as in the 1979 Fastnet, there was no obvious proce-dure that could be guaranteed to work for everyone. Two yachts were rolled when lying a'hull, and most – it would seem wisely – did their best to avoid this situation.

It is noteworthy that more boats found comfort and safety heading into the seas than the more popular tactic of running before them. Heaving-to under sail or engine was successful for all the yachts that tried it. A fourth reefing slab in the mainsail and an inner forestay was often an advantage when hove-to. The 10.4m (34ft) steel yacht *Sabre*, as we have already seen, remained hove-to under deep-reefed mainsail for the duration of the storm without any significant prob-lems. *Por Vida*, a 13.1m (43ft) Westsail ketch, went through the worst of the storm by motoring straight into the wind and sea at two-thirds throttle. She lost her storm jib and anchor from the pulpit, which carried away the hawse pipe leaving a hole to be plugged. Otherwise she had no problems. The 13.1m (43ft) Morgan-designed cutter *Hippo's Camp* spent part of the storm hove-to under storm jib, with her helm lashed to steer to weather. She used her engine in the windless eye of the storm to motor 'around' the waves, but later found the wind blew the boat flat under her storm jib. Then she lay successfully to a plastic drogue, though it is not clear whether this was led over the bow or the stern. *Kiwi Dream*, a 10.7m (35ft) steel Ganley sloop, suc-cessfully hove-to under a backed scrap of headsail and deep-reefed main, and *Swanhaven*, a 14.6m (48ft) Roberts ketch, hove-to successfully within the area of the strongest wind. Finally, *Sula II*, a 13.7m (45ft) Clark-designed cutter of 12 tons, was sailed close-hauled under trysail and her speed maintained at 3 or 4 knots by feathering into the wind. The effect of feathering took speed down to a comfortable level and brought the bow closer into the wind than would have been achieved by heaving-to. She experienced no rolls or knockdowns, but might be considered outside the strongest wind area. Kim Taylor points out, interestingly, that all these vessels were in the moderate or heavy displacement category.

It was disappointing to an analyst that the two yachts carrying parachute anchors did not deploy them, but their reasons were understandable. By the time they had come to realize that it was parachute anchor time, conditions had become very risky for working on deck. In the moderate conditions just prior to the storm, *Ramtha*, the catamaran, had spent a night lying to a sea anchor on a 91m (300ft) warp from her bows, but in the morning the sea anchor was found hanging vertically rather than holding her into the wind and sea. For some reason the sea anchor could not be tripped and, as there was only a twosome on board, winching it in proved very heavy work. Consequently, it was cut loose and abandoned. The catamaran *Heartlight* did have a 5.5m (18ft) Para-Tech parachute on board, but the skipper felt that a drogue was more suitable in the extreme conditions prevailing due to varying angles of the seas. Only when the drogue line fouled his propellers was the parachute deployed. Not finding it an advantage, the skipper said he would have cut it adrift had it not been his desire to remain in one place so he could be found more easily.

After *Silver Shadow* had been dismasted and later rolled, her crew managed, much to their credit, to release their broken mast and, following various experiments, lay from the bow a sea anchor made from a No 4 genoa. Then they rigged a jury mizzen sail which was enough to hold the yacht into the seas some of the time, and which seemed to help to prevent further capsizes.

A variety of drag devices was used over the stern, either warps, warps and chains, or drogues. Six yachts were either rolled or knocked down when trailing drag devices, two of them while being hand steered and four when not. The 12.5m (41ft) cutter *St Leger* was the most successful. Her crew deployed a Galerider on 76m (250ft)

polypropylene while under vane steering. Though the boat steered well and the speed was comfortable, the line went slack when the boat was in the troughs and it was found necessary to shorten the line to 24–27m (80–90ft). For the next 60 hours with winds over 60 knots the drogue remained stable and effective. *Destiny* towed a Sea Squid drogue using 61m (200ft) of line and 3.7m (12ft) of 10mm ($^3/_8$in) chain that proved to be very satisfactory at first. With hand steering dead downwind, the drogue kept *Destiny* at a 'comfortable' speed of 3–8 knots, but as conditions became worse the drogue broke out from the surface on two occasions, allowing the boat speed to become dangerously fast. They felt with hindsight that a longer line was necessary, but one could also imagine that more weight of chain could have helped. As it happened, *Destiny* was pitch-poled in spite of her drogue. *Quartermaster* was probably towing drogues, and was under engine and autopilot when she was last heard of in an attempt 'to get seas to come in over the back quarter' which 'seemed to be working'. *Silver Shadow* was running under storm jib and autohelm when she was struck by a breaking wave, 30° more towards the port beam than the usual seas, and this brought down her mast. At least four yachts were neither rolled nor knocked down when on autohelm or vane steering.

These records, once again, may not indicate anything very strongly, but there seems to be more than a tendency in favour of hand steering. For example, *Pilot*'s skipper felt that he would have been able to avoid the 360° roll if he had been hand steering, and *Waikiwi II*'s skipper wished he'd had more storm-skilled helmsmen. *St Leger*'s skipper felt that the quick reaction of a helmsman was essential to avoid a broach. An experienced sailor at the helm is influenced by what he can see or hear coming at him. He is influenced by speed, acceleration, angle of heel and waveform. On the other hand, the automatic helm has no anticipation and is merely influenced by the angle off course, which may occur too quickly to make any difference at critical times. Thus it could well be that the hand-steered yacht is safest, provided that the helmsman is alert, strong and competent for the task. This was also a finding from the 1979 Fastnet.

A useful point made by several skippers was that, when lightly crewed, only one tactic might be feasible. Once a severe storm has developed, one may be stuck with whatever tactic was chosen first. This point underlines the case for experimentation in moderate conditions.

One wonders how much crews are influenced when choosing their tactics by the direction in which they happen to be already going. It is easier to carry on along roughly the course one had originally intended than not. It requires a very definite decision to change course from going into it to running away from it, and a yet more bold and confident decision to turn into the wind and sea having been running away from it. In this storm the quickest route out of it was the same direction as the fleet was heading. Thus those on the western side of the storm track tended to run with the wind astern and those on the eastern side were more inclined to head into it.

As noted above, perhaps one of the most significant aspects of the storm was the surprisingly high number of problems encountered by yachts running before the sea compared to those heading into it. On the face of it, the time-honoured technique of

Australians Bill and Robyn Forbes, both aged 53, being hauled aboard HMNZS *Monowai* from their 11.6m (38ft) catamaran *Ramtha*. Photo: CPO AHS Lindsay Turvey (RNZN)

'heaving-to' under sail appears to have been the safest tactic for moderate- or heavy-displacement yachts. On the other hand, modern, lightly constructed yachts do not always heave-to comfortably under sail, as *Arosa*'s crew decided. Many are too lively, make too much leeway, and do not 'look after themselves' as traditional yachts do, so an alternative has to be found. Running before the seas under hand control and drogue or heaving-to under engine and helmsman may be the solution if a strong crew is carried. Alternatively, one has to consider lying to a parachute anchor.

Liferafts

During rescues, hand-held VHFs were useful on board. A waterproof hand-held VHF will be even more useful if a crew is forced into a liferaft. Several crews were tempted to inflate their liferaft as a precautionary action. *Waikiwi II* had two on board, and one of these was inflated in case of immediate need. After four hours it was 'blown to bits' and eventually was torn away. *Destiny*'s only liferaft was also inflated and lost when the painter parted. Two other liferafts were ripped from their deck mountings and were later found inflated and, presumably, some considerable distance from where they had been lost.

These events suggest that one should keep the liferaft in its container, stowed until required in a purpose-made deck locker or down below in an easily accessible position, and rely on regular maintenance to ensure it does inflate when really needed. One should note that *Quartermaster* carried an eight-man liferaft and a crew of only three. Liferafts are designed to perform best with their full complement weighing them down, and it could be that the *Quartermaster* crew was lost because of this. It would be normal for an owner to have a liferaft for the maximum number of crew he is likely to have on board. However, some liferaft vendors advise that it is preferable to have one person too many in the liferaft rather than one too few; this suggests that the size should be for one person less than the likely minimum crew. Short of hiring a liferaft for the appropriate number each time crew size changes (an unlikely solution), the owner is left in an unfortunate dilemma. Larger craft often have two four-man or two six-man liferafts; this is a tidy, if rather expensive, solution to the problem. Alternatively one supposes, if at all possible, an oversize liferaft should be ballasted with whatever sensible means comes to hand. A point well made by Kim Taylor in his *Storm Survey* is that the crews who asked to be taken off were in more danger during the transfer than at any other time. Besides, they were putting other lives at risk. Another key point is that, once abandoned, the boat may be considered a hazard and deliberately sunk. So, as in the past, everything points to staying with the boat and keeping her afloat as long as possible.

Useful equipment

Useful miscellaneous items of equipment cited were: strobe lights, ski goggles, cyclume sticks, hot water bottles, wetsuits and cyclists' helmets. Commander Larry Robbins, commanding officer of HMNZS *Monowai*, mentioned that *Mary T*'s strobe light was very, very effective. He makes the point that the strobe is much more visible than standard navigation lights and, as it can't be mistaken for prescribed lights, the strobe could become a useful safety aid, as with aircraft. Pilots say that the powerful strobes of commercial aircraft can be seen at distances up to 40 miles, and they have to switch them off on the ground to avoid dazzling everyone. Perhaps when the entire crew is stormbound down below would be a good time to switch on a strobe. Anyone who has tried to look to windward from a small craft in force 10, both with or without goggles, will vouch for their value. Goggles have become standard equipment in the BT

Global Challenge, the race around the world the wrong way. As Alby Burgin said after Cyclone Emily, 'If I'd held my head up the wind and water would have cut my eyes out.' Cyclume sticks provide a source of light when everything electrical has failed. Could this ever happen? Given bad enough conditions and the hostility of salt water to all things electrical, the answer has to be yes.

Even in the relatively warm waters in which the storm originated, hypothermia was a problem. Dampness works its way into the insulating layers, reducing their efficiency, and forced inaction does nothing to keep the body warm. One can become uncomfortably cold even on the equator if one has no protection from heavy rain. *Pilot* had a hot-water bottle on board, and this came in handy when Greg Forbes started suffering from hypothermia. *Mary T*'s crew found space blankets good for keeping warm in the damp conditions. A wetsuit can often be worth a place on board. For example, Bill and Robyn Forbes wore wetsuits when they were hauled aboard HMNZS *Monowai*. Apart from using a wetsuit for leisure diving, it can be used, for example, when clearing a fouled propeller.

A wetsuit's survival capabilities are illustrated by a story of many years ago, when a fishing boat capsized at night in a winter storm some miles off Iceland. No one else realized what had happened until one of the crew, who was wearing a wetsuit top, fetched up alive on the beach. He was the only survivor. Drysuits have now become cheaper, easier to put on, and can be made of breathable fabric. Consequently, they are worthy of consideration, but probably more worthy are the survival suits that are coming onto the market. Sailing people are not likely to invest in clothing that may only be used once, so survival suits that have a dual purpose are the ones likely to be best value.

As for cyclists' helmets, one can see the virtue of head protection in almost any sport. The 'Boombanger Club' can be even more disastrous than the '360° Club' and a helmet could be a major benefit. However, most people feel self-conscious about wearing helmets aboard a boat, so not everybody will be seen wearing one, but this attitude could change in time.

External support

Nine yachts, which ranged from 9.8–13.7m (32–45ft), put out Mayday calls. All except one of these was fully equipped with safety equipment, and all had either reasonably experienced or very experienced crews. Most of the crews that were rescued had actuated their EPIRBs. Not only can a 406MHz EPIRB alert shore authorities of a Mayday, it will identify the boat and give its position. Then,

Silver Shadow from HMNZS *Monowai* as her four crew were taken off. *Photo: PO AHS Lindsay Turvey (RNZN)*

when rescuers are within a few miles, they can home in on the EPIRB's transmissions. This equipment, *from a rescue point of view*, could be called the outstanding device of the event. New Zealanders will remember the story of *Rose Noelle*, a catamaran bound for Tonga in 1979 at exactly the same time of year. She capsized in a storm, eluded the search, and drifted with her crew for five months before going ashore on Great Barrier Island. The event makes a good case for the 406MHz EPIRB, though it has to be said that *Rose Noelle* was carrying an older-type EPIRB, but this was not heard.

Judging by the recordings of the radio conversations, many boats used Kerikeri shore radio – incidentally now closed down – for meteorological advice. As the storm developed some leaned heavily on the radio station for comfort and the general support that was readily given. Indeed, Jon and Maureen Cullen, who used to provide their service as a hobby, managed to stay on the air for the duration of the storm. While SSB is a superb product of the technological age, and the Cullens provide a wonderful service – especially during this storm – ideally one will not want to depend too much upon advice from someone who is not present and therefore cannot be expected to appraise the situation fully. It can be argued that the ability to talk to those ashore, and the existence of an EPIRB on board, could possibly divert attention from the primary task in severe weather and to give a false sense of security. One cannot pass responsibility on to someone else over the radio. Nor, equally, should one give up trying to take control of the situation just because the EPIRB has been activated. On the arrival of a rescuer it must require a lot of courage to announce that help is no longer required. Such decisions need finely balanced judgement, not easily found in an over-tired, over-stressed mind. Nevertheless, assuming one does decide to do without help and lives to tell the tale, it

should be remembered that one can always show one's gratitude properly and explain the circumstances to the would-be rescuer at a later date. A good seaman will understand entirely and may be glad not to have to attempt a difficult rescue.

Another form of a false sense of security can be given by the presence of other friendly yachts in the vicinity. While there are circumstances where this situation can be of advantage, in a violent storm, there is little chance of assistance from other small craft. Crews have to cultivate a sensible level of self-reliance.

Finale

One might be disappointed, but one should not be surprised to find that, once again, there was no obvious panacea, no one piece of equipment or single tactic identifiable that would have enabled all the yachts to lie quietly for the duration of this storm while their crews slept. If only a bow-led parachute anchor had been deployed we would have learnt a lot more about the capabilities of this device compared to other techniques, but none were used.

So we are left with the conclusion that to survive a rare and tremendous storm like the tropical depression of June 1994 one must have some fundamentals right, such as tactics proven for each individual yacht as a result of experiments with a strong crew on a daysail. One must also put into effect many detailed preparations for prolonged bad weather. Once caught out in a severe storm one must avoid becoming over-tired and over-stressed, and ruthlessly separate 'nice-to-have' actions from those upon which survival is likely to depend. Even then, a measure of luck may be necessary to avoid extreme breaking waves, perhaps coming from an unexpected quarter.

21

A winter storm off the south-west coast of Australia

DEBORAH SCHUTZ

A letter to the Australian magazine Cruising Helmsman, *seeking accounts of the use of parachute sea anchors in severe storms, led to Deborah Schutz's description of how* Prisana II *rode out sustained winds of hurricane strength off Perth. The story shows whether a parachute sea anchor is capable of doing its business when it really comes on to blow.*

PRISANA II IS A GLASSFIBRE KETCH. SHE is a Tayana Surprise 45 measuring 13.7m (45ft) with two equal-height masts, both with in-mast furling. Her draft is 2.1m (7ft), displacement 13 tons, beam 4.1m (13.5ft), and her ballast 5 tons. She has a fin keel, a skeg rudder and a hydraulic autopilot-to-quadrant-wheel cable steering.

We departed from Adelaide, South Australia, in early July 1996 with six people on board. These were Steve (the skipper and my partner), myself and our son Ben (seven years old at the time), and our long-time friends Trevor, Sam and Patrick. Steve has sailed for most of his life. Ben and I have been sailing for the six years since Steve and his father purchased *Prisana II*. Trevor had considerable sailing experience and was mechanically minded (like Steve). Sam had sailed previously, but Patrick had no previous sailing experience. Our plan was to cruise the Western Australian coastline and offshore islands for six months. We expected the Great Australian Bight would test us – especially as it was the middle of a southern winter. I had

visited the Bureau of Meteorology a couple of weeks before we left and was warned that we were about to cross one of the worst seas in the world for storms.

With this in mind, we decided to set up our 5.5m (18ft) Bass Strait 18 Para·Anchor, manufactured by Para·Anchors, Australia in Sale, Victoria,* parachute anchor before we left port. The parachute anchor – with a 18mm ($^3/_4$in) stainless steel swivel – was shackled to the rode which was 125m (410ft) of 18mm ($^3/_4$in), three-strand nylon contained in a deployment bag. The other end of the rode was shackled to a 12mm ($^1/_2$in) chain link welded to the ship's main anchor that is stowed on the bow in a custom-made stem fitting. To give added security, the anchor was held by a 10mm ($^3/_8$in) Ronstan rigging screw, secured to a 10mm ($^3/_8$in) stainless steel plate bolted under the windlass. Winch and plate were fastened by six 10mm ($^3/_8$in) stainless steel studs. Both the fixing point to the anchor and to the plate were backed up by secondary systems. A slack chain from the nylon rode was attached

---

* This sea anchor was incorrectly described as a Para-Tech anchor in previous editions.

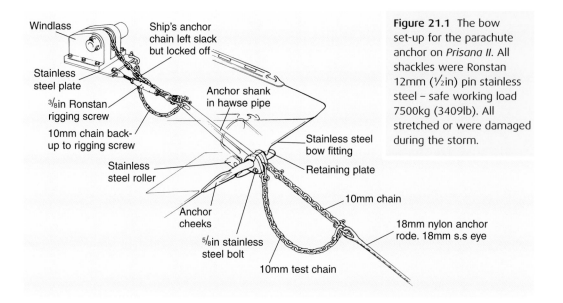

Windlass

Ship's anchor
chain left slack
but locked off

Stainless
steel plate

³⁄₈in Ronstan
rigging screw

10mm chain back-
up to rigging screw

Anchor shank
in hawse pipe

Stainless
steel roller

Stainless steel
bow fitting

Retaining plate

10mm chain

Anchor
cheeks

18mm nylon anchor
rode. 18mm s.s eye

⁵⁄₈in stainless
steel bolt

10mm test chain

Figure 21.1 The bow set-up for the parachute anchor on *Prisana II*. All shackles were Ronstan 12mm (½in) pin stainless steel – safe working load 7500kg (3409lb). All stretched or were damaged during the storm.

to a 16mm (⁵⁄₈in) stainless steel bolt passing through the anchor cheeks, and another short length of chain was secured between the anchor shackle and the 10mm (³⁄₈in) plate bolted under the windlass. We used a partial trip line – two floats and two 15m (49ft) lines with swivels (see Fig 21.1).

Fortunately we crossed the Bight within a high-pressure system. After eight days, we sighted Cape Leeuwin, the south-western-most point of mainland Australia and one of the world's great navigational landmarks. A wide berth is required to round the Cape, as immediately west and north of the lighthouse lies an extensive area of reefs. The area is known for rogue breaking waves and strong tides. We encountered choppy seas, much large shipping and a falling barometer. Winds increased up to 30 knots from the north. As the day progressed we headed farther out to sea while the weather deteriorated. During the night, gusts reached 40–45 knots as we beat into a westerly, by now 80 miles out from Cape Leeuwin.

Near nightfall on Sunday 14 July we were almost abeam of Cape Naturaliste. Our weatherfax showed a complex low was fast approaching. Growing darkness, our position, the unfamiliar coastline and the wind direction (a 40 knot north-north-east) meant that it was inadvisable to look for an anchorage. We

had already considered using our sea anchor, but owing to the number of ships in the vicinity we decided to keep going. We reduced sail, expecting the winds to swing south-west with the approaching front, which we would use to get us to Fremantle. We were wrong! Throughout the night, Mother Nature unleashed a storm of unrelenting fury, with the wind increasing to 50 knots from the north-north-east with large seas, leaving us little choice but to head out to sea.

At first light on Monday 15 July we came about. Perth Radio issued another gale warning. The barometer read 996mb (hPa) and was falling. By evening, the wind had become a strong westerly, the barometer now read 990mb (hPa), though the sea had moderated. As the night progressed, squalls reached 60 knots and lightning could be seen behind us as we sailed in a northerly direction. Eventually the anemometer was off the scale at over 65 knots and the seas were rising dramatically. At approximately 0300 a huge wall of white water knocked us over to starboard. The helmsman (thankfully harnessed) was chest-height in water, and our masts were horizontal in the sea. Ben and I were asleep below and we were both flung out of our bunks.

Steve, Sam and Trevor deployed the sea anchor, using a flying set. Even in the dark,

Prisana II is a sturdy Tayana Surprise 45.

BELOW **Figure 21.2** Track of *Prisana II* during the storm, July 1996.

this was relatively easy. Deployment simply involved reaching from the safety of the cockpit to the rode deployment bag, unlacing the top, removing the end of the rode, and shackling it to the parachute anchor. Trip line and float buoys were fed overboard, followed by the parachute anchor in its deployment bag. Within about 30 seconds, we had taken up all the rode and were gently pulled head-to-wind, allowing us to furl the sails entirely. They were to remain furled for the rest of the storm. Then we put an 18mm (³/₄in) bridle line on the rode, with a view to lying to the parachute at an angle in the manner described by Larry and Lin Pardey, but the bridle broke almost as soon as it was tensioned. So we gave up that idea and contented ourselves with leaving the rode to lead straight out over the bow. After that it was all crew below with hatches battened. At this point we were 30nm to the west of Rottnest Island.

During the morning of Tuesday 16 July I ventured into the cockpit and was immediately awestruck. The seas were incredibly huge. I soon retreated below, after taking a couple of photos. I later found out the seas were reported to be 11m (36ft) on top of a 9m (30ft) swell – a total of around 20m (64ft). When the parachute rode emerged as it spanned a trough, it sliced

The parachute sea anchor is taking the strain during the storm while the crew take to their bunks. *Photo: Deborah Schutz*

through the water like a knife, and one could see massive tension come on it as *Prisana* surged forward and back with the waves. A lot of white water was being swept from the tops of the swell, with large rolling crests of white water underneath. *Prisana* took many loads of white water across the deck, and even some green water. The conditions were such that it would have been foolhardy to be anywhere on deck. We used a safety harness when visiting the cockpit, otherwise almost all of our time was spent down below.

At that time we felt that we had plenty of sea room as we drifted in a southerly direction in the Leeuwin current on a west wind for 24 hours. This current runs southward down the Continental Shelf from Indonesia, bringing masses of warm water. It begins flowing around April each year through until October, and seldom moves faster than 1 knot in a band approximately 50km (31 miles) wide. Throughout the storm our drift rate averaged 0.9 knots. The parachute anchor held us while the winds screamed at over 70 knots. The noise was incredible! We

rolled heavily from gunwale to gunwale and it appeared that we yawed about 45° on one side to 35° on the other. Occasionally, we felt the rode become slack as the bow paid off somewhere over 45°, then there would be a tremendous jerk as the rode became taut again. This may have been due to rogue waves coming in on a different angle, but we believed that it was because the boat yawed a lot and surged on the huge swell. It was hard to tell from down below.

Steve awoke at dawn on Wednesday 17 July to see a ship on our stern, only 0.8 miles away. We tried to make contact using VHF, and an Australian vessel promptly answered, but he was 6 miles away. He informed us that the other vessel was a foreign ship, along with mentioning that he didn't envy us one bit. For 15 long minutes, we tried to make contact. We were losing sight of the whole ship (approximately 125m (400ft) long with an extensive bridge structure) behind the seas. Finally, a man's voice responded in broken English causing us a minor panic. He didn't seem eager to alter his course, telling

Sam heading for Perth after the storm. The steering was damaged but still functioning. *Photo: Deborah Schutz*

us he had no ballast and that he couldn't even see us. We managed to persuade him to alter course a little and, after ensuring that he could see our spotlight, we saw him pass 0.4nm away on our radar.

We had drifted almost as far south as Bunbury when we began to drift east and believed we were in an eddy of the Leeuwin current. We appeared to have been caught up in a typical anticlockwise flow that took us inshore and then northwards along the coast.

The weather remained unchanged. All day long the winds continued to blow over 70 knots. We heard that a large cargo ship had just lost 30 containers off Cape Leeuwin. The Adelaide media reported that a cyclone had hit Perth.

By Thursday 18 July conditions were moderating, the wind was now down to 50 knots and the barometer slowly began to rise; the seas were still large and getting steeper with shallowing depth as we crept closer to the coast. Concerned about running out of sea room late in the afternoon, we decided to retrieve the parachute anchor. This wasn't

easy. Noise from the wind and sea made it difficult to hear the skipper's instructions from the helm to the bow. Trying to use the engine to pick up the recovery float, we fouled the rode on the propeller. When we finally retrieved the parachute anchor, we found two large well-frayed holes in two separate panels between the vent hole and the skirt. We have no doubts about the manufacture or design of the parachute, nor do we believe that it was snagged during recovery, so it is probable that the holes were caused by flotsam. By the time we set a course for Rottnest Island the wind was down to 30–40 knots, which felt like a gentle breeze.

Around 1030 on Friday 19 July we motored into the Fremantle Sailing Club, grateful that we had decided to buy a parachute anchor. With it we were able to ride out and survive the storm with our bow held into the seas. During the storm, Bunbury and Fremantle Harbours were closed and the harbourmaster at Fremantle said they were the largest seas he could ever remember. Rottnest Island, 12 miles off the coast of

Figure 21.3
Weatherfax chart for 17 July 1996 showing the deep low south of Cape Leeuwin and the packed isobars between the two.

Fremantle, had holidaymakers stranded there for three days as the ferries were unable to make the crossing. When he docked at Fremantle on 19 July the captain of the ship that had lost 30 containers off Cape Leeuwin said, 'In all my time, I've never seen seas like those.' In addition to the unusually strong winds, what the weather bureau in Perth described as a rare winter tornado, which had formed at high altitude somewhere around where *Prisana* was on the night of 15 July, had struck south Perth with 200km/h (108 knot) winds.

We spent the following three to four weeks in Fremantle repairing *Prisana*. She had suffered quite some damage. The rudder shaft had been twisted, the forward bulkhead damaged, and four stanchions had been ripped from the deck, to name but a few of her problems.

During the storm both our primary systems to take the load of the rode at the bow had failed. The Ronstan rigging screw had broken, stripping eight turns of thread, and the chain/link welded to the ship's anchor had torn off. Thankfully, in both systems, the back-up held but, when the rigging screw broke, the anchor was free to smash around,

which caused some damage to our stainless steel bow fitting. We also found that our 125m (410ft) of 18mm (³/₄in) rope had stretched an extra 20m (66ft).

Prisana's rudder shaft had about a 15° twist in the 50mm (2in) diameter 316-grade stainless steel shaft at the point where the quadrant is fixed. It definitely wasn't twisted before the deployment of the parachute anchor. The rudder lashings holding the rudder on the centreline at the quadrant had broken twice during the storm. We managed to hold it, third time lucky, on spare 18mm (³/₄in) nylon anchor rode. The forward bulkhead was damaged, mostly due to a design fault rather than the conditions.

To the question, 'Did the sea anchor save the boat?' the answer is, 'Absolutely!' In the conditions we were caught in, we believe that having the parachute anchor set up before departure was crucial to its safe and easy deployment. Had we not had it (an awful thought) we would probably have tried to find shelter behind Rottnest Island by sailing on a broad-reach, possibly dragging warps as we were not carrying a drogue. I believe our chances of surviving had we done so would have been extremely slim.

Comment

It seems that *Prisana II* must have experienced hurricane strength winds for about 48 hours. That she survived in the way she did brings credit to her crew and their parachute sea anchor. It is one of the most testing accounts of a parachute sea anchor deployment, and goes to show that a parachute can work in very extreme weather. It is significant that the parachute sea anchor was set up before the yacht left harbour, in anticipation of bad weather.

The parachute system appears to have been taken to its limit. The canopy was damaged, the rode stretched, and the primary method of securing the parachute line at the boat end failed, possibly during recovery as the damage was not in a stressed part.

As is normal, the parachute did not give a comfortable ride: *Prisana* rolled from gunwale to gunwale and yawed about 80°. Then there was the time when the parachute line would become slack and then take up with a jerk. Having two masts, *Prisana* had more windage aft than a sloop and therefore just about managed without a riding sail at the stern. It is probable that she would not have yawed as much, nor would the parachute line have snatched, had one been used. The Pardey method of lying to a parachute, which was conceived to improve comfort, was tried without success in that the bridle line broke. This is not surprising due to the huge loads the bridle line has to take when the vessel is as big as *Prisana*.

It is noteworthy to find that *Prisana* was in danger from other shipping. A lookout in a yacht in storm conditions cannot easily look to windward without eye protection. Even then, spume can obscure visibility almost entirely. Looking from most enclosed bridges of ships in a storm does not improve visible range by much. The windows are continuously spattered with spray that blurs the view entirely between sweeps of the wiper. Only just after the wiper has passed is there a split second of good vision before the window blurs over again. This allows a brief view in one narrow direction. Radar is not much help either, as a yacht's echo may well be completely lost in the wave returns. Thus there is no better chance that a yacht will see a ship than vice versa. Salvation comes in the form of VHF, and it is wise to make a regular Sécurité call, giving position and circumstances.

Did the parachute save the boat? We don't know what would have happened if the crew had been forced to adopt other storm tactics, but at least we do know that by using the parachute the crew of *Prisana II* survived to tell the tale.

22

Black Velvet's bothersome return from Iceland

EWEN SOUTHBY-TAILYOUR

IT WAS JULY 2001. The mountaineers had flown back to Iceland from Greenland. I had hoped to deliver them to Scoresbysund in Greenland, then support and collect them from their expedition, but that is not what happened. The *storis*, or sea ice, of summer 2001 had been too thick for *Black Velvet*, my Tradewind 35, a 12-ton, gaff cutter even though she had been strengthened for ice.

The subsequent climbing in Iceland had been testing, but the mountaineers' greatest concern was a six-day trek to get help if necessary. Neither they, nor *Black Velvet*, had long-range communications and nor had we wanted them; our collective view was, and remains, that there is far too much reliance on outside help and advice these days and achievements are diminished for that. Conversely, long-range communications would not have prevented our eventual situation, but at least I could have had a weather report and known that the end was not in sight!

The one mountaineer who elected to sail back to Plymouth in England was Dave Wilkie, a strong man but with no sailing experience; he was a crocodile breeder in Australia and crocodile hunter in East Africa. I warned him that just because it was the return journey, there was no guarantee that it would be easy. As a climber he was well aware that 'down-climbing' to base camp can produce the greatest dangers. As far as a

yacht is concerned, after a two-month expedition in hard weather, un-surveyed waters and with no shore support, gear is probably worn, spares are running out, the engine and associated mechanics – including steering gear – need servicing. There is also a certain relaxation, as all eyes focus on the homecoming.

We sailed on 24 July with a fine forecast that should have taken us a good way towards the north-west Irish coast where, after six days or so, I had planned to telephone home via a coast radio station with our, very approximate, ETA in Plymouth. Thank goodness the Irish have not closed down this safety facility. If I had known what the weather was actually going to do, I would either have delayed sailing or headed due west from Reykjavik in order to give me maximum sea room over an arc of 270°.

About 120 miles south of Heimaey the wind starting backing to the south before we had cleared either end of Iceland. I altered course southeastwards but after only 20 miles the wind continued backing to the southeast so we started sailing as fast as we could to the west; but only for another 20 miles as the wind then veered back to the south. We now headed north-east (not an ideal course but, in theory, a safe one) to get clear of that end of Iceland instead; any closer to the wind in those confused seas and the bluff-bowed heavy *Black Velvet* would stop in the water.

The Reykjanes headland and the associated shoals that stretch for 45 miles south-west were a constant worry as we could not afford to be embayed between them and Heimaey. However, after another 20 or so miles the wind increased dramatically. After handing the log, we ran north trailing four warps in a very heavy, breaking sea.

I had two very long warps carried for mooring to the shore; these certainly stretched back over two wave formations. Two other warps were streamed in bights and, in extremis, I planned to ask Dave if we could use his precious climbing ropes, knowing that they would, of course, then have had to be written off.

To begin with we had enough sea room (110 miles) as I did not believe the wind would stay in any one direction for long – as had

RIGHT *Black Velvet* racing off Cowes.

BELOW *Black Velvet* showing her traditional underwater profile.

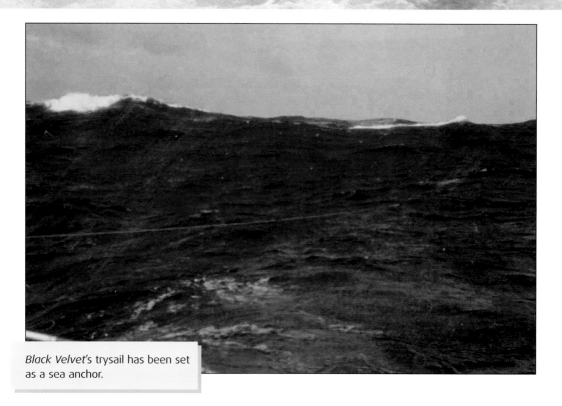

Black Velvet's trysail has been set as a sea anchor.

already been demonstrated. After about 40 miles I was planning to see if we could make Heimaey but steering under warps is not a precise art and, with the seas that were running at the time, I doubted that under storm sails we could have made a safe landfall.

Eventually the wind not only moderated but it also shifted to the west again, and for a brief period we were making a course towards Stornoway – albeit with some danger to the upper deck gear. In nearly 24 hours we managed only 8 miles over the ground thanks to the steep seas, a fickle wind, *Black Velvet*'s heavy displacement and short waterline length.

Then, at 0730 on 29 July and following a sharp rise after low pressure (lowest – 994 mb), the wind backed to the south again and this time increased to an average of 55 knots with powerful gusts on top of that. The seas were far too dangerous to do anything other than face them with our bows and so a makeshift sea anchor was rapidly made out of the trysail. Because of its asymmetric shape we could not get this to open like a

parachute and so it was, effectively, never more than 'semi-inflated'. There does not seem, in practical terms, any substitute for the real thing and if we had had the real thing we might have stopped in the water; on the other hand while the 2 knots we were making to the north did not help the 'lee-shore aspect' they did help to take some of the sting out of the breakers – aided, of course, by the presence on the near surface of the sail itself.

When we started this exercise we were almost exactly 60 miles south of Iceland's southern coast and 'aiming' for a point about 25 miles east of Heimaey. Unable to reduce this 'leeway' to less than two knots I considered what other options were open to me and the only solution I could come up with would be by courtesy of the Almighty! Any wind shift now had to allow us to sail over 60° either side of our downwind track: an angle of 135° that was opening quickly. On the other hand, at that moment, we could not, with safety, have sailed either side of our track by about 20° due to the steepness of the seas.

No matter what we threw over the bows

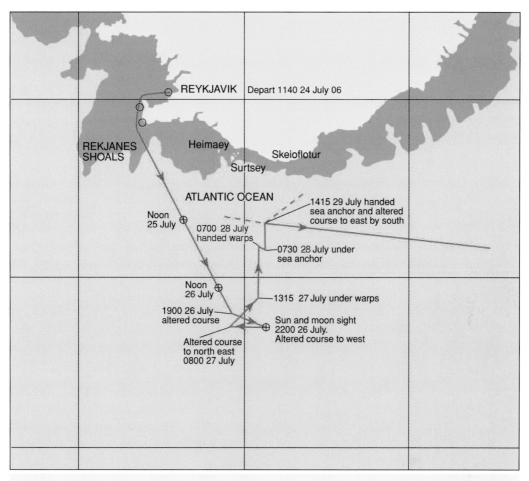

REYKJAVIK | Depart 1140 24 July 06

REKJANES SHOALS

Heimaey

Skeioflotur

Surtsey

ATLANTIC OCEAN

Noon 25 July

0700 28 July handed warps

1415 29 July handed sea anchor and altered course to east by south

0730 28 July under sea anchor

Noon 26 July

1900 26 July altered course

Altered course to north east 0800 27 July

1315 27 July under warps

Sun and moon sight 2200 26 July. Altered course to west

Black Velvet's track from Reykjavik showing where she trailed warps and deployed a sea anchor in heavy breaking seas. The dotted lines represent courses drawn to clear land.

we could not reduce our drift. In the deeper troughs, *Black Velvet*'s bows would pay off by about 70° and then, as she began sliding backwards down the forward edge of an approaching wave, the sea anchor would bite and usually – but only just in time – bring the bows back to face the breaking crests. Sometimes this did not happen on cue, causing me real concern that we would be rolled to port. For much of this time the whole port side up to the mast was under water. It was too dangerous to be on deck because a breaking sea had removed much of the cockpit gear, including an inflatable dan-buoy. I had lashed the helm hard to starboard, hoisted

the storm jib up the windward running backstay (with a Spanish-reef in it to reduce the sail area – but it made little difference to our weather-cocking and was really only more windage), and went below.

As time moved on and Iceland moved closer I had few plans left to guarantee our eventual survival. Although we were not in distress, clearly we were going to be in about 30 hours' time so I began putting out an 'all stations' call every 30 minutes. Not, I hasten to add, to ask for help but merely to seek a weather forecast.

For seven anxious hours we waited for a wind shift while watching every slightest variation on the barometer – and for seven hours no one answered our calls.

As we approached the land and, thus, I hoped, within communications range of somebody, I was prepared to set off the EPIRB and transmit a Mayday. When beaching became inevitable I intended lowering two of the three anchors, but not to their full scope in order to be able to pay out more cable if they found the bottom. The seas were, of course, horrendous otherwise we might have tried sailing across them; seas would be building up even more as the water shoaled. I doubted that the anchors would be of any value at all but had to keep my mind active.

With only 45 miles to go to the lee shore, a wind-shift did occur and, conveniently, through almost 120° towards the northwest. With it also came a marked reduction in wind speed. Nevertheless, I allowed one more hour of precious sea room to be lost before deciding to haul in the sea anchor and

everything else that was streaming from the bow. With the heavy weather jib (and extra worries about the bowsprit), no stays'l and three reefs in the main, we managed to claw to the east slowly. As the seas became more confused but less dramatic we were able to make a course of east-by-south. It was not comfortable nor was it entirely free from the possibility of being rolled but it was preferable to beaching. We could have headed slightly further south but I wanted to get as much easting under our keel as possible. Two days later we were at last east of the eastern end of Iceland and thus, if necessary, with sea room all the way to the Arctic ice.

It had taken us eight days to clear the island and instead of arriving home three weeks before my son's wedding we arrived with five days to spare. We had been less than 24 hours from being wrecked on a rockbound lee shore, so we were glad to arrive at all.

Comment

Even with ever improving computers and skill it should be accepted that weather forecasting is not an exact science. Therefore it should be expected that the weather could occasionally be other than as forecast. Taking the argument further, it should be expected that the wind will occasionally be completely opposite in both strength and direction to that forecast. Ewen Southby-Tailyour is too experienced a seaman to put too much reliance on his forecast, yet he came close to annihilation in a sound and sturdy sea boat in just these circumstances.

It is sometimes jokingly said that 'Gentlemen do not go to windward', but sailors would be unwise to assume that they never need to go to windward. Modern yacht design is often influenced by the racing requirement of excellent windward ability, but Ewen Southby-Tailyour's attractive heavily built gaff rigged yacht is probably not in the first league when making to windward.

Black Velvet was built to be bomb proof and ice proof. It is debatable whether the wind strength given in this account was such that no craft of *Black Velvet*'s size could have made much ground to weather.

The best remedy in the circumstances would have been an effective sea anchor. A correctly constructed, and appropriately sized, parachute sea anchor will usually reduce drift to less than one knot, water not being compressible, so Ewen Southby-Tailyour's attempt to make an ad hoc sea anchor from a trysail was the right tactic to adopt, although a sail with more equal length of sides could have been preferable. Makeshift sea anchors have been made out of sails that, if sufficiently large and strong, are probably not much less effective than commercially available, purpose-made parachute sea anchors. However, a sail-formed sea anchor needs to have rigging lines that are both long enough and of the correct disposition for the sail to fill and remain stable. The lines should be equidistant from the

Black Velvet trailed four warps in heavy breaking seas. *Photo: Safehaven Marine*

centre of effort, which can be found by bisecting the angles at each attachment point and clearly this is best done before the situation has become desperate. Once a sea anchor has been deployed it is neither easy nor wise to try to recover the system until the weather has abated, so it has to work first time. Indeed the only time to experiment is in moderate weather in a non-threatening situation.

With gift of hindsight, Ewen Southby-Tailyour was remiss in not adequately testing out his makeshift arrangements beforehand, especially with a vessel with not-so-good heavy weather windward capability. Had he done so he might have established the lengths of rigging line on his trysail, or other sail, that worked efficiently. In all other respects he did all that could be done. Indeed he applied a cool and logical approach to a most difficult situation. Nevertheless, his experience should be a salutary lesson to those whose yachts simply do not even have suitable sails to go to windward or the means to hoist them, and have given little thought – apart from unwisely assuming that their engine will be effective in a storm force seaway – as to how they would deal with a lee shore situation should it unexpectedly come on to blow from an unexpected direction.

23

The loss of *Reliance AC*

RICHARD HEATH

I LEFT MY FAMILY HOME IN ROMSEY, Hampshire, UK in December 2003 to join a delivery crew who were to take a new 15m (49ft) yacht from Les Sables d'Olonne, a fishing port and holiday resort on the North Biscay coast in France, to St Lucia in the West Indies. I was 23 and had been sailing for five years. The yacht, *Reliance AC*, was a Jeanneau Sun Odyssey 494. She had just been built and launched at Les Sables d'Olonne, and was specifically designed for the charter business. She was of light displacement with a relatively low draught and had a pleasantly spacious interior. She carried a low rig and just two sails: a mainsail with two reefing points, and a furling genoa. She was also equipped with a 75hp Volvo diesel engine along with a three-bladed propeller.

Our skipper was Alasdair Crawford, a Scotsman from Kirkcudbrightshire. At 24, he was already an experienced yachtsman with over 50,000 miles under sail to his credit, including five transatlantic crossings. Alasdair and I met for the first time just before Christmas 2003 on the ferry journey across to France. Once we arrived at Les Sables d'Olonne we spent a week preparing the yacht for our voyage. Much of this work involved laboriously taping plastic sheeting over the newly varnished surfaces, so protecting them from damage; mousing all the shackles, and putting anti-chafe material on the rigging. As might be expected of a new

boat destined for charter in the West Indies, *Reliance AC* was short of equipment, and Alasdair used some of his lump sum payment to buy crucial items for the delivery such as charts, an EPIRB and hand-held red flares. He also had his own hand-held Garmin GPS for navigation, and a sextant.

After Christmas, Kasper (Mick) Dieperink, from Bussum near Amsterdam in the Netherlands, joined the crew. Although only aged 17, he, too, was an experienced sailor and the three of us were all qualified Yachtmasters. We would have had a fourth crew member (a Spaniard) on board when we left Les Sables d'Olonne, but his oilskins had been delayed in the Christmas post so we arranged that he would join us at La Coruña, the first planned port of call after our south-westerly course towards the Spanish peninsula. Given fair winds, we expected this initial passage to take three days and, once Mick arrived after Christmas, we were waiting for a window in the weather to leave. We were all very keen to sail south to warmer climes as soon as possible.

On 27 December it seemed that a weather window had appeared. The daily synoptic chart posted in the marina office window showed the pressure to be 1006mb, with loosely spaced isobars across the Bay of Biscay. The nearest 'low' was just east of the Orkney Islands, and it seemed reasonable to expect that a ridge of high pressure was

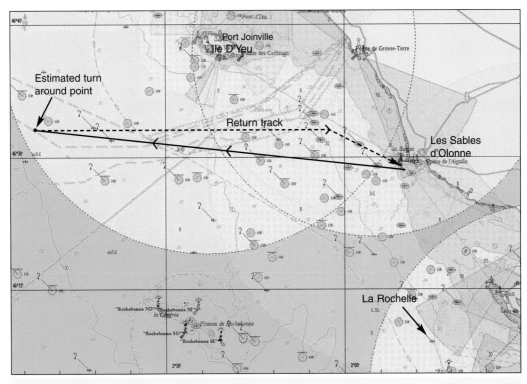

The passage back to Les Sables d'Olonne.

heading our way from the 'high' over the Azores. However the French verbal forecast was not quite so benign. It was offering SE force 6–7, veering NW. The weather that day at Les Sables d'Olonne was warm, dry and sunny with 15 knots of breeze from the SW. There was a moderate swell and although the forecast suggested an uncomfortable first night, there might be in winter an even longer wait for better weather conditions. We decided to leave at midday.

Mick and I had every confidence in our skipper and, indeed, some confidence in the size of our vessel. We were not to know that a revised French forecast was issued at 1300, one hour after we had sailed, giving SW veering NW force 8–9, nor did we have a long wave radio on board that would enable us to receive BBC Shipping forecasts, which were predicting much the same thing for Biscay. None of us spoke French so we were unable to use the French radio fore-

casts or understand the VHF radio warning when we were at sea, which announced an imminent storm.

We left the harbour, in good conditions, with two reefed slabs in the mainsail but we soon took these out and made reasonable progress on a course slightly north of west. This heading took us between the Rochbonne Plateau and the Ile d'Yeu. We were sailing to windward, which was not the yacht's best point of sailing as she did not sail very close to the wind, nor did she seem fast or responsive. The swell built up steadily and after two hours the wind increased, gradually at first, and then quite dramatically. We put two reefs back in the mainsail and furled the genoa down to just a scrap of baggy and ineffective sail as it had entirely lost its aerofoil shape.

The wind increased to 45–55 knots, with some much greater gusts. I saw the anemometer register 58 knots in a gust and Mick saw it reach 85 knots. Waves built up on the ever-increasing swell and broke over the boat with water pouring down below through the main hatch. We were knocked down twice. The yacht was not easy to handle in these conditions, as without a possible third reef in the mainsail, we were over-canvassed. Then one of the new genoa sheets parted and we had little alternative but to furl the genoa entirely. We all felt seasick.

At about 1800 Alasdair decided that we should turn back for Les Sables d'Olonne. A position was plotted using Alasdair's hand-held Garmin GPS and a course laid off, but inaccurately, as we made a landfall somewhat north of our destination. I was off watch during much of the passage back to Les Sables d'Olonne but I do remember hearing the engine being started. When I came on deck I took over the navigation while Alasdair remained on the helm. Visibility was quite good between rain showers, but when we were in the troughs of the huge waves we could not see any lights, making their identification difficult. I felt sure that we identified the lights of Petite Barge and Nouch Sud buoys correctly, as we left them close to port and I put a fix on the chart from the GPS. However, I did not read in the almanac that the south-western approach channel should not be used in bad weather as waves break over the Barre Marine even in moderate seas. The lights of the town were showing clearly but I did not pick out the leading lights at Potence. After heading in on the town lights our course should have altered to port towards the harbour entrance for which there were fixed red leading lights. I never saw those but I did see a red flashing light, which was marked on the chart at the end of the harbour wall. We headed for that. By then the waves were much bigger than I had ever experienced, and on this new course they were approaching from the port beam. Suddenly, an even bigger breaking wave was heard and, at the last moment, seen. This huge wave lifted the boat and rolled her over, breaking the mast off in the process.

Our safety harnesses dragged us all underwater. Mick told me later that he had cut his harness with a shark knife that he kept strapped to his leg, then disentangled a rope wrapped around his feet and finally surfaced. That rope helped him to stay close to *Reliance AC*. When another wave came the boat was rolled upright again and Mick was able to climb aboard as the partially waterlogged boat rolled towards him. While still submerged I tried to inflate my lifejacket and detach my safety harness. Something finally gave way and I arrived at the surface after about a minute without a lifejacket and having swallowed much seawater. Later it was revealed that a clip on my lifejacket had failed. Alasdair was nearby in the sea and full of reassurance. He had not lost his lifejacket as, I was to discover later, the clip on his safety harness had failed, which had been holding him underwater.

At this point the partly submerged boat was already 100m (328ft) away. I was astonished and dismayed to see how far away she had drifted from us in so short a time. We swam backstroke towards her, coming within about 15m (50ft), close enough to shout to Mick onboard, over the noise of the wind and waves. Alasdair told Mick to set off the EPIRB and the red flares. We saw Mick ignite one of the red flares that Alasdair had bought, and at the same time he activated the EPIRB. Alasdair was still most encouraging, and positive that we would come through the ordeal, but the boat drifted faster than we could swim and we soon lost sight of her. After hitting the rocks for the first time, *Reliance AC* lost her keel, but remained upright and continued to be carried over the rocks towards the shore. Alerted by the EPIRB, in due course brave Frenchmen from the local search and rescue team, led by Monsieur Vincent Castin, wearing flippers and diving suits, swam out to *Reliance AC* and persuaded Mick to swim ashore with them. The time was 0247 and the wind was NW 45 knots.

At some time after we lost sight of *Reliance AC*, I thought that I could see a rescue boat to seaward, searching for us. Later I heard that the sea temperature was 11°C.

Reliance AC's capsize and final position.

Alasdair and I clung together for warmth, with waves breaking over us continuously, hoping that the rescue boat would come our way. But this boat may well have been an illusion, as I did not see her again. I could, however, see a fixed red light on the shore and decided to swim for this while helping Alasdair, who was now showing signs of acute hypothermia. The few words that he did utter were very slurred. We lost contact in the breaking waves but eventually both of us reached the shore. At this stage we had been in the sea for about an hour, and I was almost totally exhausted, having had to finally drag Alasdair through the waves to the shore. Alasdair then stopped breathing and I did not have the strength to pull him out of the water. I gave him mouth-to-mouth resuscitation on the beach but soon gave up,

feeling that our predicament was so desperate that I had to go and find help. I put Alasdair on a rock with his head out of the water and then I crawled, and then staggered, up the beach. There was no sign of anybody ashore, but I managed to break into a deserted house at a beach caravan site and found some blankets. I peeled off my oilskins, wrapped the blankets around myself and sank into a coma.

At 0800 the next morning, I woke up and went to look for Alasdair but I could not find him. I then made my way towards the marina office, obtaining a lift from an uncomprehending driver. At the marina office, I learned that *Reliance AC* had been found on the shore and that Mick was alive and well. Alasdair, tragically, had been found dead on the beach.

The French Search and Rescue helicopter searching for survivors on the night of the storm. The flash of La Grande Barge lighthouse can be seen over *Reliance AC*.
Photo: Jacques Archambaud

Comment

This harrowing story poignantly illustrates the acute difficulty and danger of trying to reach an unfamiliar port in safety, on a lee shore and in a storm.

The results were tragic, but much can be learnt from the event. The Maritime Accident Investigation Branch's finding was that a yacht equipped for cruising in the Caribbean would not necessarily be equipped with items needed only on the delivery voyage. UK yachts that are used in sailing schools, or for charter, have to comply with Maritime and Coastguard Agency Codes of Practice, whereas none of the safety measures apply for delivery trips. The most hazardous part of this voyage was in the first few hundred miles. A concession to safety was the provision of a liferaft, and the flares and an EPIRB supplied by the delivery skipper, Alasdair Crawford, himself. Attention was drawn to the lack of a long wave radio, a storm jib and a trysail, and the final suggestion was that it probably would have been safer to stay at sea.

Following the Maritime Accident Investigation Branch's very reasonable findings, there are other relevant matters to consider.

Should *Reliance AC* have left Les Sables d'Olonne when she did? With the gift of hindsight, obviously not. After the week of preparation, probably 'harbour sickness' – a form of crew boredom brought about by having a boat and going nowhere – was taking effect. Sailors' minds need to be sharply focussed at times, for example when entering a strange port at night. The same minds may need to be re-focussed, or de-focussed, when they have been concentrating for too long on the pressing need for departure. A suitable diversion may have to be introduced, such as a visit to a local point of interest, such as a castle or a museum. The important objective is to break the 'bent-on-leaving' mindset. When Drake was allegedly determined to finish his game of bowls before taking on the Spanish Armada, his action may have been intended to prevent a disorganized mad rush to sea by his fleet.

Pleasant though the weather on the morning of 27 December was, just acceptable though the French verbal forecast may have seemed, and encouraging though the synoptic chart appeared, there was a good case for waiting a day for the wind to come round to the north-west, giving a reach to La Coruña rather than 'one uncomfortable night' at sea with the wind from ahead. This would have given a chance for the ridge of high pressure to assert itself, if that is what it was going to do. The synoptic chart did not tie up with the forecast and that, in itself, was grounds for caution. When under pressure to leave, there is a temptation to grasp any favourable indication, and ignore unfavourable information. One is reminded of the autumn Biscay storm of September 1993, described in an earlier edition, when a remote favourable Danish forecast was preferred to the other far less optimistic and more local information, with calamitous consequences.

Actually, 27 December would have been a good day to go to sea to try out the new boat and new crew that had never sailed together before. It might have given some bones to a retreat strategy, in the event of things going wrong later, by revealing the two different lines of approach to the harbour entrance, and exposing the disadvantage of having no navigational information displayed on deck. A two-hour outing might have exposed the strengths and weaknesses of each of the crew that otherwise had to be measured by their ability in harbour. It might have exposed how well the yacht went to windward and the nature of her handling qualities in a blow.

The crew, having failed to obtain every possible weather forecast, though BBC long wave transmissions are obtainable clearly but faintly at Les Sables d'Olonne, was caught in a decidedly difficult situation when the storm came. As with many yachts, *Reliance AC* was not supplied with sails that were suitable to make to windward in a blow, and the crew had few resources on board to fall back upon. So what else could they have done rather than run for Les Sables d'Olonne? The well-furled genoa was

clearly useless to windward, and if it had been used on the starboard tack and if the other sheet had failed, which it clearly might have done, the whole sail might have unfurled. In the prevailing wind strength the full sail would have probably torn itself to ribbons before long, but whatever happened, the task of lowering and bringing the sail below, torn or not, would have been fraught with difficulty and danger. Three men would not have been enough to hold on to the sail and, had they tried, there would have been an unacceptable risk of losing one or more crewmen overboard. It is probable that they could not have hove-to successfully with a mainsail that could not be reduced below the double reefed state. We read, also, how difficult the big yacht was to handle as the wind freshened.

The crew did not have the materials for any sort of drag device, and the lee shore of Ile d'Yeu was only 20 miles away. They might have considered taking shelter behind Ile d'Yeu. Port Joinville is on the eastern side of the island, and offered a sheltered approach. At low water on 27 December there was enough depth above chart datum for the harbour to have been accessible for *Reliance AC* at any state of the tide. However, had they been unable to make to windward from the lee side of Ile d'Yeu, another nasty lee shore of the French coast lay not far away, and the approach to Port Joinville at night would not have been easy. Even so Port Joinville would have been a better option than Les Sables d'Olonne. La Rochelle, some 60 miles away, with its tricky approach and shallow entry, would have been a less attractive option than Port Joinville, but certainly better than Les Sables d'Olonne. Generally the mainland French coast of the Bay of Biscay is one long dangerous lee shore, so the lee shores of the offshore islands have their uses in westerly storms. Port Joinville would have served well though Alasdair's decision was almost certainly influenced by lack of large-scale charts.

Lying a'hull is dangerous. Without the swell, the wave height would not have had time to grow to more than 2 metres. But the swell had built up as the day had worn on, and the combination of swell and wind-developed waves would have been big enough to roll the boat unless the bow was held into the sea.

What about using the diesel engine? *Reliance AC* had a 75hp Volvo with a fixed three-bladed propeller. Having taken down the mainsail and lashed it thoroughly to the boom, the crew could have used the powerful engine to keep the bow into the sea until the storm was over. It would have been a long, wet and cold night, but not life threatening. Heaving-to under engine is a perfectly valid option while the engine is working and while there is fuel in the tank. The tactic is much used by fishermen who, by virtue of their job, are often caught out in storms. They call it 'dodging'. As it turned out, the weather had moderated to a manageable NW force 5 by the morning. They could have rehoisted their two-slabbed mainsail and, given calmer seas, might later have had a chance to re-reeve the genoa sheet, enabling them to continue on to La Coruña in relatively good shape and on schedule.

Accepting that Les Sables d'Olonne was not a wise port to return to in the circumstances, what actually went wrong during the approach? Richard, who was doing the navigation, felt reasonably confident that he had identified the Nouch Sud buoy, but from that moment on matters are not entirely clear. The fact of the matter was that Richard was trying to find the entrance of a harbour surrounded by shoal water in the most difficult possible circumstances: at night, towards low tide with an onshore gale blowing and against a confusing background of town lights. Since navigation was of vital importance at this stage, Alasdair should have handed the helm over to Mick. Richard should have been plotting the boat's position from down below using the

hand-held GPS, and should have been reading the almanac carefully, and Alasdair should have been the one to interpret Richard's information against the lights he could see on deck and pass instructions to Mick at the helm. It is customary for the skipper to take the helm on entering and leaving harbour, and with good reason, but in the prevailing circumstances and when a navigational mistake was the most likely and potentially disastrous occurrence, Richard needed help with the navigation. The skipper should be involved with the most difficult decisions and be in a position to check data for himself. Had the skipper handed over the helm to Mick there would have been more time to plan the entry into Les Sables d'Olonne, which could have been made easier by some key GPS waypoints to guide them in.

Having passed the Nouch Sud buoy, a red flashing light was spotted and they steered for it assuming it was the red light on the port-hand entrance pier. Even if it had been the correct light and they were on the chosen approach bearing, with the large waves on the beam it is quite possible that the boat would have been rolled, as entry from the south-west is only recommended in calm weather due to the presence of breaking waves on the Barre Marine. However, the green light on the starboard-hand pier which has the same intensity as the red light on the port-hand pier was not observed, nor were the leading lights at La Chaume seen, which should have been in the same direction and which have lights of greater intensity. Moreover, the flashing red light that the crew was steering for was not the ultra-quick flashing light described in the almanac as being on the port mole.

The only other red flashing light, and the one that most nearly matches Richard's description, has a characteristic of two flashes every ten seconds, and that was the Grande Barge lighthouse offshore to the northwest. It has a range of 17 miles and was less than 2.5 miles away. The course to

The wreck of *Reliance AC* well up the beach on the morning after the storm, having lost mast, keel and rudder. Her single remaining genoa sheet can be seen. The Grand Barge lighthouse is on the horizon above the bow.
Photo: Jacques Archambaud

the Grande Barge would have been 15° different from a course to the harbour entrance lights. In the circumstances, a tired crew could have overlooked such a discrepancy. The consequence of heading for the Grande Barge was that *Reliance AC* would have passed over the dangerous shoal bank of Le Nouch, or possibly Le Noura. Unless she had hit one of the odd rocks, there would have been three or four metres below her keel in calm conditions but, in the prevailing stormy conditions, rather less in the troughs of the waves. The tidal stream that would have been flowing nearly south-west at this point, combined with the shallow water, would have caused the waves to build up massively and to break. In these conditions, a sailing vessel would almost inevitably have been rolled and lost her mast on the seabed. Plotting back from where *Reliance AC* went ashore, allowing for the north-west-going tide and her drift rate, which we know was faster than a man can swim in rough water, it does seem probable that she was heading for the wrong light.

After the capsize, Mick's ability to remove his safety harness which was holding him underwater was much helped by having a knife at hand, and one is reminded of the old adage 'Every good seaman always carries a knife'. All three of the crew had difficulty in releasing their safety harnesses, and one is reminded of the sinking of *Waikikamukau* (see Chapter 17), when a member of the crew went down with the yacht because he was unable to release his safety harness. Safety harnesses must have a clip at both ends, and the old tradition of carrying a readily accessible knife remains valid.

Whilst agreeing with the Maritime Accident Investigation Branch's findings, additional conclusions are that *Reliance AC* should not have set off on passage on 27 December, and that day would have been better used for sea trials. Having been caught out in an unexpected storm, the crew could have used the engine to keep the bow into the sea and perhaps make slow progress further offshore, or make for Port Joinville in the Isle d'Yeu. Having unwisely decided to run for Les Sables d'Olonne, they approached using a dangerous channel and then, with insufficient navigational information, they probably altered course for the wrong light, taking them to certain disaster.

It is easy to criticize with the gift of hindsight. Alasdair and his crew got it wrong, but there may be some of us, in similar circumstances, who would have done exactly the same. The account serves to reinforce the advice in Chapter 11.

24

'Bombed' in the Tasman Sea

PETER COOK

I JOINED *RED* IN EDEN ON THE SOUTH-east coast of Australia. She was to take us to Nelson on the northern tip of the South Island of New Zealand, some 1100 miles across the Tasman Sea, known for its tempests. The owner of *RED* was Kevin Hansen from Alaska. Normally he just had his wife Beth with him, but on this first occasion in many years of cruising Beth was unable to come, so in her absence Kevin had recruited me, a yacht delivery skipper. We had met before in Tasmania.

RED is a steel cruising cutter, waterline length 14.6m (48ft) and about 20 tonne displacement, in which the Hansens have been cruising since 2000. When she was built for them in 1998, all their best ideas were put into her, gleaned from 12 years of cruising the Pacific in a Valiant 40. *RED* is a solid vessel built for serious ocean cruising and, after careful preparations in case of a stormy passage, we left Eden on 8 February 2004, expecting to take a week for the passage to Nelson. *RED* has an excellent sailing performance so we slipped along at over 7 knots with a light breeze off the port quarter. The first five days of the passage went well, with a few changes to the number of reefs as the wind went up and down.

At 1800 on Friday 13 February, Kevin and I enjoyed a meal together in the cockpit. The wind was blowing 20–25 knots from the NNE, our heading was due east and the boat was nicely settled with two reefs in the main, and the staysail set. The sea state was comfortable and our boat speed was up around 8 knots. There was about 50 per cent cloud cover with nothing unusual. Kevin went below at 1815, as we were doing three hours on and three hours off. The barometer showed 1008mb and we were expecting the wind to veer more to the south as a forecast shallow low passed overhead during the night.

At 1900 I was in the cockpit facing aft doing a little reading when I heard a rumble, not unlike a Boeing 747 taking off, and poked my head over the dodger to see what the noise could be. To the south I saw a huge wall of foaming swirling whiteness, like a blizzard, heading directly in our direction and it was obvious that there was a fair bit of wind about to hit us. I put the autopilot to standby, grabbed the wheel and started to turn *RED* to run off wind to lessen the impact. I was not quick enough, and the wind hit with all the force of a cyclone, *RED* gybed and was laid over to about 70°. After a couple of seconds she came upright, I got some steerage way and *RED* screamed off downwind, planing like a skiff. I could sense the force of the wind stressing the rig. There was no chance to alert Kevin, however I figured he would notice some commotion sooner or later. I remember glancing at the true wind indicator, which read 94 knots. The sound was incredible, now a close-by

278

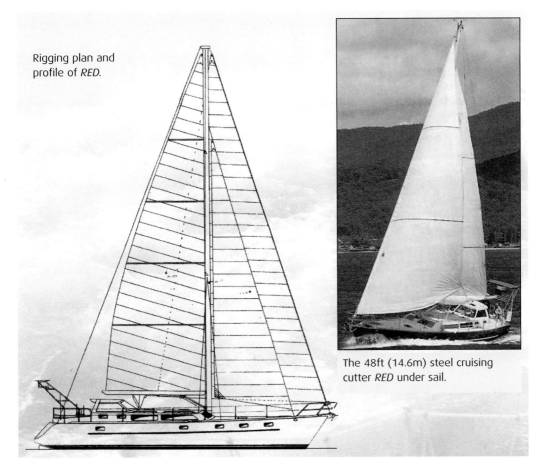

Rigging plan and profile of *RED*.

The 48ft (14.6m) steel cruising cutter *RED* under sail.

747 on take off, but mingled with the scream of the wind in the rigging and a sound that I could feel in the pit of my stomach. There was no rain. I was waiting for the rig to collapse: *RED* was way over-canvassed for these conditions, and I thought at the time that something surely had to give. That it did not indicates the integrity and generous factor of safety built into the rig of this fine yacht.

Then Kevin emerged in the companionway, wearing only his underpants, and his eyes were popping out of his head. I said to Kevin 'You had better come up as we have a bit on at the moment', which Kevin later described as the understatement of the century. Kevin quickly put on his foul weather gear and harness, and joined me in the cockpit. Just as he did so *RED* rounded up into the wind, this time staying at around 50° angle of heel with the stanchions well submerged on the lee side. She was pinned broadside to the wind, which was still blowing on the high side of 80–90 knots. It was now probably only about 10 minutes from when the first gust hit us. Kevin and I started to crawl to the foredeck to lower the staysail. The roar of the wind was incredible and the water was boiling all around us. It was not possible to look into the wind, and the spray was like being sand blasted. I have sailed a lot of offshore miles and experienced high winds before, but this was something else. I remember the struggle I had just to make it to the foredeck. Crawling forward on top of a car doing 100mph would be a good likeness; the spray from the sea was painful against the back of my head and around the back of my ears (I was only wearing a polar fleece and my foul weather trousers and harness, as it had been such a nice evening before the blow). We finally made it to the foredeck and struggled to lower the staysail. Once down, we lashed the staysail to the lifelines. At no time was a word spoken between Kevin and myself, indeed it was pointless to try, such was the noise. Having secured the staysail I made my way to the main. Happily, the boom on RED is low, which makes handling the mainsail easy and safe. She is set up with Harken luff cars, which help, and she has good lazy jacks, too. Kevin had made his way back to the cockpit to secure it and retake control. Now under bare pole, Kevin was able to bear away and run off with the wind, with the result that he was steering north. The wind was still in the high 80s. We were running at over 10 knots with a fairly violent sea starting to develop. We were largely in control, though we occasionally broached.

I took the opportunity to use the video camera in spite of near darkness. We have subsequently watched the video several times and we still find that the sheer strength of the wind leaves us in awe. It was just amazing to see what Mother Nature can do without warning. While filming, Kevin asked what the wind speed was, and I swung the camera to show the wind speed at 86 knots apparent, and our boat speed at 10 knots. The boat was travelling far too fast for the conditions and the rapidly developing waves from the blow were throwing us around. It was time to trail some warps. Ready for use in each aft locker RED has two 91m (300ft) lengths of 14mm ($\frac{1}{2}$in) warp in milk crates. We took three turns around the primary headsail winches and slowly eased the warps out over each quarter. This had the effect of slowing RED from 8–10 knots to 4–5 knots. The warps were trailed straight out as I have found in the past that when trailing them in a bight they occasionally skip out of the water when the vessel starts to surf. With lots of sea room (we were about 400 miles west of the South Island of New Zealand) we had no need to slow the boat further. At 4–5 knots we still had good water flow past the rudder and therefore the vessel steered well. We were able to activate the autopilot, which held a

good, comfortable course. With the transom presented to the sea we took some water in the cockpit but with RED's good storm boards, we never took any water down below.

With everything under control we went to write up our hourly log when I noticed that it was now 2125, so it had taken us around two and a half hours to recover control and settle the vessel. We were wet, cold and tired, and it was nice to be down below, insulated from the extremes of the weather. It was still blowing hard up top, however you would never know this below decks in RED with her comfortable motion and well-insulated hull. After five hours the wind had eased to around 60 knots, and by morning it seemed almost peaceful. We retrieved our warps using the winches, tidied up a little, set the headsail and set ourselves back on course. The top batten of the main had broken so we sailed the last 400 miles to New Zealand under headsail alone. But with the wind from the SE often up to 40 knots we made good progress close-hauled, sometimes under the storm jib and sometimes motorsailing to make good our course. We arrived at Nelson at 2100 on Sunday 15 February.

Curiously we had received a weatherfax at the moment the blow hit us that showed no change in the weather we had been experiencing. Moreover, the barometer did not show any change until three hours after we were hit, but then showed that the low had deepened from 1008mb to 985mb. Later we saw our depression, which we believe is described as a 'low-pressure bomb', appear on the weatherfax over our position. Twelve hours later, the weatherfax showed our low, now of 986mb, sitting over the top of the Cook Strait in New Zealand. The New Zealand weather bureau described this storm as the worst since 1976, and a 1-in-40 year storm for February, which is normally one of the most settled and fine months of the year. The weather was severe enough to stop ferries sailing the Cook Strait, close Wellington airport, create widespread flooding that shut off 18 stretches of state highway and, sadly, claimed the lives of two fishermen.

Comment

The unusually intense squall that hit *RED* in the Tasman Sea might appear to be rare, though one wonders how many vessels have been lost without trace as a result of a similar event. A meteorological 'bomb' is a quasi-scientific term that describes a low that rapidly intensifies, sometimes also called explosive deepening. *RED*'s experience could well have occurred because she was in the '*comma-shaped*' arc in the cold air behind the cold front as described in Chapter 8 on Meteorology by Richard Ebling.

It would seem that *RED* was a sound craft to be aboard in such circumstances. She was of praiseworthy design; her steel construction, her strong rig, her warps stowed ready for trailing, her small crew of experienced seamen, Kevin Hansen and Peter Cook, all smack of a wise owner who keeps his boat and crew ready for all eventualities.

To survive such a blow, the crew has to stay on board; the boat has to be structurally strong, stiff (ie have a good righting moment) and have a rig with a large factor of safety. It is noteworthy that in a hurricane force wind on the beam, just one man could lower the double-reefed mainsail fitted with its 'good cars' and low boom.

The video shots reveal the usual photographic fact at sea in extreme winds, namely that there is too much water about at low level to catch anything in sharp relief.

Moreover, darkness fell soon after the squall hit. Nevertheless, the video bears out Peter Cook's account.

Some owners continue to use the time-honoured technique of trailing warps to slow down to a comfortable speed when running under bare pole, while others use a small strong drogue for the same purpose. The advantages of the drogue are that it does not take up so much stowage space, and is cheaper to purchase and it is arguable as to whether it would have been better for *RED* to have trailed a drogue. Peter Cook has no doubt that *RED* was better off trailing her warps, and clearly the warps worked well in this case. He says that a drogue can skip out of the water, depending on the sea state and length of line; and that one cannot vary the amount of drag with a drogue – too much drag and the boat is pooped, too little and there is insufficient control. He believes that trailed lines are less vulnerable to chafe, easier to manage using primary winches, and can be staggered to change the angle the stern presents to the sea. He does not like to trail the line in the form of a loop, as the loop tends to skip the sea at times like a drogue, resulting in variable drag.

One could add to Peter Cook's remarks in favour of trailing warps, rather than using a drogue by saying that a drogue is more committing than warps. Once deployed a drogue cannot easily be recovered, and if it is necessary to cut the drogue line then a valuable line as well as the drogue is lost for ever.

25

Berrimilla braves 80-knot winds in the South Atlantic

ALEX WHITWORTH

DESIGNED BY PETER JOUBERT IN THE mid 1960s, *Berrimilla* is a 10m (33ft) masthead sloop, solidly built of GRP in 1977 and owned by myself since 1993. She had a displacement of about seven tons in her world circumnavigation trim, and her point of vanishing stability occurs at 143°, so she is unusually stiff by modern standards. Before this account, in my term of ownership, *Berrimilla* had sailed in 13 Sydney–Hobart Races including the especially stormy 1998 race, in which she won the Performance Handicap System (PHS) class overall. She had also sailed in eight Gosford–Lord Howe Island races, again winning the PHS class in 1999.

On Boxing Day, 2004, we set off for Hobart in the 2004 Sydney–Hobart Race with a crew of six, but this time with a difference. We intended to finish the race, drop off four of the crew in Hobart, turn left and sail for England via Cape Horn and the Falkland Islands. In England, we planned to race in the Two-handed division in the Fastnet race and then sail back to Sydney via the Cape of Good Hope in time to start in the 2005 Sydney–Hobart. In the event, all this was achieved.

We set off from Hobart on 10 January, 2005 for the Horn with Peter Crozier, also in his 60s, as my co-skipper. All went according to plan, except for a near inversion in a storm south of New Zealand that destroyed the masthead instrument fittings and severely dented my ribs, causing an unscheduled stop in Dunedin, South Island, New Zealand, for repairs to both. We eventually rounded Cape Horn on 11 March and berthed in Port Stanley, Falkland Islands, three days later.

We left Port Stanley at 1300 on Good Friday, 25 March after an adventurous final

The sturdy *Berrimilla* is a Brolga 33 10m (33ft) sloop built using a very adequate number of GRP laminates. In Alex Whitworth's hands, she has competed in every Sydney–Hobart Race since he bought her from 1993 to the present date, 2007.

Figure 25.1 This is the GRIB forecast valid for midnight on 28/29 March. Our weather had been coming from the west and I have selected a forecast area that takes in the area to the west of our position. There is no sign of the low forming to the east.

Richard Ebling says that with a north-westerly and from the shape of the isobars it looks as though the low was centred near to East Falkland, with a central pressure of about 1000 hPa (mb). It would have been very difficult to know what would happen next, but as the south-westerly winds behind the front are stronger than the north-westerlies ahead it would have been wise to be prepared for increasing winds.

X = position of *Berrimilla*

day in the harbour, during which a 50-knot north-easterly tried very hard to smash the boat against a big commercial jetty. The intention after departure was to head north-east towards the more useful winds on the eastern side of the South Atlantic high and avoid the southerly current down the South American coast.

Things did not quite happen that way and on 28 March we found ourselves a long way further west than intended, sandwiched between a big high pressure system over South America and a tight low developing about 1000 miles east of Montevideo.

I had pulled in the low-resolution weather file for our general area via *Sailmail* for midnight on 28 March (Fig 25.1), and it was not particularly startling. Indeed our actual conditions favoured optimism and complacency. The sun was out after days of damp weather and Pete was actually wearing his shorts.

However, 24 hours later (Fig 25.2), there was a different story. We had worked out while in the South Pacific that the GRIB* weather files were reasonably accurate for predicted wind direction and barometric pressure but that it was sensible to double the predicted strength to get an idea of the actual gusts to be experienced. On that basis, Fig 25.2 predicts a south-westerly with a maximum strength of 70 knots, and this was not to be ignored. *Berrimilla* is not fast enough to go hunting for favourable weather systems and we had no option but to ride out what the weather had in store for us.

---

*GRIB (Graphics in Binary) files associate a specific weather datum (eg wind velocity or atmospheric pressure) with a geographic position. Because the resulting file is a collection of these points and the required forecast area can be selected precisely, the files can be kept very small and so are ideal over slow links such as Sailmail. They are transmitted as data, not text, and are reconstructed by the receiving laptop software to appear as a chart with wind arrows, predicted wind strength and pressure data embedded in them.

Figure 25.2 24 hours later and the prediction is quite different, putting *Berrimilla* in the dangerous quadrant of the low to the east, with predicted SW winds of 35 knots. Experience told us to double the predicted wind strength and, in the event, this turned out to be an underestimate.

Richard Ebling says that GRIB March 30 now places the deepening low some 600nm to the north-east or ENE having moved at a speed of about 25 knots, which is normal.

X = position of *Berrimilla*

Figure 25.3 And another day later, the centre of the low is now 600 miles to the south-east and deepening. *Berrimilla* is in light breezes and sunshine, but still with a big south-westerly swell.

X = position of *Berrimilla*

Figure 25.4 This wind direction hedgehog figure shows *Berrimilla's* track as a series of data points heading north-east then north during the storm; each point colour-coded for wind strength according to the colour scale at the top left corner. The orange/red dots are the 75+ knot gusts.

The blue lines show true wind direction for each point, with the wind blowing towards the track. They are purely directional and their length is not significant. The boat is on the west side of a southern hemisphere low pressure system and the prevailing wind veers from east to south-west as the storm arrives and remains south-west to west for the duration.

Note the change in wind direction as each gust arrives. The blue lines connecting to each red datum point are about 40–60° veered from the prevailing wind.

Richard Ebling says that traditional theory has always been that in the Northern Hemisphere the wind veers in gusts, *viz* that the wind direction in a gust is nearer than that in the free atmosphere rather than backed to blow in towards low pressure under the effect of friction. In the southern half of the globe this of course would be reversed and so the expectation would have been for the wind to back.

Work done by Mike Brettle has shown that this is not necessarily so, but the *Berrimilla* record is the first time that I have seen an instrumental plot of wind shifts experienced by a boat over open waters that were contrary to that theory.

Figure 25.5
Berrimilla's data logger for wind speed indicates how quickly a storm can arise. It also shows its typical gusty nature. Peak gusts of over 80 knots are extreme for a summer storm.

Data from midday on 29 March to midday on 31 March. The wind drops to less than 10 knots at about 1700 on 29 March, then rises to over 80 knots by about 2200 and stays above 70 knots for the next 12 hours through the night and the next morning. Compare this with the hedgehog for the same period to see the changes in wind direction.

Pete wrote in his journal in the morning of 29 March:

We now have a very steep, mostly short, beam sea, which rolls the boat continuously. It has been blowing 40 knots here this morning but now that has passed through. We are left with very little wind but the sky is clear. We have had quite a lot of rain in the last 12 hours. The wind is due to go south tomorrow and blow up to 45 knots.

About three hours later he wrote:

The wind has come up quite strongly, and we have gone down from the No 4 headsail and two reefs in the mainsail to the No 5 headsail and three reefs in the mainsail. All was okay for a few hours then the wind increased to 45 knots so we decided to get rid of the main, and stay with the No 5 headsail. By the time we got on deck to do the change, the wind was howling so we lowered both the main and the No 5 headsail,

and continued downwind under bare pole.

It is now another hour later, and we are running downwind at 4–5 knots, still under bare pole, with the wind gusting to 60 knots. It is almost dark and this wind does not look like it will abate. I have entered our position of 45° 27' south and 49° 36' west in the log, just in case things get worse. This is the strongest wind we have had. The wind is now regularly above 70 knots: Alex said he just saw 82 knots.

A bit later Pete wrote:

The waves are not as bad as in the Southern Ocean. The fetch would only be 300–400 miles from the South American coast but, if this wind strength holds, it could produce some terrible waves later. Alex just saw 86 knots; he has stopped looking now, and is making a cup of tea to take our mind off the wind instruments. We have been hit by a few bad waves but have not yet been knocked down badly. The wind is really howling in the rigging. This is going to be a very long night and I can't see us getting much sleep.

The low intensified very quickly and the wind had risen from about 5 knots to 80+ knot gusts in about 5 hours. Fig 25.5 shows the wind strength over 48 hours and Fig 25.4 shows graphically the wind strength and direction on our track for the same period. Our Fleming self-steering gear was coping well with the wind on the quarter. There was a following south-west swell to begin with, but this came on the beam as we turned north to keep the wind abaft the beam.

At 2005 UTC on 29 March I wrote:

Those of us who thought things would get easier this side of the Andes could not have been more wrong. Lots of wind this morning, then none, and now we are in a ferocious little storm that we were sort of expecting but at much lower strength. Quite scary at the moment – wind screaming at different levels in different bits of the rig, big waves building up, boat bare-poled, wind on the quarter as much as possible. Wind 60–80 knots in gusts, waves crashing against and across the boat. There is too much tension and noise to sleep ... this is very nasty indeed. All we can do is sit it out and hope nothing breaks. It's gusting 80 knots and the waves are crashing over the boat – she's only little. Grey knuckles till it abates, and no sign of that at the moment.

In a lull a short time later I wrote:

Hi again – I'm taking a punt that it's decided to abate a bit – and I need to write a situation report as a distraction. It is still a steady 65–70 knots but the really big gusts seem to be further apart. You know things are really bad when the wind is so strong it flattens the tops off the waves and the boat has stopped rolling.

The lull did not last and later in the night I felt a change in *Berrimilla*'s attitude and motion so I peeked out of the storm board flap with the big lantern. It was very dark, with horizontal spray, and I could see a quivering white line stretched astern from above my head. This could only be the liferaft painter, so the raft was trailing astern somewhere, and threatening to write off the self-steering or the turbine line; the turbine being an impeller on the end of a 40-metre floating line to drive our generator.

We were both already partly dressed in wet weather trousers and thermals, so a rapid upgrade into full gear with combined lifejacket and harness was relatively easy. Both of us clipped on by reaching into the cockpit over the bottom storm board and climbed into the cockpit where we replaced and secured the top storm board immediately. The boat was rolling through a huge arc and big waves were breaking across the coachroof and decks with the cockpit continuously half full of water. The spray was blasting across in solid sheets and it was impossible to look upwind. The torch showed glimpses of reflective tape at some distance astern, sometimes high above, sometimes way below. The water-activated light on the raft was lit but mostly obscured by what turned out to be the torn canopy. The liferaft was clearly hindering the boat's progress and ability to ride the waves, but *Berrimilla* was coping.

The painter had snagged on the starboard secondary winch but I managed to bring it onto the primary winch and, by judging wave motion and surges, winched it in bit by bit to just off the starboard quarter. It was very heavy through being full of water, and the canopy was only barely attached. The ballast bags were, of course, full and were causing a lot of drag.

It might have been possible to keep the liferaft close under the quarter if we could have left the cockpit to attach a second line on it from a forward cleat, but it was simply not safe to do so. We decided it was probably best to let it trail aft again and assess the risk of damage – all seemed to be OK, although

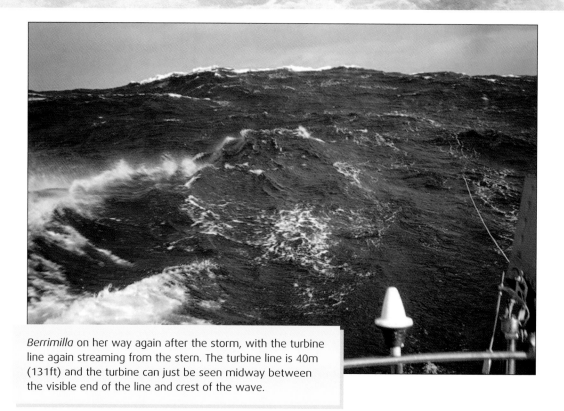

Berrimilla on her way again after the storm, with the turbine line again streaming from the stern. The turbine line is 40m (131ft) and the turbine can just be seen midway between the visible end of the line and crest of the wave.

Berrimilla became very sluggish when raft and boat tried to move in opposite directions. I thought it unlikely that the liferaft would last the night but if it did there might be a better chance to retrieve it in daylight. I put a sharp knife within reach of the storm board flap in case we needed to get rid of the liferaft urgently, and we returned below, staying in our wet weather gear for what became a very long night indeed. The liferaft only lasted until the next big wave train, when the painter attachment tore away from the raft fabric. This was obvious from the change in motion as *Berrimilla* surged off the bigger waves. I duly reported the drifting liferaft with its *Berrimilla* identity number, on my satellite phone.

Our survey at first light revealed a badly bent stanchion, presumably caught by the liferaft capsule as it became detached, and the self-steering was still working, albeit sluggishly, with the liferaft painter wrapped around the actuator arm and paddle, as well as the turbine line of the wind generator. The

liferaft lashings were undamaged but the pelican clip was open, with its slider jammed in the closed position.

By 1000 on the morning of 30 March, the wind was starting to abate and the barometer was rising but the waves, which were covered with flying foam and spray moving at the speed of the wind, were as big as we had seen off Cape Horn. I sent an e-mail report at 1600 to our web minder in Hobart, assessing the maximum wave height we were experiencing as about double *Berrimilla*'s mast height, which would have been nearly 30m (98ft), but this was difficult to judge with any accuracy.

We felt that the self-steering made a significant contribution to our safety by keeping the wind and waves on *Berrimilla*'s quarter and allowing us to remain below and have some minimal rest and an occasional cup of tea. Had we become beam-on to the numerous big rolling breakers, we would have had a lot more knockdowns, or worse. In an e-mail report I emphasized the importance of having a drill or checklist for critical operations so they become instinctive. We had them for man overboard and heavy weather spinnaker drops but we did not have a drill to ensure that the laptop is always tied down and covered before leaving the nav table to go on deck. It became airborne during one of the knockdowns and its rugged frame once more preserved it from serious damage. I am writing on it now, more than a year later.

We had saved a guardrail stanchion from the Dunedin repair and we were able to fit it on 31 March, by which time the weather had become warm and sunny with a following wind. Neither of us had been hurt in this rather nasty episode and the boat was otherwise unharmed, apart from a missing spinnaker block and some seawater and disarray below. In my analysis I stressed the importance of good preparation for a storm such as we had just experienced, citing our sturdy storm boards, good harnesses and well-positioned strong points to attach them. The satellite phone had obviously been of benefit and I suggested that emergency numbers be programmed into the phone, as there is little opportunity to look them up in such circumstances. Clearly, a single pelican clip is insufficient to secure a liferaft and additional lashing is necessary with a serrated knife at hand to cut the lashing in emergency. How the clip opened remains a mystery. I am sure it was closed before the storm.

Epilogue

Sadly *Berrimilla* was rolled and lost her mast on her return from the Sydney–Hobart Race in January 2007. Whilst running under bare pole at night through the Bass Strait in winds gusting to 60 knots (according to the Met Bureau, though much higher wind strengths were also reported), accompanied by very steep and confused seas she was, without warning, caught by a breaking beam sea and was rolled. *Berrimilla* quickly righted herself, as one might expect for such a stiff design, but the mast collapsed shortly afterwards. The helmsman, Peter Crozier was thrown into the sea, held by his lifeline, and then was tossed back onto the pushpit from where he could climb back on board. The coachroof was dished inwards and holed, and the starboard aft window above the galley had been broken. The boat was flooded to about a foot above the cabin sole.

The EPIRB was actuated, though the Mayday was later cancelled by satphone. When help arrived, a tow was wisely declined as conditions were dangerous and the engine was working. *Berrimilla* made her own way to the shelter of Gabo Island, after which a water police boat towed her to Eden. She has now been repaired ready for the next Sydney–Hobart race.

Comment

It is impossible not to admire Alex Whitworth and Peter Crozier's extraordinary feat in putting a Fastnet Race between two consecutive Sydney–Hobart Races, and sailing all the way between in a 1960s 10m (33ft) design, backed only by modest resources. Their courage and determination was complemented by thorough planning and preparation, which justifies describing their voyage as an outstanding and unique achievement in the class of historic world-girdlers.

Plentiful credit is also due to the designer and builder of their *Berrimilla*. The event seems to have taken the sailing world by surprise, as there is simply nothing to compare.

The storm that is described probably had the greatest wind strength of their circumnavigation, and is of particular interest as the wind speed and direction is recorded throughout. One is impressed by the rate that the wind speed increased, but also the occasional sudden and major changes in wind direction during the storm. The *Berrimilla* crew were alerted to the prospect of a storm by the GRIB file that shows a synoptic chart on the screen of their laptop. This is a most valuable facility in remote areas though the small GRIB file scale will probably not show incipient or small depressions. Other ocean voyagers have also found that the forecast wind strength needs to be doubled to obtain the strength of prolonged gusts.

Alex's and Peter's tactics were simple and effective. With ample sea room they ran before the wind under bare pole, leaving their wind vane to keep the wind and seas at a comfortable angle on the quarter. They spent most of the ferocious storm in the relative shelter and comfort of the cabin.

Short-handed yachts need to rely heavily on their wind vane, and well-designed and constructed wind vanes seem to have no upper limit to the amount of wind with which they can cope.

Regarding the loss of the liferaft, it can only be said, once again, that liferafts stowed on deck are tremendously vulnerable to major wave action. How water can bend steel is mystifying, but it does, and how deck-stowed liferafts continually carry away in heavy weather is equally mystifying but, as will be found in several places in previous editions of this book, they do. Occasionally stainless steel fastenings break and are found to have been made of 312 grade stainless steel which is not a marine grade, as 316 is, though it is usually sheer wave force that causes the problem. To avoid losing liferafts, one remedy is for designers to add a liferaft deck locker, as some do, that will ensure that the liferaft is both well protected and also available on deck at short notice. In the meantime, small craft with limited storage capacity below decks need to have enormously strong holding down arrangements which, in some cases, may entail strengthening the coach roof. The liferaft needs to be secured so effectively and cunningly that there is an apparent excess of strap, which can be quickly removed in emergency. If this latter arrangement requires a knife then this should be stowed permanently adjacent to the liferaft.

Bibliography

1994 Pacific Storm Survey, Kim Taylor, Quarry Publishing 1996
All Weather Yachtsman, Peter Haward, Adlard Coles Nautical 1990
Alone Through the Roaring Forties, Vito Dumas, Adlard Coles (UK) 1960, International Marine (USA) 2004
Around the World with Ridgway, John & Marie Christine Ridgway, Heinemann, 1978
Because the Horn is There, Miles Smeeton, Grafton Books 1985
Blue Water Sailing Manual, Barry Pickthall, Adlard Coles Nautical (UK) and International Marine (USA) 2006
Cape Horn: The Logical Route, Bernard Moitessier, Adlard Coles Nautical (UK) and Sheridan House (USA) 2003
Deep Sea Sailing, Erroll Bruce, Stanley Paul 1953
Desirable and Undesirable Characteristics of Offshore Yachts, J Rousmaniere, WW Norton 1987
Drag Device Database, Victor Shane, Para-Anchors International 1998
Drogues: A Study to Improve the Safety of Sailing Yachts, Carol Hervey & Donald Jordan, Marine Technology 1988
The Eight Sailing Exploration Books, HW Tilman, Diadem Books, an imprint of Hodder & Stoughton
Fastnet Force 10, John Rousmaniere, Nautical Books 1987
Fastnet Race Enquiry Report, RORC & RYA 1979
Fatal Storm, Rob Mundle, Adlard Coles Nautical (UK), International Marine (USA) and HarperCollins (Australia) 2001
Halsey's Typhoons, Adamson & Kosco, Crown Publishers, New York 1967
Handling Small Boats in Heavy Weather, Frank Robb, Frank Robb, PO Box 1804, Cape Town, South Africa 1965
A Manual of Heavy Weather Cruising, Jeff Toghill, Adlard Coles Nautical (UK) and New Holland Publishers (Australia) 2000
Heavy Weather Cruising, Tom Cunliffe, Fernhurst Books 1996
Heavy Weather Guide, Kotsch & Henderson, US Naval Institute Press 1988
Heavy Weather Tactics Using Sea Anchors and Drogues, Earl Hinz, Adlard Coles Nautical (UK) and Paradise Cay Publications (USA) 2004
How to Cope with Storms, D von Haeften, Adlard Coles Nautical 2006
Ice Bird, David Lewis, Adlard Coles Nautical (UK) and Sheridan House (USA) 2002
My Lively Lady, Alec Rose, Adlard Coles Nautical 1988
North Atlantic, K Adlard Coles, Robert Ross 1950
Offshore, Captain J Illingworth, Adlard Coles 1963
Offshore Racing Council Special Regulations, Offshore Racing Council
Offshore Special Regulations Handbook, Alan Green, Adlard Coles Nautical 2005
The Parachute Anchoring System and Other Tactics, J Casanova, V Shane, DC Shewmon & G Macmillan, Chiodi Publishing 1985
Rogue Storm, Tony Farrington, Waterline 1995
Seaworthiness: The Forgotten Factor, CA Marchaj, Adlard Coles Nautical 1986, 2007
The Sea Anchor & Drogue Handbook, Daniel Shewmon, Inc. 100 Harbor Lake Drive, Safety Harbor, FL34695-2310 USA. Fax (813) 797 5708
Storm Tactics Handbook, Lin & Larry Pardey, Pardey Books 1995
This is Rough Weather Cruising, Erroll Bruce, Nautical Books 1987
Venturesome Voyages of Captain Voss, JC Voss, Grafton Books 1988
Yachting Casualties 3–8 June 1994, Maritime Safety Authority

Index